A History of the Khipu

This book begins by proposing a theoretical model that reconciles orality-literacy studies and media theory to avoid the specious dichotomization of societies into those with and those without writing. The more relevant issues are the ways in which a given society distributes semiotic functions among the various media that it employs and the forms of economic and political integration within which such media function. This theoretical model then informs a history of the Andean khipu from pre-Columbian times through the first 120 years of the colonial period. The first half of the book examines early Andean media and their socioeconomic and political contexts, culminating with the emergence of Wari and subsequently Inca khipu. The second half of the book documents and analyzes the continued use of khipu by indigenous individuals and communities in their interactions with Spanish officials, chroniclers, and priests. The study corrects many common misconceptions, such as the alleged mass destruction of khipu in the late sixteenth century. Even more important, it highlights the dialogue that occurred in the colonial period between the administrative and historiographic discourses of alphabetic Spanish and those of native Andean khipu genres.

Galen Brokaw is Associate Professor of Romance Languages and Literatures at the University at Buffalo. He has previously taught at Lafayette College and as a visiting professor at Harvard University. Brokaw has received fellowships from the National Endowment for the Humanities, the Social Science Research Council, the American Council of Learned Societies, and the David Rockefeller Center for Latin American Studies at Harvard University. His articles have been published in *Latin American Research Review*, *Colonial Latin American Review*, *Centennial Review*, the *Bulletin of the Comediantes*, and other journals.

CAMBRIDGE LATIN AMERICAN STUDIES

General Editor
Herbert S. Klein
Gouverneur Morris Emeritus Professor of History, Columbia University
Director of the Center of Latin American Studies, Professor of History,
and Hoover Senior Fellow, Stanford University

94
A History of the Khipu

Other Books in the Series

(*Continued on page 301*)

A History of the Khipu

GALEN BROKAW

University at Buffalo

CAMBRIDGE
UNIVERSITY PRESS

CAMBRIDGE UNIVERSITY PRESS
Cambridge, New York, Melbourne, Madrid, Cape Town, Singapore,
São Paulo, Delhi, Dubai, Tokyo

Cambridge University Press
32 Avenue of the Americas, New York, NY 10013-2473, USA

www.cambridge.org
Information on this title: www.cambridge.org/9780521197793

First published 2010

Printed in the United States of America

A catalog record for this publication is available from the British Library.

Library of Congress Cataloging in Publication data

Brokaw, Galen, 1966–
A history of the khipu / Galen Brokaw.
p.   cm. – (Cambridge Latin American studies ; 94)
Includes bibliographical references and index.
ISBN 978-0-521-19779-3 (hbk.)
1. Indians of South America – Peru – Languages – Writing.   2. Quipu – History.
3. Literacy – Peru – History.   4. Indians of South America – Peru – Politics and government.
5. Indians of South America – Peru – Social conditions.   6. Spaniards – Peru – History.
7. Peru – Politics and government.   8. Peru – Ethnic relations.   9. Peru – Social conditions.
10. Peru – Antiquities.   I. Title.   II. Series.
F3429.3.Q6B765   2010
985′.01 – dc22   2009045435

ISBN 978-0-521-19779-3 Hardback

Contents

Illustrations

Figures

Maps

Color Images

Color images follow page 128.

Preface

This project originally grew out of research on the native Andean chronicler Felipe Guaman Poma de Ayala, who claimed to have relied on the Andean khipu in the composition of his *Nueva corónica y buen gobierno*. Most of the published analyses of the alphabetic portion of Guaman Poma's text have tended to focus on the way in which it participates in the discursive space of European culture. In my research on Guaman Poma, I attempted to broaden this perspective by examining the indigenous dimension of his discourse. One part of that project identified a discursive structure that characterized both Guaman Poma's history of the Inca Empire and that of another text that claimed to be a direct transcription of khipu. As I investigated this topic further, I became more and more interested in the khipu itself. Rather than publishing my study of Guaman Poma as a book then, I completely reconceptualized the project by inverting this relationship. In the new study, Guaman Poma's text would still figure in the analysis, but the primary focus would be the khipu. This new project was to consist of two sections: the first would contain a series of chapters dealing with theoretical issues related to writing and alternative forms of communicative media; the second section would present several textual analyses of colonial texts derived in one way or another from khipu. These texts would include Guaman Poma's *Nueva corónica* and other chronicles but also numerous other published and unpublished documents from the colonial Andes. After completing many of the initial drafts for the chapters of this project, it occurred to me that I ought to include a chapter on the history of the khipu at the beginning of the book to provide a context that would ground the theoretical arguments and textual analyses. At the time, I was familiar with the few short historical studies that had been published by Carlos Assadourian, Carmen Loza, Tristan Platt, and Gary Urton, and I suspected that my chapter would do something similar. However, what I thought was going to be a short historical study that would serve to contextualize the main themes of the book soon became so long and thematically varied that I had to split it into two chapters. These two chapters then turned into four, at which point it became apparent that the historical portion of the project required a book of its own. I also realized that the historical research had important implications for the theoretical discussions that formed part of the original project. Rather than returning to the original manuscript, then, I decided to finish the historical research first, most of the results of which constitute the present book.

The title of this book identifies it as "historical," but it is an interdisciplinary project. Given the general move in academia toward interdisciplinarity, it is becoming increasingly, although perhaps not yet completely, unnecessary to justify such work. Throughout the process of conducting this research, presenting the findings at conferences and symposia, and sharing drafts with colleagues, it has become very clear that scholars from different disciplines often engage in, and conceive of, interdisciplinary work in different ways. In addition to, or perhaps because of, the fact that academic disciplines delimit their fields of inquiry at least partially in relation to other disciplines, they tend to have different notions of what constitutes evidence for particular research questions, and they employ different methodologies and different styles of argumentation. Moreover, even where fields of inquiry may overlap, they tend to ask different types of questions. My own graduate training at Indiana University was very interdisciplinary in nature, including history, anthropology, and linguistics; but I was based primarily in a department of literary and cultural studies. The University at Buffalo where I currently teach is also a very interdisciplinary environment, but I am still based in a literary and cultural studies department. I situate myself in this regard not in an attempt to preempt any criticism of the theoretical perspectives or methodological approaches that inform this book, but rather to help clarify my relationship to them. I am sure that my own form of interdisciplinarity is inflected by the institutional position in which I was trained and from which I teach and engage in research.

A common complaint about the interdisciplinarity practiced in literary and cultural studies is that it does not provide the kind of methodological rigor required to produce the same kind of knowledge as the more traditional social sciences do. For "literary" cultural studies, then, the interdisciplinary dialogue often tends to be one-sided: erstwhile literary scholars rely on historical, anthropological, and sociological research to inform their cultural-studies projects, but the reverse is not nearly as common. Even radically interdisciplinary cultural-studies research that focuses on objects and practices other than literature may often exhibit an interest in, or an emphasis on, issues that are tangential to the traditional interests of the social sciences. I would argue, then, that the problem is not one of methodological rigor but rather of disciplinary differences about what constitutes relevant or even interesting knowledge of the particular objects, practices, or phenomena under study. My sense is that these differences derive in large part from the fact that interdisciplinary scholars working from the discipline of literary and cultural studies draw from a long tradition that does not view interpretive analytical work as necessarily an attempt to make definitive statements about the object of study. In fact, these fields often celebrate the inherent ambiguity and polysemy of language and other signifying practices. With the exception of some branches of anthropology that have been influenced by many of the same theoretical perspectives as literary and cultural studies, the social sciences tend to engage in work that aspires – whether explicitly or implicitly – to more objective and definitive knowledge claims.

These disciplinary differences do not always necessarily enter into conflict. In fact, I would suggest that they can, and often do, complement each other. In a field where the status of knowledge in a particular area may not be sufficient to allow further advances using the traditional methodologies of the social sciences, methodologies developed in the humanities offer the opportunity to flesh out or call into question what is known, to produce further knowledge, and to explore possibilities for further investigations. The difference has less to do with the rigor of the methodology than it does with the nature of the knowledge produced. Furthermore, the combination of these methodologies is not new. Even the most rigorously scientific archaeological research, for example, rarely, if ever, produces knowledge that does not involve conjectural or speculative interpretation; and this type of interpretation has much in common with the interpretive methods of the humanistic disciplines.

However, even a cursory comparison between archaeological and cultural studies publications reveals that these two disciplines place different emphases on distinct modes of research: archaeological research has traditionally dedicated more time and space to the description and documentation of its object than it has to interpretation. This is not a criticism of the discipline, and it does not mean that interpretation is not an essential feature of archaeological research. In fact, even the description of archaeological sites and objects inherently requires a certain level of interpretation, and publications in archaeology are not limited to empirical analyses. But the very nature of the field demands a great deal of description and documentation before more comprehensive interpretation can take place. Cultural studies, in contrast, originated in the analysis of more "historical" phenomena for which different kinds of evidence is available and about which much more is known beforehand. Thus, the interpretive and theoretical dimensions of cultural studies projects often seem to predominate over empirical description. For a practitioner of cultural studies, then, traditional archaeological research can often seem to get bogged down in the minutia of physical description, whereas for an archaeologist, cultural studies can often appear to be ungrounded in empirical evidence and hence somewhat superficial. This is an admittedly broad generalization that does not capture all the nuances of each discipline, but I would argue that it accurately describes some of their general tendencies.

This study engages with archaeological research but also with anthropology and history. The topic and the temporal range of this book require an interdisciplinary dialogue. The execution of this project would be impossible from within the boundaries of a single discipline. Previously, the comparison and contrast between archaeology and cultural studies is useful, because they occupy different ends of the scale indicating the traditional ratio of empirical description to interpretation and theorizing or the degree to which these activities are integrated. Anthropology and history would probably fall somewhere in between. Again, this classification carries no implication of value, effectiveness, or legitimacy. In many ways, discipline-specific methodologies have developed in response to the particular constraints inherent in their disciplinary objects or time periods.

The first several chapters of this book deal with Andean cultures prior to the conquest. Thus, I rely extensively on archaeological research to construct a history of the Andes with an emphasis on the relationship between the development of socioeconomic complexity and the emergence of secondary media. I attempt to present a history of several Andean polities in the service of both a larger theoretical argument about the development of secondary media in conjunction with the emergence of socioeconomic complexity and a hypothesis about the origins of the khipu. The second section deals with the history of the khipu in the colonial period, and thus it relies on the analysis of colonial documents. In both cases, much of this history is conjectural and speculative, and it is informed by certain theoretical premises that I set forth in the Introduction and revisit throughout the book. In general, the project focuses on a particular set of questions without regard to the limitations of the disciplines within which I primarily work at the institutional level. I have attempted to construct a history of the khipu by drawing from, and contributing to, a number of relevant disciplines. I am sure that other scholars will point out the extent to which my methodology, interpretive framework, or theoretical foundation may entail a lack of rigor or a flawed logic from the perspective of a particular discipline. And this is as it should be. Such a dialogue will contribute not only to our knowledge of the history of the khipu but also to the interdisciplinary mode in which this history must be constructed.

I should make it clear that this project does not attempt to forge a completely new interdisciplinary space within which to operate. Many other scholars have contributed to opening up this interdisciplinary space in Andean studies and in Latin American studies more generally. In the process of conducting the research for this book, I have very conscientiously solicited feedback from scholars from other disciplines. I have profited

immensely from dialogues with scholars in history, anthropology, archae-
ology, art history, and literary studies. It would be impossible to produce a
comprehensive list of all those who have contributed in one way or another
to this project, but I would mention Rolena Adorno, Marcia and Robert
Ascher, Bob Bradley, Carrie Brezine, Gordon Brotherston, David Castillo,
John Charles, Tom Cummins, Alan Durston, Bill Egginton, Paul Firbas,
Sabine Hyland, David Johnson, Jongsoo Lee, Yolanda Martínez-San Miguel,
Mónica Medelius, Jeffrey Quilter, Rocío Quispe-Agnoli, José Rabasa, Alejo
Rojas, Frank Salomon, Gary Urton, and Nicolás Wey-Gómez. During the
2006–2007 academic year, I learned much about Andean art and archaeology through my participation in the Andean Art History and Archaeology
Group at Harvard University led by Gary Urton, Tom Cummins, and
Jeffrey Quilter. Gary Urton's extensive work on the khipu over the last
fifteen years has helped raise the profile of khipu studies and push it in new
directions. He has been an incredibly generous colleague and friend from
whom I have learned a great deal. The community of scholars in Peru have
also been extraordinarily welcoming and helpful. Marco Curatola and Juan
Ossio of the Pontificia Universidad Católica del Perú and Carmen Arellano
Hoffman, the director of the Museo Nacional de Arqueología, Antropología
e Historia del Perú, have been generous hosts and valuable interlocutors. In
Peru, I also enjoyed the support and intellectual and social companionship
of Alejo Rojas, Monica Medelius, José Carlos de la Puente, and the late
Hugo Sánchez. Herb Klein, the editor of the series of which this book
forms a part, and Frank Smith from Cambridge University Press provided
valuable feedback on the manuscript. Bob Bradley and John Charles read
initial drafts of Chapters 1 and 7, respectively, and Frank Salomon, Jeffrey
Quilter, Sabine Hyland, and Alan Durston all read the entire manuscript.
I revised the manuscript extensively in the light of their insightful comments and critiques. Even in cases where I disagreed on certain points with
the critiques offered by friends and colleagues who read the manuscript
or listened to lectures, their comments invariably helped me refine the
presentation of my arguments.

In the course of the research for this book, several museums generously
allowed me to examine their khipu collections: Manuela Fischer at the
Völkerkunde Museum in Berlin, William Wierzbowski at the University
of Pennsylvania, Elizabeth Peña at the Buffalo Museum of Science, and
Carmen Thays Delgado and her staff of the Textile Department at the
Museo Nacional de Arqueología, Antropología e Historia del Perú. During
several research trips, I also profited from the generous help offered by the
staffs of the Peruvian National Library, the Departmental Archives of Cuzco,
the National Archives of Peru, and the General Archives of the Indies in
Seville. A National Endowment for the Humanities Institute fellowship
exposed me more directly to archaeological work and to a wider variety of

Andean archaeological sites. At the University at Buffalo, research grants from the Baldy Center, the College of Arts and Sciences, and the McNulty Chair held by Dennis Tedlock allowed me to travel to Peru to conduct research, and the Julian Park Fund paid for the color images included in the book. During a visiting research fellowship at the David Rockefeller Center for Latin American Studies at Harvard University, I was able to complete comprehensive bibliographic research related to the khipu and Andean studies more generally. A research fellowship from the American Council of Learned Societies funded in part by the Social Science Research Council and the National Endowment for the Humanities allowed me to take time off from teaching to dedicate to research and writing.

Although the historical project presented here is in a sense twice removed from my original dissertation research, my graduate mentors at Indiana University have influenced it both directly and indirectly in many ways. I benefited immensely from conversations with Arlene Díaz, Edward Friedman, and John McDowell. I was particularly fortunate to be able to work directly with Gordon Brotherston and Kathleen Myers, both specialists in colonial Latin American studies who have been constant intellectual interlocutors, generous mentors, and friends since the beginning of my graduate studies more than fifteen years ago. They have both pioneered different kinds of interdisciplinary work from the institutional position of literary and cultural studies. Brotherston's work, which deals with both pre-Hispanic and colonial indigenous traditions, has been particularly inspiring as it relates most directly to the nature of my own project. I can only hope that this book will make a similar contribution to the kind of interdisciplinary space he and many of the other scholars mentioned here have pioneered.

Introduction

Traditionally, writing has been considered a major benchmark in the development of human societies: its appearance marks the boundary between history and pre-history, on the one hand, and the corresponding disciplines of history and archaeology, on the other. In more contemporary scholarship, however, the term "pre-historic" does not have the same currency as in the past, because it often implies a qualitative deficiency that is no longer politically correct. In colloquial use and increasingly in academic discourse, "history" is normally conceived as a more general term referring to past events regardless of whether or not they are documented with written texts. Nevertheless, the existence or absence of writing in a given society has inherent implications for the methodological approaches available for investigating the past. Archaeologists can certainly apply the methodology of examining the material remnants of human cultures to a period after the advent of writing. In fact, this is a very productive endeavor that attests to the fact that written documentation can never tell the entire story. The historical method of reading and analyzing documents, however, is restricted to periods in which written documentation exists. In the investigation of societies with a form of writing that is no longer in use and the knowledge of which has been lost, efforts to decipher their writing systems and to study their texts present a unique challenge that often attracts researchers from various disciplines: archaeologists and historians, of course, but also linguists, art historians, and anthropologists as well. When the system of writing is tied to verbal language, as in the case of the Maya syllabic script, researchers have a natural tendency to develop and articulate their projects in interdisciplinary terms: thorough archaeological research of the Maya area, for example, now demands training in Maya language and epigraphy. Writing systems whose conventions are either partially unknown or not tied directly to verbal language open up an interdisciplinary space with less-defined methodological constraints. The freedom of this interdisciplinary space can be extraordinarily productive for stimulating theoretical reflection, but it also has its limitations. Even partial ignorance of the underlying principles of a writing system means that decipherment projects are hindered not only in the analysis of written conventions but also in the very recognition of conventions as such. These cases are doubly problematic, because they raise the question of what constitutes the threshold between writing systems and other forms of media. Nowhere has this issue been more controversial than in the case of Andean societies and their use of the knotted, colored cords known as khipu (also spelled *quipu*).

A khipu, which means "knot" in Quechua, is a device of knotted cords used by the Incas and other Andean cultures to record various types of information. Throughout this book, I will refer to the Andean string device in both singular and plural forms as khipu. Although I recognize, as Tristan Platt has pointed out, that the Aymara also employed knotted cords that they called *chinu* (Platt 2002), they are part of the same larger Andean tradition. I spell the term "khipu" rather than "quipu," not for any ideological reason nor to give priority to one dialect over another, but merely because this has become the more common spelling in recent scholarship.[1]

Although museums and private collections around the world preserve hundreds of khipu, much about this device remains unknown. Khipu cords are normally made from cotton or camelid fiber. The basic structure of a khipu includes a main cord, often displayed horizontally in museum exhibits, to which are attached any number of vertical pendant cords. In many cases, pendant cords also have their own attachments, normally called subsidiary cords. These subsidiary cords, in turn, may have their own subsidiary cords, and so forth. In most cases, the number of subsidiary cord levels is limited to one or two, but in theory a khipu could have any number of such levels. Some khipu also exhibit top cords, which are similar to pendant cords, except that they extend in the opposite direction. These top cords serve to summarize the information of a group of pendant cords with which they are associated through proximity or attachment. The colors of khipu cords include all the natural hues available in the cotton or wool itself as well as a number of colors produced using dyes. Cords may be either solid or a combination of two or more colors using various different methods to produce distinct patterns. Any given cord on a khipu, including in rare cases the main cord, may also contain knots. Although khipu exhibit a few uncommon or idiosyncratic knots, in general, they employ three types: (1) a knot tied in such a way that it creates a figure-eight pattern; (2) simple overhand knots; and (3) long knots created by

---

1 In the colonial period, the term was always spelled "quipu" or "quipo." The disadvantage of this spelling in English language publications is the tendency for those unfamiliar with Spanish to pronounce it KWEE-POO. In the past, some scholars have also spelled the term "kipu." The aspiration indicated by the "h" in "khipu" reflects the way this word is pronounced in Cuzco and areas to the east and south (Alan Durston, personal communication).

wrapping the cord around itself normally from two to nine times and then pulling the end through the loops.

The only dimension of the khipu that has been deciphered is a decimal system, documented thoroughly with archaeological khipu for the first time in the early twentieth century by Leland Locke. Locke demonstrated that the knots function in a decimal place system to convey numbers in a relatively unambiguous way. According to this system, knots and knot groupings appear at different positions along the pendant, subsidiary, and top cords. These positions correspond to decimal values. The lowest position records the value for the single units or the "ones." Following an empty space, the next knot or grouping of knots corresponds to the tens position, the position after that signals hundreds, and so forth for higher powers of ten. Any position left blank indicates a zero value for the decimal power to which it corresponds. The lowest position, which corresponds to the single units, contains only one knot, either a figure-eight knot or a long knot; and these two knot types normally do not appear in any other position. The figure-eight knot signals a value of 1, and the various versions of the long-knot indicate values two through nine according to the number of turns in the knot. All other positions may contain anywhere from one to nine overhand knots grouped closely together. Each overhand knot indicates a single unit of the decimal value of the position in which it appears. Two overhand knots in the tens position, for example, would correspond to a value of twenty.[2]

Many khipu, however, appear to violate this system in one way or another: figure-eight knots and long knots, for example, may appear in positions higher than the single units. Urton argues that such khipu are extranumeric: that is to say that they convey other types of information such as narratives (Urton 2002c; 2003: 55, 97–98). Another possibility is that such conventions record multiple numbers on a single string.

Since Leland Locke documented the khipu decimal system in the early twentieth century, most research on the khipu has focused on the material conventions of this medium, its semiotic capacity, and the related debate about whether or not it constitutes a system of writing. Pioneering work by Carlos Radicati, Marcia and Robert Ascher, and more recently Gary Urton and Frank Salomon has greatly enhanced our understanding of the materiality of the khipu and many features of its conventional use. Here,

---

2 Using only the figure-eight knot and the long knots in the single units or "ones" position helps avoid the possible ambiguity of even decimal units (e.g., 20, 30, 100, etc.): if the last knot or knot grouping on the cord is a simple overhand knot, then you automatically know that the value of the "ones" position is zero. This is often useful because the actual position of each decimal power across a khipu can vary somewhat.

I do not propose to analyze directly the material conventions of the khipu but rather the history of this medium. The nature of khipu conventions is a fascinating and important question, but it has had a tendency to displace equally important and interesting questions about its history.

Nevertheless, any historical investigation into the development of a record-keeping system inherently must discuss at times the process through which material media convey meaning. Given that we still know relatively little about khipu conventions and even less about what gave rise to them, the discussion of this process will necessarily often remain at a fairly general level. Throughout this book I employ the term "semiosis" and its adjectival form "semiotic" in order to refer in a general way to the transmission of meaning. The only alternative would have been "representation," which I use in reference to iconographic modes of semiosis but otherwise try to avoid. In addition to being somewhat awkward in certain contexts, the notion of "representation" brings with it a great deal of conceptual baggage that can interfere in any attempt to understand the nature of non-Western media in both their synchronic aspects and their diachronic development.

The history of the khipu can be divided into at least two distinct periods: the first, from its origins through the Spanish conquest, and the second from the conquest through the present. Each of these periods poses different questions and calls for different theoretical perspectives and methodological approaches. Accordingly, this book is divided into two sections. But the analysis of any form of communicative medium also raises the larger theoretical issue of the very way in which it is conceived. Before discussing the issues that arise in the historical analysis, then, it may be useful to make explicit the theoretical perspective that informs it.

The Khipu and the Dialogic Model of Media

Although this project does not focus directly on the conventions employed by the khipu to record information, the historical analysis of this medium requires a dialogue between an attempt to understand the semiotic conventions of the material object, on the one hand, and its historical contexts (social, cultural, political, etc.), on the other. What is at stake here is not the issue of whether or not Andean cultures had a form of writing that would make them "historical." I find the continued use of the term "prehistory" highly problematic, but the distinction between periods in which alphabetic documentation exists and those in which it does not is certainly significant. Although we may have moved beyond a teleological perspective of history, writing is still considered a benchmark, and in many respects justifiably so. Most scholars agree that the development of extended, complex sociopolitical organizations such as states or empires is not possible without some form of writing.

However, pre-Columbian American states such as the Aztec and Inca Empires have always presented certain problems for this theory: they were sociopolitically and economically complex, yet they did not appear to possess a writing system. The Aztec case is relatively easily explained by their use of a form of iconographic script. The Inca Empire, on the other hand, is more problematic, because it is much more difficult to identify an Andean medium that qualifies as writing as traditionally defined. The most common solution to this problem, normally offered by scholars who do not focus on the khipu directly, involves a rather brief assessment of the khipu as a kind of anomaly, perhaps a form of "proto-writing" that somehow facilitated the development of a complex state.

The interdisciplinary field of knowledge within which this type of investigation is normally carried out supplies terms such as "writing," "literacy," and "orality." In most cases, debates about the nature of the khipu revolve – whether explicitly or implicitly – around the question of whether it constitutes a system of writing. At one level, this is a semantic issue that depends on the particular definition of writing that one adopts. In some cases, to insist that the khipu be considered a form of writing may be a necessary political strategy to counter ethnocentric perspectives that relegate societies without writing to an inferior position (Boone 2000:29–30). An even more radical approach, however, would be to refuse to submit to the terms of the debate. The concepts designated by the terms "writing," "literacy," and even "orality" originated in the particular historical context of alphabetic literacy and from the perspective of a literate mentality that has been unable to deal with the implications of other forms of semiosis. If the only two categories of society are those with alphabetic writing and those without, the Inca Empire does not fit into either of them. Researchers who seriously study the khipu and other non-Western media tend to recognize that they demand a reevaluation both of traditional historical and anthropological theory and of writing itself.

I would argue that the problem presented by Andean polities, and the Inca state in particular, reveals a blind spot in traditional anthropological and historical theories of the relationship between writing and political complexity. The main weakness of such theories stems from the fact that they do not problematize sufficiently the concept of "writing." Scholarship on writing abounds, but it tends to allow the cultural and historical determination of the concept to dictate the terms and parameters of the investigation. The problem is not merely that a universal concept of writing is difficult to define, but also that the notion of "writing" already imposes certain premises and biases that hinder such a project. The only truly successful attempt along these lines is Derrida's recognition that the essential nature of writing resides in its iterability (Derrida 1974). To the frustration of many, however, iterability is also the essential feature of perception and cognition in general, which means that if we follow Derrida, anything at all can be considered a form of writing. One might argue, then, that Derrida's notion of writing renders the concept useless as a critical tool for projects not engaged in some form of Derridean deconstruction.[3] However, Derrida's work does not deny the possibility of making *empirical* distinctions between different types of writing. Nor does it deny the historical and anthropological importance of *alphabetic* writing in the development of modern societies. Rather, it calls into question the universality of this development and reveals that anything is potentially codifiable into a more formalized semiotic or communicative system.

Certain universal characteristics of the human mind and the material world make some developments in communicative media more likely than others. Oral language is arguably a universal in human societies, but even in this case, all languages do not codify the available features of oral acoustics in the same way. Languages like Chinese and Zapotec, for example, make use of tones to determine literal semantic meaning, whereas most other languages do not. Even more important, the universal is not located in any specific feature of oral language or even in oral language itself but rather in the conditions conducive to its development.

The same can be said of what I would call secondary media. All societies engage in a variety of communicative interactions through various channels. Here I draw a distinction between primary media, which inherently involve interpersonal contact such as speech or sign language, and secondary media, which do not. In other words, primary media depend on the presence of, or some form of contact between, the participants in the communicative interaction, whereas the communication made possible by secondary media may take place without such contact. Alphabetic writing, of course, would be an example of a secondary medium that does not require the presence of, or direct contact between, the parties involved. I do not wish to emphasize this distinction in any rigorous way. I realize that it is not sustainable in all contexts,[4] but it nonetheless has important implications for the possibilities of social, economic, and political developments. This is because secondary media can store and transmit information over time and in most cases across space. The association between knowledge and power means that the use of such media has the potential, and perhaps inevitable tendency, to impinge on the socioeconomic and political landscape; the more versatile

3 Actually, to say that this concept of writing is absolutely useless serves to illustrate Derrida's point. From a rigorously philosophical perspective, absolute uselessness amounts to the same thing as absolute usefulness.

4 The reason this distinction is not sustainable in all contexts is because the classification focuses on the material object rather than the practice associated with it. Thorough knowledge about any secondary semiotic system and its effects requires an understanding not only of the material medium but also of the way in which it was used. Semiosis does not occur outside of social practices.

the secondary medium, the more extensive its ability to store and manage various types of knowledge and hence its importance for socioeconomic and political development. This is not to suggest a causal relationship between the development of any particular form of secondary medium and particular socioeconomic or political changes: as I will explain in more detail below, these two domains are each inextricably caught up with the other. The point here is that formulating the issue in terms of secondary media without specific reference to writing attempts to avoid the problems caused by the conceptual baggage that accompanies the latter term.

Moving from an emphasis on writing to one on secondary media is complicated by the fact that both the social sciences and the humanistic disciplines have had a tendency to dichotomize human societies into those that are literate and those that are oral. This dichotomy served as the original basis for the emergence of the field of orality-literacy studies, and to some extent it is still a dominant model in that field. In the early twentieth century, Milman Parry and Albert Lord inaugurated the field of orality-literacy studies with their pioneering comparative work on Homer and the Serbo-Croatian epic. Parry and Lord compared the features of the contemporary epic tradition to those of Homeric verse and concluded that the Homeric epics were originally oral compositions that had been set down in writing (Lord 1960). Subsequently this work gave rise to three related fields of study: (1) it generated a general interest in forms of oral literature, particularly poetry; (2) it served as the basis for the field of orality-literacy studies, which informed (3) the emergence of media studies and the Toronto School of Communication. The first field essentially engages in anthropologically informed literary research with a particular emphasis on poetry.[5] Orality-literacy studies, on the other hand, focuses on the differences between oral and literate discourses as well as their cognitive, sociocultural, and political implications.[6] The third field, media studies, also takes as its point of departure the theoretical implications of the historical transition in Greece from orality to phonographic literacy, but it also acknowledges that different forms of media correspond to different modes of thought with their own particular social and political implications.

Unfortunately, since the 1960s these three fields have developed more or less independently. In so far as studies of oral literature are interested primarily in the features of specific oral discursive traditions, they would not necessarily benefit from the insights of the other two fields. Orality-literacy studies and media studies, however, are both fundamentally based

---

5 See Foley 1981, 1987, 2002.
6 See work by Havelock and Hershbell 1978; Havelock 1963, 1982, 1986; Goody 1968, 1977, 1986, 1987, 2000; and Ong 1967, 1977, 1982.

on the theoretical argument that orality and literacy correspond to different modes of thought. The conceptual relationship between these fields has always been clear, but they have tended to focus on different contexts and to ask different questions. Orality-literacy studies tend to be historical and anthropological, whereas media studies deal with more contemporary sociological and technological issues.

A research question involving communication in apparently "non-literate" cultures such as the Inca and other Andean groups would normally adopt the critical and theoretical framework of orality-literacy studies. However, the lines of inquiry within orality-literacy studies that I am interested in here have remained locked for the most part within the binary opposition between alphabetic literacy and orality. Over the last forty years, for example, Jack Goody, one of the most prominent scholars in this field, has produced a series of books and articles developing various dimensions of this orality-literacy opposition and defending the premises of the field (Goody 1968, 1977, 1986, 1987, 2000). Such work has made significant contributions to our understanding of literacy in modern societies and of certain oral traditions. The theoretical model of orality-literacy studies works very well for understanding the nature of modern phonographically literate societies in contrast to those that do not employ such writing systems. However, it does not account for the function of other forms of media that are not recognized as writing. The orality-literacy dichotomy essentially homogenizes all societies without a medium that qualifies as writing (however this term is defined). It effectively defines "oral" societies in terms of what they are not rather than what they are.[7] For this very reason Walter Ong rejects the term "illiterate" and uses "non-literate" instead (Ong 1987: 374). However, this problem is inherent to the oral-literate opposition itself.

The analytical category of "oral cultures" obscures the fact that no society limits its communicative interactions to those that take place through oral language. The point here is not to equate other forms of media with alphabetic writing, but rather to recognize the way in which they function within the societies that employ them. If we maintain the comparison between "us" and "them," the relevant opposition is not always between alphabetic literacy and orality but rather between alphabetic literacy and Mesoamerican iconography, alphabetic literacy and the Andean khipu, alphabetic literacy and Innuit pole carving, and so forth. If writing effects a cognitive transformation in the modes of thought of those who employ it, then it stands to reason that other dominant forms of semiotic or communicative media would correspond to different cognitive transformations.

---

7 Margaret Jackson makes this same argument specifically in reference to Moche iconography (Jackson 2008).

Orality-literacy theory, restricted as it is to the binary opposition indicated in its very name, is not able to address this issue;[8] but this is precisely the type of question that media studies attempts to answer.

Although media studies have focused primarily on the effects of modern electronic media, the fundamental theoretical basis of this field holds that the use of any given medium has particular personal and social effects (McLuhan 1994: 7). I would argue that this media-studies model, which acknowledges the transformative effect of all media, is more successful in resolving the problem identified by Ong of defining a culture in terms of what it is rather than what it is not. The application of this theoretical model to non-phonographic historical and anthropological contexts is more difficult, because typically the nature and type of communicative interactions that take place through non-phonographic media differ from those mediated by alphabetic scripts. Furthermore, the communicative functions of societies without a form of writing as traditionally defined tend to be distributed more evenly across a number of different media. In fact, this is one of the reasons why the emergence of alphabetic writing was so significant historically: it corresponded to a dramatic increase in the communicative interactions that took place through a single secondary medium. The transformation in modes of thought associated with alphabetic literacy are not due merely to the nature of the medium but also to the fact that this medium acquired such prominence, that so much semiotic activity came to be concentrated in it. Of course, the two are linked: the undeniable versatility of phonographic scripts lend themselves to use in a variety of functions and contexts, whereas most other traditional media are more limited.

The nature of the medium, however, is only one part of the equation. Some scholars have argued that orality-literacy theory often gives too much credit to the role of writing, and this same criticism could be leveled at foundational media theory as well. Orality-literacy theorists such as Jack Goody and Walter Ong appear to discuss the role literacy plays in cognitive and sociopolitical transformations in causal terms: for them, writing *causes* transformations in thought, *leads to* political domination, and so forth. Ruth Finnegan argues to the contrary that the technological nature of writing or any other medium for that matter does not determine the uses to which it is put or the consequences that will follow (Finnegan 1981: 335–336; cited in Street 1987: 97). Brian Street identifies this causal argument, which treats writing as if it were an autonomous force in the transformation of society, as the autonomous model of literacy. In opposition to this autonomous model, Street proposes an ideological model of literacy, according to which the effects of literacy derive from its ideological use. For

8 For a cogent critique of the theoretical foundations of orality-literacy theory, see Biakolo 1999.

Street, literacy "is a social process, in which particular socially constructed technologies are used within particular institutional frameworks for specific social purposes" (Street 1984: 97). From this perspective, cognitive and social transformations often associated with literacy are results of cultural and ideological institutions rather than the technological features of the medium.

It is unfortunate that the autonomous and ideological models of literacy developed in opposition to each other. They both offer interesting and valid insights for understanding the nature and effect of literacy. Many of the differences between these two models stem from the different contexts that they examine. The effects of alphabetic literacy in modern societies are the result of a long historical process in which literate technologies and practices developed in a dialog with the institutions that employ them. Literacy functions very differently in a society where it develops more or less organically over time as opposed to a context where it is introduced, adopted, or imposed, often in conjunction with political or economic imperialism. Here again, the notion of "organic development" is not meant to be overly rigorous. If, as Benjamin asserts, "there is no document of civilization which is not at the same time a document of barbarism" (Benjamin 1968: 256), then the development of writing always involves some sort of political and economic domination. The essential questions have to do with the nature and function of the institutions that employ writing and how they develop over time. Literate practices perpetuated by institutions of political control will naturally function differently than those developed by institutions of resistance, for example. One cannot generalize about the effects of literacy without taking into account such contextual differences. The technological features of a given medium are certainly conducive to certain types of use and certain cognitive transformations, but they are not restricted to those that manifest themselves in a particular sociohistorical trajectory. No universal laws determine the nature of that development: it is a dialogic process involving numerous variables, many of which we may never be able to identify. But among those variables both the nature of the medium and the ideological institutions that employ it figure prominently.

I would argue that more adequate than the autonomous or ideological models of literacy, then, is a dialogic model of literacy that acknowledges the roles of both the technology of writing and the ideological institutions that develop and use it.[9] Furthermore, in thinking about societies that do not employ a form of alphabetic writing, the media-studies model that I have proposed broadens the field by substituting "media" in place of "writing." This implies a dialogic model not just of "literacy" but of media

---

9 This theoretical model explicitly invokes Bakhtin's theory of dialogism (Bakhtin 1981; 1986), but it is also influenced by Heidegger's onto-epistemology, elaborated most thoroughly in *Being and Time*.

in general: any given form of media develops in a dialogic relationship to the ideological institutions with which it is associated. The dialogic model of media does not attribute sociopolitical and economic transformations solely to a secondary medium or to ideological institutions but rather to both of them as well as to other factors in their dialogic relationship as it evolves over time. This historical process also influences the nature of the medium and its associated institutions. In other words, media and their ideological institutions are mutually constituting and interdependent.

However, I have suggested that the most diagnostic historical phenomenon marking the cognitive, sociopolitical, and economic transformations normally associated with the development of complex polities is not the emergence of a medium like writing or institutions of literacy per se but rather the concentration of a large number and a high frequency of semiotic functions in a single medium, or perhaps in some cases a limited number of media. Alphabetic, and more generally phonographic, writing is clearly versatile, more versatile perhaps than any other known secondary medium. By versatility, I refer to a medium's ability to take on different functions, to record different types of information, and so forth. Phonographic scripts certainly have their limitations. Other media are better suited for some types of semiosis, but the versatility of phonographic scripts gives them a much more dynamic role in the dialogic relationship within which they develop. I would suggest that this versatility is precisely what allowed alphabetic writing to support such a high concentration of semiotic functions. Differences between cultures, then, are evident not only in the type and number of secondary media that they employ but also in the way in which semiotic functions are distributed among them. In European societies, alphabetic script gained such importance, because the versatility of the medium supported the development of a large number and wide variety of semiotic functions, many of which were caught up either directly or indirectly in the exercising of political and economic power.

The rise to prominence of alphabetic writing does not mean that other media disappear, but that their semiotic functions remain less explicit, less rigid, and less regulated by social norms relative to alphabetic writing. All societies employ multiple forms of media to one degree or another. Even in modern societies, in addition to oral language, writing, and visual media such as painting and film, a great deal of information is conveyed through clothing, hair styles, architectural structures, and so forth. The diversity of media in Andean cultures also includes pottery, textiles, architecture, and even the landscape itself. One might argue that the communicative function of such objects as clothing and architectural structures is merely incidental to their primary role of providing individual and collective shelter, protection, storage capacity, privacy, and so forth. They certainly do not appear to record the kind of knowledge that alphabetic writing does. In theory it would certainly be possible for these media to encode information to the same extent as a medium such as alphabetic script, but their pragmatics and their inherent limitations constrain them from developing in this way. Nevertheless, in the Andes these types of media can, and often do, play a much larger role in social interactions than they do in modern Western cultures. Susan Niles has argued, for example, that certain Inca architectural structures served as a kind of enduring historical record (Niles 1999).

The rise to prominence of one medium in relation to others may involve the transfer of functions to it from other media, but it also implies the emergence of new, original functions. In other words, the development of new media may affect the distribution of existing semiotic functions in addition to introducing new functions that develop in conjunction with them to create a new pattern of distribution. However, the greater prominence of a single medium such as alphabetic writing implies a reduction in the relative importance of other media and their semiotic functions.[10] In most cases, societies that did not develop a phonographic writing system do not seem to concentrate as many semiotic functions in a single medium, but this does not mean that they distribute their semiotic activities symmetrically. The dialogic model of media leaves open the possibility that other forms of media might also support a high enough concentration of semiotic functions to create the potential for a dynamic analogous to that produced by alphabetic script in relation to its associated institutions.

According to the dialogic model, the relationship between a medium, its institutions, and other factors both inform the process that leads to the concentration of semiotic activity in a single medium and are in turn affected by it. If the development of a certain level of sociopolitical and economic complexity depends on some form of secondary medium that supports a high concentration of semiotic functions and vice versa, then the existence of one implies the existence of the other. This line of reasoning leads William Burns to conclude that the Inca must have had a form of alphabetic writing, which he then locates in the textile designs known as *tocapu* and in the khipu (Burns 1990; 2002). The problem with this portion of Burns's larger argument is not its form but rather the specific content of one of its premises. He assumes that only alphabetic writing is versatile enough to make possible the kind of complexity evident in

---

10 The rise to prominence of one secondary medium in relation to others in a society does not mean that the resulting distribution pattern of semiotic functions will remain static. Marshall McLuhan has argued that the advent of new electronic media in modern societies (radio, television) effected a new pattern of distribution that has profound social and political effects (McLuhan 1994). These shifts are as much due to socioeconomic, technological, and even political changes as they are to the proliferation of new forms of media, but this is precisely the point. These domains are inextricably connected.

the Inca Empire. The nature of the Inca Empire certainly may imply the existence of a secondary medium that would facilitate the administration of goods and services, but the assumption that this medium must necessarily be alphabetic is unjustified.

According to the theory that I have outlined here, a sufficiently high degree of sociopolitical and economic complexity may imply the existence of a secondary medium; but it cannot determine a particular threshold of complexity nor predict the particular form of medium that will develop. To the extent possible, a history of secondary media must consider the nature of the secondary semiotic functions of a society and the way in which these functions are distributed among the various media that they employ; or to put it another way, the way in which a society deploys media to fulfill its semiotic functions. No credible evidence has surfaced to suggest that the khipu originally employed alphabetic conventions, but archaeological research and sixteenth-century historical documents make it very clear that pre-conquest indigenous Andean societies concentrated a significant number of semiotic functions in the khipu.

Historical Research and "Pre-historic" Media

Several major obstacles impede any investigation into the history of the khipu prior to the Spanish invasion. The historical or diachronic analysis of a secondary system of communication must posit connections between the semiotic conventions of the material medium, or at the very least its material features, and the objects and practices from which they developed. In the case of the khipu, the material nature of the textile medium did not lend itself to preservation. In contrast, the primary sign carrier involved in early Mesopotamian economic transactions that eventually gave rise to alphabetic writing consisted of dried clay tokens, which are extremely durable (Schmandt-Besserat 1992). There is a trade-off, however, between the more durable medium of dried clay and the more flexible and operable textile medium of the khipu. Clay could be inscribed only once before drying, whereas the cords of the khipu might potentially be coded and repeatedly recoded using knots. Although on occasion nonoperable sign carriers such as the Mesopotamian clay tokens might have been reused, in most cases they were probably either stored or discarded. Thus, the material nature of molded and/or inscribed clay imposes certain limitations on its use while at the same time insuring a significant and enduring archaeological record that provides evidence from which a history of writing can draw substantive inferences. Khipu, on the other hand, are made from cotton or camelid fiber, which deteriorates naturally over time, especially when not preserved in some fashion. For this reason, archaeological khipu come predominantly from the coast where the dryer climate is more conducive to the conservation of these materials and almost exclusively from grave sites where they have benefitted from the careful storage and preservation procedures involved in burial customs.

The fact that almost all surviving khipu come from grave sites poses a problem not only because it limits the number of archaeological specimens, but also because it may imply a generic limitation in the khipu corpus. Erland Nordenskiöld argued that ancient Peruvians would have interred only khipu with some kind of cosmological significance (Nordenskiöld 1925a; 1925b). Nordenskiöld's premise led him to search for and find cosmologically significant numbers recorded in the knots of archaeological khipu, but his argument remains highly conjectural. Nevertheless, whether or not it is true that the semiotic content of archaeological khipu are limited to cosmological figures, it is certainly possible that only one type of khipu or set of khipu types would have been interred in a grave. Thus, we cannot assume that archaeological khipu recovered from graves constitute a representative sample of this medium.

Another problem has to do with the fact that most of the khipu known or assumed to have come from grave sites have no specific contextual or provenance information that would possibly constitute clues or suggest directions for analysis. Many of the khipu located in museums were originally obtained and sold by looters who had no interest in keeping provenance records; and even those khipu with known geographic provenance are rarely accompanied by more detailed information about the specific site or other associated objects from the same grave. The late nineteenth- and early twentieth-century archaeological expeditions that acquired the majority of such specimens were often more concerned with amassing a collection of artefacts for European and American museums than they were with documenting their excavations in ways that might have yielded valuable information about the objects they were collecting. The separation of khipu from their archaeological contexts also makes it difficult to establish a stylistic chronology that might inform an understanding of the nature of this medium and the direction in which it developed. The limited number of khipu specimens that have undergone radiocarbon dating has begun to shed light on certain aspects of the chronological development of this medium between the Wari and Inca periods. However, the relatively imprecise nature of radiocarbon dating, the rather short period of Wari and Inca dominance and the evidently rather rapid nature of khipu development will probably make it difficult to identify a more detailed developmental chronology based on stylistic and/or functional differences.

The paucity of archaeological specimens, especially from the pre-Inca period, and the lack of contextual information make it difficult to identify and establish links to material precursors and their associated semiotic practices. Even in the case of Inca-era khipu, specimens of which appear to be the most prevalent and about which there exists the most information, we have only a basic understanding of the decimal system that makes possible a numeric reading; but this is only one dimension of khipu semiosis. Moreover, the knots of many khipu, or in some cases sections of khipu, do not conform to the standard decimal conventions. It is possible that these anomalous khipu employ knots in a non-numeric way (Ascher, M. 2002; Urton 2002a, 2003; Urton and Brezine 2005); but even if this is the case, we currently have no way of knowing for sure what the specific nature of these conventions might be. Our ignorance of how the khipu functioned constitutes a significant obstacle in determining its historical development. Arguments about how the khipu developed are limited to inferences about its material relationship to other textile products, brief speculations about diachronic changes in material features, comparative analyses that consider possible analogies to the development of secondary media in other civilizations, and conjectural hypotheses that are difficult to confirm.

Without an understanding of the nature of khipu semiosis or its relationship to other media in relation to which it developed, a history of this medium must make certain assumptions about the historical processes involved. Thus, several premises underlie the history of the pre-conquest period presented here. The first is that as a general rule, semiotic systems are not invented from scratch: they build on previously established cultural products and practices (Collon 1990: 14; Houston 2004: 234; Jackson 2008: 7). The emergence of any semiotic medium as complex as the khipu takes place through developmental processes of increasing sophistication that build on pre-existing practices and technologies. Second, as explained in the previous section, at the very least a general, if not universal, correlation exists between the emergence of a certain level of socioeconomic complexity and developments in secondary media; and this relationship may provide a basis for interpreting the significance of various material remains from the archaeological record. However, a corollary to this premise is that, as explained above, the development of secondary media takes place in a dialogic relationship to the development of social, economic, and political institutions. In other words, the question of which came first does not make any sense, and not just because it is difficult to tell which is the chicken and which is the egg. The chicken and the egg are both mutually dependent products of a long interrelationship, the origins of which would not be identifiable as either a chicken or an egg. Socioeconomic and political institutions and the secondary media through which they function are mutually determined. Moreover, the nature of any given stage of their development does not provide a basis for predicting further developments. Neither the specific nature of the relationship between socioeconomic institutions and their secondary media nor the specific form of their complexity is universal.

Traditionally, historians of alphabetic writing have argued that writing originated with a form of mimetic pictography that eventually evolved into a system of abstract signs. In this model, the transition from mimetic representation to phonography takes place through the discovery of the rebus principle according to which a pictographic or iconographic image is employed for its phonetic rather than its mimetic value. Denise Schmandt-Besserat has argued, however, that pictography was an intermediate stage of development and that the long path eventually leading to the emergence of alphabetic writing began in Mesopotamia with economic record-keeping practices that employed clay tokens to represent quantities of a particular commodity (Schmandt-Besserat 1992). These Mesopotamian tokens are merely a more complex variation, if not a direct descendant, of the earliest known secondary medium of notched bone, which begins appearing in the archaeological record at least from the middle paleolithic (Schmandt-Besserat 1996: 90–91). The long historical process that eventually gave rise to alphabetic writing, then, began with a simple numerical record-keeping system that arose in the context of economic institutions.

As with the origins of alphabetic writing, the set of semiotic practices associated with the khipu would have emerged originally from the communicative and record-keeping needs of the economic and political institutions that motivated their development. Tristan Platt suggests that the khipu originated in the hunting and herding practices linked to the domestication of Andean camelids (Platt 2002: 226). Certainly, the context of the Andean economy was very different from that of Mesopotamia, but any form of economic exchange, partnership, cooperation, or reciprocity creates a context in which secondary media become very useful if not absolutely necessary. Ultimately, complex sociopolitical institutions are founded on, and developed in conjunction with, such economic activities. In fact, some scholars have suggested that as a matter of course, the numeracy involved in the numerical nature of early recording media has historically preceded other forms of literacy (Harris 1986: 133; Gaur 2000: 12). Thus, as Schmandt-Besserat has argued, part of the history of alphabetic writing involves the transition from a primarily numerical medium to one that in one way or another builds in other kinds of semiosis. This is particularly relevant in considering the history of the khipu, because one of the few certainties that has been established is the numerical nature of this device.

The fact that khipu were numerical in nature does not mean that they correlate to the early, numeric stage evident in the history of alphabetic writing in the Middle East and Europe. Again, the histories of secondary media do not all follow a universal trajectory. The development of both socioeconomic systems and semiotic media can take a wide range of possible paths. Traditional histories center on socioeconomic and political changes, but Harold Innis, Marshall McLuhan, and others have argued that communicative media play an important role in the particular nature of such developments (Innis 1951; McLuhan 1964). The approach taken here does not displace the socioeconomic in favor of an exclusive focus on media.

Rather, it attempts to identify the essential relationship between them. Social, economic, and political phenomena all take place through communicative interactions. Thus, an historical interest in media necessarily involves the communicative interactions of which they are a part. In order to emphasize this connection, the historical analysis in the first section of the book follows a chronological sequence in which Andean polities are discussed together with the media they employed.

Although there has been very little radiocarbon dating of archaeological khipu, it appears that most surviving specimens are from Inca times. The Wari period, five hundred to one thousand years prior to the emergence of the Inca Empire, produced khipu with distinct material features, and archaeological specimens appear to reveal a link between the Inca and Wari khipu traditions. Currently we have no confirmation of the existence of khipu or khipu-like devices prior to the emergence of the Wari Empire in the first millenium CE, but various types of semiotic media of one kind or another were used. Even if we cannot identify the specific conventions employed in the early practices that eventually led to the late Inca khipu just prior to the Spanish invasion, we can identify in the archaeological record a general outline of different forms of social, economic, and political complexity that constitute the contexts within which Andean secondary semiotic media developed. Furthermore, the general features of early Andean media suggest intriguing interrelationships among themselves and with both Wari and Inca khipu.

Andean Media Prior to the Spanish Conquest

The first chapter of this study reviews the archaeological research on the emergence of early Andean civilizations and the implications for the development of secondary media. It then discusses in some detail the semiotic practices of the Moche evident in the fine-line drawings that appear on ceramics from the first millennium CE. The Moche arguably developed significantly more complex socioeconomic and political institutions than many of their precursors. The Moche also seem to have employed a number of different media. I argue that they distributed a number of semiotic functions across several, possibly interrelated, secondary sign systems. The most compelling of these systems was a mimetic style of fine-line painting that appears on ceramic vessels. Of course the fine-line painting itself constitutes a secondary medium, but these paintings also depict other media such as textiles, ceramic pots, and sets of inscribed beans. Although it is difficult to ascertain all the ways in which these media functioned, in some cases it is possible to make limited inferences.

The various media of any given culture function in different contexts to convey different types of information, but in some cases an overlap occurs.

This redundancy appears to be particularly evident in societies in which semiotic functions are more evenly distributed across various secondary sign systems. Such redundancies may also facilitate the transpositioning of the semiotic function of one medium into that of another in their dialogic inter-action with socioeconomic and political developments. By transpositioning, I refer to a complex relationship between two or more signifying systems by virtue of some commonality in semiotic function, which may involve common referents as well as certain semiotic conventions or principles.[11] I would argue that this commonality often derives from the reworking of conventions in one medium that were originally developed in another.

The pervasive nature of material media in everyday life means that mimetic arts inevitably transposition other media incidental to the mimetic operation. The iconography of Moche fine-line painting, for example, trans-positions the secondary media of textiles, ceramic vessels, and inscribed beans, thus constituting a kind of meta-semiosis in which the object of representation is representation itself. I argue that this phenomenon is highly significant in the history of media, because it indicates a more self-conscious awareness of the nature of semiosis as such.

In Chapter 2, I examine possible evidence of another kind of transposi-tioning in the Middle Horizon Period during the Wari and Chimu Empires. The specific nature of the Wari administrative state is not entirely clear, but Jeffrey Quilter argues that this is the first Andean polity to integrate large-scale religious, political, and economic activities; and it is at this point that the khipu first appears in an unambiguous way in the archae-ological record (Quilter 2002b: 213–214). Middle Horizon Wari khipu are different from later Inca khipu in that their pendant cords are wrapped with colored thread to produce chromatic patterns (Image 14). Although in some cases, these khipu also contain knots, others do not. The knotless Wari khipu, then, appear to rely almost exclusively on the colored bands pro-duced by the thread wrappings. These colored bands resonate in interesting ways with a colored checkerboard pattern that appears on ceramic vessels associated with the economic production of the Wari state (Image 13). This checkerboard pattern, in turn, suggests a relationship to the account-ing device/practice known as *yupana*, which involves the manipulation of small stones, kernels of corn, or some other smallish objects (Images 5 and 6). And the *yupana* appears to be related to certain accounting practices

---

11 Julia Kristeva originally coined this term as an alternative to the notion of intertextuality, which had come to be understood in an overly simplistic way. Studies of verbal discourses normally limit the use of this concept to the identifiable relationship between specific texts, but it is much broader and more complicated than that. Kristeva explains it as "the passage from one sign system to another" (Kristeva 1984: 59). Kristeva did not have different writing systems in mind, but the use of the concept in this context is not formally inconsistent with the phenomenon she is attempting to describe.

evident in the archaeological investigation of Chimu storage facilities. These relationships are particularly important for understanding the history of the khipu, because colonial sources establish that the khipu was used in conjunction with the *yupana*, and both the Wari and Chimu influenced the development of the Inca Empire.

The apparently non-numeric nature of most Wari khipu does not necessarily mean that the khipu originated as a non-numeric device. If the development of complex recording systems takes place gradually in a series of stages, then simpler numeric khipu practices would have predated the fully developed decimal system evident in Inca khipu. I would argue that the khipu did in fact originate as a simple numeric medium, probably in the context of the administration of economic activities analogous to those that motivated the use of clay tokens in Mesopotamia. The color bands of the Wari khipu may indicate the transpositioning of a color symbolism originally employed in the storage and accounting practices associated with the *yupana*-like checkerboard image on the Wari ceramic vessels and the Chimu architectural structures mentioned above. Prior to this point, the khipu would have been a comparatively more simple medium used in less centralized and hence less regulated contexts.

In his analysis of changes in Chimu architectural structures over time, John Topic argues that the administration of economic resources shifts from a model of stewardship to one of bureaucracy (Topic 2003). This shift is signalled by the distancing of architectural accounting and control mechanisms from the resources with which they were associated. In other words, the material medium that conveyed and regulated certain types of knowledge acquired a greater level of independence from its referents. Based on the evidence currently available, the Chimu do not seem to have employed khipu, but the development of the Wari state also would have involved the emergence of a form of bureaucracy. If the shift from the Chimu stewardship model resulted from pressures exerted by an emerging bureaucracy, then analogous pressures in the Wari state may have inspired the adaptation of early khipu devices for use in more centralized administrative practices. In any case, the complex chromatic conventions and the fully developed decimal place system of the Inca khipu may be the direct result of the convergence between the numeric conventions of earlier knotted string records and the paradigmatic information structures and color symbolism used in the kind of accounting and storage practices evident in Chimu architectural complexes and the images on Wari ceramics.

It is clear that the Inca Empire implemented the use of the khipu on a much larger scale than their Wari precursors, if for no other reason than that they controlled a much larger territory. The larger, more complex nature of the Inca state would explain the innovations in khipu construction that apparently occurred in the Late Horizon during which the Inca Empire flourished. Many alphabetic texts and documents from the colonial period contain detailed information about Inca history and culture collected from, or in some cases written by, native Andeans. The criteria according to which native Andeans formulated their histories were very different from those of the colonial Spaniards, but even the alphabetic histories of the Incas produced by Spaniards in the colonial period provide valuable information that often can be taken together with archaeological data to produce significant insights into the history of the Inca Empire and the khipu medium on which it relied.

Ironically, in some ways less needs be said about the khipu in the Inca period, because the importance of this medium and the uses to which it was put are so well documented in the colonial chronicles. The Inca clearly used the khipu to record numerical data related to demographics, tribute, and some form or forms of calendrics. Many colonial texts also refer to the use of the khipu for recording laws, rituals, and even histories. No real controversy exists over the idea that there was a relationship between khipu and these various types of discourse. The controversial question has to do with the nature of that relationship, that is to say the specific nature of the relationship between the material conventions of the khipu and its discursive rendering. The specifics of khipu semiosis is not the primary focus of this study, but the expansion of khipu record-keeping practices to such varied domains has important historical implications. In Chapter 3, I briefly survey what colonial chroniclers wrote about the Inca khipu, and I identify what may have been a certain historical memory of the expansion of khipu practices in conjunction with the expansion of the Inca Empire. I also propose a theory about the nature and development of imperial khipu historiography.

Colonial accounts of khipu practices make it fairly clear that these devices were associated with various types of information: goods and personal belongings, censuses, laws, and ritual sacrifices and huacas. Numerous accounts also mention the khipu in relation to narrative histories. Each of the different categories of information types corresponds to a different official record-keeping functionary referred to generically as *khipukamyuq*. Many of the categories of information, such as commodities, censuses, and so forth, are inherently numeric in nature. Others, such as laws and lists of religious sites known as *huacas*, might have been incorporated into a numerical scheme, but they also would have involved other types of conventions. If narrative khipu were not merely simple mnemonic devices, as many have argued, then they certainly would have used a much more complex system of conventional signification.

Either way, however, the different types of information recorded on khipu would have involved not only a difference in what was signified but also a difference in the nature of the signifying system itself. In other words, the khipu appears to have been semiotically heterogenous, by which I mean that it employed different kinds of conventions in order to convey different kinds of information. Most complex media have a certain degree of semiotic heterogeneity. Even alphabetic script, which is based primarily on the principle of phonemic representation, also incorporates non-phonemic conventions such as arabic numerals, punctuation marks, formatting patterns, and so forth.

We tend to think of the development of writing as a series of successive stages in which one set of practices and objects supplanted an earlier one. But this was not necessarily the case with the khipu nor with alphabetic writing for that matter. The conventional sophistication of the khipu may have developed at different levels of society, leaving previous practices in place. The innovations in khipu conventions carried out by state-level institutions for the administration of tribute, for example, would not necessarily have affected the conventions of pastoral khipu that had probably already been in use in one form or another for hundreds, perhaps thousands, of years. Thus, the various domains in which the khipu served to record information involved distinct genres that may have corresponded to different levels of khipu literacy with conventional values specific to each level, and in some cases with unique conventions.[12] Numerical data may have been central to most, if not all, of these genres, but the significance of color, cord configuration, the non-numerical use of knots, and other non-numerical conventions would have differed from one genre to the next. Furthermore, different levels of khipu literacy may have exploited different material features of the khipu for conventional use.

The Khipu in the Colonial Period

It is important to keep in mind the nature of khipu literacy and its various genres or levels when attempting to understand colonial descriptions of the khipu. What we know of Inca khipu practices comes primarily from the reliance on these pre-Hispanic records by Spanish officials in the process of incorporating indigenous populations into the colonial system. After the conquest, information about khipu comes from specific social, economic, and political contexts that affected the way in which they were perceived and represented. The second section of this book traces the history of these contexts in order to document the continuity of khipu genres involved in the recording of demographic data, tribute payments and obligations, and historical narratives. It also identifies certain adaptations of the khipu to the new social, political, and religious contexts of the colonial period.

---

12 For a discussion of diversity and standardization of khipu, see Quilter 2002b: 200–204.

Immediately following the arrival of the Spaniards in the Andes in 1532, one of their more pressing ideological tasks was the determination of the legal status of the Indians. In theory, if they were natural lords, then they would not be subject to conquest.[13] The determination of whether or not the Incas were natural lords required a historical investigation into the history of the Inca Empire. This was ironic for two reasons: first, the conquest was mostly over by that time, and second, the outcome was all but predetermined. Although the Spaniards would never have relinquished their control over the former Inca Empire, the historical investigation was still necessary in order to appease their collective conscience and to determine the status of indigenous nobility in the colonial order as well as the privileges of various different ethnic groups. Chapter 4 discusses the use of the khipu by Spaniards who conducted and wrote up these historical investigations as well as histories motivated by other concerns throughout the sixteenth and early seventeenth centuries; and these writers consistently reveal that their native informants employed khipu.

After the Viceroy Francisco de Toledo's definitive inquests of the 1570s, the number of histories produced as a result of official investigations decreases dramatically. However, the khipu continues to inform histories written by Spaniards who wished to gain fame or fortune and by mestizo and indigenous chroniclers interested in promoting their personal and political agendas. By the mid-seventeenth century, however, even these historiographical khipu disappear from the documentary record. Several factors contribute to this disappearance, first and foremost perhaps was the demise of this particular khipu genre. At the same time, seventeenth-century historiography became more and more concerned with the history of the sixteenth-century colonial enterprise than the Inca past; and most of the seventeenth-century chroniclers who dealt with indigenous history relied primarily on written documents and earlier chroniclers, particularly Garcilaso de la Vega, rather than indigenous informants.

The semiotic heterogeneity of khipu semiosis, the various khipu genres with their unique conventions, and the socioeconomic structure of the Inca Empire meant that khipu literacy was not an independent institution to the same extent as is modern alphabetic literacy. Khipu genres were dependent on the institutions that, in turn, depended on them. The dissolution of Inca political institutions, then, made inevitable the obsolescence of

---

13 A "natural lord" was defined as "a lord who, by inherent nature of superior qualities, goodness, and virtue, and by birth of superior station, attains power legitimately and exercises dominion over all within his lands justly and in accord with divine, natural, and human law and reason, being universally accepted, recognized, and obeyed by his vassals and subjects and acknowledged by other lords and their peoples as one who rightfully possesses his office and rightfully wields authority within his territory" (Chamberlain 1939: 130).

the particular khipu genres on which they depended. The historiographic projects of the Spaniards in the sixteenth century may have prompted the perpetuation of imperial Inca khipu historiography to a certain extent, but Spanish institutions would not have regulated these accounts the way the Inca had done. This may explain the rather idiosyncratic khipu that appear to inform several early seventeenth-century chronicles. In any case, whatever support that the colonial Spanish administration might have given to the institution of imperial khipu historiography incidental to its historical investigations was very limited, because the colonial regime provided no incentive or impetus for perpetuating this practice in any formal or regulated way.

Administrative khipu studied in Chapter 5, on the other hand, were vital not only to the Inca but to the colonial Spaniards as well. Immediately after the conquest, the Spaniards were faced with the task of integrating the indigenous population into a colonial government. In most cases, this meant dividing the land up into *encomiendas* and charging the Spaniards to whom they were granted with evangelizing the Indians who lived there in exchange for the right to exact tribute. The process through which colonial officials granted *encomiendas* was supposed to involve an official *visita* or inspection that included a census of the population and an investigation of its productive capacity. But *visitas* were time consuming and expensive, and the turmoil of the early years after the conquest made it difficult to dedicate the resources necessary to carry them out in a thorough way. Whenever the Spaniards actually began such *visitas*, however, they discovered that the Indians already had khipu accounts of precisely the information they needed. In many cases, Spanish inspectors relied exclusively on khipu censuses in the determination of population figures. Khipu also provided data on both pre-conquest Inca tribute and the fulfilment of post-conquest obligations.

Colonial records that transpositioned khipu accounts into alphabetic script make it evident that local record-keeping practices did not depend on Inca institutions. Local communities certainly produced khipu for their interactions with the Incas, but in many cases, khipu record keeping was already a vital part of internal community administration. The *reducciones*, which forced the population of a region to settle in an urban center, contributed to breaking down traditional socioeconomic structures, but many communities preserved the use of khipu in their internal administration. Colonial documents attest to these types of enduring khipu practices well into the eighteenth century. Frank Salomon's work on the patrimonial khipu from Tupicocha indicates that in at least this case, community *khipukamayuq* actively employed khipu at least through the end of the nineteenth century and possibly into the early twentieth (Salomon 2004).

Whereas Chapters 4 and 5 trace the history of specific khipu genres or sets of genres in their relation to the colonial administration, Chapter 6 explores a more general perspective on this same relationship. This is necessary, in part, because the few studies that have been published on the history of the khipu in the sixteenth century have introduced or reinforced certain misconceptions. Building on earlier work by Pierre Duviols (Duviols 1971) and based on a very limited number of colonial documents, Carmen Loza has argued that the khipu passes through a series of stages in its relationship to the colonial legal system. The progression through these stages involves the gradual acceptance of the khipu by Spanish officials, a process of legitimation and adherence to the khipu, and later a rejection of this medium (Loza 1998a, 2000, 2001). Although Loza's argument has a certain logic, it is based primarily on just four sets of documents and what I would argue is a misreading of both Toledo's ordinances and the Third Lima Council's allegedly universal condemnation of khipu issued in 1583, which are the primary bases for establishing the temporal limits of the most important historical stages in her model. Although Loza explicitly delimits her study to the history of the khipu in the colonial legal system, the implications of her argument extend to sixteenth-century khipu in general. This is not to take away from the valuable contribution Loza has made to our understanding of the khipu in the sixteenth century. Loza's work has had a tremendous influence on the way other scholars, including myself, think about the history of the khipu. For this very reason, however, a critical engagement with her analyses is so important. Chapter 6, then, proposes a revision of Loza's model in which the history of the khipu in its relation to the Spanish administration is much less tidy and without such clear-cut stages.

One of the most common misconceptions regarding the history of the khipu in the colonial period is that in the latter part of the sixteenth century they were universally condemned by the Spaniards, sought out, and destroyed. This view has had surprising acceptance despite abundant evidence to the contrary. Most early claims along these lines were offered with no substantiating evidence. In *La poesía quechua*, Jesús Lara alleges that the *Extirpación de la idolatría del Perú* (1621) by Joseph de Arriaga describes the destruction of khipu (Lara 1947: 50). Although a rather late work from the second decade of the seventeenth century, this is precisely the type of text where one would expect to find references to the destruction of idolatrous khipu. But I have been unable to find any such account in this text. Arriaga does record an episode in which a number of idolatrous objects are burned, but he does not list any khipu among them. Lara may have misread the term *quepa* [a kind of trumpet], which does appear in Arriaga's list (Arriaga 1621: 94). Only a few pages earlier, however, Arriaga actually advocates the use of khipu for confession (Arriaga 1621: 89).

More rigorous scholars like Pierre Duviols and Carmen Loza have unwittingly associated assertions such as that made by Lara with a statement issued in 1583 by the Third Lima Council establishing a relationship between certain khipu records and idolatrous practices, and ordering that the khipu be destroyed (Duviols 1971: 243; Loza 1998a, 2000, 2001). In the historical investigation of phenomena for which there exists relatively little documentation, scholars have had a tendency to place an inordinate amount of weight on isolated pieces of evidence because they are often the only bases on which to construct a historical narrative and from which to draw conclusions. The assertion that the Third Lima Council issued a universal condemnation of khipu in 1583, for example, is based on a single statement taken out of its larger context. I argue that the Third Lima Council's order was not a universal condemnation of khipu. In fact, the Third Lima Council itself explicitly advocated the use of khipu for confession.

Of course, the Third Lima Council was a religious body focusing on religious issues, and its attitude with regard to the khipu was not entirely positive. Chapter 7 places the Third Lima Council's order in its larger context and examines in a more thorough way the reaction to the khipu by Spanish priests. The fact that the Third Lima Council did not issue a universal condemnation of all khipu does not necessarily mean that there was not a widespread campaign in which many khipu were destroyed. The Council's order probably indicates that the Spaniards had been destroying what they saw as idolatrous khipu for many years prior to 1583. The issuance of the order in the instructions formulated by the Third Council attests to the fact that they already knew about the idolatrous nature of some khipu genres and how to best deal with them. In fact, it seems that by 1583, for the most part the campaign against such khipu had already run its course. Thus, the Third Council's order was most likely more a vestige from the early days after the conquest than an urgent call to arms.

Those who would have been engaged in identifying and destroying idolatrous khipu would have been priests and missionaries; and their actions were not documented in the same way nor to the same extent as the *visitas*, especially in the early chaotic years during and immediately following the conquest. Even in those early years, it is clear that no general condemnation of the khipu was in effect, but Spanish missionaries may very well have been destroying "idolatrous" khipu at the same time colonial officials were drawing on khipu records in their *visita* inspections. The *khipukamayuq* who were the target of the extirpation campaign would have either abandoned their "idolotrous" khipu practices or begun hiding them from the Spaniards. Either way, this would explain the absence of any account of the destruction of such khipu in later colonial records. What sixteenth- and seventeenth-century religious texts and documents do reveal is the widespread adaptation of the khipu for Christian ecclesiastical purposes.

These sources reveal a consistent record of support for such practices, even by extirpators of idolatry, the documentation of which begins possibly as early as 1560 and running at least through 1650.

The history of all khipu genres presented in this book leaves off around this same time in the mid-seventeenth century, but this date is not intended to signal the temporal boundary of a stage or period in the history of the khipu. After 1650, tracing the history of the khipu becomes more difficult because known documentary evidence of khipu practices drops off dramatically at this point. This does not mean that after 1650 the khipu falls into disuse. The few references that are known make it clear that many Andean communities continued to use khipu throughout the eighteenth and nineteenth centuries and, in some cases, into the twentieth. The lack of known sources after the mid-seventeenth century does not even necessarily mean that there exists no documentation of enduring khipu practices in subsequent periods. In fact, I am fairly confident that many historical documents from the late colonial and early republican periods lying in the archives of Seville, Cuzco, Lima, and other Andean cities contain references to the khipu and that they collectively reveal a great deal about the history of this medium.

Traditional methodologies of historical research carried out by a single individual do not lend themselves to the historical investigation of khipu record-keeping practices. The evidence of these practices consists of brief references dropped here and there in a variety of different documents dispersed among numerous archives. It is not difficult to find such references to the khipu as one peruses archival collections. Anyone who has spent any significant amount of time reading colonial Andean documents has come across them. But collecting single references here and there makes this endeavor prohibitively inefficient. The paucity of historical documentation for khipu practices after 1650 may be due merely to the fact that there has not been nearly as much historical research into this period and that far fewer primary sources have been edited and made available in print.

Although the extensive research focusing on the sixteenth and early seventeenth centuries has uncovered numerous pertinent documents, surely many more remain undiscovered in this early period as well. In researching the colonial history of the khipu, I have discovered a few relevant sources by reading at random in archival collections, but by necessity the vast majority of the archival sources on which I rely were made known through the archival work of other scholars. Although I have consulted many of the original archival documents themselves, most of them have been published. What is needed now is the on-going collaboration of numerous scholars who are willing to take note of and share any references to khipu they come across as they work on other topics. To scholars engaged in researching other issues, most references to khipu in colonial documents seem rather trivial and insignificant, but taken in conjunction with other sources they often constitute valuable clues that contribute to a more thorough understanding of this medium. It is very clear that many historically important sources lie unnoticed or unheeded in colonial archives. The history of the khipu presented here, then, must necessarily be a provisional account subject to revision and expansion as additional sources come to light.

A book attempting to trace the history of the khipu, whether in the pre-Hispanic or the colonial period, is in a certain way both premature and long overdue: premature because we still know so little about this medium; and overdue because the historical information that is available on this topic has never been presented in a unified or thorough way. The absence of extensive historical investigations of the khipu is not merely an unfortunate oversight. It has led to a tendency to implicitly dehistoricize the khipu and divorce it from its social, economic, and political contexts in ways that obscure both the possibility of constructing a history of this medium and the contribution that such an historical perspective might make in understanding khipu semiosis and possibly in devising decipherment strategies. Sociocultural and historical understandings generate perspectives that may have vital implications for our understanding of how the khipu worked and hence for devising possible methods, directions, or the very questions asked in decipherment projects. I would not suggest that constructing a history of the khipu will necessarily provide any immediate or easy solutions to identifying or deciphering specific khipu conventions, but in some ways it may shed light on the general nature of the medium as a system of secondary communication or artificial memory and possibly the principles on which it is based. However, regardless of whatever contributions a history of the khipu might offer to an understanding of khipu semiosis, it has a value in its own right as an essential dimension of indigenous Andean society.

PART I

Andean Media Prior to the Spanish Conquest

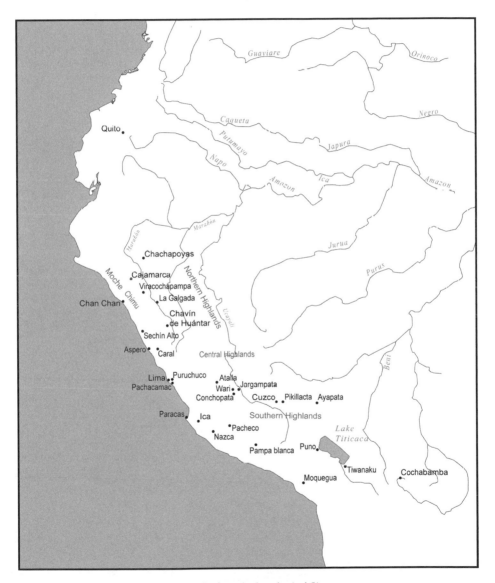

Map 1. Andean Archaeological Sites.

Early Andean Societies and Semiotic Practices

It may seem that a history of the khipu should start with the point at which this medium first appears in the archaeological record. However, the earliest unambiguous khipu specimens, which first appear between 700 and 900 CE, already exhibit the features of a well-developed medium that would have derived from earlier objects and practices. Although we have no access to earlier khipu, such media originally develop in conjunction with socioeconomic and political institutions, on the one hand, and other forms of media, on the other. As explained in the Introduction, one of the premises of this study is that all cultures employ a wide variety of media in their semiotic interactions. In other words, communicative functions are distributed across a number of different channels. More complex forms of socioeconomic and political integration, however, tend to reconfigure the nature of this distribution; and this reconfiguration often involves the transpositioning of communicative functions from one medium into another. Therefore, prior to focusing on the period in which khipu actually begin appearing in the archaeological record, it may be useful to review the history of major Andean societies together with the material media that have survived. In this analysis, I suggest that the archaeological record of early Andean societies contains subtle traces of the processes involved in the redistribution of semiotic functions and the intermedia relationships established in the process of transpositioning.

The Emergence of Complex Andean Polities

Archaeologists who invest a large amount of time and energy excavating and analyzing data from Andean societies often argue for identifying them as states. Andean archaeologists have never posited a city-state model such as that which existed in Mesoamerica. Rather, the model of Andean statehood involves the organization and control of, or influence over, an extended geographic area. Archaeological analysis must deal with several issues in constructing a geopolitical history of pre-conquest Andean states. First, it must establish a geographic unity, normally through the identification of common material elements such as styles of pottery and architectural designs in the archaeological record. Second, it must determine the nature of the relationship indicated by this evidence, a notoriously difficult task. The spread of pottery styles, for example, might be the result of any number of social, religious, economic, or political interactions. Furthermore, the constitution of political and economic systems may follow any number of possible trajectories. For the purpose of this discussion, it is not necessary to debate the criteria used to identify a state society. I am not as concerned with determining the threshold that distinguishes state from non-state political organizations as I am with relative degrees or different types of social, economic, and political complexity.

In constructing a pre-Columbian Andean history of socioeconomic and political institutions, archaeologists generally employ, with slight modifications in some cases, John Rowe's chronology of Peruvian "pre-history" that identifies a series of periods based on archaeological benchmarks in the Ica valley. The names of these periods with rough dates are as follows: the Preceramic Period lasting until around 1800 BCE, the Initial Period from 1800 to 900 BCE, the Early Horizon Period from 900 to 200 BCE, the Early Intermediate Period from 200 BCE to around 600 CE, the Middle Horizon Period from 600 to 1000 CE, the Late Intermediate Period from 1000 to the early 1400s, and the Late Horizon Period from the early 1400s to the Spanish conquest in 1532.[1] This model is based on the identification of cultural influences that appear in the archaeological record of the Ica valley. Each of the Horizons corresponds to the arrival in Ica of the cultural influence of what was ostensibly a major Andean civilization: the Early Horizon begins with the arrival of cultural traits that originated from a point normally identified as the ceremonial center of Chavín de Huántar in the north-central highlands; the Middle Horizon Period begins with the arrival in the same valley of characteristics associated with the Tiwanaku and Wari civilizations from the area around Lake Titicaca and from what is now Ayacucho, respectively; and the advent of the Late Horizon marks the arrival of Inca influence. The spread of material objects and practices appears to indicate that the cultures from which they originated enjoyed a high level of socioeconomic and political prominence.

It should be noted that the term "Intermediate Period" does not necessarily imply any general qualitative difference from Horizon Periods outside of the Ica valley. One might infer from the terminology that the Intermediate Periods correspond to times when no major civilization flourished, but Rowe's period model merely reflects the fact that the art styles of cultures from these periods did not extend to the Ica valley. Styles such as those

---

1 See Rowe 1960, 1962. Rowe's model did not originally include dates. In fact, the lack of accurate dating techniques constituted one of the motivations for the use of models such as this.

associated with the Moche and the Nazca are local compared to Chavín, Tiahuanco, and Inca, but this does not necessarily mean that the socioeconomic and political institutions of these cultures were qualitatively less complex than those of the Horizon cultures. Indeed, archaeological research has made it clear that the Early Intermediate Moche and the Late Intermediate Chimu also exhibited a high degree of complexity.[2]

The geopolitics of Andean civilizations originally arose out of the nature of smaller-scale economic practices developed at community and regional levels. In many areas of the world, trade networks that often motivated military conquest and political consolidation developed as a way of acquiring luxury items or goods that supplemented an existing subsistence economy. In the Andes, however, exchange relationships were often an essential part of the subsistence economy itself. Based almost entirely on archaeological evidence, the political economy of pre-conquest Andean societies is difficult to determine with any degree of specificity. However, from very early in the archaeological record, Andean societies appear to evince the fundamental principles of corporate labor and reciprocity that were the essential basis of most indigenous Andean economies at the time of the Spanish conquest (Moseley 1975, 1978: 505, 509–513, 1982: 10; Burger 1992: 28, 54–55).

This early model of local economic integration differed greatly from what emerged in the Middle East and Europe. The Andean geopolitics of this early stage characterized by lateral relationships inherently affected the nature of later hierarchical structures that built on them. Many analytical models fail to account for the determining relationship between these early lateral economic and political relationships and the later hierarchies of Andean states. They often adopt narrow definitions of categories like "civilization" and "state" and thereby assume the universality of a particular set of hierarchical types based on historical developments in Europe and the Middle East.

The geography of the Andean region constitutes one of the major factors in determining the nature of economic systems in this area. The steep incline of the Andes and the high altitude of the flat altiplano regions are not naturally conducive to a significant level of population density, because specific locations have a low degree of ecological diversity. Subsistence in such an environment requires the exploitation of different ecological

2 I should point out that this is not a weakness of the period model put forth by Rowe, as some have claimed. The period model based on the local sequence of the Ica valley is merely a heuristic device used to facilitate analysis. The model itself carries with it no inherent implications of phenomena outside of the Ica valley. Many scholars have mistakenly viewed the period model as if it were a stage model, which is precisely what Rowe was trying to avoid. See Rowe 1962 for a detailed explanation of the methodology and its differentiation from the stage model.

zones. In other words, a community must have access to the goods produced in several locations. Two general methods for acquiring this access developed among Andean communities in many areas. The community either specializes in products supported by their ecological zone and establishes trade networks with other communities from other zones in what David Browman has called the altiplano model of economic integration (Browman 1984); or it creates its own outposts in the ecological zones to which it needs access in what John Murra has identified as the archipelago or vertical model of economic integration (Murra 1971). Michael Moseley has argued that the vertical control model is evident from the earliest Andean societies (Moseley 1978: 506–507). It appears that both methods were employed in different areas of the Andes at different times, but they both relied on, and reinforced, communal institutions.

In the northern part of Peru, a large area adjacent to the coast possesses a much greater diversity of resources than in the south. This environment is capable of supporting a much higher population density than in other areas of the Andes. But even there, in the Initial Period prior to the spread of Chavín influence from the northern highlands, the apparent shift in some areas from a primarily coastal, marine subsistence economy to inland agriculture involved the adaptation of communal institutions that already existed, as indicated by the archaeological remains of what apparently could only have been corporate labor projects (Moseley 1978: 513–515; Burger 1992: 28, 71). Furthermore, an emphasis on inland agriculture did not completely eclipse the importance of coastal communities. In fact, recent research suggests that even during the Preceramic Period, coastal communities already functioned within a network that involved inland agricultural sites (Shady 2000; Shady and Leyva 2003).

Rowe's organization of temporal periods in the Andes, based on what had been discovered at the time, privileges the periods following the introduction of ceramics. This bias is perhaps a natural result of the heavy reliance on ceramics in establishing dates and chronologies in archaeological research. Most scholars assumed that prior to that point, there existed no major socioeconomic or political institutions of the type that characterized Chavín in the Early Horizon. In part, this assumption derived from the premise that social complexity arose only from an agricultural economy. Beginning in the late 1950s, Andean archaeologists such as Frédéric Engel and later Edward Lanning, Thomas Patterson, and Michael Moseley began questioning this premise, arguing that maritime coastal societies exhibited a complexity greater than that normally associated with nonagricultural subsistence (Engel 1957, 1958, 1966; Lanning 1964; 1967: 57–59; Patterson 1971; Patterson and Lanning 1964; Patterson and Moseley 1968). In the 1970s, Michael Moseley's work on the coastal society of Aspero at the mouth of the Supe River further developed the argument that maritime resources served as the foundation for subsequent developments in socioeconomic and political complexity (Moseley 1975).

More recent work by Ruth Shady has identified Aspero as part of a larger civilization possibly centered at the inland site of Caral. Shady and her team argue that in the third millennium BCE, the Supe valley on the north central coast witnessed the development of a complex civilization with urban centers and corporate labor projects (Shady 2000; Shady and Leyva 2003). Moseley maintains that Shady's discovery does not refute the hypothesis that identifies a maritime foundation of Andean civilizations according to which the emergence of social complexity occurred during a time when marine resources constituted the majority of protein consumption (Moseley 2005). However, at the very least the situation in the Supe valley appears to present an interdependent relationship in which the development of maritime communities depended on the agricultural produce of inland sites, specifically the cotton used to construct fishing nets, and the inland sites depended on the protein acquired from marine food sources on the coast.

Based on recent claims, the work at Caral would be particularly relevant to the history of the khipu, because Shady has announced the discovery of a khipu at the site. Previously, the oldest datable khipu came from around 700 CE in the Middle Horizon Period (Conklin 1982: 71). A khipu from Caral would predate Middle Horizon Wari khipu by almost 3,000 years. However, the object from Caral poses several problems, the first of which is its very identity as a khipu or even as a semiotic medium. Although the Caral object is very different from Wari khipu, a generous analysis might identify the basic structure of a main cord with attached pendants. The "pendants" consist of cords wrapped around small sticks, thus resonating in a certain way with the wrapped cords of Wari khipu. In some cases, these cords extend beyond the end of the stick, with or without knots. However, it is possible that this object has nothing to do with khipu whatsoever. One of the Caral publications presents another object that also has a main cord and wrapped pendants extending from it, but this object is identified as a necklace (Shady 2007: 55). It is unclear, then, what the criteria are that lead to the identification of one of these objects as a khipu and the other as a necklace. To further complicate matters, at the site of Caral itself, a placard announces the discovery of a stone on which allegedly appears a painted image of a khipu. The rather blurred image does, in fact, look kind of like a khipu, especially if the viewer is prepared before hand by the caption of the photograph. Nevertheless, any definitive identification of such objects is difficult to make on the basis of a single specimen in an isolated context and the ambiguity of an alleged petroglyph.

Another problem presented by the identification of the Caral object as a khipu is the fact that no other knotted-string devices have appeared in the archaeological record spanning the approximately 3,000 years between Preceramic societies such as Aspero-Caral and Wari. The lack of archaeological khipu in this intervening period does not necessarily mean that they did not exist. In theory, the apparent affinity between the Preceramic Caral object and the later Wari and Inca khipu could indicate a genealogical relationship between these devices. Several explanations for such a gap in the archaeological record are possible. The context of use in which khipu developed and the nature of the medium, for example, may not have been conducive to preservation. Khipu were not inherently fixed in the same way as the clay tokens used as a secondary medium in early Mesopotamia: cotton and woolen strings could be added, removed, or cut; knots could be untied and retied; and over time, the cords of the khipu would have deteriorated as a result of normal wear and tear. Colonial sources, certain features of archaeological specimens, and modern ethnographic data suggest that khipu practices took advantage of the inherently operable nature of this medium.[3] Such practices involve the continuous use and recycling of khipu. Thus, if this operability characterized ancient khipu practices, then the archaeological record would contain very few if any complete khipu.

Without reverting to reductive versions of universalist assumptions about the relationship between writing and complex societies or civilizations, the existence of khipu at Caral would mean that the historical development of the khipu takes place simultaneously with an increase in social, political, and economic complexity on the north coast of Peru, which also occurs at roughly the same time as the developments of secondary media in Mesopotamia that eventually gave rise to alphabetic writing. As I argued in the Introduction, the development and use of secondary media, on the one hand, and an increasing level of social complexity, on the other, always occur in a dialogic relationship to each other. In particular instances, the essential questions concern the nature of the media and the correlation

---

3 Some cords on archaeological khipu are kinked, for example, indicating that a knot was untied (Conklin 2002: 80). Urton explains that in some cases, the type of knot can even be inferred or reproduced based on these kinks (personal communication). In some cases, the pendant cords have been cut off for some reason. Furthermore, one of the very first references to khipu indicates that they were operable in this way. Hernando Pizarro explains that when they requisitioned supplies from native storehouses, an indigenous official would untie the knots on one string and retie them on another: "A estos pueblos del camino vienen á servir todos los caçiques comarcanos; quando passa la gente de guerra tienen depóssito de leña é mahiz é de todo lo demás é cuentan por unos nudos en unas cuerdas de lo que cada caçique ha traydo. E quando nos avian de traer algunas cargas de leña ú ovejas ó mahiz ó chicha, quitaban de los nudos de los que lo tenian á cargo, é anudábanlo en otra parte: de manera que en todo tienen muy grand quenta é raçon" (Pizarro [1533] 1920: 175). The modern ethnographic khipu from Tupicocha studied by Frank Salomon appear to confirm this as well – at least at the community level (Salomon 2001: 121–122; 2004).

between their development and that of related social, economic, and political institutions. Thus, the existence of khipu at Caral would contribute an additional dimension to the social, economic, and political complexity of the Aspero-Caral civilization identified independently on the basis of the other archaeological evidence presented by Shady and her team; but the social complexity itself does not require the corroboration provided by the discovery of an early form of khipu.

Caral has received a lot of press recently because of the extensive nature of the excavations and the public relations campaign associated with the project, but the existence of large-scale ceremonial complexes produced through corporate labor and the interdependence of coastal and inland sites was a fundamental characteristic of many Preceramic societies (Williams 1985).[4] Other Preceramic sites will undoubtedly exhibit many of the same characteristics as Caral once they have been excavated to the same extent. The socioeconomic and political complexity of Aspero-Caral and other Preceramic societies may certainly have been conducive to the development of a secondary medium; and later societies such as Chavín, Moche, and Chimu would also have benefitted from such devices. Of course, no clear dividing line distinguishes simple from complex societies. The issue has to do rather with degrees and/or types of complexity. But neither is there any universal path of development that would allow the identification of a particular degree or type of complexity with the emergence of a corresponding level of sophistication in some sort of secondary medium. The association between a particular type of socioeconomic and political complexity and the development of a sophisticated secondary medium appears to be a general tendency that may manifest itself in a variety of different ways in different contexts. The specific nature of the medium – when it emerges, how it is used, and so forth – has less to do with a universally determinable degree of socioeconomic and political complexity than it does with the particular way in which knowledge and power are controlled and distributed in the society under question. This is why the socioeconomic and political hierarchy that emerged in the Middle East and Europe may not be the best model for understanding Andean societies or predicting the relationship between socioeconomic and political development, on the one hand, and the emergence of a sophisticated secondary medium, on the other.

As explained above, one of the defining characteristics of many indigenous Andean societies was the unique model of economic integration based on a lateral rather than a vertical distribution of power motivated by the need to exploit different ecological zones located at different altitudes and often separated by considerable distances. Although the central and north coast societies are not subject to the same conditions as the highlands,

4 Also see the other studies in Donnan 1985a.

the relationship between the inland sites, such as that of Caral, and coastal communities, such as Aspero, appears to exhibit a coastal version of this type of socioeconomic and political structure. Work at other sites like La Galgada confirms that subsistence patterns along the coast involving lateral relationships between communities specializing in irrigation agriculture in inland valleys and coastal villages exploiting marine resources emerged earlier than previously thought. These patterns are further developed in the Initial Period, where they are evident along the entire coast (Burger 1992: 97).

Initial Period societies in the central and southern highlands do not exhibit monumental architecture on the scale that exists along the coast and in the north, but smaller-scale public centers constructed by corporate labor are evident. Thus, during the Preceramic and Initial Periods both in the highlands and along the coast, the construction of public architecture indicates the emergence of ideological institutions that bound together communities and made possible the organization of corporate labor within an extended region. These geopolitical relationships appear to have constituted a network of economic exchanges between small, weakly stratified communities with no overarching political authority (Burger 1992: 75, 104). In such a context, it may be misleading to make a strict distinction between local and regional levels of socioeconomic organization. It appears that the local was always already caught up in the regional. This interdependence is consistent with the logic of Andean principles of reciprocity and the unique nature of Andean models of economic integration that also emerge later in the highlands.

The political economy of late Preceramic and Initial Period societies may have been conducive to the development of some form of secondary medium, but the lateral distribution of power would have meant that the impetus for, and hence the locus of, this development would have been the community in its relationship to affiliated communities. This appears to run contrary to the premise that identifies a dialogical relationship between the development of state-level institutions as traditionally conceived and the emergence of sophisticated material media such as writing. The Inca, and apparently the Wari, clearly employed khipu in the administration of an extended empire with institutions more conducive to the preservation of such records; but even the archaeological specimens of Inca khipu are primarily limited to those found in graves. As I will argue in Chapter 3, several of the various khipu genres employed by the Inca may have been fairly recent developments; and at the time of the conquest some of these khipu practices were in a somewhat precarious position. However, the accounting khipu, on which the Inca Empire relied most heavily in its administration, clearly corresponded to a fairly ubiquitous and well-established institution of record-keeping practices. The well-attested fact that these practices did not disappear with the dissolution of the Inca Empire suggests that the institutions on which they relied were primarily local. Thus, although the Inca state employed a form of centralized political hierarchy, the administrative model appears to have involved the linking of pre-existing local institutions to create a network that served, but was not dependent on, the central authority. The independent local institutions, then, appear to date from much earlier periods.[5] In some areas, especially those that were conquered militarily, the expansion of the administrative state may have required the imposition of these local record-keeping institutions, but this is peripheral to the main concern regarding the initial relationship between socioeconomic complexity and secondary media.

One of the problems with traditional analytical models of the relationship between early state formation and writing is the assumption that the movement from local to regional and pan-regional organization necessarily involves a corresponding increase in socioeconomic and political complexity, which then induced the development of writing. It should be noted that the Maya civilization, which developed a syllabic script, was never a unified empire but rather a network of city-states. In the Andes, the particular nature of even smaller-scale, local socioeconomic development was already such that it may have induced the emergence of a complex secondary medium prior to the appearance of larger, more unambiguously state-like polities. Furthermore, a situation in which local societies already exhibit a high degree of complexity does not lend itself to the same kind of political domination that characterizes the assimilation of relatively simple social units within a more complex political system. In fact, the local levels that were integrated into Andean states in many cases appear to have been more complex than the state apparatus that subsumed them.

Thus, in the Andean context, the extraordinarily high degree of socioeconomic complexity at the local level results in a different model of state formation and possibly a different relationship to the secondary media on which such development relied. In the case of social, economic, and political organization, this meant that pre-Hispanic Andean polities transformed local principles by adapting them to the exigencies of regional and pan-regional government; and by the same token, it also meant that in one way or another this government was consistent, or at least resonant, with local socioeconomic institutions that for the most part remained intact. In

---

5 The Andean term that normally refers to the basic unit of socioeconomic and political organization at the community level is *ayllu*. I do not employ the term *ayllu* here, because it is unclear when these local communities acquire the features that would qualify them as such. See Isbell 1997 for a discussion of this issue. Throughout this study I will use the more universal term "community," because for my purposes it makes no difference if or when a particular community conforms to all of the features of what would later be known as an *ayllu*.

the case of secondary media, this means that a ready-made medium may have both facilitated larger state-level administration and constrained the ways in which that administration developed. The conceptual paradigms corresponding to Andean socioeconomic models and to the semiotic nature of the secondary medium or media would have predisposed any further development to the direction established by local products and practices. This is not to deny the possibility or indeed the inevitability of innovation, but innovation is always a process that relies and builds on pre-existing elements.

In any case, the network model of local/regional organization emphasizing the lateral distribution of power that characterized early Andean societies may explain the lack of archaeological khipu prior to the Wari period. For, although the khipu may not date as far back as Caral, it surely originated long before archaeological specimens begin appearing in grave sites. In the case of a perishable medium like the khipu, the existence of an archaeological record would depend on the existence of institutional practices involving the preservation and archiving of recorded information. Such practices imply a certain ideology that may have been inconsistent with the institutions that developed in the lateral model of Andean socioeconomic organization. If power and the control of information are intimately linked, then the lateral distribution of power that characterized early Andean societies would have meant that the control of information was also distributed laterally. This is not to say that no centralized hierarchy existed but that such centralization took place within the context of more lateral relationships as opposed to a more strictly vertical hierarchy. Thus, the institutions associated with recording administrative information also would have been controlled primarily at the local level within the context of lateral relationships with other components of the community or with associated communities. If the evidence of khipu practices inferred from the patrimonial khipu and *ayllu* books of the modern community of Tupicocha is any indication, many local communities may have maintained their khipu records on a year-to-year basis. Salomon explains that in the modern community of Tupicocha, the khipu record had a target of zero assets and zero debits at the end of the year (Salomon 2004: 202, 206). In other words, the system was designed to facilitate the management of community obligations from year to year rather than to serve as an historical record. Even if there were outstanding service obligations at the end of a particular year, these could always be transferred to the following year's khipu. Thus, there may not have been any practical or ideological reason to keep any kind of archival record of these accountings. In fact, from the ideological perspective of many Andean communities, maintaining an archive of such records may have been undesirable. I am not suggesting that early Andean societies necessarily functioned according to the same ideology or employed the same type of administrative system as the modern community of Tupi-cocha. The point is merely that administrative models exist that would not have been conducive to the preservation of early khipu specimens.

Extraordinary circumstances might have led to the abandonment of khipu to the archaeological record, but even in such cases, the perishable nature of cotton and wool would have made them highly susceptible to disintegration over time. The coincidental convergence of diverse factors may lead to isolated instances of preservation, but in most cases preservation depends on some sort of institutional storage practice. The vast majority of Inca khipu, for example, come from grave sites along the coast. The combination of the careful storage practices associated with burial customs and the dry coastal climate helped delay the process of disintegration, but even so, many of these khipu are extremely fragile and are susceptible to disintegration when handled. No other knotted-string devices have appeared in the archaeological record prior to the Middle Horizon, but the geographical context of the Andes and the models of economic integration devised in response to it would have been conducive to the spread of such a medium both on the coast and in the highlands. Thus, the khipu may have functioned at various socioeconomic and political levels at different times and places.

Chavín de Huántar

The most prominent society of the Early Horizon Period has been associated with the northern site of Chavín de Huántar. Moseley argues that the ecological diversity of the north coast area produced little incentive for societies there to expand into the highland regions to the south (Moseley 1978: 506–507, 516, 521), but the Early Horizon site of Atalla in the central highlands constitutes an exception to this tendency. Burger and Matos Mendieta explain that Atalla exhibits a Chavín pottery style and large-scale, public masonry projects consistent with the site at Chavín de Huántar. As Burger and Matos Mendieta point out, the largest mercury deposits in Latin America are located near Atalla. Thus, this extension of Chavín influence into the central highlands during the Early Horizon was probably motivated by a desire for access to cinnabar, a mercury sulfide used in red pigments, which would have been a luxury product in the north (Burger and Matos Mendieta 2002: 153).

With the exception of such cases as this, the lowland communities of the north may have had little incentive to expand to higher altitudes, but in the highlands the more limited ecological diversity appears to have motivated a marked downward thrust in the vertical control model. The ecology of the highlands led to slower socioeconomic development, but as highland communities domesticated more high-altitude plants and developed more complex economic institutions, there would have been a strong impetus to expand into the more ecologically diverse lowlands (Moseley 1978: 506–507). In the south, where the coastal areas are narrower and support lower population densities than in the north, this impetus resulted in a long history of close ties, and often subordination, to highland societies (Moseley 1978).

In the north, however, with its wide coastal plain with abundant water and a high degree of ecological diversity, the development of state or state-like institutions takes place earlier and is more evenly distributed between coastal and highland societies. At this point, no definitive statements may be made with regard to the use of khipu prior to the Wari in the first millenium BCE. However, other media and the characteristics of material culture from the intervening period between the Preceramic Period and the Middle Horizon Wari may relate in one way or another to the same principles that inform the development of the khipu.

Leading up to and during the Early Horizon Period, Chavín-style ceramics spread throughout a large geographic area. Burger explains that the construction of Chavín de Huántar implies the mobilization of surplus labor on a large scale from the surrounding region; and the population around the site itself eventually grew to several thousand people (Burger 1992: 181). At the same time, Sechín Alto, a site along the central coast, grew to a size many times larger than Chavín de Huántar (Moseley 1982: 12). Burger argues that although many of the inhabitants of such sites would have been farmers, many also would have been engaged in some sort of service economy in support of ritual activities and pan-regional pilgrimages. For Burger, the diffusion of a common ideology, the increased urbanization of ceremonial centers, the economic diversity resulting from the spread of trade networks, and other economic developments all point to the emergence of state-like institutions in which a priest class would have acquired an increasingly more important role in the administration of social and economic affairs. During this period, however, these religious/political institutions would have been relatively fragile, dependent as they were on the hegemonic prestige of a religious ideology and uncoerced tribute in the form of gifts (Burger 1992: 181).

The ideology on which these early polities depended would have emerged out of the lateral, reciprocal economic relationships characteristic of many Andean societies. Burger explains that Chavín iconography expresses this ideology through the themes of harmony, balance, and the resolution of opposites (Burger 1992: 180). Such ideological motifs are consistent with the geopolitics of the Initial and Early Horizon Periods, and they are conducive to the accommodation and consolidation of ethnically diverse groups within a network of social and economic exchange. As individual sites grow into urban centers, the increased population density unavoidably results in new social structures that induce a dialogic development of existing ideological institutions. In the Western model, urbanization also involves a shift from a kin-based to a class-based economic and political structure resulting in social inequality. Here again, however, it may be misleading to impose this model in the Andean context, especially given the fact that the later Inca urban centers maintained a more essentially kin-based system. Nevertheless, the material and economic changes involved in urbanization inevitably would have produced some sort of class structure — albeit highly kin-inflected — with corresponding shifts in social ideologies and institutions designed to prevent social disintegration. Burger argues that the cohesiveness of what he identifies as a regional Chavín cult that spread throughout both the northern highlands as well as to the north coast was religious in nature with more social and economic than political implications (Burger 1992: 213). But the religious cohesion is a parallel development that does not completely explain the social and economic changes that would have necessarily accompanied it, at least in the urban center itself.

The disintegration of the Chavín cult's widespread dominance in the third century BCE may have resulted from the lack of strong, coercive, political institutions necessary for long-term stability. The process of urbanization around regional religious sites like Chavín de Huántar would have involved a social transformation in which specialized labor created a situation characterized by economic interdependence and the possibility, at least to a limited degree, of accumulating individual wealth. The emergence of some sort of class distinction as a result of social differentiation constitutes a gradual shift from a system in which religious elites were tied to regional sites with little or no direct involvement at the local level of government to one in which political elites belonged to, and participated directly in, local levels. Christina Conlee has recently identified precisely this sort of shift in the Nazca drainage during the Late Intermediate Period (Conlee 2003). It may be misleading to identify this shift as a secularization of society, because the elites probably retained a significant link to religious authority. In this context, secularization refers merely to economic and social transformations resulting in an increased complexity of the material, economic infrastructure not only at the proto-urban sites themselves but also at the regional and pan-regional levels. At the local level of regional religious sites like Chavín de Huántar, this shift may have taken place gradually as a result of its function as a center of regional and pan-regional activity and its associated urbanization. Richard Burger suggests that the ever-increasing complexity of economic and social relationships may have induced the incipient development of more centralized control mechanisms that, though necessary for long-term stability, were incompatible with the Chavín cult's ideology and the established institutions through which it had originally spread. Local levels, where economic, social, and political structures were more closely linked, may have been able to resolve this incompatibility; but it evidently proved impossible at the pan-regional level, which erupted into military conflict, as evidenced by the construction of military fortifications during the period of Chavín's disintegration. Thus, as Burger explains, "Chavín civilization was doomed by its very structure" (Burger 1992: 229).

In spite of the return to regional spheres without significant interaction after the collapse of Chavín, the socioeconomic stratification persisted and in some areas even intensified (Burger 1992: 229). The shift from a politically weak pan-regional religious/ideological orientation to politically strong local and regional systems resulted in the dissolution of Chavín influence, but at the same time it laid the groundwork for the later emergence of the more centralized Moche state in the Early Intermediate Period.

The Moche and Their Media

The archaeological history of the Peruvian Andes bears witness to the rise and decline of major societies such as Chavín, Moche, Tiwanaku and Wari, Chimu, and finally Inca. It is important to point out, however, that the decline of a dominant group does not necessarily signal a complete dissolution of the social and economic principles and practices on which it was based. As in the case of Chavín, the disintegration of pan-regional relationships may have been the natural result of progressively more complex local developments. In this Andean model of sociopolitical change, the fundamental principles that inform local and regional developments are often unsustainable at the pan-regional level. Nevertheless, an eventually unsuccessful impetus toward pan-regionalism may have effected certain local and regional adjustments that made subsequently more stable institutions possible. This is an admittedly very general model that does not explain the detail and variety that characterizes the complex processes of sociopolitical development, but the concern here is of a very general nature: the relationship between large-scale sociopolitical developments – whatever their nature – and secondary media. And with the emergence of Moche polities from the remains of Chavín, we find evidence of what may have been more complex secondary semiotic systems.

As with other pre-Hispanic cultures, the specific nature of Moche society continues to be a topic of debate. Some researchers argue that it was a highly centralized polity that wielded considerable economic, military, and/or ideological influence of one sort or another over an extended geographic area along the north coast (Billman 2002: 371). One of the reasons for this argument is the identification of mita-style labor systems and associated storage facilities administered by a central authority very similar to that of the Inca (Moseley 1975, 1978: 526; Moseley and Day 1982;

Figure 1.1. Presentation or inspection of food stuffs (After Larco Hoyle 1939: I, 188. Courtesy of Museo Larco, Lima, Peru).

Day 1982). Others, however, see no evidence of any administrative centers (Isbell 1986: 194). More recent work has confirmed the existence of storage facilities without necessarily viewing this as evidence of a unified polity. In fact, the tendency in recent scholarship has been moving toward a less unified model involving disparate polities with common cultural and ideological practices and beliefs. Regardless of whether the Moche was a conquest state, two independent regional polities, a federation of loosely allied groups, or a number of culturally related but independent polities,[6] at least in the final phase of its dominance, the Moche appear to have built on fundamental principles of local Andean cultures to develop mechanisms capable of maintaining networks, whatever their specific nature, involved in the organization of labor and the production of commodities (Bawden 1996: 137).

An image on a Moche ceramic vessel at the Museo Arqueológico Rafael Larco Herrera depicts what may be a ritual related to these activities (see Figure 1.1). Rafael Larco Hoyle argues that this scene presents a banquet of visiting dignitaries (Larco Hoyle 1939: II, 142–149), but Donnan maintains that the represented activity is not clear (Donnan 1976: 77). The individuals involved do not seem to be participating in a feast. In the middle of the image, there appear several rows of slightly anthropomorphized pots, with each row containing a different product, as indicated by the contents that protrude from the top of each container. On the right-hand side of the image, another three rows of ceramic jugs are differentiated by their design and their disposition. The jugs in the top row are plain with what appears to be some sort of carrying rope used primarily to facilitate transport.[7] In addition to these ropes, three of the four jugs on the second row exhibit a decorative design. The three jugs on the bottom row

6 For impartial surveys of these various arguments see Shimada 1994: 105–112 and Quilter 2002a: 158–161.

7 Archaeological specimens of such jugs often still have these carrying ropes attached (Jeffrey Quilter, personal communication).

have both the carrying ropes and the decorative design; and they are also portrayed in a horizontal position with their contents pouring into bowls. The activity presented in this image may have involved the consumption of goods, but it may also correspond to the storage and administration of goods and services. The anthropomorphic legs of the ceramic vessels in the middle of the image may serve to indicate that the goods are the product of labor service. Other ceramic vessels depict similarly complex socioeconomic and political activities.

The development of such administrative mechanisms is often indicative of the kind of socioeconomic complexity characteristic of what are often identified as state societies. Chavín may require a revision of the binary opposition between states and non-states, and Moche certainly inherits many uniquely Andean qualities. But Moche regional polities also appear to begin evincing features more characteristic of the traditional "state" category, and these conditions are conducive to the further development of, and innovations in, secondary communicative media. It may be no coincidence, therefore, that more extensive evidence of such systems appears with the rise of the Moche.

The Moche employed several different types of media for different purposes. One of the most prominent and compelling of these media in the archaeological record is the imagery that appears on ceramic vessels as well as murals. As evident in Figure 1.1, Moche ceramic vessels reveal a highly developed pictorial form of realistic representation (Donnan 1976: 21–22; Donnan and McClelland 1999: 22–23). Jeffrey Quilter explains that the highly mimetic quality of Moche art is relatively rare in the pre-Columbian Americas and probably unique in the Andes (Quilter 2001: 21).[8] The mimetic nature of Moche art makes it ostensibly fairly straightforward in its presentation, but this is not to say that the pictorial mode is a passive medium that merely reflects a reality over which it has no influence. The sociocultural, economic, and political motivations for categorizing and distinguishing between classes of persons – for example, through the use of dress – although initially independent of any secondary medium of representation, might very well have been reinforced and even transformed once it emerged as a convention in Moche iconography. Inevitability life will always imitate art to some extent, because every presentation is always already a re-presentation.

Furthermore, even a strict mimeticism is not free of conventionality specific to its own medium. In most mimetic representations, for example, metonymy functions as actively as in verbal language. Traditionally,

---

8 This is not to say that it does not derive from a broader tradition. Quilter notes elsewhere that Moche art participates in a larger tradition of representational styles appearing as far north as Ecuador (personal communication).

metonymy is identified as the essential mode of linguistic description and narration as opposed to the more complete representation possible in painting: hence the saying "a picture is worth a thousand words." But most forms of mimetic representation also employ metonymy in that they are not exhaustively mimetic: they select elements to represent and rely on them to invoke a larger material and cultural context. Although the mimetic mode of Moche art makes it fairly easy to recognize most images, many of the details remain obscure because they relate to cultural objects and practices that are no longer observable. Nevertheless, it is clear (and in any case inevitable) that the represented objects function within a particular system of cultural signification. Any mimetic pictorial mode of representation inevitably incorporates the cultural codes inherent in the segments of everyday life depicted. In other words, the mimetic mode has at its disposal ready-made systems of signification that are incidental to the mimesis itself. The dress and ornaments that characterize certain figures and the activities in which they are engaged would have made them easily identifiable to any one familiar with the cultural context of Moche society.

Such iconographic metonymy involving multiple figures and objects and the relationships between them inherently requires some kind of self-consciously conventional framework. In fact, the common understanding in much current scholarship is that any image is inherently conventional (Mitchell 1980; 1986: 8, 26). Although at first glance the conventions of Moche art do not appear to be as complex as those of Mesoamerica, they share many of the same features. In Moche art, the physical appearance of individual figures, the bodily disposition, the clothing, accoutrements, and associated symbolic images, for example, are reminiscent of Mesoamerican iconographic conventions.

This complexity calls into question the way in which Moche imagery is often conceived. The term "art" often suggests a primarily aesthetic intention devoid of the kind of a priori systematicity that characterizes language and writing. However, in his analysis of Moche fine-line painting, Donnan defines art as a more general category that includes, among other things, all types of pictorial representation including those whose primary function may not be limited to aesthetic pleasure (Donnan 1976: 5–10). In one of the foundational theories of Western aesthetics, Kant also defines art in this broad sense, making a distinction between mechanical art, created primarily to make its object of representation actual, and aesthetic art, which has the primary goal of inducing pleasure (Kant [1790] 2000: 184). This distinction appears to correspond to determinant or rational judgments, on the one hand, and aesthetic judgments, on the other. A rational judgment is one based on the schematized relationship between perception and a priori concepts. In contrast, an aesthetic judgment gives its own rule to the artistic representation. Even in Kant, except perhaps in the case of the sublime, this distinction is not sustainable in any absolute sense: linguistic production can have an aesthetic dimension; and any form of mimetic representation has a rational aspect. But according to Kant the cognition of rational thought differs fundamentally from the cognition that occurs in response to, or in the production of, art – whether it be linguistic or plastic. This difference, however, inheres not in the actualized objects of cognition themselves but in the cognitive procedure through which they are perceived or generated.

In many ways the difference between mechanical or rational judgments and aesthetic judgments depends on originality. In everyday communication, even in the many cases in which linguistic utterances are original in their particular syntax, there is no expectation that linguistic performance be original in the way it employs the general system of language, the rules according to which it actualizes its objects. In fact, communicative effectiveness depends on it not being original in this sense. From a Western perspective, however, art, whether verbal or visual, is expected to be original. In Kantian terms, it is expected to give the rule to its representation; and this is the criterion used to evaluate it. This notion of originality, however, is a modern concept that has a relatively short history. The institution of Moche art certainly does not emphasize originality in this modern sense. The selection and syntactical arrangement or configuration of the images that appear on Moche ceramics varies from one to another, but the signs they employ are highly standardized and conventional (Jackson 2008).

This has led Donnan to identify Moche ceramic art as a type of iconographic writing (Donnan 1976). Donnan uses the term "iconography" here in its more literal etymological meaning of "writing with icons" rather than "the study of images." Both etymologically and in Peircian semiotics, an icon is a sign that refers to its object by virtue of its own qualities, by its similarity to its object (Peirce 1955:104–107), and "graphy" derives from *graphein*, originally meaning to scratch but extended to refer to alphabetic writing. Although any form of visually mimetic inscription is iconic in nature, the term "iconography" as used here is reserved for a system of conventional iconic signs that exhibit a form of systematicity such as a syntax or grammar. Donnan describes Moche iconography as a type of writing because he sees it as "a symbolic system that follows consistent rules of expression . . . similar to the symbolic system of a language" having the iconographic equivalent of nouns, verbs, adjectives, and adverbs (Donnan 1976: 5–10, 21–34). The various scenes that appear in Figure 1.2, for example, depict a variety of individuals, actions, places, and so forth with which analogies to the elements of verbal grammar can be established.

Margaret Jackson develops this line of reasoning even further in terms of both its theoretical foundations and its supporting analysis (Jackson 2008). Jackson begins with a theoretical discussion that recognizes the

Figure 1.2. Image of Moche handling of prisoners of war (Drawing by Donna McClelland).

semiotically heterogenous nature of all sign systems, and she goes on to argue that in addition to strictly mimetic conventions, Moche iconography appears to employ logographs and rebuses. She also identifies compound icons "embedded with various modifiers (symbols, locators, informants, and indexes)... capable of creating and recording new narratives by means of combining and disassembling variable iconographic units" (Jackson 2008: 148–149.

The point is not that this iconography is necessarily a form of writing in the same sense as alphabetic script. Posing the question in terms of an alphabetic standard is not very productive, because it imposes a taxonomy with implicit, unexamined, theoretical premises that I would argue are misleading.[9] The more important questions have to do with exactly what kind of information this medium actually conveyed, how it did so, for what purposes, and in what contexts. This is a sociohistorical and ideological question as well as a semiotic or theoretical one, but it does not begin with a rigidly preconceived conceptualization of semiotic possibilities. Certainly, this type of iconography is theoretically capable of conveying a wide variety of information types. Modes of mimetic representation are much more versatile than a Western perspective normally recognizes. If the sign carriers of Moche iconography were limited primarily to ceramic vessels, limitations of time and energy would suggest that this medium was not adapted for communication or record keeping to the same extent as Mesoamerican iconography or the khipu; but this does not mean that it was necessarily any less communicative within the context of its use.

9 In the history of this debate, the application of the term "writing" to indigenous American media such as the khipu or Mesoamerican iconography has been, and continues to be, useful for political reasons. But ultimately, this is a semantic issue that can often obscure the underlying theoretical issues involved.

In the case of Mesoamerican iconography, there clearly appears to be a dialogic relationship between the symbolism of both ritual and everyday life, on the one hand, and iconographic conventions, on the other; and this may have been true of Moche iconography as well. From an alphabetic perspective, such a system involves rather ambiguous and polysemic practices, but in some ways it makes possible a higher degree of specificity. In his study of Moche public art, Quilter argues that the increased simplicity in the Moche art style may be related to the need for an iconography that was more "readable" by the general population and hence more efficacious in conveying the dominant ideology of larger, complex polities (Quilter 2001: 41).

One of the principles of this type of iconography may have involved the format of the objects depicted. Jackson argues that Moche iconography exhibits a configurational, as opposed to a linear, syntax that "operated in a simultaneously horizontal and vertically layered manner" (Jackson 2008: 149). Even in early Moche research, Larco Hoyle maintained that the images of individuals in Figure 1.1 are arranged according to a rigorous hierarchy (Larco Hoyle [1939] 2001: 187–189). Another type of mimetic hierarchy in this image may have related to the goods produced and stored. The products in Figure 1.1, for example, are separated and organized neatly into rows in a systematic way. Of course, in the case of human figures and other realistic objects, this type of mimetic hierarchy probably corresponded to an organizational system independent of, or at least equiprimordial with, the conventions of the secondary medium. In other words, the organizational conventions of the secondary medium probably reflect actual practices involving political and cultural principles of categorization and organization as opposed to merely arbitrary conventions of the secondary medium itself. Nevertheless, the very use of such iconography inherently involves the adaptation of the mimetic intention to the exigencies of secondary representation, which induces a greater level of self-reflexiveness with regard to the mimetic codes that require adaptation to the secondary medium. In this case, the transpositioning of a rigorous hierarchy that characterizes the culturally determined relationships between both people and objects appears to have produced a corresponding convention in the secondary medium involving what we might call paradigmatic information structures.

Such conventions may relate directly to ethnocategories associated with Wari ceramics (Isbell 1977: 53) and Inca khipu records (Murra 1981). It may be too much of a leap to jump immediately from the apparent information structures in Moche iconography to those that characterized khipu records, but only in that the semiotic medium involved is so different. As I will explain in more detail in Chapters 4 and 5, khipu records associated with both tribute and narrative histories of the Inca Empire also employ paradigmatic information structures (Brokaw 2003). Thus, there seem to be certain conventional homologies between these media. It is precisely this type of intermedia relationship that appears to characterize Andean semiotic practices in general. This relationship is evident in other types of semiosis that may have served to bridge the gap between the mimeticism of Moche iconography and the nonmimetic dimensions of the khipu.

First, as already explained, Moche art itself is not exhaustively mimetic in that it relies heavily on metonymic contextual indicators. Much of the symbolic significance in Moche iconography derives from the cultural symbolism and implied context inherent in the mimetic representation of such figures as priests, warriors, and hunters in their characteristic garb.[10] Whether or not they dressed in this way when they were actually engaged in the represented activities is another question. In some cases, the scenes depicted in Moche art are rituals, and in the excavation of tombs, Donnan and others have been able to identify certain individuals because they were buried in the garb and with the objects that appear in Moche fine-line paintings (Donnan and McClelland 1999: 23; Donnan and Castillo 1992, 1994; Donnan 1985, 1988; Alva and Donnan 1993). But in Moche art, human figures wear elaborate garb even in scenes depicting quotidian activities such as hunting and fishing. Donnan argues that the incompatibility between the dress and the activity suggests that these scenes also correspond to ritual enactments and therefore that Moche art is of a nonsecular nature (Donnan 1976: 130–137). On the other hand, as Donnan explicitly recognizes, the distinction between secular and religious activities is not sustainable in the context of such cultures as the Moche. Even more important for understanding the iconographic conventions is that the realism of Moche art is not a guarantee that it portrays objects, people, and events exactly as they appear in real life. The elaborate garb of hunters and fisherman in Moche art may depict the dress of ritual practices and at the same time represent the quotidian activity of hunting and fishing. The elaborate dress may be an iconographic convention rather than a mimetic correspondence to the way in which these real-world activities were normally carried out. Such conventions are still mimetic in that they depict people, objects, and actions, regardless of whether the scenes themselves correspond exactly to the reality of the activity represented. In this type of iconography, the objects and actions represented are essentially first degree or primary mediations transpositioned into a secondary medium. In the case of ritual activities, it would seem that such iconographic representations transposition the primary mediation of the ritual, which would already be a performative representation, although still primary, of quotidian activities.

10 See the analysis, for example, in Donnan 1976: 118.

It is important to keep in mind that the distinction between primary and secondary mediation is a heuristic strategy that is not rigorously sustainable. In some sense, any cognition is always already secondary, but the cognition of an object or phenomenon differs significantly from the cognition of a representation of that object or phenomenon. One might argue that the elaborate dress of a priest and hierarchical structures are representations, but they are primary in the sense that they function in the direct interpersonal relationships of the individuals who participate in Moche society. The essential difference between primary and secondary mediation, then, often has to do with the transposition from one medium into another. Moche art re-represents these objects and phenomena by transpositioning them from their primary context into the secondary iconographic medium of murals and painted ceramics in configurations that might not necessarily correspond completely with any given instance of the original practice.

Many ways to codify abstractly the rules and categories of Moche iconography surely exist, but systematic codification may be misleading because it suggests a rigid, independent code that is inconsistent with what is inherently a more flexible and integrated phenomenon. Nevertheless, some distinctions are heuristically productive in analyzing the possible development of this medium over time and its relation to the semiotic principles of other media forms such as the khipu. For example, it may be useful to distinguish between the transpositioning of primary media such as mimetic objects and characteristic garb and the transpositioning of other secondary media. The use of ceramics and textiles in Moche art, for example, appears to employ more discrete, and in some cases apparently arbitrary, nonmotivated semiotic conventions that were transpositioned into the iconographic medium. The style and decoration of ceramic vessels, for example, may have served an important semiotic function. The designs that serve to differentiate ceramic containers in Figure 1.1 may be primarily arbitrary signs possibly used to identify the contents of the vessels that are then transpositioned into the iconographic medium incidental to the mimetic mode.

The iconographic use of ceramics and textiles is even more suggestive in Figure 1.3, a well known fine-line drawing of what appears to be a textile workshop (Campana 1994). The scenes depicted on the vessel present eight weavers and six additional individuals associated in some way with the workshop. Alongside each of the weavers there appear anywhere from four to eight spindles of yarn, a ceramic vessel, and in some cases a completed textile. One might hypothesize that the ceramic vessels represent payment, reciprocity, supplies, or something similar, but the variety of shapes, styles, and decorative markings suggests that they have more than merely a single, generic iconic significance. This variation may reflect some merely aesthetic principle; but if different types and styles of ceramic vessel

Figure 1.3. Moche textile workshop (Drawing by Donna McClelland).

were used for different purposes, then they may convey more specific information in these drawings. Furthermore, in the case of the multiple images of identical spindles of yarn, the variation in quantity may be a semiotic rather than merely an aesthetic convention. It is important to keep in mind, however, that this type of iconography calls into question the very distinction between aesthetic and rational thought that informs the conceptual difference between art and more self-consciously conventional modes of semiosis such as writing.

Of course, the distinctive patterns of the textiles that appear in Figure 1.3 may correspond to items, perhaps articles of clothing, identifiable by members of Moche society. It is clear that Moche iconography employs clothing styles both to differentiate between classes of people and to identify specific individuals. The use of distinctive garb to identify individuals is no less conventional and arbitrary than the use of ceramic styles and decorative designs. From a semiotic perspective, however, the difference is subtle but significant. The distinctive garb means something only in the integrated context in which it is worn. It makes no difference that one could recognize the garb without a body, because it would not normally function in a disembodied context. The garb is only one element in what is an essentially integrated context that also includes the position of the figure and its relationship to other images in the scene. The disembodiment of the textile, however, makes possible the re-signification of the image. Given their disembodied nature, the textiles in Figure 1.3 do not function to indicate an identity as they may when actually worn. In this case, they appear to represent themselves as units or categories of economic production, and as such they take on a new semiotic function that was probably more closely related to the function of the images of distinctive ceramic containers in Figure 1.1.

The use of such signs may not be as qualitatively distinct from the semiotics of the iconographic mode as is the use of the rebus principle in Mesoamerican iconography, but it is no less significant. A rebus is a type of iconographic pun in which a mimetic image is used for its phonetic rather than its mimetic value. Thus, it is a type of semiosis that is dependent on, but fundamentally different from, mimetic iconography. The rebus principle would have had a precedent in the use of verbal puns in oral language, but the iconographic puns used for toponyms and personal names as they appear in Mesoamerican script was an innovation inherently specific to the iconographic medium. The use of iconographic puns effectively incorporates a phonographic mode of semiosis into the otherwise primarily iconographic script, producing a higher degree or an additional dimension of semiotic heterogeneity.

One might argue that other uses of mimetic signs in nonmimetic ways, such as the function of ceramics and textiles discussed above, do not constitute an analogous development, because they merely transposition pre-existing media incidental to the mimetic mode. The representation of ceramic pots is mimetic in that these iconographic objects are employed for their mimetic value (i.e., to represent themselves), but they function within a larger, pre-existing semiotic system at the level of primary social and economic interaction. It may be an exaggeration to call these signs arbitrary, because they are intimately linked to their referents within the integrated context of primary mediation, but even in that context they already have the essential features of an arbitrary sign. In the mimetic mode of the iconographic medium itself, these signs are metonymic in that they served to invoke the referents with which they were associated as such in the primary mediation of social interaction, but in many cases the association itself is semiotically (i.e., logically) arbitrary. The particular abstract design on a ceramic pot or a Moche headband, for example, appears to have no motivated or logical relationship to the function or the content of the pot or to the identity of the individual wearing the headband, respectively.

The nature of this arbitrary relationship is nothing unusual or extraordinary. All cultures use logically arbitrary signs in one way or another, and the development of some form of secondary medium, even if to a very limited degree, is also arguably universal. In theory, the use of any arbitrary sign – whether in the context of primary or secondary mediation – would create the potential for a greater self-reflexive awareness of the semiosis involved, which in turn would be conducive to further innovative developments. The degree to which this self-reflexive awareness arises, the extent to which it induces semiotic innovations, and the direction that those innovations take depends on a variety of factors: the specific nature of the media, the types of semiosis that they employ, the nature of the ideological institutions in conjunction with which they develop, and so forth. The possibility that the conditions conducive to raising the level of semiotic self-reflexivity will emerge are dramatically greater when a transpositioning of logically arbitrary signs takes place from the primary mediation of social (to include economic and political) interaction into the secondary mediation of a material sign system.

This is not to say that Moche iconography did not have a social function, but that the semiosis itself was not necessarily a social phenomenon in the sense that it was not necessarily limited to an interpersonal context: it could occur merely between an individual and the medium itself. In fact, the heuristic distinction between primary and secondary media that I have drawn here depends precisely on the extent to which semiosis may occur between a "reader" or "writer" and a "text" divorced from a context of direct interpersonal communication. Regardless of whether or not the semiosis typically occurred in such a context, the secondary nature of the medium and the epistemological shift involved in the process of transpositioning would have been conducive to the emergence of a greater awareness of the semiotic principles involved. This awareness would in turn be conducive to semiotic innovations, particularly when the transpositioning involves the isolation of logically arbitrary signs.

Initially, these innovations may include an adaptation of mimetic resources to a different form of semiosis, as in the case of the iconographic pun or rebus. Moche iconography clearly exhibits a rather sophisticated process of transpositioning of signs from the primary mediation of social interaction to the secondary medium of iconographic script, and the use of distinctive ceramics and disembodied textiles in Figures 1.1 and 1.3 appears to isolate logically arbitrary signs indicating precisely the kind of conventional innovation consistent with a move toward a more self-consciously conventional semiosis. Margaret Jackson has also argued for the possibility that Moche iconography employs rebuses (Jackson 2008), which would have contributed even further to the cognitive sophistication of this medium.

Such secondary media develop over time; and I would argue that even if they are originally abstract in nature, they are usually parasitic in one way or another on the mediation of primary semiotic phenomena. This is why some form of mimetic medium is common to most if not all cultures. In other words, semiotic principles are not invented from scratch: they develop dialogically in relation to (1) the primary mediation of their referents, (2) the nature of the secondary medium, and (3) other media employed by the same society. This is not to say that invention and innovation does not occur but rather that it occurs in the context of this dialogic relationship. Even the alleged invention of the Korean phonemic script was informed by principles already inherent in the Chinese logographic writing system that it was designed to supplement.

Furthermore, it may be misleading to conceive of the development of any single medium as a linear, one-dimensional progression from its immediate precursors in isolation from other forms of semiosis. The dominance of alphabetic script in modern Western cultures makes it difficult to conceive of this medium as *merely* one among others in an essentially multimedia context, but this is what it originally was and in fact continues to be. Widespread literacy is a relatively recent phenomenon even among European societies. The nature of alphabetic script may make it less susceptible to intermedia relationships, or perhaps it merely makes these relationships more subtle and therefore less perceptible. It is true that the particular dialogic development of alphabetic script and Western institutions has tended to isolate alphabetic writing from other media, although this has been changing with the emergence of electronic media. Nevertheless, no single medium has ever completely dominated social interaction; and in most cultures, a much more intimate relationship exists between the various media employed than in modern Western society prior to the advent of electronic media.

At least two or three other forms of nonmimetic media seem to have interacted in one way or another with Moche iconography. Perhaps the clearest example of nonmimetic semiotic practices consists of the use of what have been called makers' marks on adobe bricks to indicate the individual or group who made them (see Figure 1.4; Hastings and Moseley 1975: 199). Such marks are also common in Europe and Mesopotamia as well. In most cases, these marks are believed to have served to identify the producer of the object (brick, carved stone, pot, etc.) or as a method of signifying ownership or keeping track of the labor performed. Although the systems of marks were essentially the same in semiotic function, the European and Andean economic systems that gave rise to these conventions differ significantly.

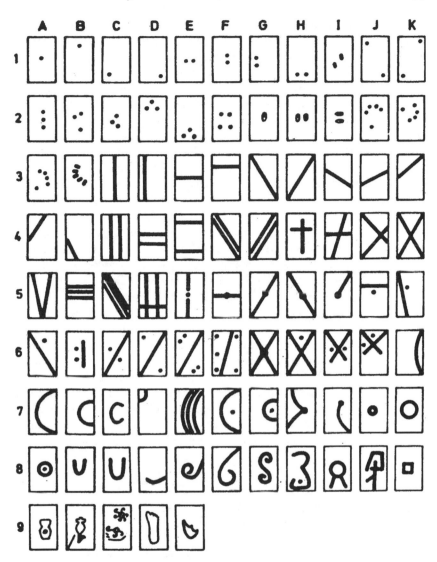

Figure 1.4. Assortment of makers' marks (From Hastings and Moseley 1975: 199). Reproduced by permission of the Society for American Archaeology from *American Antiquity* 40.2 (1975): 199.

Andean corporate labor projects involved the contribution of labor in a system of reciprocity and redistribution. Even more suggestive is the fact that the function of the makers' marks as a record of labor contributions coincides precisely with the kind of information that would be recorded in the administration of community labor obligations. Whether or not the Moche marks identified individuals or groups, they would have effectively allowed the determination and assessment of labor contributions.

Although these marks constitute a relatively simple system with a limited function, they may have informed more complex practices. The more elaborate, mimetic dimension of Moche iconography is more complex stylistically, but the nonmimetic nature of the makers' marks involves a different kind of semiotic operation. These marks may relate in one way or another to the use of the textile icons discussed above and to the development of more complex systems such as the square textile designs known as *tocapu*. These identifying marks seem to have a clear stylistic relationship to certain textile conventions that would eventually culminate in the *tocapu* designs of the Incas. The "S" pattern of the mark located at G-8 in Figure 1.4, for example, is very similar to Guaman Poma's drawing of the *tocapu* on the tunic of Manco Capac (Figure 1.5; Guaman Poma de Ayala [1615] 1980: [86] 86), and the mark at H-8 is virtually identical to one of the *tocapu* designs on the tunic of Topa Inca Yupanqui (Figure 1.6; Guaman Poma de Ayala [1615] 1980: [110] 110). There may be a dialogic relationship, then, between these makers' marks and the textile *tocapu* designs. In the past, I may have been too dismissive of the line of argument that identifies the *tocapu* as participating in a complex semiotic system (Brokaw 2005: 572). Researchers such as Thomas Barthel (1970, 1971), Victoria de la Jara (1970), and William Burns (1990, 2002) have argued that the *tocapu* were part of an elaborate writing system, but the fallacious nature of their arguments obscured, for me at least, the possibility of the kind of more nuanced interpretations offered more recently by Carmen Arellano, Rocío Quispe-Agnoli, Mary Frame, and others (Arellano 1999; Quispe-Agnoli 2005; Frame 2007).

Another possibly related example of a complex semiotic system employed by the Moche involves the inscription of designs on lima beans studied by Rafael Larco Hoyle (1939, 1942, 1943a, 1943b) and Victoria de la Jara (1970). Larco Hoyle argues that certain images of inscribed lima beans on Moche ceramics suggest the existence of an ideographic writing system. It is important here to distinguish between Larco Hoyle's more radical assertion that the inscribed beans were a system of writing capable of recording historical narratives and the more limited argument that they constituted some kind of semiotic system. He begins his analysis of the iconographic evidence by affirming his premise that a complex civilization like that of the Moche must have had some kind of writing system, because civilization and writing go hand in hand. In spite of Larco Hoyle's predetermined conclusions, his presentation of the evidence itself is very suggestive.

Figure 1.5. Manco Capac (From Guaman Poma de Ayala 1615: 86. Courtesy of the Danish Royal Library, Copenhagen).

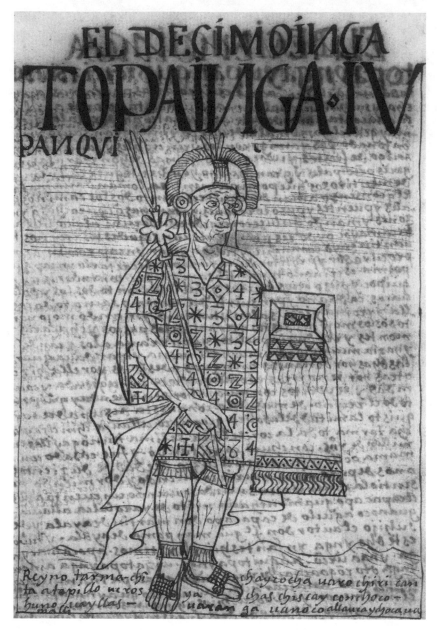

Figure 1.6. Topa Inca Yupanqui (From Guaman Poma de Ayala 1615: 110. Courtesy of the Danish Royal Library, Copenhagen).

Figure 1.7. Bean runners (After Larco Hoyle 1939: I, 95. Courtesy of Museo Larco, Lima, Peru).

Larco Hoyle identifies a Moche iconographic theme involving figures that appear to be runners carrying small bags (see Figures 1.7 and 1.8). The runners are also associated with lima beans that exhibit often intricate designs inscribed on their surfaces (see Figure 1.9). Larco Hoyle argues that the bags served to hold the inscribed beans, which functioned to record

Figure 1.8. Close-up of bean runner (After Larco Hoyle 1939: I, 87. Courtesy of Museo Larco, Lima, Peru).

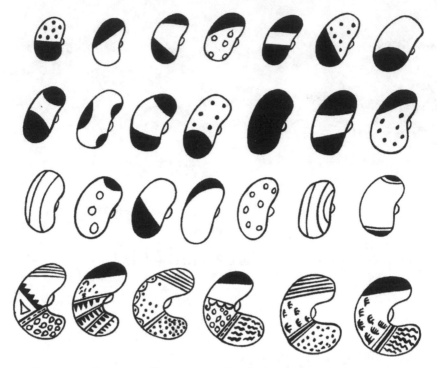

Figure 1.9. Assortment of bean patterns (After Larco Hoyle 1939: I, 94. Courtesy of Museo Larco, Lima, Peru).

messages. He identifies these runners as messengers that participate in an institution that would later give rise to a Chimu equivalent, which in turn would influence the Inca *chasqui* system (Larco Hoyle 1939: II, 122–123). Larco Hoyle was able to match up both the images of beans and those of the bags with actual archaeological objects (Images 1, 2, and 3). The beans and the messengers also appear in scenes in which two people handle and discuss them. The scene in Figure 1.10, for example, portrays the bean readers themselves as zoomorphic beans who handle distinctively inscribed beans and deploy them in specific configurations in the context of what appears to be a communicative interaction. Furthermore, Larco Hoyle explains that modern individuals and communities in the highlands continued to employ similar objects such as kernels of corn organized into bags as an accounting system to keep track of crops and livestock and that along the coast they used lima beans for the same purpose. He suggests that these practices are vestiges of an ancient, more elaborate Moche ideographic writing system that was not limited to accounting records (Larco Hoyle 1939: II, 119–120).

Figure 1.10. The reading of beans (After Larco Hoyle 1939: II, 147. Courtesy of Museo Larco, Lima, Peru).

Other scholars argue that the use of these beans as indicated in Figure 1.10 is actually related to some sort of game or divination as opposed to writing or record-keeping practices (Régulo Franco, personal communication). However, even if such beans were employed in some kind of game or for purposes of divination, this does not necessarily mean that they did not constitute a semiotic medium. That would be like saying that because Boggle and Scrabble are games, the letters on the respective cubes and tiles of these games are not part of a writing system. In fact, these games depend on the writing system. Furthermore, limiting these objects to the context of games does not have the same explanatory force as Larco Hoyle's hypothesis. It does not take into account, for example, all of the contexts in which the beans appear in Moche iconography.

Likewise, the use of these beans in divinatory practices supports rather than undermines their status as a semiotic system. Historically, many different cultures have attributed magical properties to alphabetic writing as well. Frank Salomon has even documented the use of khipu in divination practices – what he calls khipumancy – in the modern community of Tupicocha (Salomon 2004: 225–231). Of course, in this case, the mundane semiotic conventions of the khipu are no longer employed productively, but the members of the community are very aware of the semiotic nature of the medium. In some cases they even have a folk understanding of how some of the material features of the khipu functioned. In any case, divination inherently involves the identification of signs, albeit esoteric, that tell the future; and semiotic media constitute sign systems. Thus, in a society that both possessed a secondary system of communication or record keeping

Figure 1.11. Decorative bean pseudo-signs (After Larco Hoyle 1939: I, 114.
Courtesy of Museo Larco, Lima, Peru).

and engaged in divinatory practices, it would be surprising if they did not
associate the two in some way. If the scene in Figure 1.10 actually represents
some form of divination, then this would only lend further support to the
possibility that this medium constituted some form of secondary semiotic
system.

One of the principal problems with Larco Hoyle's assertion that the bean
system recorded narratives is that any given scene contains a rather limited
number of designs. Figure 1.11, for example, is a reproduction of the bean
images on a single ceramic container, all of which appear to be virtually
identical (see also Image 4). If these beans functioned in a semiotic system
complex enough to convey narrative information, one would expect there
to be a large number of distinct designs. One might argue that the image
of these beans on a ceramic vessel is a meta-representation that may not
have been intended to reproduce an actual message. Similar phenomena
have been identified in the Maya context, where what have been termed
"pseudo glyphs" appear on ceramic vessels. In other words, the image of
the beans may have merely been a convention used to denote semiosis in
general rather than the specific content of a communicative interaction.
The image of a number of identical beans may have functioned in the same
way as images of alphabetic documents that contain a series of wavy lines or
Guaman Poma's representation of accounting and astrological khipu with
no knots (Figures 1.12 and 1.13; Guaman Poma de Ayala [1615] 1980:
[360] 362, [883] 897): a transcendental reduction that represents the
medium as such without any content necessarily pertinent to the particular
context of the representation. On the other hand, the number of dots on
each bean varies, possibly indicates a numerical dimension of these signs,
whether transcendental in this case or not. Other images include beans
with a variety of distinct designs, but even so it is impossible to determine

Figure 1.12. Khipu accountant (Guaman Poma de Ayala 1615: {360} 362.
Courtesy of the Danish Royal Library, Copenhagen).

Figure 1.13. Khipu astrologer (Guaman Poma de Ayala 1615: [883] 897. Courtesy of the Danish Royal Library, Copenhagen).

if they are deployed according to some form of syntax or what they are designed to signify.

Furthermore, the fact that Moche fine-line painting was not the primary sign carrier of this system means that the designs that have survived may constitute only a very small percentage of those in actual use. Given the perishable nature of the beans themselves, we may never have access to a corpus of "bean texts" sufficiently diverse enough to provide a basis for decipherment projects. Nevertheless, the extant evidence from the media that transpositioned these beans suggests that they participated in some form of semiosis.

Victoria de la Jara, the only other scholar to follow up on Larco Hoyle's hypothesis, divides the beans into four different categories based on stylistic features and temporal periods. She reverses the direction of influence posited by Larco Hoyle, arguing that the oldest beans are from Paracas, which then give rise to their use by the Nazca, followed by two periods identified as Mochica A and Mochica B (Jara 1970: 32). Recognizing the problem presented by the limited number of distinct designs, Jara argues that these beans may have had at least two different uses: (1) the images of identical beans may have been used as part of a game, as argued by other researchers; and (2) the images containing a variety of distinct designs may indicate a writing system. Jara focuses on the idea that they constitute a writing system, and she identifies two classes of beans that she labels signs and ciphers. The signs would correspond to words or ideas and the ciphers would represent numbers. Jara also suggests that the medium of inscribed beans is closely related to the *tocapu* designs that appear on textiles as well as on drinking vessels called *keros*. She claims that the Mochica B system is the most complex and that it is related to the Inca writing system, by which she means the *tocapu*. Jara argues further that this Mochica B system also developed a separate method for representing numbers that is related to the khipu (Jara 1970: 32). According to Jara's argument, the Moche beans informed both a logographic *tocapu* writing system and the numerical record-keeping system of the khipu (Jara 1970: 29, 32).[11]

The arguments about semiotic beans presented by Larco Hoyle and further developed by Jara are very suggestive, but they are also problematic. For the most part, Larco Hoyle's discussion and analysis of the archaeological evidence is sound, and the correlation he establishes with contemporary

11 In their attempts to prove that the *tocapu* constituted a logographic system of writing, Jara and Thomas Barthel claimed to have deciphered some of the *tocapu* signs, but their analysis is based on inexplicable logical leaps and unsupported assertions that make their work even more problematic than Larco Hoyle's. The fallacious reasoning seems to have eclipsed whatever legitimately valuable insights their analysis might contain. Furthermore, it is difficult to discern what might be well founded, because their entire discussion consists of provocative assertions without any supporting explanation or argument.

cultural practices is illuminating. Unfortunately, the radical assertion about narrative capability that he makes in the introduction and conclusion of his discussion does not follow from the actual analysis of the evidence. The issue is not whether the inscribed beans of the Moche actually did record historical narratives but rather whether the evidence supports this assertion; and Larco Hoyle's argument does not even address this issue. Larco Hoyle was convinced that the Moche must have employed a complex writing system, because they were a complex society; and according to prevailing wisdom, complex societies are made possible only by the development of a writing system that can record historical narratives. Given the problematic nature of Larco Hoyle's syllogism, his actual discussion and analysis is surprisingly constrained, objective, and logically consistent. He focuses primarily on the presentation and discussion of the material evidence. Certainly, his interpretation is not definitive. Alternative explanations are possible, but Larco Hoyle presents a convincing analysis for the more modest conclusion that the inscribed beans used by the Moche were a kind of semiotic medium. The disjuncture between the unfounded premise and exaggerated conclusion, on the one hand, and the actual analysis, on the other, may have discouraged later scholars from giving due credit to a more limited version of his argument.

The medium of inscribed beans may not have recorded and transmitted historical narratives in the way Larco Hoyle believed, but the variety of inscription designs and the contexts in which they appear suggest that they were indeed part of a semiotic medium that functioned on a more self-conscious level than the general codes of cultural life. The stagnation of this line of research may stem more from the lack of evidence than from the rejection of Larco Hoyle's and Jara's unfounded and rather grandiose claims. Given the limited number of these inscribed beans found in the archaeological record and the relatively limited nature of the iconographic contexts in which they appear, there may be no way to corroborate even the limited version of Larco Hoyle's hypothesis, much less decipher the beans themselves. Although there have been no advances in this line of research, neither have there been any convincing alternative theories offered about these images and their associated archaeological objects. Furthermore, Jara's otherwise dubious analysis suggests at the very least a relationship between this medium and other forms of Andean semiosis such as the *tocapu* and possibly the khipu.

The semiotic media employed by the Incas, then, may have had their roots in Moche developments on the north coast. At the very least, the practice of using these beans seems to exhibit a formal relationship to the use of colored stones or kernels of corn employed by Inca and colonial-era Andean societies, often in conjunction with khipu accounting. Guaman Poma's drawing of a khipu accountant includes an image of a grid whose

Figure 1.14. Moche bean runners (After Larco Hoyle 1939: I, 106. Courtesy of Museo Larco, Lima, Peru).

boxes contain different quantities of black and white circles (see Figure 1.12; Guaman Poma de Ayala [1615] 1980: [360] 362). This grid is normally identified as relating to the accounting practice and the device referred to as *yupana* (Images 5 and 6). Thus, Jara's assertion that the allegedly numerical signs of the Mochica B bean inscriptions were related to the khipu is intriguing, but unfortunately she provides no evidence or explanation of this relationship.

One possible piece of evidence that may establish a link between these media among the Moche appears in Figure 1.14. Larco Hoyle points out that the object held in the hand of the individuals depicted looks an awful lot like a khipu and that this is the same context in which the beans appear. The figures are runners who are dressed in the same way and with the same or similar headdresses as the bean runners in Figures 1.7 and 1.8. The identity of the object in question is not exactly clear, but it is certainly possible that it is a stylized representation of a khipu. The perishable nature of the khipu may mean that it was in use for hundreds or even thousands of years prior to its appearance in the archaeological record. It may be that the khipu and the semiotic beans originally functioned in different contexts but then began to converge as the development of Andean societies placed increasingly greater demands on their record-keeping practices. Even if we assume that the Moche employed khipu at some level of society, it would seem that the inscribed beans were clearly the more important medium. The number of distinct bean designs discovered on ceramics and textiles is larger than what one would need if their use were limited to numerical calculation. The diversity of these designs documented by Larco Hoyle would have been sufficient for some form of record keeping. The extent to which the Moche used this medium to record different types of information is impossible to determine with any certainty; but they appear to constitute a much more semiotically sophisticated and complex system than the mimeticism of strict iconography.

Later, the Wari and Inca states evidently shifted the emphasis to the khipu while maintaining the use of beans or other small objects often as an ancillary or complementary system that facilitated calculations. The advantages and disadvantages inherent to each type of medium make this shift understandable. The inscribed beans would have been more conducive to short-term semiotic operations, whereas the khipu lends itself to longer-term record keeping. In any case, as Wari and Tiwanaku emerge as the dominant polities of the Middle Horizon Period, bean imagery loses the prominence it had in Moche fine-line painting.

Before moving on to discuss the Middle Horizon Period, it is important to point out that my treatment of these early periods is not an attempt to be exhaustive. Chavín and Moche were not the only cultures to emerge during these periods. On the southern coast, for example, Nazca flourished at the same time as the Moche, and Paracas before them. These cultures developed their own ceramic and textile media that also exhibit some of the same phenomena. Interestingly, both Larco Hoyle and Jara point out that the bean iconography actually appears on Nazca textiles (Larco Hoyle 1939: II, 123–124; see Images 7–10) and both Nazca and Tiwanaku-style ceramics (Larco Hoyle 1942). A comprehensive investigation of this bean imagery in Moche, Nazca, and Tiwanaku cultures may be productive in furthering the argument made by Larco Hoyle, but such a project is beyond the scope of this study.

Around 500 or 600 CE, the dominance of the Moche began to wane. As in the case of Chavín, it is difficult to determine the cause of the Moche collapse. In an argument similar to that of Burger's hypothesis about Chavín's demise (Burger 1992: 229), Garth Bawden suggests that although one or more catalysts probably contributed to the decline of the Moche, an inherent structural paradox in the way Moche polities had developed resulted in a social and political instability that was inevitable from the start (Bawden 1994; 1995; 1996: 271–275, 309–319). In any case, as the Moche sphere of influence began to diminish along the northern coast, the locus of dominant pan-regional social, economic, and political activity shifted to the southern highland societies of Tiwanaku and Wari.

The complex highland polities of Tiwanaku and Wari did not emerge out of the remnants of a previously pan-regional socioeconomic order as did the Moche from Chavín. Although later in time, the emergence of these highland states appears to be an independent but parallel development. However, the Moche may have influenced sociopolitical and economic developments in the highlands, especially with regard to Wari, in ways that are not yet completely apparent. As Moche waned and Wari grew, there appears to have been significant contact between the two cultures. Initially scholars argued that an expansionist Wari state was one, if not the, factor that caused the demise of the Moche (Shady 1982), but this view has given way to more nuanced perspectives that see Wari's influence as much less direct (Quilter 2002a: 160; Topic 1991; Castillo 2001). Whether or not Wari was responsible for the Moche collapse, substantive contact with the coastal polities' storage and distribution systems would have had an influence on the emerging pan-regional economy in the highlands; and it is at this point that a type of khipu reappears in the archaeological record.

2

Middle Horizon Media and the Emergence of the Khipu

In the Middle Horizon Period, knotted cord devices first begin appearing unambiguously in the archaeological record (Conklin 1982; Shady, Narváez, and López 2000). I have argued that the first evidence of archaeological khipu does not coincide with the invention of this medium but rather with the development of socioeconomic and political institutions conducive to its preservation. Such institutions originally have a number of different media on which they can draw; but as institutions become more complex, they tend to concentrate their semiotic activities into fewer media with often simpler yet more sophisticated conventions. In this chapter, I argue that this is precisely what occurs in the Middle Horizon and Late Intermediate Periods and that the archaeological record contains traces of the relationship between the various media involved. I suggest that both the Wari and the Chimu emphasized different forms of media related to the administration of goods and conducive to their respective economic and political systems. In both cases, the principles that inform certain types of architecture and the practices involved in the storage and distribution of commodities exhibit structural affinities with what we know of khipu conventions and the associated device known as *yupana*.

Tiwanaku and Highland Political Economy

As in the case of Chavín and Moche, studies of the subsequent Middle Horizon Tiwanaku and Wari cultures in the southern highlands often engage in the same debates about state versus non-state status; military versus economic expansion; direct political control versus more indirect, economic relationships; centralized versus decentralized political organization; and so forth. Such debates are difficult to resolve, because research on Tiwanaku and Wari encounter the same difficulties in interpreting the archaeological record that characterize studies of Chavín and Moche societies. Initial work on Tiwanaku assumed that the spread of a common iconography and the evidence of trade relationships indicated a centralized, hierarchical polity that governed a rather large geographic area. This assumption is implicitly informed by a European model of social and political development that moves from a rural, relatively egalitarian community structure to an urban society with a hierarchy of social classes and centralized political control often leading to either a system of city-states or a pan-regional polity. But this model of development derives from the specific historical form of European economic integration, which was very different from that which characterized Andean societies.

As explained in the discussion of Chavín and Moche, Andean archaeologists have discovered that Andean societies developed unique models of social, economic, and political development. The diverse geographic and environmental conditions of the Andean region led to the development of local and regional community structures conducive to the exploitation of different resources in different areas. Highland societies developed at least two different strategies for carrying out this exploitation: the vertical control or "archipelago" model and the altiplano model of economic integration. John Murra identifies the vertical model of integration as one in which communities establish their own outposts or settlements in several different ecological zones. This allows them access to the products of these zones through the internal economy of the individual community (Murra 1972). In the altiplano model of economic integration identified by David Browman, Andean communities specialize in the production of goods most suitable to their zone and establish trade networks with other independent communities in other zones in a mutually beneficial relationship (Browman 1984: 123). Browman argues that Tiwanaku society initially relied on the altiplano model of economic integration, and that the material evidence of Tiwanaku influence outside the Titicaca basin is a result of these economic relationships rather than military domination (Browman 1984).

The discovery of a separate and independent political and economic center located at Wari lent further support to the argument that the spread of Tiwanaku iconography did not necessarily indicate political unity. Much like Chavín, Tiwanaku's hegemonic model of peaceful socioeconomic and religious integration of the areas to the south of the Titicaca basin may have been based on the growth of its prestige as a sacred site. Browman explains that Tiwanaku established an economic network in the south, thereby spreading its ideology through merchant missionaries (Browman 1978: 327; 1984: 126). Recent research suggests that even Tiwanaku colonies in Moquegua and Cochabamba may have been politically autonomous (Owen 2005). This geopolitical pattern is consistent with Browman's altiplano model of economic integration based on trade relationships between independent communities as opposed to the social dispersion involved in Murra's model of vertical control, which was more common on the eastern slopes of the Andes (Browman 1984: 117–119, 123). The particular nature of the model of economic integration adopted at an early stage of local development would have had a strong influence on the nature of later regional institutions. This is not to say, however, that the possibilities are narrowly determined. There is no basis for limiting an Andean society to a single model of political or economic organization.

The horizontal trade relationships and the ideological affinity that characterized the Tiwanaku sphere of influence do not preclude the possibility of a Tiwanaku state with direct political control over the Titicaca basin (Browman 1984). Charles Stanish argues that by 400 CE, Tiwanaku had developed into a state capable of controlling domestic labor (Stanish 2001). Nevertheless, Albarracin-Jordan and others have argued that even the Tiwanaku heartland was not a centralized state but rather a group of closely related but independent sociopolitical units (Albarracin-Jordan 1996, 2003; McAndrews et al. 1997). Even so, beginning at least by 800 CE, the Titicaca basin does appear to exhibit a regional organization that constituted a distinct form of social interaction involving formal political relationship as opposed to the more strictly economic and religious emphasis at the pan-regional level (Burkholder 2001). The Tiwanaku federation in the Titicaca basin involved both kinship ties and some kind of regional sectarian authority structure (Kolata 1991; Janusek 2002: 56), whereas the pan-regional level was a more loosely related economic system with some degree of shared religious beliefs. Whatever regional sectarian political institutions existed in the Titicaca basin, however, the lack of any large-scale storage facilities may suggest that they were not involved directly in controlling economic production or redistribution (Topic 2003: 268). The Tiwanaku site itself was apparently designed to service elite social and religious activities rather than commercial mercantilism (Kolata 1993: 173–174). The control of economic production took place at the local, residential level (Janusek 2002: 45).

Any impetus for the development or adaptation of a secondary medium related to economic record keeping in this area, therefore, would probably have come from local communities. Although no archaeological evidence has surfaced for Middle Horizon Tiwanaku khipu, or *chinu* as they were called in this Aymara-speaking area, this may be due to the altiplano's environmental conditions, which are not conducive to the preservation of natural fibers. Furthermore, archival preservation may not have played a role in the institutions of khipu literacy at any level in Tiwanaku society.

Tristan Platt asserts that Aymara linguistic evidence suggests that the khipu originated with hunting and herding practices linked to the domestication of camelids (Platt 2002: 226).[1] Andean societies had domesticated camelids at least by the time of Chavín in the Early Horizon Period, well before the emergence of the Tiwanaku federation (Murra 1972: 118).

1 Platt makes this assertion, but he does not explain exactly what constitutes the linguistic evidence.

However, as Murra explains, the Titicaca basin contains "the largest concentration of domesticated as well as wild species" and is the most likely site of domestication (Murra 1975: 118; Latcham 1922: 82). Furthermore, the pastoral economy depends heavily on trade networks for subsistence (Flores Ochoa 1968: 87). So, if the *chinu*/khipu originally developed in the hunting and herding practices of the local communities and regional polities in or near the Aymara-speaking area of the Titicaca basin, the trade networks essential to pastoralism may have both motivated the development of the *chinu* and served to spread this medium to communities at lower elevations – possibly even as far as the north-coast Moche but most certainly to the area that fell under the influence of Wari, where we find the first evidence of archaeological khipu.

Wari and the Emergence of Archaeological Khipu

Jeffrey Quilter explains that the Wari and Tiwanaku civilizations of the Intermediate Period (400 BCE–550 CE) were the first Andean societies to combine large-scale religious, political, and economic activities, and that it is precisely at this point that khipu begin to appear in the archaeological record (Quilter 2002b: 213–214). Of course, this does not mean that no khipu existed immediately prior to these developments. The contexts in which such secondary media were preserved may also be linked to the same larger socioeconomic and political institutions that rely on them. What this means in terms of the development of the khipu, and Indo-European writing systems as well, is that they were originally tailored to the particular type of economic system in which they arose. In both cases, they seem to have functioned primarily as economic records to represent such information as inventories, economic transactions, possibly obligations of payment or exchange, and so on. One of the most dominant dimensions of such records would have been numeric in nature. And this is consistent with the argument made by some scholars that historically numeracy probably precedes any given form of literacy – iconographic, alphabetic, or otherwise (Harris 1986: 133; Gaur 2000: 12). Thus, the earliest khipu probably recorded mainly numeric information about flocks and perhaps commodities such as potatoes, corn, and coca involved in the relationships of trade and reciprocity in which Andean communities engaged. The development of more complex economic, social, and political institutions would have led to the need or desire to represent more elaborate relationships, transactions, and other socioeconomic activities, thus inducing the development of more elaborate khipu conventions.

Tiwanaku and Wari also may have employed a version of the Moche bean system (Larco Hoyle 1942), which led to the later Inca *yupana* practices. These beans may have had a numerical dimension, possibly analogous to the function of the clay tokens from the Middle East that eventually gave rise to other forms of writing. As socioeconomic and political institutions increase in complexity, they tend to place greater demands on the semiotic media through which they function. These demands inevitably run up against the limits of the conventions of the medium, inducing semiotic innovation, and in many cases, such innovations involve a semiotic transpositioning from one medium to another. The image of a possibly khipu-type device in Figure 1.14 may indicate such a transpositioning during the Moche period involving a reconfiguration of the relationship between inscribed beans and knotted string devices. The more versatile and operable nature of the knotted string devices may have induced it to assume a more dominant semiotic function, with the inscribed beans remaining as an ancillary medium that endured into the Inca period in the form of kernels of corn or black and white stones as depicted in Guaman Poma's illustration in Figure 1.12. At this point, it is impossible to determine exactly how or when this development may have taken place. If the Moche did actually employ khipu, their associated cultural institutions did not sustain and perpetuate their use in ways that were conducive to preservation. The Wari, on the other hand, appear to have employed khipu in ways that resulted at least to a certain extent in an archaeological record.

The Tiwanaku and the Wari polities are normally differentiated mainly through their methods of expansion: peaceful economic and religious exchange, on the one hand, and military conquest, on the other. The military nature and the extent of Wari expansion may have been exaggerated somewhat in early Wari research (Czwarno 1986, 1988; McEwan 1990), and like the later Inca they appear to have employed different strategies involving both direct and indirect control as dictated by the particular situation (Schreiber 1992). Although Wari may not have resorted to force in all cases, many scholars argue that it was an expansionist state with a military dimension (Browman 1978: 327, 1984: 126; Glowacki and Malpass 2003: 432). The political differences between Tiwanaku and Wari also affected the nature of their administrative structures and economic institutions. Whereas Tiwanaku influence is thought to mainly involve religious iconography, the Wari phenomenon was characterized by an administrative structure (Isbell 1977: 7, 53–54), architectural standards (ibid.: 53), and social reorganization (Schaedel 1966; McEwan 1989: 89). Although in some regions local institutions enjoyed a great deal of autonomy (Ponte 2000), other areas appear to have been under the direct control of a centralized administration (Anders 1989; McEwan 1989; Brewster-Wray 1989; Glowacki and McEwan 2001).

The balance between local autonomy and state control manifests itself in a variety of ways. Rebecca Stone-Miller and Gordon F. McEwan argue that Wari tunics and planned rectangular complexes such as Pikillacta are

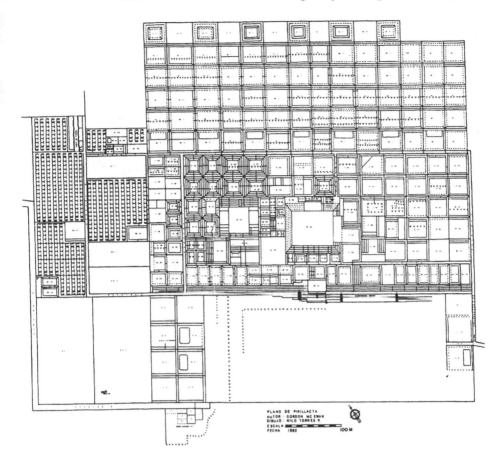

Figure 2.1. Pikillacta complex (From McEwan and Stone-Miller 1990–1991: 103).

parallel manifestations of a Wari state ideology characterized by variation within rigid parameters (Stone-Miller and McEwan 1990–1991). Both the Pikillacta complex and Wari tunics are rectangular shapes divided into smaller units creating a grid structure (Figure 2.1 and Image 11). The repetitive nature of the grid constitutes a rigid model, but the nature of the individual units within the grid vary. Stone-Miller and McEwan argue that this type of structural model had a semiotic function that expressed state power. This relationship between textiles and architecture exemplifies the way in which structural principles permeate the material dimension of Wari society.

Stone-Miller and McEwan's argument is limited to the identification of a structural principle, but the larger implication of their analysis is that specific textile or architectural articulations informed by these principles are not merely ideologically inflected aesthetic products. Here again, the very distinction between aesthetic and rational thought may be relevant only to a particularly European mode of thinking that has received its fullest expression since Kant. This is not to say that the distinction between the aesthetic and the rational is irrelevant. The reception of an architectural complex surely differed in fundamental ways from that of a khipu, for example, but perhaps not as much as we are inclined to assume. Obviously, the functionality of a khipu inherently differs from that of an architectural project, but they may share similar semiotic principles. In this case, it may be impossible to work out completely the details of Wari thought and its relationship to material media such as tunics and architecture; but other material media provide additional opportunities for reflection along these lines.

Although a centralized administration is inherently political in nature, it also necessarily involves an economic dimension. The state control of goods and services often entails, among other things, the construction and maintenance of storehouses and/or distribution facilities. John Topic argues that Wari archaeological sites exhibit no evidence of any large-scale storage facilities (Topic 2003: 268), but Isbell has identified what appear to be storage and distribution centers in planned architectural complexes such as Pikillacta, Viracochapampa, and Jargampata (Isbell 1977: 52–54). I would point out here that political control of economic production in the Andes may not have required "large-scale" storage facilities. As explained previously, the model of socioeconomic integration in the Andes often involved networks that would not necessarily require large-scale storage at centralized locations. Thus, the absence of large-scale storage and redistribution facilities does not necessarily indicate the absence of a state-level polity engaged in the control of economic production. For the Wari, smaller facilities may have been more appropriate for the kind of socioeconomic system that they administered.

The identification of Wari storehouses finds corroboration in the iconography of a certain type of Wari ceramics. Dorothy Menzel argues that the Wari engaged in a religious ritual involving the ceremonial destruction of large Wari urns (Menzel 1964: 6, 21–22, 24–25). Isbell suggests that these rituals may have been organized by the Wari state (Isbell 1977: 53). He categorizes the Wari ceremonial vessels discovered at Pacheco based on the images that decorate them. One group of vessels exclusively portrays maize in association with two figures that Menzel identifies as male and female deities (Menzel 1964: 26; Isbell 1977: 53). A second group of vessels from Pacheco contains three elements: (1) a variety of plants such as potatoes, ullucu, anu, and tarwi; (2) what Isbell identifies as intertwined felinoid snakes that are formed by, and painted on, handles placed on each side of the vessel (See Image 12); and (3) rectangular enclosures containing

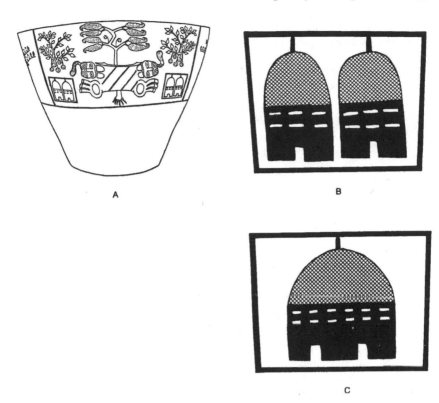

Figure 2.2. A. Large Wari ceramic vessel (After Ravines 1968: Lámina LXXXV; from Isbell 1977: 49; compare to Image 12). B. Enlarged storehouse motif (From Isbell 1977: 49). C. Variation of storehouse motif from a similar vessel (From Isbell 1977: 49).

iconic representations of buildings (Image 12; Figure 2.2; Isbell 1977: 49). Finally, a third group of vessels also exhibits three different elements: (1) representations of plants around the top; (2) the face of a deity on one side; and (3) a polychrome checkerboard with dots in some or all of the individual squares (Image 13).[2]

The plants that appear on all three types of vessel indicate the contents of the offering. The deity on the first and third types suggests the religious dimension of this economic activity. The buildings on the second group appear to be storage facilities associated with the collection and distribution of these agricultural products (Figure 2.2A–2.2C). The checkerboard design on the third type of vessel is more difficult to interpret. If these vases are

2 I have switched the order of the second and third groups in Isbell's discussion in order to conform to the order of my own analysis, which follows.

all variations of the same theme, a correlation between the elements of the three groups and the activities associated with these vessels may shed light on this checkerboard design.

Archaeological discoveries at Pacheco and other locations such as Conchopata (Menzel 1964: 23–26; Isbell 2000) and Ayapata (Ravines 1968) reveal that the ritual offerings of agricultural products associated with these large ceramic vessels correspond to the plants represented on them: maize, potatoes, tarwi, oca, quinoa, and possibly others (Isbell 1977: 53–54; Menzel 1964: 21–27). The representation of these plants was highly standardized (Isbell 1977: 53), and they are the same kind of plants that the *khipukamayuq* of the community of Huánuco listed in their tribute report to the Spaniards in 1562: potato, oca, ullucu, mashua (anu), quinoa, taures (tarwi) (Isbell 1977: 53; Bird 1972 365). We might infer, then, that these vessels were related in some way to the storage and distribution of agricultural commodities. In her revisionist interpretation of the archaeological evidence, Ruth Shady suggests that the oversized urns with their associated agricultural offerings may have been attempts to invite divine intervention in the climate, more specifically to induce rain during a long drought (Shady 1989: 13). Even if this were the case, it would not preclude the possibility that the images of storehouses and agricultural products and their archaeological correlates are also evidence of some kind of tribute collection, storage, and/or distribution system that developed as part of local, regional, and later state-level administration, whether regional or pan-regional in nature.

Isbell points out that the images of buildings within the rectangular enclosures that appear on the second group of vessels (Figures 2.2B and 2.2 C) are similar to those that appear in Guaman Poma's drawing of Inca storehouses (Figure 2.3; Isbell 1977: 54; Guaman Poma de Ayala 1615: 335[337]). Furthermore, the rectangular enclosures may correspond to the architectural structures of the same shape identified as storage and redistribution facilities at Pikillacta, Viracochapampa, and Jargampata (Figure 2.4; Isbell 1977: 49, 52–54). In particular, the rectangular enclosures in Figures 2.4 A and 2.4 B containing two adjacent buildings correspond strikingly to the structures represented on the oversized ceramic vessels. Given that these buildings are storehouses, the function of the long narrow galleries also appearing within the archaeological rectangular enclosures (Figures 2.4 B–E) would have been related to the receiving, storage, and distribution of goods as well.

Given that the third type of vessel is a variation of the other two and serves the same or a very similar function, then its characteristic images may be analogous to those that appear on the other types of vessel. All three types of vessel have plants. The first and third vessel types include representations of deities, whereas the second group depicts intertwined

Figure 2.3. Inca storehouses and *khipukamayuq* (Guaman Poma de Ayala 1615: 335 [337]. Courtesy of the Danish Royal Library, Copenhagen).

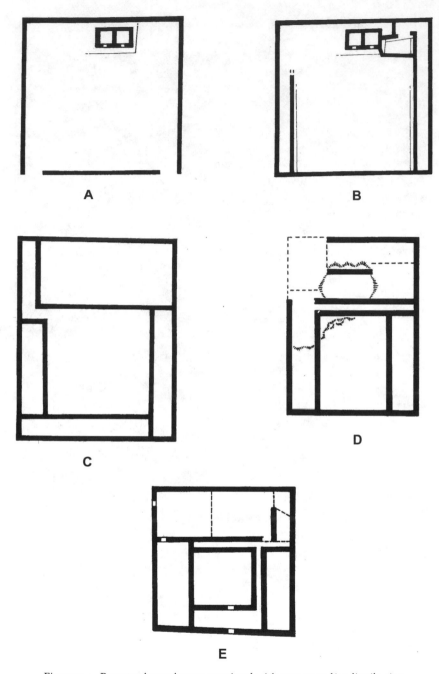

Figure 2.4. Rectangular enclosures associated with storage and/or distribution
activities. A. Jargampata North Unit, Middle Horizon 2A (From Isbell 1977: 48).
B. Jargampata North Unit, Middle Horizon 2B (From Isbell 1977: 51).
C. Viracochampa, Middle Horizon 2B (From Isabell 1977: 51; after McCown 1945:
fig. 13b). D Virú Valley, Middle Horizon 2B (From Isabell 1977: 51; after Willey
1953: fig. 57, V-297). E. Virú Valley, Middle Horizon 2B (From Isabell 1977: 51;
after Willey 1953: fig. 59, V-123).

felinoid snakes. The second and third types also contain a third element: the rectangular enclosure with storehouses and a polychrome checkerboard, respectively. Thus, if these two motifs are analogous elements, then the polychrome checkerboard that appears on the third type of vessel would relate in some way to the collection, storage, and/or distribution of agricultural commodities.

In addition to the possibility that the grid corresponds in some way to the narrow galleries discovered within actual archaeological rectangular enclosures, it also suggests the intriguing possibility that it is analogous to the drawing of the grid that appears alongside a *khipukamayuq* in Guaman Poma's *Nueva corónica y buen gobierno* (Figure 1.12; Guaman Poma de Ayala 1615: 360; Isbell 1977: 49, 53–54). Scholars who have studied Guaman Poma's drawing identify the grid as a form of *yupana*, an accounting device and technique used in conjunction with the khipu (see Images 5 and 6).[3] Colonial sources indicate that *khipukamayuq* employed small stones in conjunction with their khipu to render accounts (Pärssinen and Kiviharju 2004b: 270). Analyses of the *yupana* in Guaman Poma's drawing have yielded no definitive interpretation. In any case, as suggested in the previous chapter, the *yupana* appears to derive from, or at least relate in some way to, the same kind of record-keeping and/or accounting system in which the Moche inscribed beans participate. If the oversized Wari urns were employed in a ritual related to a system of tribute or to obligations involved in ceremonial offerings, then the checkerboard design may be an iconic representation of a *yupana* or a *yupana*-type device or practice.

This interpretation of the polychrome checkerboard as a stylized representation of a *yupana*-type device does not necessarily mean that it is unrelated to the images of rectangular storage enclosures in the second type of oversized Wari vessel. If the checkerboard on Wari urns is a representation of a *yupana*-type device related to the calculation or recording of agricultural products, then it would have emerged in a dialogical relationship with whatever other media were employed in this context, including architectural structures. A number of archaeologists, anthropologists, and theorists have argued that architecture is inherently a communicative medium. In the context of the Andes, for example, Susan Niles has explored the way in which Inca architecture gave form to historical claims (Niles 1999: 84). Even in modern society, where architectural form has been largely relegated to a realm that reconciles pragmatic necessity and aesthetics, the built environment conveys meaning even if it is merely the maintenance and perpetuation of a structure of significance (Moore 1992: 96–97; Relph 1976: 18). In cultures in which secondary semiotic operations are more dispersed among a variety of media, architectural structures may play a

3 Ansión 1990; Pereyra Sánchez 1990; Radicati 1979; Espejo Núñez 1953, 1957; Wassen 1931.

more prominent communicative role than in societies that emphasize the more strictly utilitarian and aesthetic dimensions of the built environment. Furthermore, even in modern societies storage and distribution facilities inherently employ structures of significance in their organizational systems.

As McEwan and Stone-Miller have argued in the case of Pikillacta, the built environment appears to exhibit very conscientious principles that can be reduced neither to pragmatic necessity nor to an autonomous aesthetics. Thus, the structural principles that manifest themselves both in the architectural layout of the Pikillacta complex and in the configurations of textile *tocapu* may relate to the political, social, and economic organization in which they functioned. And similar principles may underlie the relationship between the storehouses and the *yupana* device. If this is the case, then the *yupana* would have originated as an adapted model or miniature representation of an architectural structure related to the storage and distribution of goods. In other words, the architecture of compartmentalized storage systems may have served as the basis for the organizing principles of the *yupana* record-keeping/accounting device. These devices originally may have been iconic representations of the storehouses themselves, with small objects such as stones, beans, or kernels of corn used as tokens indicating quantities of goods in each compartment. The device would have reproduced the ordering principles of the storehouse, effectively converting a pragmatic practice on the level of primary interaction into a second order semiotic convention. Similar to the Mesopotamian practice of using clay tokens, which gave rise to successively more complex semiotic systems, the *yupana* would have evolved over time from a simple iconic medium to a complex system of calculation and secondary semiosis.

The *yupana*, however, whether a fixed architectural construct or a smaller, more mobile device, would have had certain disadvantages as a medium for record keeping over any length of time. Although possibly portable, moving such devices around runs the risk of corrupting or losing altogether the information encoded in them through the distribution of stones or "counters" in the various trays. For the same reason, the *yupana* would have made archiving information for any length of time somewhat awkward. Furthermore, the very nature of the device appears to inherently favor an accounting system that maintained current records rather than historical data. Thus, with a high level of socioeconomic complexity, the Wari would have had an incentive to develop or adapt some other, more versatile medium such as the khipu.

The *yupana* clearly had a numerical dimension, but if the checkerboard pattern on the oversized Wari vessels is related to this device, they may also have employed a type of color symbolism to signal the meaning of the various trays. The use of colors in this context may indicate an intermedia parallel with the type of khipu that have been called *khipu de canutos* or wrapped khipu. These khipu are similar in basic cord structure to Inca khipus, but their pendant, and in some cases subsidiary, cords have thread wrappings that create chromatic patterns, usually near the top where they connect to the main cord (see Image 14). Examples of this type of khipu appear in several early studies and descriptions of khipu (Locke 1923: 29, Plate XL; Altieri 1941: 192–197, 203); but as with the majority of khipu in museums and private collections around the world, most of these wrapped khipu have no provenance information that might have made possible even a relative chronology. However, at least two archaeological discoveries of such khipu place them in the Wari period. Conklin explains that in 1968, Yoshitaro Amano discovered a set of wrapped khipu in an excavation of Pampa Blanca, near an Hacienda in Pampa de Nasca, along with a Middle Horizon Wari mummy and Wari pottery that can be dated to around 700 CE, approximately 700 years prior to the period of Inca dominance (Conklin 1982: 267–268). More recently, Ruth Shady, Joaquín Narváez, and Sonia López announced the discovery of another Wari khipu from the Huaca de San Marcos in Lima from around the same time period (Shady, Narváez, and López 2000). Many of the pendant cords on the Huaca de San Marcos khipu are colored or multicolored, similar to the use of color on Inca khipu. They exhibit the same characteristic thickness as the Amano specimens, but the wrappings appear only on the main cord. Conklin argues that this practice of cord wrapping may derive from the textile patterning technique of warp wrapping developed around 1000 BCE by the Chavín culture. Chavín textiles use this technique to create patterned images of their most important deities, and these same deities appear to be "coherent with the deities represented during the Middle Horizon period" (Conklin 1982: 278).

The archaeological evidence suggests that the wrapped khipu preceded the Inca khipu and were used by the Wari. No one has attempted to catalog all known specimens of these wrapped khipu, but the number appears to be relatively small. Based on previously published data, at least two dozen such khipu are known to exist in museums and private collections. Assuming that all of these wrapped khipu specimens are authentic, even this relatively small corpus exhibits what appear to be significant typological differences. In addition to the apparent difference in the function of the wrapping conventions between the Amano and the Huaca de San Marcos specimens, knot conventions also seem to vary. In some cases, for example, wrapped khipu have no knots, some specimens have only simple knots, and others employ long knots. The wrapped khipus from Pampa Blanca and others studied by Conklin in the American Museum of Natural History and a private collection employ simple overhand knots but no long knots (Conklin 1982: 268–278). On other wrapped khipu, however, long knots are prevalent. The Banco Central de la Reserva in Lima, for example, possesses at least one large and rather distinctive wrapped khipu with numerous long knots. In most cases, if wrapped khipu with knots employ a decimal place system similar to that of the Inca khipu, it is not readily apparent. Many of the wrapped khipu also consist of cords that are rather thicker and shorter than those typical of Inca khipu, and unlike most later khipu, there appears to be no difference in thickness between the main and the pendant cords. But a few wrapped khipu have knot conventions and finer pendant cords that begin to approximate more closely the Inca specimens. These differences may indicate either regional variation and/or the direction in which the medium developed.

Wrapped khipu without knots appear to convey most of their information through the chromatic pattern created by the thread wrapping (Conklin 1982: 271). In cases where the cords of the khipu are all of the same natural hue, the thread wrappings may have been the only significant use of color; but in other cases the color of the pendant cords themselves varies as well. Unfortunately, without a large corpus of specimens with provenance data and associated archaeological artefacts the only way to even attempt to establish a correlation between apparent typologies and a chronology of development is through extensive radiocarbon dating, but the relatively short period of Wari dominance makes this problematic.

Wrapped khipu have received little attention from researchers, in part because they pose several problems. First, the number of specimens is relatively small, which reduces the possibility of identifying common conventions through comparison and contrast. The difficulty in establishing the conventional parameters of wrapped khipu also makes it difficult to identify possible counterfeit specimens. Eighteenth- and nineteenth-century researchers of Peruvian antiquities faced this same problem with regard to the khipu in general (Loza 1999: 51). The production of counterfeit archaeological objects has been fairly widespread, and a khipu would be relatively easy to produce. Nevertheless, the corpus of wrapped khipu is the most significant material evidence related to the history of khipu development prior to the Incas.

Although a developmental chronology of the khipu based on material conventions may be impossible to construct within the individual Wari and Inca periods, the general outline of the transition from one to the other is apparent. From a strictly formal perspective, the material differences between various wrapped Middle Horizon Wari khipu, on the one hand, and Inca khipu, on the other, appear to reflect a trajectory from (1) Wari wrapped khipu made from shorter, thicker, single-color cords with no knots or merely simple overhand knots to (2) an intermediate stage of wrapped khipu with finer, possibly colored cords and knots that then gave rise to (3) the more familiar Inca khipu normally without wrappings but with finer, multicolored cords and at least three kinds of knots. The radiocarbon dating that has been done to date on wrapped khipu lends support to this hypothesis. Although the imprecise nature of radiocarbon dating makes it difficult to identify stylistic chronologies within the individual Wari and Inca periods, it is precise enough to confirm the general distinction between the earlier Wari wrapped khipu and the later conventions of the Inca khipu (Gary Urton, personal communication, Jan. 23, 2010). In any case, the material differences between the various types of wrapped khipu also imply a corresponding difference in semiotic conventions. Of particular interest is the significance of the color wrappings, especially in the case of khipu with apparently few, if any, other significant features. The use of color in individual cords of Inca khipu to produce different visual effects described as solid, candy-striped, mottled, and joined (Ascher and Ascher 1981: 21), and the patterns created by color sequences in pendant cords (Radicati di Primeglio 1965) appear to derive from the chromatic patterns of earlier Wari wrapping conventions.

Radicati believed that the wrapped khipu were magical in nature and that they represented an initial, "primitive" stage in the evolution of this medium. According to Radicati, these khipu then gave rise to secular khipu used for accounting, history, and literature (Radicati di Primeglio 1990: 46). But the Middle Horizon wrapped khipu appears already to be a well-developed, sophisticated medium. It is also important to keep in mind that given the rather extended period during which khipu were in use and given what we know about Inca, colonial, and modern khipu, there appear to have been several different types of khipu used simultaneously in different socioeconomic and political contexts. Therefore, if certain genres of khipu were not conducive to preservation in the archaeological record, then the reconstruction of an evolutionary history of the khipu based on typological differences among extant specimens is highly problematic.

The Evolution of Khipu in the Middle Horizon Period

As explained above, the nature of Andean geography was conducive to the formation of communities that depended on relationships of reciprocity and mutual exchange, which gave rise to very resilient, non-hierarchical or loosely hierarchical institutions designed to organize and manage community endeavors and the individual responsibilities of its members. Such non-hierarchical institutions are inherently complex relative to the community level at which they develop. Furthermore, without a strong, authoritative hierarchy, community-level institutions depend largely on consensus in order to function; and without some kind of material record that would ensure accurate and equitable accounting, the complexity of Andean community institutions would have made it difficult to arrive at a consensus, thus making them unstable and susceptible to disintegration. Even the earliest Andean communities, therefore, would have been fertile ground for the development of a sophisticated secondary semiotic medium in order to facilitate the administration of socioeconomic activity.

Of course, the khipu was surely not invented at the community level as a full-fledged administrative record-keeping system. As in the case of alphabetic writing, it would have emerged and evolved gradually over hundreds and perhaps even thousands of years. The complexity of the khipu increased diachronically along with the complexity of the economic and social institutions of the communities that employed them. These community institutions would not have necessarily displaced the older khipu practices that we might label "pastoral" and "agricultural." The adaptation of the khipu to new contexts would have created different levels or domains of khipu literacy that may have employed related but distinct semiotic conventions.

The best evidence for community-level khipu comes from Frank Salomon's study of modern Tupicocha. Although Tupichocha no longer produces khipu nor uses them as a record of community administration, it maintains a set of patrimonial khipu that were replaced by alphabetic *ayllu* books in the late nineteenth or early twentieth century. Salomon explains that the *ayllu* books now serve the same function previously filled by the khipu: to keep track of community projects, the individual responsibilities of each member of the community, and so forth (Salomon 2004: 185–207). Although the details of this system may have changed over time, the basic principles of the modern Tupicochan administrative system derive from those that have been the basis of many Andean communities for hundreds and possibly even thousands of years. And community-level khipu would have developed in dialogical relation to these principles.

If khipu record-keeping practices date from before the Wari, then one might expect to find archaeological specimens from this period. At present, however, no known objects from any pre-Wari period can be unambiguously identified as khipu. Here again, any number of factors may explain the absence of khipu in the early archaeological record. The nature of khipu use at both the pastoral and community levels may not have been conducive to preservation. Unlike the clay tokens employed in Mesopotamia, the khipu is easily recyclable. If pastoral khipu were ever employed independently of community political institutions, Andean communities would have had no need to preserve them beyond the immediate context of their use; and if modern Tupicochan practices are any indication, community khipu would have been continually used and reused as a constantly changing record of the various aspects of annual community administration. Although the Tupicochans began keeping an archive of alphabetic *allyu* books in the late nineteenth century, this may be only because the nature of the alphabetic medium did not lend itself to the same kind of recycling. Furthermore, even if khipu were ever discarded, the cotton or woolen material from which they were made would have disintegrated over time if left unpreserved. Thus, the dearth of khipu in the archaeological record may be due to the fact that their contexts of use did not involve, or were not conducive to, preservation.

If this general theory about the history of the khipu is correct, then the appearance of archaeological khipu in the Wari period does not necessary indicate the advent of this medium but rather its adaptation to a new context of use that led to its preservation. Whether or not Chavín and/or Moche were state societies, Wari arguably developed political and economic institutions that were significantly more extensive with a higher degree of centralized, hierarchical control. Wari represents a benchmark of social, political, and economic development in the Andes involving massive reorganization (Schaedel 1966a; McEwan 1989: 69), extensive administrative control (Isbell 1977: 7, 53–54; 1986), and increased urbanism (Isbell 1986). These developments would have included the emergence of a bureaucracy charged with administering the day-to-day details of the Wari state. It may be no coincidence, therefore, that this is the point at which khipu begin appearing in the archaeological record (Quilter 2002b: 213–214). The conjunction of Wari, and possibly Tiwanaku, social, political, economic, and religious institutions would have served as a catalyst for innovations in the adaptation of this medium to the record-keeping needs of the state. And the context of a state bureaucracy certainly would have been more conducive to the preservation of khipu records.

The Middle Horizon Wari khipu, then, developed from what would have been an earlier, although not necessarily simpler, knotted cord device. The local economies of Andean communities, or *ayllus* as they came to be called in Quechua, were based on principles of reciprocity, or *ayni*, and these principles may have already provided the initial impetus for developing a complex secondary medium capable of handling the intricate relationships involved in community-level administration. Some aspects of Tupicocha's originally khipu-based administrative system are directly derived from Inca administration, which was influenced by the Wari probably by way of the Late Intermediate Period Chanka. Martha Anders argues that many of the features that characterize the Inca state are present at the Wari site of Azángaro: quadripartite division, ceque system, dual organization of authority, and so forth (Anders 1986, 1989); but the details of the communal administration at the local *ayllu* and moiety levels were not dependent on the Wari or the Inca state, and neither do they depend on the modern Peruvian state today.

State-level khipu would have built on khipu practices originally involved in administering the complex economic relationships of regional and local communities. With the emergence of regional and pan-regional polities in the Middle Horizon Period, local communities would have adapted their record-keeping system to new contexts; and just as the Inca would do later, the Wari state adopted this medium and adapted it to the record-keeping needs of an expanding political and economic system increasingly dependent on centralized trade and redistribution networks. The development of the khipu at this level, however, apparently took place in relation to other forms of what we might call material memory. The kind of state-level record-keeping practices that characterized the Wari state may have emerged from a convergence of, and dialogue between, architectural structures, *yupana* practices, and khipu conventions. The relationships that I have proposed – on the one hand, between the structure of the storehouses involved in the collection and distribution of goods in the administration of the Wari state and the semiotic nature of the *yupana* and, on the other hand, between the *yupana* and the khipu – constitute an even more specific kind of intertextual or intermedia relationship than that suggested by McEwan and Stone-Miller between architecture and textiles. In any case, once the Wari state dissolved, many of the record-keeping practices persisted at the local level and served as the basis for later incorporation into the Inca state.

Chimu Architectural Semiotics

Isbell has argued that the practices and institutions developed by the Wari influenced both the later Chimu and Inca states (Isbell 1986). During the later Middle Horizon, the Chimu polity developed along the north coast from the remnants of the Moche. Although the Chimu do not appear to have been conquered by the Wari (Czwarno 1989; 1988), Lumbreras maintains that they built on Middle Horizon institutions by further developing trade networks and occupational specialization (Lumbreras 1989). The main Chimu capital at Chan Chan has architectural structures indicating storage facilities and labor service similar to that of the Inca (Day 1982). Chimu administration may have been highly centralized, because these types of storage facilities are primarily found only at Chan Chan (Topic 1990: 170–171). Nevertheless, Moseley argues that the Chimu exhibit many of the institutions that will characterize the Inca state: split inheritance, which motivates military expansion and land reclamation projects, which in turn fuel mita-labor taxation systems and relocation programs (Moseley 1978: 533).

At present, there exists no confirmed archaeological evidence of any Chimu khipu, but the architecture of Chan Chan appears to exhibit structural principles that resonate with the proposed relationship between Wari storehouses and Middle Horizon khipu. John Topic has recently argued that the administrative model of the Chimu state at Chan Chan developed over time from a stewardship to a bureaucracy requiring a more accurate and detailed method of information control, and he identifies chronological changes in the distinctive architectural U-shaped structure as indicative of this development (Topic 2003: 250). These U-shaped structures appear in the various compounds or *ciudadelas* that comprise Chan Chan as well as in regional centers and rural sites (ibid.: 251). Topic explains that U-shaped structures are normally composed of three walls creating the shape of a block letter "U" (Figure 2.5; Topic 2003: 250). The Chimu employed three general types of U-shaped structures: *arcones*, which have bins; *trocaderos*, which have troughs; and *audiencias*, which have niches. Variants of each of these types evince differences "based on the number and location of bins, troughs, and niches, and the overall shape of the structure" (Topic 2003: 251).

These structures have prompted some debate, but many scholars believe that they served an administrative function, in some cases perhaps controlling access to storage areas (Andrews 1974; Moseley 1975a; Day 1982; Kolata 1982: 72, 83; Kolata 1990. 124, Topic 2003). Moore has argued that since in some cases the U-shaped structures are separated from storage areas, they would not have controlled access to these facilities (Moore 1992). However, Topic explains that the earliest U-shaped structures are associated with storage rooms and that their dissociation takes place over time in the successive building phases of Chan Chan. He argues that this change indicates a shift in the way in which information was controlled. The early periods where the U-shaped structures control direct access to the storage rooms suggest a stewardship model of administration in which the record keepers were directly involved in the management of goods. Later periods when the U-shaped structures are no longer placed at the entrance to the storage rooms correspond to a bureaucratic administrative model in which the record keepers deal primarily with information rather than the stored goods themselves. As this shift takes place, the U-shaped structures become increasingly standardized; they appear in increasingly hierarchical relationships; and there develops a rationalization of information flow as indicated by an increase in number and a change in the way they are configured within the *ciudadelas* (Topic 2003).

Topic maintains that all of these phenomena can be explained by the shift from a stewardship to a bureaucratic model of administration. Thus, although under the stewardship system the U-shaped structures may have been an administrative checkpoint associated with the physical control of goods, under the bureaucratic model, they became more of a record-keeping device. The bureaucratic facility was used to control knowledge rather than actual objects, which meant that there was no need to locate these structures near the storage areas.

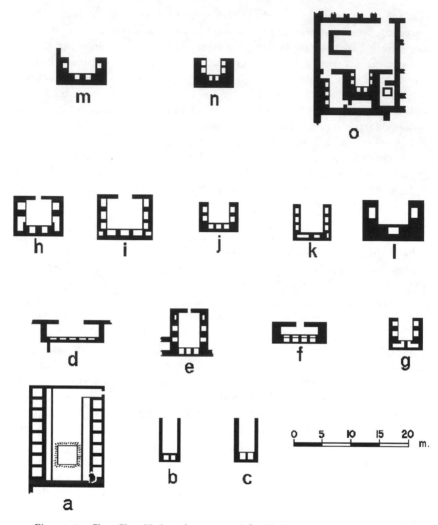

Figure 2.5. Chan Chan U-shaped structures (after Topic 2003: 250). Reproduced by permission of the Society for American Archaeology from *Latin American Antiquity* 14.3 (2003): 250.

The increased standardization of the U-shaped structures would also be consistent with this shift, because they would need to serve a more general function at a more abstract level. The earlier U-shaped structures could be tailored to a particular type or set of commodities and a particular group of storerooms. The physical dissociation of the later U-shaped structures from the storerooms themselves may correspond to a functional universalization of this device. In other words, these structures might have been used to record or manipulate information about different commodities related to different storerooms at different times. The level of abstraction involved in this process would inherently translate into a tendency toward standardization in the same way that linguistic grammar tends toward standardization with the use of alphabetic writing as a result of its decontextualization. Similar to the way written language is dissociated from the context of its production, the U-shaped structures became dissociated physically, although not semiotically, from the direct involvement with their referents.

If the Chimu built on Wari institutions as suggested by Lumbreras (Lumbreras 1989), then the niches, bins, and troughs may be the Chimu equivalents of the narrow galleries appearing along with storehouses within rectangular enclosures at Wari sites (see Figures 2.4B–E). Topic goes so far as to suggest that the Chimu U-shaped structures were also formally analogous to the khipu: "the niches, bins, and troughs had the same sort of predefined place value that we see in other Andean record-keeping devices, such as the strings of the *quipu* or the cells of the abacus [*yupana*]; similarly, then, beans, pebbles, or other markers could be placed in the niches or bins in order to record quantitative information" (Topic 2003: 251).

The record-keeping function of the U-shaped structures identified by Topic resonates with what we know about the *yupana*. Furthermore, the place system posited by Topic for these U-shaped structures may relate to the khipu in two different ways. First, it is consistent with the principles of the decimal-place system whereby the knots and knot groupings that record units and each subsequent power of ten are distinguished by their location on the cords of the khipu. Second, as John Murra has argued, based on an analysis of a khipu transcription from the colonial period, the information recorded on tribute or statistical khipu is organized into a sequential hierarchy of ethnocategories (Murra 1981). In other words, categories of information appear in a predetermined order constituting what I have called paradigmatic information structures. The nature of the U-shaped facilities would have been consonant with the administrative system involving a hierarchical set of commodities organized within just such a paradigmatic information structure.

The essential difference between the U-shaped structures, on the one hand, and the *yupana* and the khipu, on the other, is that the former were stationary whereas the latter were portable (Topic 2003: 268–269). The fact that very few storehouses or U-shaped structures appear outside of Chan Chan suggests that the political and economic activities of the Chimu Empire were concentrated in the capitol (Topic 1990: 170–171; Topic 2003: 269). This contrasts with the political economy of the Incas, who maintained storehouses throughout the empire (Levine 1992). Thus, the stationary nature of the U-shaped record-keeping/administrative structures were well-suited to the centralized political economy of the Chimu polity. The extended nature of the Inca administration, on the other hand, would have required a more portable medium. If Wari administrative practices involved both a type of khipu, as suggested by the archaeological record, and some sort of storage or control system that employed *yupana*-like devices, as suggested by the interpretation of the large ceramic vessels presented above, then the Chimu and Inca Empires may have adopted and further developed those Wari practices that most suited their particular administrative model. In the case of the Chimu, this meant a more elaborate storage and record-keeping system based on *yupana*-style practices. The Incas, on the other hand, appear to have emphasized the more versatile khipu while at the same time maintaining ancillary *yupana* practices.

3

The Khipu and the Inca State

Inca khipu practices appear to have built on the knotted-string devices used by Wari and possibly other pre-Inca ethnic and political groups that dominated different areas of the Andes (Larrabure 1935: 125; Conklin 1982; Quilter 2002b: 213–214). Although no evidence of any Tiwanaku khipu has surfaced, the use of *chinu*, as they are called in this Aymara-speaking area, may not have been entirely an Inca imposition (Platt 2002). In any case, the only confirmed non-Inca archaeological khipu appear in Wari contexts (Conklin 1982; Shady, Narváez, and López 2002), and the Wari influenced the development of the Inca state in several ways. The Incas seem to have developed a Wari-inspired model of statecraft and strategies of imperial expansion (Anders 1986; McEwan 1989: 68–69; Isbell 1986: 197; Schreiber 1987). Wari practices also inform Inca-era ancestor worship (Gose 1993), the standardization of local organization (McEwan 1989: 69), and the conceptualization of sacred and political landscape (Anders 1986; Glowacki and Malpass 2003).

The Inca expanded into the Wari area after the Wari state had already dissolved into a loose confederation of often hostile groups known collectively as the Chanka, but according to Juan de Betanzos, these groups still employed khipu (Betanzos [1551] 1996: 90–91). However, the Inca apparently developed and extended the use of the khipu in the administration of its state to a greater extent than earlier groups. This does not necessarily mean that the khipu was not already a ubiquitous device in the Andes but that the Inca state extended its use in conjunction with the development of state institutions that required more extensive and more formalized record keeping and that resulted in archaeological preservation. More specifically, I would argue that local and state institutions generated different genres of khipu with often unique conventions specific to particular levels of khipu literacy.

Khipu Genres

Although other forms of media may have played important roles in the socioeconomic and political activities of pre-Inca societies, the material properties of the khipu appear to indicate a far greater level of versatility than is evident in the other kinds of media discussed in previous chapters. Furthermore, colonial sources reveal that the khipu supported a relatively high concentration of semiotic functions, which is consistent with the highly versatile nature of this medium. The Inca clearly adapted the khipu for statistical record keeping at all levels of the empire. Colonial sources document extensively the use of statistical khipu, and some of these practices have survived to some extent into the present in some parts of the Andes (Mackey 1970, 2002). However, colonial chroniclers claim that in addition to maintaining pastoral statistics and registering tribute, the khipu recorded personal inventories,[1] censuses,[2] laws,[3] ritual sacrifices, religious geography,[4] calendrical data,[5] and, perhaps most intriguingly and certainly most controversially, narrative histories.[6] The controversy about the khipu does not have to do with whether or not khipu records were associated in some way with the many types of information identified by colonial chronicles but rather with the nature of that relationship. In other words, the controversial question involves the nature of khipu semiosis: what the signs of the khipu explicitly recorded and how they did so. This is a much more complicated issue than it first appears.

The highly varied nature of the different types of information associated with the khipu would require distinct conventions pertaining to what Jeffery Quilter has called diverse khipu systems (Quilter 2002b: 201–202), or what I would call separate khipu genres. Even primarily alphabetic scripts exhibit clear conventional differences in the way they organize and

---

1 Bandera [1557] 1965: 179.
2 Cieza de León [1553] 1985: 74, 77–78; Betanzos [1551] 1987: 56; Capoche [1585] 1959: 138; Acosta [1590] 1986: 409; Garcilaso de la Vega [1609] 1985: I, 112–113; II, 24; Murúa [1611] 1987: 374.
3 Porras [1582] 1904: 197; *Tercer Concilio Limense* [1583] 1990: 191; Garcilaso de la Vega [1609] 1985: I, 88, 112; II, 27; Murúa [1611] 1987: 377, 407; Calancha 1638: 91.
4 Molina [1570–1584] 1989: 122–123, 127–128; Avila [1608] 1991: 112, 142; Murúa [1611] 1987: 442–443; Arriaga 1621: 88.
5 Román y Zamora [1575] 1897: II, 67–68; Gutiérrez de Santa Clara [c.1596–1603] 1963: 251; Murúa [1611] 1987: 372, 376.
6 Collapiña [1542/1608] 1974; Polo de Ondegardo [1572] 1917: 46, 91; Molina [1570–1584] 1989: 58; Santillán [1563] 1950: 43; Anonymous Jesuit [1580] 1968: 171, 173; Cabello Balboa [1586] 1951: 240; Acosta [1590] 1986: 124–125, 418; Román y Zamora [1575] 1897: 68; Anonymous [1600] 1944: 292; Gutiérrez de Santa Clara [c. 1596–1603] 1904: 548; Avalos y Figueroa [1602] 151; Garcilaso de la Vega [1609] 1985, I, 45, 67; II, 26; Murúa [1611] 1987: 373; Vázquez de Espinoza [1630] 1992: 758; Calancha 1638: 91–92; Cobo [1639/1653] 1956: II, 83.

communicate different types of information. Most of the khipu genres identified by colonial chroniclers have modern alphanumeric analogs: inventories, censuses, laws, calendars, and so forth. These modern alphanumeric texts employ different kinds of formatting, syntactic conventions, and often distinct or unique semantic values as well. Although most alphabetic discursive genres such as letters, diaries, newspapers, novels, and so forth generally adhere to the same essential grammatical and stylistic conventions, they differ significantly in their format. The written format of a newspaper, for example, is immediately distinguishable from that of a novel. If this is true of a writing system with a relatively low level of semiotic heterogeneity, then it may be even more characteristic of secondary media that rely directly on multiple types of semiotic conventions.

Although we still do not have a complete understanding of khipu semiosis, the nature of the medium suggests that it employed a number of semiotically heterogenous conventions. The khipu may have made use of many conventions of which we are unaware, but even those identified by colonial chroniclers imply the coordination of several different features with distinct semiotic functions. Colonial sources refer to the numeric value conveyed by knots, but they also mention the use of color and the format of the pendant and subsidiary cords. The potential significance of format is particularly difficult to understand from a modern perspective. Marcia and Robert Ascher, however, demonstrate compellingly that the format or configuration of a khipu can function as an essential component of khipu semiosis (M. Ascher 1983: 270, 1986: 270, 2002; Ascher and Ascher 1969, 1971).

Even a cursory examination of the corpus of archaeological khipu reveals a number of different formatting options of which the khipu availed itself. Images 15 through 18 illustrate several different string configurations that may correspond to different genres. The most obvious use of format or structure is evident through cord groupings and what Carlos Radicati identified as color seriation (Radicati 1965). Seriation can take several forms. In some cases the color sequence involves a series of individual cords of different colors that repeats along the length of the khipu main cord. This effectively creates cord groupings whose boundaries are determined at the point at which the sequence begins to repeat itself. In a more complex version of this format, the color sequence may vary from one group to the next. Another form of seriation moves from one group of pendants of a single color or color pattern to another grouping of a different color rather than from cord to cord. In other words, all of the pendant cords in each group would be of the same color or color pattern (Image 18). In both cases, the boundary between cord groupings may or may not be reinforced by leaving a space between each group (compare Images 17 and 18).

Such color seriation reinforces the paradigmatic information structures according to which categories of information appear in predetermined sequences. John Murra identified this principle of khipu semiosis in his analysis of sixteenth-century khipu transcriptions of commodity records that employ a series of what he calls ethnocategories (Murra 1981, 1982). The transcriptions present the same categories of information in the same order. Presumably, the khipu from which such records were transcribed assigned a commodity to a cord or group of cords in the predetermined sequence. On such khipu, color symbolism would reinforce the paradigmatic sequence and perhaps clarify any ambiguity or allow for some variation. The brief references to khipu conventions found in colonial sources corroborate these principles. Cieza de León explains that each cord signaled a particular category of information with an associated numerical value (Cieza [1553] 1985: 58). The Inca Garcilaso de la Vega's description of khipu conventions suggests that color allowed for variability in the order while categories that did not have an assigned color were subject to a predetermined sequence.[7]

The organization of information into paradigmatic structures involving sequences of ethnocategories may have constituted the general semiotic principle of most, if not all, community, regional, and state-level khipu in the Inca Empire. In addition to the passages from Cieza de León and Inca Garcilaso cited above, numerous other chronicles and khipu transcriptions suggest that many khipu genres relied on some sort of conventional sequence of information categories. Garcilaso explains that colors and numbers signaled laws and punishments (Garcilaso de la Vega [1609] 1985: I, 88). Other sources indicate that the Inca divided the population into age-grades (Capoche [1585] 1959: 138; Guaman Poma de Ayala [1615] 1987: I, 193[195]–234[236]). Capoche also states that this same type of ordered account characterized histories of the Inca Empire as well, which took the form of a sequence of kings and notable events (Capoche [1585] 1959: 138).

The *khipukamayuq* who serve as informants for Spanish chroniclers primarily read and describe khipu involved in the administration of the Inca Empire. However, I would argue that just as Andean state institutions derived from, and built on, local ones, state-level khipu also derived from, and built on, local-level practices. As state institutions develop and become more complex, the need for a more or less durable record of new and/or more elaborate types of information emerges. In any context in which such needs arise, pre-existing media unavoidably inform in one way or another the development of new genres, new conventions, or even new media to meet institutional demands. In this case, Inca state administrators would have adopted and adapted the secondary media that were already available.

7 "Las cosas que no tenían colores iban puestas por su orden" (Garcilaso de la Vega [1609] 1985: II, 24–25).

If, as I have suggested, the semiotic principles of the earliest local-level khipu emphasized numerical quantities, then state level adaptations would build on, expand, and perhaps revise the numeric conventions.

This process would inevitably result in differences between local, regional, and state-level khipu. In fact, I would suggest that it gave rise to a variety of different khipu genres adapted to the particular type of information they were designed to record. Thus khipu literacy was not necessarily completely analogous to alphabetic literacy, because the semiotic conventions themselves seem to vary from one khipu genre to another far more than is the case with alphabetic texts. Furthermore, these khipu genres and the institutions with which they were associated developed together and were mutually dependent. The dissolution of a socioeconomic or political institution meant that whatever khipu genre might have been associated with it would be lost as well. The genre-specific nature of khipu conventions may have been what led Bernabé Cobo to state that a khipu could be read only by the *khipukamayuq* who made it (Cobo [1639/1653] 1956: II, 143). This may have been true of some khipu, but khipu genres at both the community and state levels also would have relied on standard conventions readable at least by other *khipukamayuq* involved in that administrative level and versed in its particular genres.

Colonial chroniclers never present an authentically detailed explanation of khipu conventions, but Marcia and Robert Ascher have illustrated compellingly the versatility of the khipu based on detailed analyses of the material features of archaeological specimens (Ascher and Ascher 1981). In addition to the conventions discussed above, the knots of the khipu are also more complex than the standard decimal system indicates. Knots may not always necessarily record numbers (M. Ascher 2002; Urton 2002c; Urton and Brezine 2005). Furthermore, we still do not understand many dimensions of the khipu. If we attempt to discard the semiotic prejudices imposed on us by an alphabetic mentality, it is not difficult to see how the main khipu conventions of cord spacing, color symbolism, color sequence, and numerical and non-numerical knots, not to mention the many other conventions that often vary from one khipu to another, could record in great detail all the various types of information that colonial sources associate with this medium. It is important to begin with this understanding, because it has implications for the interpretation of the archaeological evidence and the ethnohistorical sources related to the history of the Inca Empire.

The Emergence of the Inca Empire

Any attempt to construct a history of the Inca khipu in relation to the development of Inca state institutions faces serious problems, because the vast majority of specimens have no provenance information. The generally accepted correlation between the development of writing or record-keeping systems and increased levels of political and socioeconomic complexity in human societies is important to keep in mind, but it does not provide any basis on which to devise an analytical methodology that would establish a correlation between specific socioeconomic and/or political developments and the development of any particular type of secondary semiotic practice. The developmental possibilities of human social interactions, on the one hand, and of secondary media, on the other, are so diverse that the relationship between them can be posited only as a general principle with no specific methodological implications. Thus, the empirical analysis of the development of Inca khipu would depend on the discovery of khipu in archaeological contexts associated with different stages in the emergence of social, economic, and political institutions. Unfortunately, as Brian Bauer points out, relatively little archaeological research has focused on the early formation of the Inca Empire in the Cuzco region itself (Bauer 1992: 9), and there have been no discoveries of archaeological khipu in the little work that has been done.

Archaeological khipu come almost exclusively from the coast, but they can be inferentially dated to the Inca period. The complexity of the khipu implies at the very least the existence of complex socioeconomic and political institutions conducive to preservation. Of course, even without the corroboration of archaeological khipu, the Inca Empire certainly involved complex political and socioeconomic systems. The documentary history of the Spanish conquest and colonization of the Andean region makes this very clear. The socioeconomic and political complexity of the Inca Empire suggests that in one way or another the khipu may have undergone significant development in conjunction with Inca expansion. There has been no way to date archaeological khipu from the Inca period with any degree of specificity, making it impossible to identify a stylistic chronology that might correspond to specific Inca socioeconomic and political developments. Nevertheless, archaeological research in conjunction with ethnohistorical sources suggests a correlation between certain khipu genres, the consolidation of the Inca Empire, and the political systems on which it was based.

It is important to remember that ethnohistorical sources from the colonial period do not necessarily reflect the kind of history to which modern scholarship aspires (Urton 1990: 9; Bauer 1992: 4–9). Brian Bauer attributes the problems inherent in colonial accounts of indigenous Andean history to the fact that "the indigenous peoples of the Andes did not develop any form of written records" (Bauer 1992: 7). Leaving aside the issue of Bauer's rather casual dismissal of the existence of "*any* form of written records" (my emphasis), I would point out that the development of a form of written record does not guarantee the preservation of "historical facts." I am not necessarily denying the existence of historical facts, but written documents are rarely, if ever, objective reflections of historical events.

Regardless of whether or not one wishes to define the forms of material memory employed by the Incas as writing, it is true that the indigenous informants relied on by colonial chroniclers provided often drastically different versions of the history of the Inca Empire. For some purposes, it may be pointless to attempt, as many scholars have done, to determine which of these versions was the more accurate. In a sense they are all both accurate and inaccurate: accurate in the sense that they reflect the way various indigenous groups articulated their past at that point in time; and inaccurate in relation to the modern criteria that inform the construction of historical narratives. Over the last several decades, more and more scholars have begun adopting a methodology that considers archaeological findings in relation to ethnohistorical sources whenever possible (Bauer 1992: 1–17). Without insisting on reading ethnohistorical sources as if they conformed to European expectations of historical narrative, suggestive inferences can be drawn from them. No ethnohistorical texts from the colonial period explicitly thematize the development of the khipu, but references to this medium appear to imply in one way or another a correlation between Inca expansion and the adaptation of the khipu in order to meet the demands of imperial administration and to legitimize the authority of the ruler and his ethnic group.

According to traditional interpretations of ethnohistorical sources from the colonial period, the Inca were a small, rather insignificant ethnic group until they came into serious conflict with the Chankas at some time in the early fifteenth century. At this point, Inca Yupanqui defeated the Chankas and subsequently began a campaign of conquests that were continued by his son Tupac Inca Yupanqui and, to a lesser degree, by subsequent Incas. In this version of Inca history, the rapid expansion of the Inca Empire under Inca Yupanqui and his son also would have involved dramatic sociocultural changes as well. Bauer's archaeological research in the Cuzco region, however, reveals that the regional influence of the Inca developed over a much longer period of time beginning in the early Killke period (1000–1400 CE). This is not to say that the Inca Empire did not go through a period of rapid expansion over a relatively short period of time or that there was no war with the Chankas that played a significant role in inducing that expansion. In fact, Bauer argues that the archaeological record actually confirms the assertion made in colonial sources that the political domination of the Inca ethnic group over an extended geographical area was the result of a rather late and rapid expansion that took place during the last few generations before the Spanish conquest (Bauer 1992: 48); but the archaeological evidence also suggests that these events must be understood within the larger context of "diachronic transformations in Andean social institutions" (Bauer 1992:7). What seems clear is that prior to the Chanka war, the Incas had already developed a network of political and economic relationships with other ethnic groups in which they exercised some form of leadership or authority.

It is unclear to what extent and at what levels the Inca polity employed khipu prior to the expansion that began with the wars against the Chankas, but according to ethnohistorical sources at least by this time they seem to have begun relying on khipu in the administration of their conquered territories. Based on the history of the Inca Empire recorded by the sixteenth-century chronicler Juan de Betanzos, Pachacuti Inca Yupanqui's first military campaign outside of the Cuzco region itself was to the south, where he subjugated the Chankas (Betanzos [1551] 1996: 85–86), the loose federation of ethnic groups consisting of the remnants of the Wari state; and these groups already employed khipu to record stored goods and production rates. Betanzos explains that Inca Yupanqui had the caciques from all the areas that he and his captains had conquered report on what they possessed and their production capabilities. In order to provide this information, the caciques called for their khipus (Betanzos [1551] 1987: 96–97; 1996: 90–91). Although this group of *curacas* included representatives from Condesuyu and Andesuyu (ibid. [1551] 1987: 90–91, 95; 1996: 86, 89), the only groups specifically mentioned by name are Chanka groups from Collasuyu, the area previously dominated by the Wari and conquered personally by Inca Yupanqui. After studying the records produced by the *curacas*, the Inca created different khipu for each of the conquered lords designating what they would pay in tribute to the city of Cuzco. The Inca then ordered that there be two copies of these khipus, one for lower level caciques and one for the lords (Betanzos [1551] 1996: 90–91). Regardless of whether or not the Inca already employed some sort of administrative khipu, at this point their own practices would have been influenced by the vestiges of Wari record-keeping systems that had survived at more local levels. In fact, the episode in Betanzos' history can be read as an account of the origin of the bureaucratic khipu record-keeping system employed in the Inca Empire.

The Yupanqui Dynasty and the Expansion of the Inca Empire

In *Antigüedades deste reyno del Peru* (1613), Juan de Santa Cruz Pachacuti Yamqui Salcamayhua's history of the Inca Empire seems to suggest that Inca politics began to change during the reign of the sixth Inca, Yahuarhuacac Inca Yupanqui. Pachacuti Yamqui states that this Inca began imposing a tribute on all of the nations and provinces and that in his old age he dedicated himself to conquests (Pachacuti Yamqui [1613] 1968: 295). This text implies that prior to Yahuarhuacac Inca's reign, some sort of extended Inca political system existed but that it did not exact tribute from its provinces. It may be that prior to this time, Cuzco served as a regional center with loose economic ties to other regions, as was the case with the beginnings of other Andean polities. This roughly corresponds to the revisionist model of Inca development proposed by Bauer and other like-minded archaeologists; and other chronicles seem to corroborate this general notion. Cristóbal Molina explains, for example, that at this time, the Inca controlled only the area near Cuzco (Molina [1570–1584] 1989: 58). Pachacuti Yamqui's reference to nations and provinces, then, may refer merely to what would subsequently become the pan-regional empire.

The next Inca in Pachacuti Yamqui's account, Viracocha Inca Yupanqui, is not a strong leader, but he sent two of his sons to conquer Collasuyu (Pachacuti Yamqui [1613] 1968: 296–297). One of these sons died, but the other, Inca Yupanqui, succeeded his father as Inca, conducted extensive conquests, imposed tribute throughout his newly acquired territory, and took on the additional name of Pachacuti (ibid.: 297–300). Pachacuti Inca Yupanqui ceded rule to his son Tupac Inca Yupanqui, who continued the tradition of military exploits (ibid.: 300–305). According to Pachacuti Yamqui's history, Tupac Inca Yupanqui first brought representatives of conquered groups to live in Cuzco, and he began overseeing the construction of roads and bridges, the planting of fields, the production of arms and other goods, and other activities (ibid.: 302).

Scholars disagree over which Inca was the most influential in the development of the empire. John Rowe argues that Tupac Inca Yupanqui ruled approximately between 1463 and 1493, and that he was responsible for the greatest expansion of the Inca Empire (Rowe 1985: 193). Based on ethno-historical sources, María Rostworowski states that Tupac Yupanqui organized the empire using a system of decimal units known as *guarangas* and *pachacas*, groups of 1,000 and 100 family units (Rostworowski 1990: 295). According to other chroniclers, it appears that Tupac Inca Yupanqui's father, Pachacuti Inca Yupanqui, made the most significant contributions to the development of Inca society and to the expansion of the empire. In the histories of both Betanzos and Sarmiento de Gamboa, Pachacuti Inca Yupanqui is the one who unified the area immediately around Cuzco, began conquests of other areas, built up and maintained an army, developed an infrastructure, enacted laws and other cultural practices, developed a calendar, and so forth (Betanzos [1551] 1996: 23–121; Sarmiento de Gamboa [1572] 1988: 84–127).

Regardless of who receives the most credit, if a period of Inca expansion took place over a relatively short period of time prior to the Spanish invasion as confirmed by Bauer's archaeological research (Bauer 1992: 48), innovations in khipu practices designed to adapt this medium for use by the institutions required to support and maintain the empire would have been a relatively recent phenomenon as well. Although the Incas probably employed the khipu themselves prior to their expansion, the beginning of the conquests outside the Cuzco region and the imposition of tribute may have induced innovations in khipu record-keeping practices in order to accommodate a more extensive and complex administration. Such a phenomenon would not be inconsistent with the history of other writings systems. Stephen Houston argues that scripts tend to develop in steps through rapid bursts in which major innovations appear and take hold within the span of a single lifetime (Houston 2008). Influence from the vestiges of the Wari administrative khipu record-keeping system would have further facilitated such developments. Without insisting on the "historical" accuracy of the historiographic details, this appears to be exactly what we see occurring in the episode from Betanzos's history discussed above.

Cristóbal de Molina also explicitly identifies a more extensive use of khipu accounting with the expansion and reorganization of the empire under the leadership of [Pachacuti] Inca Yupanqui (Molina [1570–1584] 1989: 58). Ultimately, for the more macrohistorical interest here, it makes no difference whether it was Pachacuti Inca Yupanqui or Tupac Inca Yupanqui who was the most active in these endeavors, or even whether these are literal accounts as opposed to metonymic condensations. The significance of these narratives of Inca expansion is that they can be correlated to the archaeological evidence of Inca expansion and that they specifically make reference to the khipu in this context. The more extensive and elaborate use of khipu would have facilitated the kind of social reforms and economic expansion that characterized the reign of these Incas.

Guaman Poma describes in even more detail the complexity of these reforms, and among them he includes the creation of administrative positions involved in khipu record keeping:

He who began to order that they prepare the royal roads and bridges. And he placed runners *hatun chasque, churro chasque*, and waystations. And he ordered that there be magistrates, *tocricoc*; constables, *uata camayoc*; hearing officers, presidents, and councils of this kingdom, *Tahuantinsuyu camachic*. And he had an advisor, *yncap rantin rimac*; procurator and protector, *runa yanapac*; secretary, *yncap quipocnin*; scribe, *Tauantinsuyu quipoc*; accountant, *hucha quipoc*. And he created other offices, and he spoke with all of the idols *huacas* each year. And he ordered that the boundary markers of this kingdom be set up for the pastures and fields and mountains and that towns be reduced.[8] And he honored the great lords and he gave them great favors and alms. And he ordered that the said ancient ordinances be observed,

---

8 "Reduced" could mean a variety of things in the sixteenth century. In this context, it appears to relate to establishing precise limits.

and afterwards he enacted other ordinances. And he began to build his estate and community and storehouses with much order, account and *quipo* in all of the kingdom. (Guaman Poma de Ayala [1615] 1987: 111[111]).[9]

The equivalency of the European terms into which Guaman Poma attempts to translate the administrative structure of the Inca Empire may be misleading, but his list of state officials is consistent with what would be expected of an extended socioeconomic and political system such as the Inca Empire. Of particular interest here is the fact that Guaman Poma explicitly identifies several officials whose function primarily involves record keeping with khipu.

In Pachacuti Yamqui's history, in addition to the explicit references to political and socioeconomic development during the four reigns of the sixth to the ninth Incas, and in particular that of Tupac Inca Yupanqui, other features of the text may indicate that this was a distinctive era. Like other chroniclers, Pachacuti Yamqui's periodization of the Inca Empire is based solely on the succession of Inca rulers; he does not distinguish explicitly between different periods based on any other criteria. However, his text implies the possibility of other types of periodization. The four generations of Inca rulers, from the sixth through the ninth in Pachacuti Yamqui's history, constitute a period of military expansion. The fact that all four of these Incas share the name Yupanqui may even reflect a recognition by the indigenous tradition that they belong to a unique period.

Linguistically, "Yupanqui" seems rather odd for a name. It appears to be a second person singular conjugation of the Quechua verb "yupay," which means "to count" related to the term "yupa," whose semantic field includes the meanings "count," "account," "value," "merit," "esteem," and "price," among others (González Holguín [1608] 1989: 371–372; Rostworowski 1981: 383; Urton 1997: 96–100; Arellano 1999:239; Kaulicke 2000: 10). The unexpected form of this name may suggest a different linguistic origin. Other languages such as Aymara and Puquina were spoken in Cuzco (Alan Durston, personal communication). I would suggest, however,

9 El que comensó a mandar que aderesasen todos los caminos rreales y puentes. Y puso correones *hatun chasque* [postillón principal], *churo chasque* [mensajero de caracol] y mezones. Y mandó que ubiese corregidores, *tocricoc*; alguaziles, *uata camayoc*; oydores, prisidente, consejo destos rreynos, *Tauantinsuyo camachic*. Y tubo azesor *yncap rantin rimac*; procurador y protetor *runa yanapac*; secretario *yncap quipocnin*; escribano *Tauantinsuyo quipoc*; contador *hucha quipoc* [contador de deudas incumplimientos]. Y puso otros oficios y hablaua con todos los ydolos *uacas* cada año. Y mandó mojonar los mojones destos rreynos de los pastos y chacaras [sementera] y montes y rreduzir pueblos. Y honrraua a los grandes señores y hazía mucha merced y mucha limosna. Y mandaua guardar las dichas hordenansas antiguas y después por ella hizo otras hordenansas. Y comensó hazer su hacienda y comunidad y depócitos con mucha horden, qüenta y *quipo* en todo el reyno (Guaman Poma de Ayala [1615] 1987: 111[111]).

that regardless of whether or not the name "Yupanqui" originally derived from another language, in Quechua it would have inevitably invoked the conceptual field associated with the term "yupa," which is also the root of the word "yupana" referring to the accounting device closely associated with the khipu (Figure 1.12; Guaman Poma de Ayala [1615] 1987: [360] 362]). Santo Tomás's *Lexicon* (1560) reveals a close connection between these concepts in his definition of "cuenta" [count; account] which he renders as both "quipposca" and "yupasca" (Santo Tomás [1560] 1951: 89). Several sources also state or imply that Inca Yupanqui instituted or expanded the use of the khipu in the Inca state (Molina [1572–1580] 1989: 58; Sarmiento de Gamboa [1572] 1988: 49; Porras [1582] 1904: I, 199; Guaman Poma de Ayala [1615] 1987: 111).

The close association between the khipu and the *yupana* makes the Yupanqui dynasty all the more significant. On one interpretation, the "Yupanqui" name is a title indicating the esteem in which the Inca was held. The name "Yupanqui" could certainly be understood to refer to the esteemed status of the Inca, but that meaning may be derived in part from the fact that it was the name attributed to this group of Sapa Incas. In other words, the connection between the notions of quantitative value and esteem that are included in the definition of *yupa* or its derivatives has a certain logic, but it may be reductive to understand the use of this term to refer to the venerated status of the Inca as merely a semantic extension. In fact, in addition to the notion of "value" inherent in the *yupa* concept, the understanding of this name may also have been related to the political and socioeconomic innovations that the Yupanquis introduced. The significance of the name Yupanqui may derive from the accounting that would have been involved in the administration of military campaigns, the construction of public works, the administrative organization of the population, and so forth.[10] All of these activities would have involved the extensive use of both khipu and *yupana*. An extension of khipu accounting practices would also have been essential in the administration of tribute obligations associated with the conquests undertaken by the Yupanqui dynasty. The dialogic relationship between the complexity of socioeconomic systems and developments in secondary media suggests that this period would have inevitably involved innovations in khipu practices. Thus, regardless of the historical etymology of the name "Yupanqui," Quechua speakers may have associated it with the recognition that these Incas instituted the semiotic practices involved in the imperial expansion and its associated administrative institutions, which included khipu and *yupana* record keeping and accounting.

---

10 Fernando Prada Ramírez implies that this was the case with Tupac Yupanqui, whose name he translates as "gran contador" [great counter or accountant] (Prada Ramírez 1995: 19).

Khipu Record Keeping

In addition to the development of the more mundane administrative enterprise during the expansion of the Inca Empire, political institutions would have expanded and become more complex, requiring more elaborate mechanisms of control and legitimation capable of perpetuating an ideology that asserts hegemonic claims to power and authority in a society with an increasingly diverse population organized into classes based on a number of different criteria (e.g., social, ethnic, and even possibly economic). One form of control mechanism would have been a legal system. Garcilaso de la Vega claims that the Incas recorded laws and punishments on khipu:

Of the sentences that the ordinary judges gave in the law suits, they gave an account every month to other superior judges and these to their superiors, which there were in courts of many levels, according to the nature and severity of the issues; because in every ministry of the republic there was an order of minors and majors up through the supreme, which were the presidents or viceroys of the four parts of the Empire. The account was so that they could see if they had administered justice, so that the lower judges would not be careless in doing so, and if they had not, they were punished rigorously. This was like a secret audit that was done every month. The way in which these reports were given to the Inca and those of his Supreme Council was by knots given on little cords of diverse colors, and they understood them just like numbers. Because the knots of such and such colors conveyed the crimes that had been punished, and certain threads of different colors that had been tied to the thicker cords signaled the punishment that had been given and the law that had been executed. And in this way, they understood, because they did not have letters, and below we will prepare a separate chapter with a longer description of the way of counting with knots that they had, which, it is true, many times has caused wonder among Spaniards to see that their best accountants err in their arithmetic and that the Indians are so correct in theirs of partitions and contracts, which, the more difficult, the more easily they are shown, because those who handle them, do not dedicate themselves to anything else, day and night, and thus they are extremely adept in them. (Garcilaso de la Vega [1609] 1985: I, 88).[11]

11 De las sentencias que los jueces ordinarios daban en los pleitos hacían relación cada luna a otros jueces superiores y aquéllos a otros más superiores, que los había en la corte de muchos grados, conforme a la calidad y gravedad de los negocios, porque en todos los ministerios de la república había orden de menores a mayores hasta los supremos, que eran los presidentes o visorreyes de las cuatros partes del Imperio. La relación era para que viesen si se había administrado recta justicia, porque los jueces inferiores no se descuidasen de hacerla, y, no la habiendo hecho, eran castigados rigurosamente. Esto era como residencia secreta que les tomaba cada mes. La manera de dar estos avisos al Inca y a los de su Consejo Supremo era por nudos dados en cordoncillos de diversos colores, que por ellos se entendían como por cifras. Porque los nudos de tales y tales colores decían los delitos que se habían castigado, y ciertos hilillos de diferentes colores que iban asidos a los cordones más gruesos decían la pena que se había dado y la ley que se había ejecutado. Y de esta manera se

Information collected in an investigation into Andean customs ordered by the viceroy Martín Enríquez in 1582 also indicates that the Incas employed the khipu in their legal institutions. As in most other cases, the investigation was based on a list of questions posed to each of the witnesses. The questionnaire included requests for information about the legal practices of the Inca and any form of writing or record keeping that might have been used to preserve knowledge. By this time, in many cases, the witnesses were Spaniards who had extensive experience interacting with indigenous societies in the Andes. In one of the surviving documents from this inquest, the first witness, García de Melo, had lived in Peru for many years and served as a judge of indigenous affairs [juez de naturales] many times (García de Melo [1582] 1925: 277). He gives the most thorough response, to which the subsequent witnesses primarily offer corroboration with some additional bits of information. In response to the fifth question, García de Melo first states that the Inca legal system essentially consisted of ad hoc judgments by the Inca. However, he goes on to list a series of laws and their punishments, which would seem to contradict his earlier statement. García de Melo also asserts that the Incas passed on the memory of their laws through songs similar to the Spanish romances. In response to the seventh question, he states that the Indians had no form of writing (ibid.: 276). The last question specifically asks about khipu, to which García de Melo responds that the khipu was limited to "counts" [quentas] and that everything else was passed on orally through song (ibid.: 277).

The second witness, Damián de la Bandera, does not respond to each question in order. Rather, he reads and confirms García de Melo's answers, but he also implicitly corrects García de Melo on a few points. After expanding on the divisions of the Inca Empire, Bandera explains that legal khipus recorded not only laws and ordinances of the kingdom but many other things as well (Bandera [1582] 1925: 279). Bandera had been in charge of a general inspection or *visita* in Cuzco and Huamanga for the viceroy Cañete in 1557, and he claims to have researched extensively this very question.

The subsequent witnesses also coincide with Damián de la Bandera. Alonso de Mesa states that the Inca did not write anything, but he also claims that the sentences imposed by Inca judges were recorded on khipu (ibid.: 282). The indigenous informants that testified along with Bartolomé

---

entendían, porque no tuvieron letras, y adelante haremos capítulo aparte donde se dará más larga relación de la manera del contar que tuvieron por estos nudos, que, cierto, muchas veces ha causado admiración a los españoles ver que los majores contadores de ellos yerren en su aritmética y que los indios estén tan ciertos en las suyas de particiones y compañías, que, cuanto más dificultosas, tanto más fáciles se muestran, porque los que las manejan no entienden en otra cosa de día y de noche y así están diestrísimos en ellas (Garcilaso de la Vega [1609] 1985: I, 88).

de Porras are the most explicit in contradicting García de Melo's testimony; and they are much less ambivalent about the nature of the khipu. They explain that Inca laws were recorded on khipu and on varicolored boards (ibid.: 284).[12] In response to the question about writing, they refer to the khipu (ibid.: 285–286). They also state, however, that neither the khipu nor the painted boards had survived, because the Spaniards destroyed them during the conquest: "Currently there are no khipu records nor boards, which as has been said, the Inca had to preserve his laws, because when the Spaniards conquered this city and kingdom, they broke and destroyed them" (ibid.: 287).[13] Of course, khipu were still clearly in use at this time. The text appears to refer only to the specific genre of legal khipus associated with the Inca state.

The most common genre or genres of khipu involved in the administration of the Inca state were probably those that recorded demographic data, resources, and labor tribute, all of which were related to the tribute system. Inca tribute was levied in the form of labor obligations rather than resource quotas. Such a system inherently involved the organization and control of the population. In the idealized system, the population broke down into decimal groups of ten thousand tributary households known as *hunu*, which were divided into two groups of five thousand households or *piska waranqa*, which in turn were divided into five groups of one thousand tributaries called *waranqa*, then five hundred or *piska pachaca*, one hundred or *pachaka*, and so on down to five households. Each of these groupings had numerical names, the most prominent of which were the even decimal units of ten thousand tributaries known as *hunu*, one thousand tributaries or *waranqa*, and one hundred tributaries or *pachaka* (Julien 1982: 123).

This organization is not strictly decimal in that each even grouping of decimal units (i.e., 10,000, 1,000, etc.) divides into two odd groupings (i.e., 5,000, 500, etc.). In other words, ten thousand households consists of an even ten sets of one thousand households, while five thousand households breaks down into an odd five sets of one thousand households. With the exception of the smallest grouping of five households, these units still have decimal components, but the division into sets of five is not inherent to the decimal system in the same way it is with the even groupings.

However, the Quechua-language number system has a cultural significance that also informs its conceptualization. Gary Urton's modern

---

12 The reference to multicolored boards raises interesting questions that are difficult to answer. A comprehensive analysis of the relevant sources on this issue is beyond the scope of this study. However, I will return to this topic in a future project.

13 Al presente no hay memoria de quipos ni de las tablas que dicho tienen tenía el Inga para memoria de sus leyes, porque cuando los españoles conquistaron esta ciudad y reino las quebraron é destruyeron. (ibid.: 287).

ethnographic research has identified a Quechua ontology of numbers with two main components: the decimal system and a model of fives in which the numbers one through five are associated with the fingers on the hand and a mother with four age-graded offspring (Urton 1997). As with all decimal number systems, the practice of counting on the ten fingers of the hands would have informed the decimal nature of the Quechua-language number system; and the division of this decimal value into two groups of five inherent to the human body further informed the Quechua ontology of numbers, producing what Urton calls the model of fives and the principle of duality in which each unit (whether a single unit or a grouping of five sets) is complete only when paired with another. As Urton argues, the principles of this Quechua ontology of numbers are also evident in the pre-Hispanic and colonial periods. The linguistic and cultural features of this numerical ontology inevitably would have informed the development of the decimal conventions of the khipu. Thus, in the Inca state, the Quechua ontology of numbers by way of the decimal conventions of the khipu would have served as the basis for the ideal organization of the population and the administrative structure through which it was controlled; and this is precisely what colonial sources indicate (Julien 1982).

Recently Gary Urton and Carrie Brezine have identified a set of seven khipu that may belong to different levels of this administrative structure (Urton and Brezine 2005). Most khipu have no provenance information, but even khipu recovered during archaeological excavations are often isolated specimens. In some cases, however, archaeologists have found sets of khipu together in the same place, what Urton calls khipu archives. Although the vast majority of archaeological khipu come from grave sites, a khipu archive consisting of specimens interred with several different mummies, as in the case of the discovery at Laguna de los Condores, may not be as useful as a set of khipu uncovered together in closer proximity in a more mundane context, as was the case with the Puruchuco and Pachacamac archives. The Puruchuco archive analyzed by Urton and Brezine consists of twenty-one khipu, seven of which figure in the analysis. They identify three different sets of khipu, the members of each of which exhibit the same or very similar cord configurations and color sequences within the set. These sets relate to each other in a hierarchy in which the information on khipu from higher levels summarizes or condenses the information on lower levels. Or if the information flowed in the opposite direction, the information on lower levels subdivides the information issued from higher up. In addition to the main body of cords, khipu on levels two and three include introductory segments of three cords with single figure-eight knots. Urton and Brezine speculate that these knots may constitute locative designators. Although they do not argue that the knot-values record population figures, demographic khipu may have functioned in the same way.

In addition to organizing the population into manageable groups, the khipu involved in the administration of the labor-tribute system would have needed to manage time. Much like other chroniclers, Cristóbal de Molina associates the expansion of the empire under Tupac Inca Yupanqui with the development of a more thorough and detailed record-keeping practice, but he also appears to identify more specifically the development of a more precise calendrical record. Molina is rather skeptical about many of the accounts of the past related by indigenous informants, but he believes that the khipu was a precise record, particularly after the reign of Tupac Inca Yupanqui:

They had in these quipus, which are like these strings that old women use for praying in Spain, only with ends hanging from them, they had such an account of the years, months, and moon that there was no error in the moon, year, or month, although not with as much order as after Inca Yupanqui began to reign and conquer this land; because until then the Incas had not left the vicinity of Cuzco, as it appears in the account that Your Reverence has. This Inca was the first to establish order and reason in everything, and he who took away and gave cults and ceremonies, and he who made the twelve month year, giving names to each one, and creating the ceremonies that they observed in each one of them, because even though before his predecessors reigned they had months and years in their quipu, they were not regulated so rigorously as after he was lord, for they were governed by the winters and the summers. (Molina [1570–1584] 1964: 10–11).[14]

Alphabetic documents from the colonial period provide little information about the nature of such khipu or their relationship to the demographic records involved in the tribute system, but Urton has identified an archaeological specimen that appears to be a calendrical and demographic tribute khipu from the Chachapoyas region (Image 19; Urton 2001). Most of the cords on this khipu are organized into twenty-four paired sets of alternating groups of 20, 21, or 22 cords on the one hand and 8, 9, or 10 cords on the

14 Tenían en esto quipos, que casi son a modo de pavilos con que las biejas reçan en nuestra España; salvo ser ramales, tenian tanta cuenta en los años, meses, y luna de tal suerte que no avía herrar luna, año, ni mes aunque no con tanta pulicía como después que Ynga Yupanqui enpeçó a señoriar y conquistar esta tierra porque hasta entonces los Yngas no avían salido de los alrededores del Cuzco, como por la relación, que Vuestra Señoría Reverendíssima tiene, parece. Este Ynga [Pachacuti Inga Yupanqui] fue el primero que empeçó a poner cuenta y razón en todas las cosas y el que quitó y dio cultos y cerimonias, y el que hizo los doze meses del año, dando nombres a cada uno y haziendo las ceremonias que en cada uno dellos hacen, porque no obstante que antes que reynasen sus antesesores tenían meses y años por sus *quipos*, no se regían con tanto concierto como después que este fue señor, que se rejían por los ynviernos y veranos (Molina [1570–1584] 1989: 58).

other. Each of these paired sets combine in such a way as to produce a total of 30 or 31 cords in all cases except the first set, which consists of 29, for a total of 730. Urton argues that this khipu constitutes a two-year calendar in which each of the cords belonging to the paired groupings corresponds to a calendrical day organized into twenty-four cycles roughly coinciding with synodic lunar months (more precisely calculated at 29.53 days). The twenty-four paired sets can be divided into two series of twelve months each containing 362 and 368 cords/days, respectively, for a total of 730 – that is, "$362 + 368 = 730 \div 2 = 365$" (Urton 2001: 137). Urton suggests that the difference in the total number of days in each year may be due to a further division of each year into two half-year periods corresponding to the perihelion and aphelion.[15] The calendrical significance of this cord configuration is very compelling, and such a two-year calendar would be logically consistent with the principle of dualism that informs the Quechua ontology of numbers.

While the number and configuration of the cords on this khipu appear to have calendrical significance, the knot-values may record demographic information. Urton explains that colonial documents from shortly after the conquest identify the leader of this region as a lord of three *waranqa*, or 3,000 tributary households, and this number corresponds almost exactly to the total knot-value of 3,005 from all the pendant cords that belong to the main structure of paired cord groupings (Urton 2001: 143). Presumably, the implication of Urton's analysis is that each tribute payer would render a labor-tribute of one day every two years. In other words, the knot-value of each of the cords corresponding to a calendrical day represents the number of tributary households assigned to work on that day.

Although Inca tribute consisted of labor-service, state administrators had to manage the goods produced through this labor. Thus, the storage and distribution of goods would have relied on khipu employing the ethnocategory conventions discussed in the section above on khipu genres. Murra's analysis of sixteenth-century khipu transcriptions from Jauja argues that khipu employ a standardized order of information categories, each presumably corresponding to an individual cord or cord grouping. The khipu transcriptions studied by Murra indicate that these ethnocategory conventions characterized records of both commodities and tribute labor (Murra 1981, 1982). If the khipu studied by Urton and Brezine record tribute as a demographic calendar, then these may constitute two different methods for registering similar information, perhaps corresponding to two different administrative interfaces.

---

15 The perihelion and aphelion refer to the number of days between the equinoxes (Urton 2001: 137).

If astronomic observations contributed to the development of complex Andean numeracy, then the seriation conventions themselves may have derived originally from calendrical records, which inherently involve a series of differentiated time units. As such conventions were adapted for recording other types of information, a need to build in other conventions would have arisen. One method for addressing this need would be to structure the cords of the khipu to reflect the calendar, and then use the knots to record the events or desired information on the relevant days or months, as in the case of the Puruchuco khipu analyzed by Urton and Brezine. It is easy to see how such a khipu would be useful for certain types of data, but other types of information recorded on khipu did not naturally correlate so evenly to calendrical units of time. Another method, as suggested by Murra, would assign each item or category of information to individual cords or cord groupings and devise some other way to indicate the temporal aspect if required for that type of record.

Khipu Historiography

Either of the methods described above could have conveyed the narrative genres mentioned by colonial chroniclers. Even the calendrical tribute khipu analyzed by Urton and Brezine would constitute a kind of narrative. This type of calendrical structure would produce a kind of annals, whereas other narrative khipu genres may have used the event sequences themselves to structure the seriation of cords. Molina's description of the calendric khipu cited above suggests that it was not merely an agricultural and ritual calendar.[16] Keeping an account of the years implies some form of historical record. In fact, the difference in the calendrical records maintained prior to Inca Yupanqui's reign and those created subsequently may reside precisely in that early khipu calendars served primarily an agricultural and ritual function, whereas later historiographic khipu drew in one way or another from calendric conventions or incorporated them in some way.

The most complex form of khipu historiography evident in colonial sources records the history of the Andes and more specifically that of the Inca Empire. According to the dialogic model of media presented in the Introduction, the adaptation of calendrical conventions for more complex historical narratives would have occurred in conjunction with sociopolitical developments. According to Sarmiento de Gamboa's history, during the expansion of the Inca Empire, Pachacuti Inca Yupanqui gathered together in Cuzco old historians from all over the Andes and produced a material record in the form of paintings. He then placed these paintings in the

16 See also Conklin 2002 for a discussion of Molina's statement.

Temple of the Sun and restricted access to them (Sarmiento de Gamboa [1572] 1988: 49).[17] Cieza de León further explains that each Inca selected three or four elders of his own nation to compose songs documenting all that happened during his reign. These historians were not allowed to perform the songs except in the presence of the Inca. After the Inca's death, they would perform the songs for the new Inca, who would choose his own historians to learn the old songs and compose new ones to document his own legacy. Cieza goes on to explain that these histories were also recorded on khipu (Cieza [1553] 1985: 57–58). What stands out in these accounts is the tight control that the Inca exercised over this historical record.

This control and the fact that the institution of khipu historiography develops during a period of imperial expansion may indicate that it was a response to the political context. The Incas originally claimed legitimacy on the basis of an origin narrative. In some versions, this involved establishing a common origin at Pacaritambo for all Andean peoples. In some cases, the origin narrative emphasizes a genealogical link between the first Inca, Manco Capac, and the sun (Urton 1999: 45–58). The details of these accounts may differ, but in all cases it seems clear that the major principle of subsequent Inca politics involved the notion that authority derived from a genealogical relationship to the original Inca, Manco Capac.

Catherine Julien argues that the genealogical politics of Inca government was articulated through the principle of *capac* status. In *Reading Inca History* (2000), Julien explains that *capac* was a hereditary status with accompanying privileges and rights granted to the descendants of the first Inca, Manco Capac, through the male line. The Inca ruler himself possessed the highest degree of *capac* status, which legitimized his authority. But other individuals and groups also held different degrees of *capac* status that determined their rank in the Inca hierarchy (Julien 2000: 23–48). In this situation, political struggles often involved competing claims about complex genealogical relationships. Julien explains that "because claims to status were contentious and because the dynastic genealogy could be recast to favor particular groups or individuals, there was a very good reason for formalizing an account of dynastic descent" (Julien 2000: 17).

The ideology of Inca politics articulated through the determination of *capac* status led to the formalization of an Inca history consisting of a genealogically linked series of Inca biographies. All histories of the Inca Empire written during the colonial period would have to derive either directly or indirectly from indigenous informants. And as Julien demonstrates, to one degree or another, all of them exhibit a genealogical/biographical format. It is not unreasonable to conclude therefore that

---

17 This reference to paintings may relate to the multicolored boards mentioned above. Here again, this issue is beyond the scope of this study, but I will deal with it in a future project.

the ideology of Inca politics articulated through the determination of *capac* status led to this particular genealogical/biographical format of Inca historiography. And colonial chroniclers often describe Inca historiography in very explicit terms as a biographically structured discourse (Collapiña [1542/1608] 1974: 21; Cieza de León [1553] 1985: 57–58; Polo de Ondegardo [1572] 1917: 46; Cabello Balboa [1586] 1951: 240; Gutiérrez de Santa Clara [c.1596–1603] 1963: 251; Murúa [1611] 1987: 373).

Certainly, these kinds of genealogical histories may have been transmitted orally, but as the classes of Inca elite expanded over time, the non-fixed nature of oral accounts would have been susceptible to challenges emerging out of power struggles, especially after the death of the ruling Inca. Oral histories are transitory and tied to the credibility and authority of the speaker. A more durable material record would have been an advantage in that it is a more permanent medium less susceptible to modification – although equally susceptible to fraud, deception, and ideological manipulation. Simultaneously, those individuals who employed the increasingly complex system of khipu semiosis within the rapidly expanding economic and political administration of the Inca Empire would have become more and more cognitively aware of, and self-reflexive about, the possibilities of secondary semiosis. The convergence of political power struggles, increased levels of technical complexity of secondary media, and a greater cognitive awareness of the possibilities of material semiosis would have created an environment conducive to the adaptation of secondary media in the legitimation projects of the ruling elite. Given the genealogical politics of the Inca Empire, it makes sense that such legitimation projects would have involved the representation of genealogical histories establishing *capac* status and tracing a line of authority back to Manco Capac.

The possibility of creating a more permanent material record that legitimized authority and the advantage of such a record evidently did not escape the Inca rulers. Sarmiento, Molina, and Guaman Poma all point to an attempt to regulate and standardize Andean history during the reign of the ninth and/or tenth Inca (Molina [1572–1580] 1989: 58; Sarmiento de Gamboa [1572] 1988: 49; Guaman Poma de Ayala [1615] 1987: 111). This roughly coincides with a later stage of Inca imperial expansion observed in the archaeological record and recounted in colonial chronicles. It is also beginning with these Incas that Sarmiento de Gamboa's apparently khipu-based history becomes much more detailed (Julien 2000); and Guaman Poma's history shifts from a mythic to an historic pace in terms of the length of the reign of each Inca (Brotherston 1992: 81). Of course, these were the most recent Incas, and the historical details of their reigns would have been preserved in the living memory of their subjects. But these developments are also consistent with what one might expect in terms of the conditions for, and results of, the adoption or expansion of some form of secondary system of representation in the use, transmission, and preservation of historical knowledge. If, as implied by the chronicles, the standardization of this level of khipu literacy was rather recent, then the Spanish invasion may have occurred at a time when the *khipukamayuq* had only recently adapted and expanded khipu conventions to the genre of biographical historiography in response to social and political exigencies.

Many other factors other than *capac* status entered into the determination of the successor to the Inca, and it is clear that these other factors also played a role in the political struggles over succession (Regalado de Hurtado 1996; Martínez Cereceda 1995). But this does not diminish the importance of khipu histories in Inca politics. Indeed, it appears that, as in other societies, the Incas were no exception to the dictum that the victors write the history. When the Spaniards arrived in 1532, the Inca Empire was in the middle of a civil war. The Inca Huayna Capac had died shortly before, and two of his sons, Huascar and Atahualpa, were engaged in a political and military struggle over the right to rule the empire. It would seem clear that Huascar had a legitimate claim to the throne. Some chroniclers suggest that Atahualpa was an illegitimate usurper, albeit in some versions provoked by Huascar's cruelty (Sarmiento de Gamboa [1572] 1988: 150–161; Cabello Balboa [1586] 1951: 26). María Rostworowski has argued, however, that Atahualpa was probably an eligible candidate, and that succession to the position of Sapa Inca was always a delicate and potentially violent affair (Rostworowski 1999: 106–134). Liliana Regalado de Hurtado maintains that both Huáscar and Atahualpa formed part of a dual hierarchical system that characterized Inca politics (Regalado de Hurtado 1996: 103–111). In any case, Atahualpa captured Huascar and had him executed. In an effort to consolidate his power, Atahualpa persecuted and killed many of the members of the ancestral kin group to which Huascar belonged. In 1542, native informants from Cuzco explained to the Spanish governor Vaca de Castro that part of this persecution included burning all of the historiographic khipu and killing all of the *khipukamayuq* that could be found (Collapiña [1542/1608] 1974: 20). Thus, the civil war was waged not only in terms of political influence and military might but also in the material record of the historiographic khipu.

Cieza de León explains that the Inca exercised control and even a kind of censorship over khipu accounts (Cieza de León [1553] 1985: 58, 137). If Huáscar and Atahualpa were both more or less viable candidates, then Huascar had probably already inscribed his legitimacy in the biographical genealogy of official Inca khipu historiography in Cuzco along with the other rituals involved in Inca succession. Thus, Atahualpa's act of destroying his rival's khipu and killing his *khipukamayuq* was a way of censoring the historical record; and Atahualpa would have had his own *khipukamayuq* "rewrite" and perpetuate a version of history that supported his legitimacy.

But while in the custody of the Spaniards, shortly after having Huascar executed, Atahualpa was also put to death. Thus, if the use of historiographic khipu had been a relatively recent development by the Incas in order to transmit and preserve historical knowledge that served to perpetuate legitimacy, the elimination of the imperial khipu and the execution of most of the official khipu historiographers would have placed the institution of khipu historiography at this level in serious jeopardy.

According to the *Relación de la descendencia y, gobierno y conquista de los Incas* – also known as the *Relación de los quipucamayos* – at least four of the official khipu historiographers persecuted by Atahualpa survived to read their khipu histories to officials employed by Vaca de Castro in 1542 (Collapiña, Supno, et al. [1542/1608] 1974: 20).[18] Elsewhere, I have argued that this *Relación de los quipucamayos* and Guaman Poma's *Nueva corónica* are the two historical accounts of the Inca Empire transcribed most directly from khipu and that they appear to reflect the seriation conventions discussed above (Brokaw 2003). As with all histories of the Inca Empire, these versions take the form of a series of Inca biographies that exhibit a structure essentially consisting of the same set of information categories appearing in the same order. Each biography includes certain categories of information such as a list of the Inca's conquests and accomplishments, the name of his queen, a list of his children, and the length of his rule. Furthermore, these information categories appear in the same order. The content of the categories sometimes differs, but the structure itself is highly stable and consistent.

Many later colonial chroniclers also mention the khipu as one of their sources of historical information; but without the sociopolitical institutions that drove its development and motivated its use, there would have been no support for the preservation and perpetuation, much less further development, of the institution of imperial khipu historiography along with whatever semiotic innovations were involved in this enterprise. The historiographic khipu practices enduring into the colonial period, which will be documented in Chapter 4 appear to be independent vestiges of the Inca historiographic tradition, in many cases dependent on the survival of pre-conquest *khipukamayuq* or their immediate successors. Without the imperial institution to give it purpose, the practice of maintaining an historiographic record of the Inca Empire appears to have largely disappeared by the mid-seventeenth century.

In addition to imperial khipu historiography, some sources, including the Inca Garcilaso's *Comentarios reales*, mention that individual kinship groups both from Cuzco and other regions kept their own historical accounts on khipu (Capoche [1585] 1959: 138–137; Garcilaso de la Vega

18 For a detailed analysis of this text and its relation to khipu historiography, see Brokaw 2003.

[1609] 1985: I, 45, II, 26), but the specific content and structure of these accounts is not as clearly described or well attested as the imperial history of the Inca Empire. It is also difficult to determine whether official Inca historiography employed unique and innovative semiotic conventions or merely a more elaborate version of the conventions used in regional histories and tribute records. Inca khipu historiography might have developed out of regional conventions; or regional khipu historiography may have developed as a result of Inca innovations; or they may have developed independently but still based on the previously established practices of khipu record keeping associated with socioeconomic relationships.

The relatively recent adaptation of the khipu for Inca imperial historiography also may have contributed to the ambivalent nature of colonial sources with regard to the specifics of this medium: colonial chroniclers often mention the khipu in relation to narrative histories, but they also insist – whether explicitly or implicitly – that it was merely a numerical device. Although colonial chroniclers clearly understood that some khipu were used to record historiographical information, the vast majority of their experience was with statistical khipu used to record more typically numeric data such as tribute. In other words, the ambivalence evident in the chronicles derives in part from the difficulty in understanding a non-alphabetic medium, but it may also stem from the fact that in the colonial period there was a disparity between what native Andeans said about the khipu and the uses to which the Spaniards were generally exposed. If the material features of the statistical khipu were not markedly different from historiographical khipu, this would have contributed only further to the confusion.

Not even the Inca Garcilaso de la Vega is immune from this ambivalence. In fact the Inca Garcilaso's comments on the khipu in his *Comentarios reales* is perhaps the best illustration of this problem. In the following passage, Garcilaso explains the various functions of khipu record keeping:

These people set down with their knots the tribute that they gave each year to the Inca, placing each thing by its genre, species, and qualities. They recorded the people who went to war, those who died in war, those who were born and passed away each year, according to the months [in which they occurred]. In sum, we say that they wrote in those knots all the things that consisted of number counts, including the battles and skirmishes that they had, even including the number of messages and how many speeches and discourses the King produced. But that which the message contained, neither the words of the discourse nor any other historical event, they could not say them with the knots, because it consists of ordered sentence spoken aloud, or by writing, which cannot be recorded on knots, because the knot says the number but not the word. (Garcilaso de la Vega [1609] 1985: II, 25–26).[19]

Garcilaso goes on to explain that the speeches constituting the contents of the "embajadas" were preserved not in the khipu but in the memory of the *khipukamayuq*. This has led many scholars to argue that the khipu was merely a mnemonic device consisting of numeric memory cues.

It is important to keep in mind, however, that Garcilaso was approximately sixty years old, having left Peru at the age of nineteen or twenty never to return. Garcilaso was a humanist whose project involved translating indigenous culture into European terms. Most important, however, as Garcilaso himself reveals, his experience with actual khipu was limited to the very specific context of his dealings with his father's Indians:

I worked with the khipu and knots with my father's Indians, and with other *curacas*, when around San Juan [June] and Christmas they came to the city to pay their tribute. Other *curacas* would plead with my mother that she send me to compare their accounts because, as suspicious people, they did not trust the Spaniards to treat them honestly in those particulars until I had certified it for them, reading them the transcriptions that they brought me of their tribute and comparing it with their knots, and in this way I knew as much about them as the Indians. (Garcilaso de la Vega [1609] 1985: II, 27).[20]

Garcilaso may very well have understood these particular khipu as well as the Indians, but this does not necessarily mean that he had a full understanding of this medium. Garcilaso himself echoes other chroniclers like Acosta and Murúa in identifying different genres of khipu used for different types of subject matter (Garcilaso de la Vega [1609] 1985: I, 112–113;

19 Estos asentaban por sus nudos todo el tributo que daban cada año al Inca, poniendo cada cosa por sus géneros, especiales y calidades. Asentaban la gente que iba a la guerra, la que moría en ella, los que nacían y fallecían cada año, por sus meses. En suma, decimos que escribían en aquellos nudos todas las cosas que consistían en cuenta de números, hasta poner las batallas y reencuentros que se daban, hasta decir cuántas embajadas habían traído al Inca y cuántas pláticas y razonamientos había hecho el Rey. Pero lo que contenía la embajada, ni las palabras del razonamiento ni otro suceso historial, no podían decirlo por los nudos, porque consiste en oración ordenada de viva voz, o por escrito, la cual no se puede referir por nudos, porque el nudo dice el número, mas no la palabra (Garcilaso de la Vega [1609] 1985: II, 25–26).

20 Yo traté los quipus y nudos con los indios de mi padre, y con otros curacas, cuando por San Juan y Navidad venían a la ciudad a pagar sus tributos. Los curacas ajenos rogaban a mi madre que me mandase les cotejase sus cuentas porque, como gente sospechosa, no se fiaban de los españoles que les tratasen verdad en aquel particular, hasta que yo les certificaba de ella, leyéndoles los traslados que de sus tributos me traían y cotejándolos con sus nudos, y de esta manera supe de ellos tanto como los indios (Garcilaso de la Vega [1609] 1985: II, 27).

Acosta [1590] 1986: 402; Murúa [1611] 1987: 373). Garcilaso's familiarity with statistical tribute khipu, therefore, does not necessarily make him an authority on the khipu in general.

Garcilaso's *Comentarios*, however, do indicate a detailed knowledge of the khipu decimal system and at least some awareness of the existence of a number of khipu genres. In his chapter dedicated to the khipu, Garcilaso presents a rather clear, albeit general, description of the decimal system used to record numbers. He also discusses the difference between what are now called pendant and subsidiary cords. In the case of some genres, such as censuses, he even provides examples of the significance of these extra-numeric elements. In his discussion of legal khipu cited above, he also refers to genre-specific color codes, the significance of pendant and subsidiary cords, and the size of knots (Garcilaso de la Vega [1609] 1985: I, 88). The use of different sized knots may refer merely to the different values of long knots, which inherently result in different sizes. But some modern khipu also use the relative size of other kinds of knots in their system of conventions (Uhle 1897). The lack of archaeological specimens that employ such conventions does not mean that they are post-conquest developments. Andean societies may have had no ideological reason to bury specimens of this khipu genre in graves.

Semiotic Heterogeneity, Khipu Genres, and Levels of Khipu Literacy

A more detailed analysis of the khipu's semiotic conventions is beyond the scope of this study, but Garcilaso's description highlights a characteristic of the khipu, the implications of which have not been sufficiently explored in modern scholarship. Modern discussions of the khipu tend to assume a high degree of semiotic homogeneity: the notion that information is conveyed using only one or a limited number of semiotic principles. This implicit perspective derives from the relatively high degree of semiotic homogeneity of alphabetic script. Alphabetic writing certainly employs a number of different types of convention, but its phonographic nature predominates. Of course, it has always been clear that khipu semiosis involved a certain degree of conventional heterogeneity: it employs knots using a decimal place system to convey numerical quantities, color to represent categories of information, and the relationship between pendant and subsidiary cords both to differentiate between information categories and to indicate their relationship. These various conventions employ qualitatively distinct modes of semiosis: they convey different types of information in different ways; and Garcilaso indicates how these different modes can function in different genres such as censuses and legal records. The implications of this semiotic heterogeneity include the following: (1) we may not be aware of all of the types of semiosis employed by khipu;[21] and (2) different khipu genres may have employed different sets of semiotic conventions. In other words, the material conventions employed by one khipu genre would not necessarily be the same as those of another.

We tend to think of the development of writing systems as a series of successive stages in which one set of practices and objects supplanted earlier ones, but this was not necessarily the case neither with the khipu nor with the practices that would develop into alphabetic writing.[22] In the Andes, different degrees of sophistication in khipu conventions may have developed at different levels of society associated with different institutions, leaving previous practices in place. Thus, we must not assume that all khipu would be uniform in the way in which they encoded information. In fact, the provisional outline of khipu development that I have proposed suggests that the khipu was a semiotically heterogenous device that employed different types of conventions for different types of information. In other words, in addition to the inherent heterogeneity of the khipu conventions, there would have been different levels of khipu literacy.

One of the lowest levels of khipu literacy probably involved pastoral and perhaps agricultural khipu designed to keep records of livestock and goods. These would have been related to the tribute and storehouse records observed by the Spaniards upon their arrival in the Andes. On another level, the statistical khipu of the empire would have shared conventions with these lower level records, but perhaps with certain adaptations. Another level of khipu literacy involved the community records used in the administration of community obligations. To the extent that these community records recorded information similar to that of pastoral and/or agricultural khipu, they too would have conventions in common. But these khipu would probably have developed additional techniques to record context-specific information related to community administration, such as any unique labor obligations.[23] These khipu also may have been related to the census records demanded by the Inca state and later by the colonial administration. If the Inca maintained legal records on khipu as indicated by some chroniclers, these would have constituted yet another level of khipu literacy with its own conventions. And imperial khipu historiography was yet another level with possibly esoteric conventions.

21 For the most extensive treatment of possible khipu conventions published to date, see Urton 2003.

22 For an argument along these lines with respect to alphabetic writing, see Schmandt-Besserat 1992.

23 In Frank Salomon's research on the patrimonial khipu from Tupicocha, he does not address the issue of semiotic heterogeneity, but his description of these khipu and their conventions seems to imply it (Salomon 2004).

Although it is important to recognize the theoretical possibility that the khipu might have employed some form of phonography, no credible evidence currently available suggests that this was a prominent feature of khipu semiosis.[24] Marcia and Robert Ascher have demonstrated convincingly that the material features of the khipu require a more sophisticated understanding of the use of color, format, and numbers than that to which we are accustomed (Ascher and Ascher 1981). Most scholars who have worked on the khipu in any detail usually come to the conclusion that the way information was encoded on the khipu and its relationship to a verbal rendition would have made it difficult to understand for colonial chroniclers from their alphabetically biased European perspective (Ascher 1986; Jara 1970; Prada Ramírez 1995: 11; Arellano 1999; Urton 2002b; Loza 2001: 61–62).

Without a more complete understanding of the khipu – both in its synchronic and diachronic dimensions – we cannot correlate specific developments in khipu conventions to specific stages in the social, economic, and political development of individual Andean societies. I would argue, however, that given what we know about the khipu and the ways in which secondary media have developed in other cultures, we can make several provisional inferences. First, the khipu as a medium certainly has the potential to employ various types of conventions – whether they be ideographic or even phonographic – and to record any given type of information or discourse structure – whether that be statistical, narrative, or otherwise (Ascher and Ascher 1981; Urton 1994, 1998; Pärssinen 1992: 31–50; Pärssinen and Kiviharju 2004a; Quilter 2002b: 201–202). Second, the social, economic, and political phenomena associated with the expansion of the Inca Empire would have created a context conducive to innovations in the pre-existing khipu medium. The link between the development of complexity in semiotic media and the emergence of complex economic, social, and political institutions implies the possibility and perhaps even the likelihood that the Inca developed khipu conventions that would have recorded the kinds of narrative histories transcribed by colonial chroniclers.[25]

24 Some researchers claim to identify phonographic conventions in the khipu. The most well-known cases are put forward by William Burns and Laura Laurencich Minelli, respectively. Burns's work consists of a series of hypothesis based on dubious assumptions and leaps of logic (Burns 2002). Laurencich Minelli's work is based on the controversial Naples documents, the authenticity of which is also highly dubious (Laurencich Minelli 1996).

25 I am well aware that making such a claim begs a more theoretical investigation into the relationship between the material medium and its oral rendering. Such a discussion is beyond the historical focus of this study, but I will address this issue in a later work focusing on theoretical issues and textual analyses.

The khipu is a textile product, and the trajectory from Early Horizon textile warp wrapping to Middle Horizon wrapped khipu to Late Horizon Inca khipu appears to indicate – albeit in very general terms – a line along which textile techniques converged and developed with increasing degrees of semiotic complexity. As is well known, the organic development of Andean society was interrupted with the arrival of the Spaniards in 1532. Although the Spaniards left intact the network of indigenous communities, they immediately displaced the larger imperial administration and its constituent institutions. The civil war between Huascar and Atahualpa had already weakened the institution of imperial khipu historiography, and the dissolution of the Inca state transformed the sociopolitical context conducive to its recovery. In fact, the *khipukamayuq* who participated in Vaca de Castro's inquest in 1542 may have belonged to the last generation of imperial khipu historiographers to have employed this particular genre in the context of the Inca institution that perpetuated it. Furthermore, the legal khipu practice to which Damián de la Bandera and other Spanish and indigenous witnesses refer appears to have dissolved along with the Inca Empire.

The history of the khipu, however, does not end here. Even without institutional support, *khipukamayuq* continued maintaining khipu records of various sorts throughout the fifteenth and sixteenth centuries; and some levels of khipu literacy continued to function for centuries after the conquest in traditional contexts in the service of indigenous institutions that remained intact and functioned either autonomously or subordinate to the Spanish colonial government. Cultural practices are resilient, and social, economic, and political upheavals always involve a measure of continuity. The following chapters will attempt to trace that continuity in the changing context of the Andes during the early colonial period.

PART II

The Khipu in the Early Colonial Period, 1532–1650

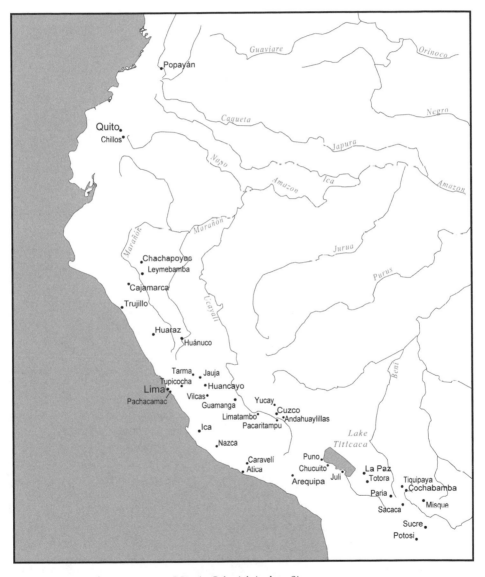

Map 2. Colonial Andean Sites.

4

Historiographic Khipu and Colonial Chronicles

Given the inherent relationship between the khipu and Andean socioeconomic and political institutions, one would expect that the history of the khipu would change radically with the conquest. Of course, as explained in Chapter 3, even prior to the arrival of the Spaniards, a civil war between Huascar and Atahualpa had erupted over who would succeed the previous Sapa Inca, Huayna Capac. The Incas waged this conflict both on the battle field and in the ideological field of Inca genealogical historiography recorded on khipu. If Atahualpa had not burned khipu and killed *khipukamayuq* prior to the conquest by the Spaniards, colonial chroniclers might have written a very different story about the Inca Empire; and they might have had much more to say about the khipu. Unfortunately, the Spanish conquest resulted in the dissolution of the political institutions that supported and perpetuated imperial khipu historiography precisely at the time when Atahualpa was engaged in his apparently revisionist project. The conjunction of the Inca civil war and the Spanish conquest, then, had a profoundly negative impact on the survival of such khipu. However, cultural practices are also linked to the individuals who engage in them, and they often persist long after their original motivation disappears.

In one way or another, all colonial alphabetic accounts of indigenous history derive from what was originally an indigenous discourse, and in many cases this discourse is associated with the material medium of the khipu. It is impossible to ascertain all of the details of the post-conquest history of these khipu, but their relationship to the historiographic projects of the Spaniards provides a very general outline and suggests that historiographic khipu genres persisted in one form or another at least until the first decades of the seventeenth century. Colonial chronicles written by Spaniards, mestizos, and native Andeans contain traces of the interaction between the khipu and alphabetic discourses. The historiographic discourses of the khipu and alphabetic script enter into a dialogue, albeit asymmetrical, in which each exerts a transformative influence on the other.

The Khipu and Early Colonial Chronicles

In the early colonial period, the Inca institutions that originally gave rise to imperial Inca historiography had dissolved, but the Spaniards immediately began searching out the Inca *khipukamayuq* to serve as informants in an attempt to reconstruct the indigenous past in order to satisfy requests from the king (Esteve Barba 1992: 513). From the very beginning of the colonial enterprise in the New World, Spain was ambivalent about the enslavement of native Americans. Early in the colonial enterprise, Francisco de Vitoria and Bartolomé de las Casas advanced legal arguments defending the rights of Indians and calling into question the legality of Spanish conquests. In response, the Crown enacted new laws in 1542 that attempted to bring colonial practices into line with legal principles. Although the intent of peninsular Spanish officials may have been sincere within the context of the period, from a modern perspective changes in colonial policy such as the move from *conquista* [conquest] to *pacificación* [pacification] or from an emphasis on *encomiendas* to one on *repartimientos*, for example, appear to be merely creative means of justifying the continued domination and exploitation of the indigenous population. Although on paper the New Laws inspired by Las Casas represented a substantive improvement in the status of indigenous peoples, more often than not, official Spanish policy differed significantly from actual colonial practice. In Peru, early attempts to actually enforce the new policies incited civil war.

Even after colonial authorities reestablished order and allegedly began enforcing the New Laws, the debate about indigenous rights continued. According to the sixteenth-century version of international law, Spain's right to sovereignty over New World peoples was related to whether or not the indigenous rulers were natural lords. In sixteenth-century Spanish political thought, "natural lord" was defined as "a lord who, by inherent nature of superior qualities, goodness, and virtue, and by birth of superior station, attains power legitimately and exercises dominion over all within his lands justly and in accord with divine, natural, and human law and reason, being universally accepted, recognized, and obeyed by his vassals and subjects and acknowledged by other lords and their peoples as one who rightfully possesses his office and rightfully wields authority within his territory" (Chamberlain 1939: 130). Of course, in the most rigorous interpretation of this definition, it is doubtful that any ruler would qualify as a natural lord. One could argue that the vague nature of the criteria allowed for whatever determination was most politically expedient. The ultimate outcome may have been predetermined, but this question, among others, prompted the Crown to repeatedly request information about the history of indigenous American cultures even after 1542.

Image 1. Inscribed bean (Courtesy of Museo Larco, Lima, Peru).

Image 2. Reverse of inscribed bean (Courtesy of Museo Larco, Lima, Peru).

Image 3. Moche bean bag (Courtesy of Museo Larco, Lima, Peru).

Image 4. Moche ceramic vessel with bean pseudo-signs (Courtesy of Museo Larco, Lima, Peru).

Image 5. *Yupana* device (Courtesy of Museo Larco, Lima, Peru).

Image 6. *Yupana* device (Courtesy of Museo Larco, Lima, Peru).

Image 7. Nazca textile with bean imagery (Courtesy of the Museo Nacional de Arqeuología, Antropología e Historia del Perú).

Image 8. Close-up of Nazca textile with bean imagery (Courtesy of the Museo Nacional de Arqeuología, Antropología e Historia del Perú).

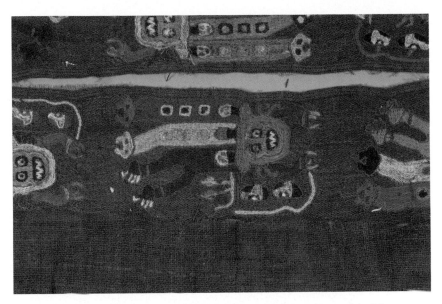

Image 9. Close-up of Nazca textile with bean imagery (Courtesy of the Museo Nacional de Arqeuología, Antropología e Historia del Perú).

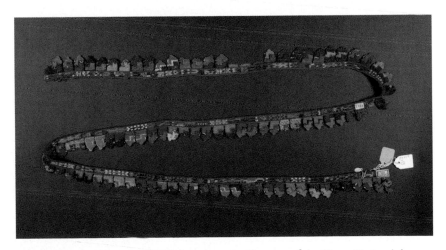

Image 10. Nazca textile with bean imagery (Courtesy of the Museo Nacional de Arqeuología, Antropología e Historia del Perú).

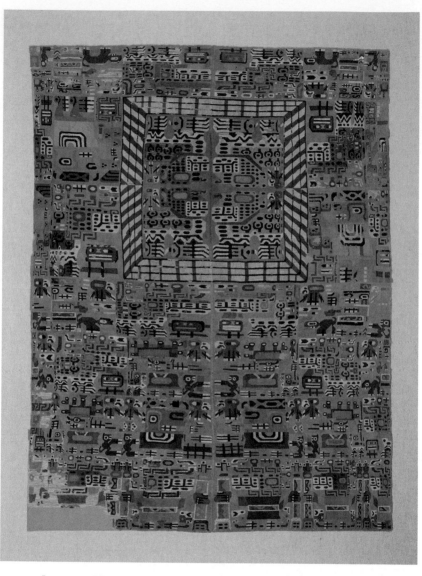

Image 11. Wari textile (© Dumbarton Oaks, Pre-Columbian Collection, Washington, DC).

Image 12. Large Wari ceramic vessel, category 2 (Courtesy of the Museo Nacional de Arqueología, Antropología e Historia del Perú).

Image 13. Large Wari ceramic vessel, category 3 (Courtesy of the Museo Nacional de Arqueología, Antropología e Historia del Perú).

Image 14. Wari-style wrapped khipu (Image #5068, courtesy of the Library,
American Museum of Natural History).

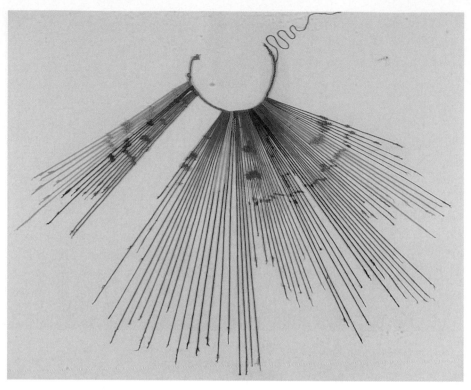

Image 15. Inca-style khipu (Courtesy of the Museo Nacional de Arqeuología, Antropología e Historia del Perú).

Image 16. Inca-style khipu (Courtesy of the Museo Nacional de Arqeuología, Antropología e Historia del Perú).

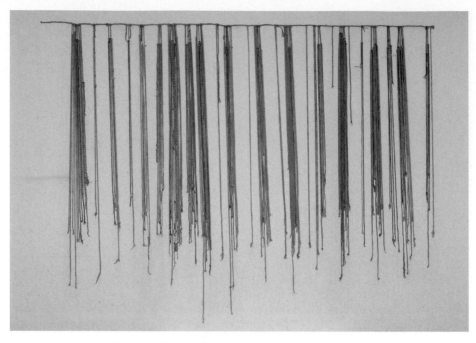

Image 17. Inca-style khipu (Museo Nacional de Arqeuología, Antropología e
Historia del Perú).

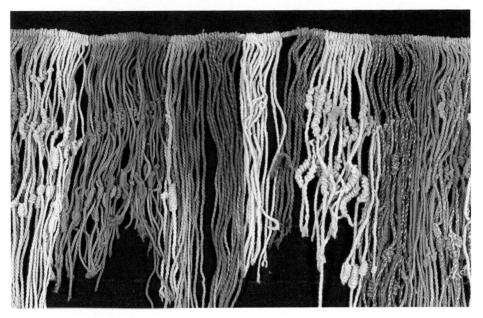

Image 18. Inca-style khipu (Courtesy of the Museo Nacional de Arqeuología, Antropología e Historia del Perú).

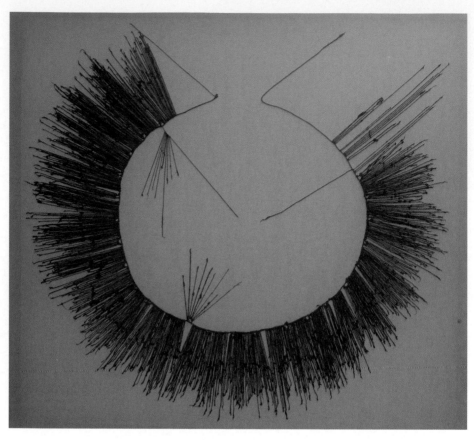

Image 19. Inca-style khipu from Chachapoyas. Quipu CMA. 1889/LC1.052.
Centro Mallqui, Leymebamba, Peru. (Photo by Gary Urton).

In the conquest of Peru, Francisco Pizarro was more concerned with consolidating his power and distributing *encomiendas* than he was interested in the history of the indigenous inhabitants of the Andes; but several of his successors were more diligent in their attempts to establish the legality of Spain's colonial enterprise. In 1542, Pizarro's immediate successor, the governor Cristóbal Vaca de Castro, ordered the first inquest into the history of the Incas. The results of this investigation have survived only in the form of a copy incorporated into a text produced in 1608, commonly referred to as *Relación de los quipucamayos* or *Relación sobre la descendencia, gobierno y conquista de los Incas* (Collapiña, Supno, et al. [1542/1608] 1921, 1974). Most scholars accept that the first section of the 1608 manuscript containing a history of the Inca Empire is based on an original document produced in 1542 as part of Governor Vaca de Castro's interview with several *khipukamayuq* (Duviols 1979: 589; Porras Barrenechea [1952]1986: 748; Urton 1990: 45).

According to the *Relación*, Vaca de Castro gathered together the oldest inhabitants of Cuzco and the surrounding area and asked them to give an account of their origins and history. The responses that he received varied greatly and often contradicted each other. Perceiving the frustration of the Spaniards, these *ancianos* [elders] suggested that they consult the *khipukamayuq*. As discussed in Chapter 3, these elders explained that during the civil war that was going on when the Spaniards arrived in Peru, Atahualpa had attempted to kill all the *khipukamayuq* in Cuzco and burn their khipu. A few of these *khipukamayuq*, who presumably belonged to the administration of Atahualpa's rival, Huascar, had survived Atahualpa's extermination campaign by fleeing to the mountains. The viceroy tracked down four of these *khipukamayuq* and had them brought to Cuzco with their khipu. He then separated them and posed the same questions to each one individually in order to determine whether their khipu-based accounts were in conformity. According to the *Relación de los quipucamayos*, all four conveyed essentially the same information. Several authorities on indigenous language and culture, including Juan de Betanzos – an interpreter and the author of *Suma y narración de los Incas* (1551) – were tasked with the translation and transcription of the khipu historiography conveyed by these *khipukamayuq*.[1] As explained in Chapter 3, this text draws from

---

1 "Al tiempo que gobernó en este reino del Perú el Licenciado Vaca de Castro, pretendiendo con mucha solicitud saber la antigualla de los indios deste reino y el origen dellos, de los ingas, señores que fueron destos reinos, y si fueron naturales desta tierra o advenedizos de otras partes, para averiguación desta demanda, hizo juntar y parecer ante sí a todos los ingas viejos e antiguos del Cusco y de toda su comarca, e informándose dellos, como se prentendió, ninguno informó con satisfacción sino muy variablemente cada uno en derecho de su parte, sin saber dar otra razón más que todos los ingas fueron descendientes de Mango Capac, que fué el primero inga, sin saber dar otra razón más que todos los ingas fueron descendientes de Mango Capac, que fué el primer inga, sin saber dar otra razón,

an established tradition of imperial khipu historiography that took the form of a series of Inca biographies. It also reveals a significant difference in terms of consistency between the oral accounts produced by ordinary informants and the khipu histories conveyed by the *khipukamayuq* (Brokaw 2001, 2002, 2003).

Subsequent governors, viceroys, and other colonial officials also conducted their own inquiries into the history of the Andes in response to requests from the Crown. In addition to enforcing the New Laws of 1542, Blasco Núñez Vela, the first viceroy of Peru, who arrived to replace the interim governor Vaca de Castro in 1544, was instructed to comply with all previous orders and requests for information (Hanke and Rodríguez 1978: I, 20–36). Núñez Vela's rather dogmatic adherence to the orders of the king provoked a rebellion and eventually led to his death at the hands of the rebels in 1546. Polo de Ondegardo, who arrived in Peru with Núñez Vela (González and Alonso 1990: 11), may have been involved in whatever inquests took place. Polo de Ondegardo's known writings on indigenous culture are normally dated from 1559 to the early 1570s, but Porras Barrenechea states that Ondegardo's texts are known to have circulated in Peru for many years in manuscript form prior to that time (Porras Barrenechea 1986: 326). In a document from 1561, Polo explains that he had carried out many other investigations previously, and he explicitly refers to the khipu as the source of pre-Hispanic history:

Many times, for other reasons, I have dealt with this method in different parts of this kingdom, and I have informed myself about the old Indians. . . . In that city today are found many old officials of the Inca, [officials] of religion and government, and another thing that I would not have believed if I had not seen it, was that laws and statutes were represented using threads and knots, the one just like the other, and the succession of kings and the time that they governed, and those who were charged with these [records], which were not a few, can still be found, and I even clarified somewhat the statutes that were enacted in the time of each one [of the kings], and from there to when they had introduced and observed customs pertaining to idolatry and government; and those [customs] that they had in their

no conformando los unos con los otros. E vístose apurados en esta demanda, dixieron que todos los ingas pasados tuvieron sus "quipocamayos", ansí del origen y principio dellos, como de los tiempos y cosas acontecidas en tiempo de cada señor déllos; e dieron razón que con la venida del Challcochima e Quisquis, capitanes tiranos por Ataovallpa Inca que destruyeron la tierra, los cuales mataron todos los quipocamayos que pudieron haber a las manos y les quemaron los "quipos", diciendo que de nuevo habían de comenzar (nuevo mundo) de Ticcicápac Inga, que ansí le llamaban a Ataovallpa Inga, e dieron noticia (de) algunos que quedaron, los cuales andaban por los montes atemorizados por los tiranos pasados. Vaca de Castro envió por ellos, y le trujeron antél cuatro muy viejos. . . . Los que trujeron ante Vaca de Castro pidieron término para alistar sus quipos, y se les dieron y en partes cada uno de por sí apartados los unos de los otros, por ver si conformaban los unos con los otros en las cuentas que cada uno daba" (Collapiña, Supno, et al. [1542/1608]1921:3–5).

marriages, in which they had their prohibitions and order, and in the succession of the women. (Polo de Ondegardo [1561] 1940: 128–130).[2]

Polo de Ondegardo drew from khipu sources during an inquest he carried out in 1559, which will be discussed below, but he also states that he was involved in many such investigations. It is likely, therefore, that he produced reports for several viceroys, possibly beginning with Núñez Vela.

Shortly after Nuñez Vela's death in 1546, Pedro de la Gasca arrived in Peru to assume the presidency of the Audiencia. Pedro Cieza de León, a soldier who would become another important chronicler, joined the force gathered by La Gasca to put down the rebellion led by Gonzalo Pizarro. After defeating the rebels, La Gasca served in place of the viceroy until 1550. An anonymous account from 1550 titled *Relación de todo lo sucedido en la provincia del Pirú . . .* and recently attributed to Polo de Ondegardo explains that Pedro de la Gasca carried out an extensive census and inspection of indigenous communities (Anonymous [1550] 1870: 192–196). This investigation involved interviews with indigenous informants requesting the kind of information normally recorded on khipu. If Polo de Ondegardo and Pedro Cieza de León were not directly involved in these inquests, their own writings were probably inspired and influenced by them. It would appear that both Cieza de León and Polo de Ondegardo were predisposed to the kind of historical and cultural investigations that they undertook, and most scholars view their work as among the most reliable sources from the early colonial period. It is all the more significant, therefore, that they both identify the khipu as the source of their information (Polo de Ondegardo [1561] 1940: 129–130; [1572] 1917: 46, 91; Cieza de León [1553] 1984: 220).

Some debate exists about whether La Gasca actually appointed Cieza de León as his official chronicler,[3] but Cieza clearly conducted an extensive

2 "Muchas vezes para otros efectos he tractado desta manera en diferentes parte deste Reyno y me he informado de los yndios viejos. . . . En aquella ciudad se hallan oy muchos viejos ofiçiales antiguos del inga, así de la Religión como del gouierno, y otra cosa que no pudiera creer sino la uiera, que por hilos y ñudos se halla figurada las leyes y estatutos, así de lo vno como de lo otro, y las sucçesiones de los Reyes y tiempo que governaron, y hállase los que todo esto tenían a su cargo que no fué poco, y avn tuue alguna claridad de los estatutos que en tiempo decada vno se avían puesto, y dende a quando se avían entroduzido y se guardavan las costumbres, así en lo que la ydolatría como en lo del gouierno, y las que se tenían en los matrimonios, en los quales tuuieron sus prohibiçiones y orden, y en el sucçeder las mugeres los vnos de los otros" (Polo de Ondegardo [1561] 1940: 128–130).

3 No clearly unambiguous evidence exists to corroborate Cieza's appointment as official chronicler. Marcos Jiménez de Espada claimed that Cieza was named official chronicler (Jiménez de la Espada 1877: cii–ciii), and other historians have accepted his assertion (Ballesteros 1984: 18–19; 1985: 12). Franklin Pease argues, however, that although La Gasca certainly facilitated and perhaps even sponsored Cieza's project, it is unlikely that he appointed him as his official chronicler (Pease 1984: xxvi–xxii).

investigation into pre-conquest Andean history. Although La Gasca certainly facilitated and possibly sponsored the project, Cieza appears to always have been actively engaged in recording information and events during his entire time in the Indies (Pease 1984: 23–24). He says himself that he began his chronicle in 1541 while still in Cartago and Popayán, before joining La Gasca's forces (Cieza de León [1553] 1984: 403–404). In the fourth part of his chronicle, Cieza reveals that even early on he was intensely interested in indigenous culture, and he based his research on interviews with numerous indigenous informants (Cook and Cook 1998: 9).

At first glance, the relationship between Cieza's work and khipu sources is somewhat ambiguous. On the one hand, in the first part of his chronicle, Cieza explains: "all of the information that I write regarding the events and things of the Indians, I relate and treat by means of the account of everything that they gave me themselves; who, because they lacked letters, and so that time would not consume their happenings and feats, had a genteel and elegant invention, as I will explain in the second part of this chronicle" (Cieza de León [1553] 1984: 220).[4] Cieza makes this statement in the context of a narrative history of the Inca past. It would appear that "a genteel and elegant invention" refers to the khipu, which implies that the oral accounts conveyed to Cieza by his informants were read off from khipu. On the other hand, in the second part of his chronicle, he seems to suggest that he had very limited firsthand experience with khipu accounts. Cieza explains that many times he had heard about the khipu and about how accurate they were, but that he did not believe it. Thus, on one occasion he asked Guacrapaucar, a Huanca leader from Jauja, to explain the khipu to him. Guacrapaucar showed Cieza a set of khipu that recorded all the goods the Spaniards had taken from storehouses in Jauja since their arrival (Cieza de León [1553] 1985: 59–60). If this is the only experience Cieza had with khipu, then he must not have relied on khipukamayuq informants in the investigation of indigenous Andean history.

This apparent contradiction may reflect merely a certain narrative anachronism in Cieza's text. Cieza clearly conceived of his work as a totality, but the first part was not necessarily written prior to the second. Cieza's account of his encounter with Guacrapaucar is not part of a chronological narrative. Thus, his statement about having heard of the wondrous khipu but not believing it may refer to a time prior to his arrival in Peru. One of the first places in Peru where Cieza spent any amount of time was precisely

---

4 "Todas las materias que escribo en lo tocante a los sucesos y cosas de los indios lo cuento y trato por relación que de todo me dieron ellos mismos; los cuales, por no tener letras ni saberlas, y para que el tiempo no consumiese sus acaescimientos y hazañas, tenían una gentil y galana invención, como trataré en la segunda parte desta crónica" (Cieza de León [1553] 1984: 220).

the valley of Jauja. After arriving in Peru, Jauja served as La Gasca's base of operations, from which he mounted an offensive against Pizarro (Espinoza Bravo 1962: 166–167). Furthermore, immediately after the defeat of the rebels in the valley of Sacsahuana, near Cuzco, Cieza traveled to Lima in advance of La Gasca (Ballesteros 1984: 17), which would have taken him through the valley of Jauja again. Given Cieza's inherent curiosity about indigenous culture and his propensity for research and writing, therefore, it is most likely that his encounter with Guacrapaucar took place during one of these early visits to Jauja in 1548 before he began his more extensive, formal investigations encouraged by La Gasca.

At some point between late 1549 and 1550, with the help of the *corregidor* of Cuzco, Juan de Saavedra, Cieza began an investigation of Inca history for which he gathered together and interviewed a group of Inca nobles in Cuzco, including Cayu Tupac, the last known descendant of Huayna Capac (Cieza de León [1553] 1985: 41–42).[5] Some scholars claim rather casually that these informants were *khipukamayuq* (Cook and Cook 1998: 15), but Cieza does not identify them as such; nor does he mention the khipu anywhere in this chapter. On the contrary, Cieza de León actually identifies the medium through which they conveyed the information he requested as "cantares" [songs] (Cieza de León [1553] 1985: 41–42). As is the case in many other chronicles, the implication here seems to be that the primary medium was not khipu but rather oral discourse, which took the form of songs in some cases.

However, this does not necessarily mean that Cieza's informants did not provide him with information from khipu. The vast majority of colonial texts with indigenous content are rather vague about the actual media on which the informants themselves relied. Pierre Duviols claims that reference to khipu sources became an ubiquitous rhetorical device adopted to lend authority to colonial accounts of indigenous history (Duviols 1979: 589), but this is a gross exaggeration. Many chroniclers mention the khipu, but relatively few of them explicitly identify the khipu in specific terms as the source of their information. After his experience translating and transcribing khipu histories for Vaca de Castro in 1542, Juan de Betanzos would presumably have drawn from this experience and/or sought out *khipukamayuq* informants in the composition of his *Suma y narración de los Incas* (1551), but he does not explicitly identify the khipu as one of his sources for this history. Furthermore, the chroniclers who do specifically cite the khipu do not normally privilege this source in the way one would

---

5 In a note in his edition of Cieza's text, Ballesteros dates these interviews to early 1550, but he provides no documentation (Cieza de León [1553] 1985: 41, n.46). Nevertheless, it must have taken place in 1549 or early 1550. La Gasca did not appoint Juan de Saavedra *corregidor* of Cuzco until 1549, and Cieza returned to Spain in 1550.

expect if it were a gesture designed to bolster the authority of their texts. Furthermore, many colonial records of statistical information that could have come only from khipu sources make no mention of this medium either (see Chapter 5).

The uncritical distinction often drawn in contemporary scholarship between an oral account and a khipu record tends to forget that these two media are not mutually exclusive. Andean oral traditions certainly played an important role in the communicative practices of native Andean societies; but any information recorded on a khipu would also by necessity have to be rendered orally for the Spaniards.[6] The epistemological barrier inherent in the alphabetic bias of a European mentality may have led the Spaniards who witnessed such oral renderings of khipu to emphasize the oral dimension of the performance, because they found it difficult to conceive of how it might relate in any significantly semiotic way to the material object of the khipu.

Furthermore, in most cases, the information provided by *khipukamayuq* informants would have been mediated by a translator. The Spaniards would have interacted more directly with the translator and thus would not necessarily have been paying much attention to the details of what the actual informant was doing. It is a mistake, then, to assume, as Duviols does, that references to khipu sources are merely rhetorical devices, and it is equally problematic to assume that the khipu is mentioned in every document that transpositioned information from this Andean medium into alphabetic script.

Perhaps the best evidence that Cieza's interviews in Cuzco involved *khipukamayuq* comes from Polo de Ondegardo's report in 1561 to Briviesca de Muñatones, in which he clearly identifies his informants for his own 1559 inquest as previous Inca officials who employed khipu (Polo de Ondegardo [1561] 1940: 129–130). As explained above, Polo de Ondegardo's 1559 report relies on earlier interviews with Inca *khipukamayuq*. Thus, the investigations to which Polo refers may be the very same ones conducted by Cieza. Even if Cieza and Polo were not collaborators, their interviews in Cuzco took place more or less in the same time period. It is virtually certain, therefore, that they would have spoken with at least some of the same informants.

Unfortunately, Cieza de León does not appear to have pursued any further the curiosity about the nature of khipu semiosis that he manifested in his visit with Guacrapaucar in Jauja. Perhaps his extensive travel and writing

---

6 This does not mean, as many claim, that the khipu was necessarily mnemonic in nature. The necessity of an oral rendering to which I refer is merely due to the fact that the Spaniards could not read the khipu for themselves.

during his relatively brief sojourn in Peru gave him time to focus only on the content rather than the medium of Andean discourses. Cieza returned to Spain in 1550 and died in 1554, having published only the first part of his work, which appeared in 1553. The second part, which focused most directly on the history of the Inca Empire, was not published until the nineteenth century.

Polo de Ondegardo, however, would continue his investigations for many years. Ten years after the New Laws of 1542 had been enacted, the administration of Felipe II had yet to receive a satisfactory report on indigenous history and culture that would serve as the basis for determining the status of various classes of indigenous societies in the socioeconomic order of the colony. Even after the death of Gonzalo Pizarro and the rescission of a portion of the New Laws in 1542, there was considerable unrest among the colonial Spaniards opposed to the reforms. Rebellions and continued political turmoil did not prevent Cieza de León from conducting in-depth inquiries into Andean history and culture, but it seems to have detracted from the incorporation of these findings by official policy makers. In 1553, after the Valladolid debate between Las Casas and Sepúlveda, the Crown prepared a new questionnaire requesting specific socioeconomic and historical information about Andean society prior to the conquest. This questionnaire explicitly instructs colonial officials to verify the oral accounts of their indigenous informants using whatever material media through which they might have recorded such information (Santillán [1563] 1968: 101). Ten years later, in 1563, in direct response to this *cédula*, Fernando de Santillán produced his *Relación del origen, descendencia, política y gobierno de los Incas*, in which he both explains that the Peruvians employed khipu records and identifies the khipu as one of the principle sources of information about pre-conquest Andean history (Santillán [1563] 1950: 43, 66). Porras Barrenechea argues that in the composition of his work, Santillán also drew directly from other chroniclers such as Damián de la Bandera and probably Polo de Ondegardo (Porras Barrenechea 1986: 326).

In 1558, the viceroy Andrés Hurtado de Mendoza, marqués de Cañete, appointed Polo de Ondegardo *corregidor* of Cuzco, and he charged him with investigating questions relating to indigenous history and religion. Ondegardo appears to have conducted a rather thorough investigation that has led some scholars to identify his methodology as "anthropological" (González Pujana 1993: 65–66). As a result of this investigation, Ondegardo discovered Inca mummies that had been hidden from the Spaniards, and in 1559, he produced the document titled *Tratado y averiguación sobre los errores y supersticiones de los indios* (1559), which was later incorporated into the record of the Third Lima Council in 1583 (*Tercer concilio Limense* [1583] 1990).

These same investigations would also inform Ondegardo's later writings for at least two subsequent viceroys. In 1560, Diego López de Zúñiga y Velasco, conde de Nieva, is sent to replace Cañete as viceroy. Nieva's instructions from the Crown express concern over the perpetuity of the *encomiendas* (Hanke and Rodríguez 1978: 56). Here again, the Crown requests information about indigenous Andean communities in order to provide the basis for an informed decision. After arriving in Peru and assuming his duties as viceroy in 1561, Nieva and one of his officials, Briviesca de Muñatones, showed this order to Polo de Ondegardo and ordered him to provide the information requested (Polo de Ondegardo [1571] 1990: 36–37). In response, Ondegardo produced a report dated the same year and directed to Briviesca de Muñatones. At this time Ondegardo was in Lima and did not have access to his papers from the inquest from 1558–1559, but he explicitly refers to this earlier investigation as well as various others that he had carried out. He explains that the most reliable sources of information about the Incas were the oldest surviving Indians in Cuzco, who had served as administrative officials in the Inca administration and who still maintained khipu records of Inca laws, statutes, the succession of the Inca kings, the length of their reigns, and what laws and customs each one had instituted. He marvels at the nature of these records, saying that it is impossible to believe without actually seeing it. Ondegardo does not have complete faith in the historical accuracy of the khipu accounts, but he explains that if the elderly Inca *khipukamayuq* had died and their khipu had been lost, he would not have been able to conduct his research at all (Polo de Ondegardo [1561] 1940: 128–130).

In the early colonial period, the Spaniards were not the only ones to rely on khipu records in the production of alphabetic texts containing narratives and/or ethnographic information. Native Andeans also relied on these records to support their own legal cases. In the Inca civil war, in addition to killing many *khipukamayuq* and burning their khipu, Atahualpa also persecuted those Inca lineages who supported Huáscar, the most notable of which perhaps was that of Tupac Inca Yupanqui. After the conquest, the Spaniards confiscated the lands occupied by surviving members of Tupac Inca Yupanqui's descent group and assigned it to Spanish *encomenderos*. In 1569, members of the descent group, who were the grandchildren of those who had been slain by Atahualpa, requested that the colonial government in Cuzco consider a petition for the recognition of their status (Rowe 1985). The colonial administration in Cuzco agreed to consider their petition, and it was duly submitted. The petition included two sections normally referred to as *Memoria de los nietos* and *Memoria de las provincias*. The *Memoria de los nietos* identifies twenty-two members of Capac Ayllu, further subdivided according to internal lineages that correspond to the hierarchy of the three ceque-line categories, Collana, Payan, and Callao, with which they were associated.[7] The *Memoria de las provincias* contains a list of provinces, fortresses, and kings conquered by Tupac Inca Yupanqui and his brothers. John Rowe argues that the presentation of the information in these *memorias* exhibits a rigid structure that conforms to principles of organization based on Andean cultural logic and consistent with what is understood of khipu conventions (Rowe 1985). These texts make no explicit mention of the khipu, but they would have had no reason to explicitly identify this medium as the original source text. As Polo de Ondegardo explains, the Spanish judicial system was based on the testimony of witnesses rather than historical documents, and native Andeans quickly learned how to work this system (Polo de Ondegardo [1561] 1940: 129). The petitioners in this case were well aware of this criterion for authentication, and they provided ten witnesses to testify to the truthfulness of the information they presented.

Unfortunately, the viceroy Francisco de Toledo took office in 1569 around the same time the original petition was submitted. Although Toledo was a strict enforcer of royal decrees who instituted sweeping reforms designed to reign in the abuses of the Spanish *encomenderos*, he did not share Las Casas's views on indigenous rights. His primary concern was with enforcing the authority of the Crown, particularly with regard to the economic obligations of the Spaniards. Although many of the reforms Toledo instituted were designed to protect indigenous rights, these actions were merely incidental to the imposition and consistent enforcement of royal authority in the colonial system. Whether or not Toledo had already made up his mind about the status of native Andeans prior to the beginning of his inquest, it quickly became clear that he did not consider them natural lords. Thus, in the new political environment of Toledo's administration, the petitioners from Tupac Inca Yupanqui's descent group had no hope of success (Rowe 1985: 193).

Although various governors and viceroys took up the task of investigating the history of the Andes to one degree or another, Toledo conducted the most systematic and extensive inquiry during his tenure as viceroy. Las Casas had been unable to convince the Crown to adopt all of his proposals, but official policies were clearly more in line with Las Casas's perspective than that of Sepúlveda, his opponent in the debate at Valladolid in 1550–1551. Francisco Esteve Barba argues, following earlier nineteenth-century scholars such as Mendiburu, Clements Markham, and José Riva Agüero, that Toledo's anti-Lascasian leanings motivated him to seek out information from diverse sources, including, or perhaps especially, from non-Inca groups who might lend support to a history that would undermine the

7 For a description of the ceque system, see Zuidema 1964 and Bauer 1998. For a discussion of Inca social hierarchy in Cuzco and how it relates to genealogical politics and the ceque system, see Zuidema 1977.

Incas' status as natural lords (Esteve Barba 1992: 519). Roberto Levillier, on the other hand, claims that Toledo's investigations were objective and truthful (Levillier 1956: 37–40, 42, 51). In either case, from October of 1570 through at least February of 1572, Toledo and his entourage traveled throughout the highlands meeting with and interviewing groups of up to one hundred informants in places such as Jauja, Huamanga, Vilcas, Yucay, and Cuzco (Toledo [1570–1572] 1921: 105–143; Levillier 1956: 41–42). It may be unlikely that all of the hundreds of indigenous informants interviewed by Toledo's inspectors were *khipukamayuq*, but it is equally unlikely that none of them were. Although Toledo's report seems to point explicitly to traditions passed down orally and preserved by memory, as in the case of Cieza, this may merely reflect the structure of the investigational method that depended on translators and the epistemological barrier that impeded an understanding of the khipu as a medium of material memory. Many of the informants are referred to as *curacas* or *caciques*, and in similar inquests, these leaders are also identified as *khipukamayuq*. Toledo's report from Yucay, in fact, identifies one of the *curaca* informants as having been the *khipukamayuq* of Huayna Capac (Toledo [1570–1572] 1921: 124).

In addition to the economic and cultural information used to determine specific details of Toledo's reforms, the reports from these investigations also led to the production of narrative histories. Pedro Sarmiento de Gamboa may have actually participated in Toledo's inquests, and he produced his *Historia índica* (1572) at Toledo's request. Consistent with Spanish legal procedures, Toledo's interviews were rigidly structured by a pre-formulated set of questions. More than thirty years later, The Inca Garcilaso de la Vega would criticize such procedures, because they were not effective in uncovering the truth. To one degree or another all such questionnaires presuppose or delimit the nature of the information sought. Garcilaso explains that Inca judges, in contrast, would ask their witnesses to divulge everything they knew of the issue or case in question and then let them answer without interrupting: "under oath, they let him say all that he knew of the case, without cutting him off or saying 'I didn't ask you that, but rather this other thing' or anything else" (Garcilaso de la Vega [1609] 1985: 65).[8] In other words, the problem with the Spanish system is that the official conducting the inquiry won't shut up and let the witnesses explain what they know. The methodology employed by Toledo, then, forced native informants to provide only the information explicitly requested and in the order dictated by the questions.

Of course, the type and order of information categories requested in Toledo's questionnaire would not have coincided with the respective information categories and structure of the khipu. Thus, the *khipukamayuq*

8 "Debajo de su promesa la dejaban decir todo lo que sabía del hecho, sin atajarle ni decirle 'no os preguntamos eso sino estotro,' ni otra cosa alguna" (Garcilaso de la Vega [1609] 1985: 65).

who were surely involved in the interviews would not have consulted their khipu in response to questions whose answer did not require it. And even when the information solicited in the question was recorded on the khipu, the way in which such an inquiry demands the isolation and extraction of data from the context of its larger discourse may mean that the *khipukamayuq* would have consulted the khipu only in an intermittent and cursory fashion, and in some cases perhaps not at all. The particular nature of this interaction, then, would inevitably inform the way in which the interviewer and those observing the interview understood the relationship between the khipu and the information reported. In such cases, it would have been natural to infer that the khipu was an auxiliary device, perhaps a kind of aid for remembering information that was essentially retained in natural memory.

Sarmiento would have drawn from the reports produced during Toledo's inquests, in which he may even have participated, but the immense difference in detail and substance between these documents and the *História índica* suggests that Sarmiento also conducted his own independent investigations and produced his own documents (Levillier 1956: 65). In fact, at one point he appears to refer to these documents explicitly:

And thus examining from all levels of society the most prudent and elderly of all conditions and states, who are the most trustworthy, I got and compiled the present history, referring the declarations and statements of one group to their enemies, that is to say the opposing faction, because they group together in factions, and asking each one for their own account of their lineage and of that of their adversaries. And these accounts, which are all in my possession, referring them and correcting them with their adversaries and lastly ratifying them in the presence of all the factions in public, under oath by the authority of a judge, and with expert translators, and very curious and faithful interpreters, also under oath, what is written here has been perfected. (Sarmiento de Gamboa [1572] 1988: 49–50).[9]

The methodology described by Sarmiento is consistent with that of Toledo's interviews. Initially, Toledo prepared a set of fifteen questions that were used in the interviews with native informants in Juaja and Huamanga. In the inquests carried out in Vilcas, Pina, Limatambo, Mayo, Cuzco, and Yucay, however, Toledo drafted additional questions eliciting explicit confirmation or denunciation of the information obtained from the informants in Juaja

9 "Y así examinando de toda condición de estados de los más prudentes y ancianos, de quien se tiene más crédito, saqué y recopilé la presente historia, refiriendo las declaraciones y dichos de unos a sus enemigos, digo del bando contrario, porque se acaudillan por bandos, y pidiendo a cada uno memorial por sí de su linaje y del de su contrario. Y estos memoriales, que todos están en mi poder, refiriéndolos y corrigiéndolos con sus contrarios y últimamente ratificándolos en presencia de todos los bandos en público, con juramento por autoridad de juez, y con lenguas expertas generales, y muy curiosos y fieles intérpretes, también juramentados, se ha afinado lo que aquí va escrito" (Sarmiento de Gamboa [1572] 1988: 49–50).

and Huamanga (Levillier 1956: 47–60). Thus, Sarmiento's practice of cross-checking among different groups may refer to Toledo's interviews. However, the reference to documents in Sarmiento's possession containing memorials that he requested from "each one" may allude to the results of his own, less rigidly structured inquests as part of his historiographical project. If Sarmiento also engaged his informants in a less structured dialogue similar to the Inca methodology described by Garcilaso and possibly indicated by Sarmiento's reference to "memoriales," the *khipukamayuq* informants would have presented an account of their historical and cultural knowledge using their own methods and discursive structures. In other words, in such a context, the *khipukamayuq* informants would have presented their information in a much more organic relation to the khipu. The depth and detail of Sarmiento's text suggests that he probably relied on information acquired using both methods.

The two different methodologies employed by Sarmiento would have resulted in very different relationships between the khipu and the oral discourse of the *khipukamayuq*, which in turn would influence the way the Spaniards conceived of khipu semiosis. The difference between the role of the khipu in the accounts elicited by these two methodologies, then, may contribute to the equivocation with regard to this medium that is evident in the writings of many colonial chroniclers, including Cieza, Ondegardo, and Sarmiento himself. Similar to Cieza and Ondegardo, Sarmiento implies that native Andeans preserved historical knowledge through an independent oral tradition, while at the same time he recognizes that the khipu was associated with this oral tradition and that this medium was able to record information in incredible detail (Sarmiento de Gamboa [1572] 1988: 48–49). As Toledo's official chronicler, in practice if not in name, and given the date of his text, Sarmiento's investigation would have been able to draw on the same administrative resources of the colonial government that were dedicated to Toledo's general inspection. If Sarmiento was not always directly involved in the actual transcription and translation (or vice versa) of the discourses produced by the *khipukamayuq* informants, then his inferences about khipu semiosis would be even more problematic.

Toledo's interviews with *khipukamayuq* also informed, either directly or indirectly, the production of several other texts. Miguel Cabello Balboa's *Miscelánea austral* (1578–1586) explicitly cites the khipu as the primary repository of Andean history, and Carlos Assadourian argues that these references to khipu-based information refer to Toledo's investigations in 1571 and 1572 (Assadourian 1998: 27).[10] Whether or not Cabello Balboa had access to all of Toledo's reports, it would seem clear that he relied

10 Cabello Balboa is not explicit about the specific nature of his immediate sources. His reliance on Toledo's reports may only be indirect by way of the work of Sarmiento and Molina. Porra

directly on Sarmiento's *Historia* (Porras Barrenechea 1986: 351). Cristóbal
de Molina, *el cuzqueño*, on the other hand, may have actually participated
directly in Toledo's inquests, and he would have drawn on the results in
the production of his *Historia de los Ingas*, now lost but possibly completed
sometime between 1570 and 1574.[11] Although no copy of Molina's *Historia*
has ever been found by modern researchers, other colonial chroniclers such
as Cabello Balboa, José de Acosta, Blas Valera, and Bernabé Cobo seem to
have had access to it (Porras Barrenechea 1986: 351). In his *Relación del
Cuzco* from 1649, Vasco de Contreras y Valverde appears to refer to Molina's
Historia as having been ordered by Toledo, and he identifies Molina as a
"scrutinizer of khipus" [*escudriñador de quipos*] (Contreras y Valverde [1649]
1982: 34). We know that Molina's text was circulating in Peru as late as
the first half of the seventeenth century, because in his *Historia del Nuevo
Mundo* (1653), Bernabé Cobo states that he acquired Molina's account
(Cobo [1653] 1979: 100). Porras Barrenechea suggests the possibility that
both Cabello Balboa and Sarmiento drew heavily from Molina's *Historia*
(Porras Barrenechea 1986: 351). If this is the case, it may be an additional
factor in the apparent contradiction in Sarmiento's description of what was
recorded on khipu. If Molina was the one who collected the more detailed
memoriales mentioned in the *Historia índica* based on a more organic reading
of the khipu, then the ambivalence in Sarmiento's text may derive from the
difference between his personal experience with the khipu in the context
of Toledo's inquests and an ostensibly more direct relationship between the
khipu and the discourse of Molina's *Historia de los Ingas*.

On the other hand, Molina shares the same alphabetic bias as other
Spaniards,[12] and his surviving text, *Fabulas y mitos de los Incas*, exhibits the
same ambivalence with regard to the khipu. In this text, Molina compares
the khipu to strings used by women in Spain in reciting prayers, and he
seems to imply that they are limited to numerical information. At the same
time, however, he explains that the khipu was an extremely accurate device
used to record all the things that had happened in the Andes for the last
five hundred years and by which "the smallest thing was not forgotten"
(Molina [c. 1570–1574] 1964: 10). Relatively speaking, Molina appears to
be one of the more objective chroniclers of the early colonial period, and

---

Barrenechea explains that portions of Cabello Balboa's text come directly, in some cases verbatim,
from Sarmiento's *Historia* (Porras Barrenechea 1986: 351).

11 Porras Barrenechea states that Bishop Lartaún, who arrived in Cuzco in 1573, instructed Molina to
write the history of the Incas; and Molina's *Fabulas*, which was probably finished in 1575, makes
reference to this earlier text (Porras Barrenechea 1986: 350–351). Porras Barrenechea presumably
bases this assertion on Bernabé Cobo's statement in *Historia del Nuevo Mundo* (1653) that Lartaún
ordered Molina's investigation (Cobo [1653] 1979: 100).

12 Molina has often been identified as a mestizo and a native speaker of Quechua. Porras Barrenechea
demonstrates that, in fact, he was a Spaniard (Porras Barrenechea 1986: 349–350).

the nature of his inquiry into indigenous religion meant that he would necessarily have had to engage in a more open dialogue with native informants. Although the *Historia de los Ingas* was primarily a historical text, *Fabulas y ritos* is more ethnographic in nature, produced at the request of Bishop Lartaún (Cobo [1653] 1979: 100; Porras Barrenechea 1986: 351) and motivated by the need to understand indigenous religion in order to better root it out.

In undertaking this project, Molina organized a new *junta* of elderly informants who "saw and did" in the time of Huayna Capac, Huascar, and Manco Inca (Molina [c.1570–1574] 1989: 49). In this work, Molina claims to have relied in part on pictorial texts that were traditionally kept in Poquen Cancha, the temple of the Sun, and that recorded the origin of the Incas and the lives of each Inca ruler. Given his involvement in the investigations, Molina probably would have been present, along with Polo de Ondegardo,[13] at the reading of Sarmiento's history and the exhibition of the paintings that Toledo had commissioned to accompany it. In any case, it is unclear to what extent the information collected in *Fabulas y ritos* derived from khipu. This type of ethnographic knowledge might not have been as systematically recorded as the dynastic genealogies of the Incas that would have informed in one way or another his previous work. It is unfortunate, therefore, that Molina's *Historia de los Ingas* is lost, because it may preserve the original nature of a khipu-derived discourse to a greater degree than his more ethnographic text or other chronicles written from a more ideologically inflected perspective. Even if Molina's lost *Historia* is not as direct a transcription of khipu as the *Relación de los quipucamayos* appears to be, it might provide additional information both about indigenous forms of knowledge and about the interaction between khipu and alphabetic script in the colonial period.

Molina also participated in an inquest conducted by the subsequent viceroy, Martín Enríquez, who ruled for about a year and a half from late 1581 until his death in May of 1583. As in the case of other viceroys, Enríquez also received orders to investigate the customs of the Indians, in particular those relating to law and government, in order to determine the best form of colonial rule. By this time, peninsular officials were well aware of the khipu and its role in indigenous record keeping; but they did not know how it worked nor the extent to which it was able to record different types of information. The *cédula* ordering Enríquez's investigation specifically mentions the khipu, illustrating the same kind of ambivalence evident in the chronicles. After inquiring about laws, the sixth question of the inquest asks if there existed written records of such laws so that

---

13 Levillier claims that Gonzalo Jiménez read what had been written on the *paños* to Polo de Ondegardo (Levillier 1956: 66), but I have found no evidence to support this.

the judges would not err in their application and so that there would be uniformity (Levillier 1921–1926: IX, 270). The seventh question then asks whether the judgments and sentences were written or how they were remembered over time, who was in charge of this, and with what kind of ceremony they were carried out (ibid.: 270). The final question of the inquest also asks more generally if there are any signs or khipus or other materials that corroborate or verify the information provided in the informant's testimony (ibid.: 271). This investigation was much more limited than Toledo's, and it relied primarily on Spanish witnesses. The testimonies recorded in the case come from García de Melo, Damián de la Bandera, Cristóbal de Molina, Alonso de Mesa, Bartolomé de Porras, and "some Indians." The witnesses disagree with regard to the use of the khipu in pre-Hispanic times (see Chapter 7), but it appears to be clear that even those who maintain that the information in question was originally stored on khipu are not drawing directly from khipu records in order to answer the questions posed by the inquest. Of course, this was a much more specific inquiry related to Inca laws and legal procedures; and, as the two indigenous witnesses explain, there no longer existed any specimens of this genre of khipu (ibid: 287).

Post-Toledan Chronicles

Beginning around 1580, roughly coinciding with the end of Toledo's tenure as viceroy, khipu sources in historiographical texts are much less prevalent. Some scholars cite the Third Lima Council's order in 1583 to destroy khipu as a pivotal event that led to the disappearance of this medium among many Andean communities. As I will explain in more detail in Chapter 7, this order applied only to idolatrous khipu. It had no apparent effect on administrative or historiographic khipu practices at all. Several factors contributed to the decline in the visibility of this medium at this point. By the 1580s, the legal issues motivating the official inquests of the early colonial period gave way to the more pressing exigencies of the day-to-day colonial administration. A few *visitas* took place in the late sixteenth and early seventeenth centuries, but they were neither as extensive nor as intensive as those conducted previously. Furthermore, they tended to focus on the more specific data pertinent to the immediate administrative matters of the time rather than the larger legal issues such as whether or not the Incas had been natural lords, which required delving into the history of the Inca Empire. For all intents and purposes, Toledo definitively resolved these larger questions to the extent that they would influence colonial policy. From this point on, colonial histories of the indigenous past appear to be motivated more often by the interests of a particular individual or group: priests investigated indigenous history and culture in order to better evangelize the Indians; and indigenous and mestizo writers produced texts to vindicate their cultural heritage and to legitimize legal claims within the colonial system. Very few historiographic texts from this later period can be tied in any definitive, direct, or unambiguous way to a contemporary khipu source. However, those texts that do cite the khipu are often even more intriguing than earlier sources.

José de Acosta's *Historia natural y moral de las Indias* from 1590 cites the khipu as his source of information on Inca history (Acosta [1590] 1986: 418), but Acosta's experience with khipu records may date from much earlier. The Inca Garcilaso de la Vega's *Comentarios reales* (1609) contains a description of the khipu that exhibits an apparently unintended ambivalence, but this work also cites regional historiographical khipu from which Garcilaso drew indirectly by way of his correspondence with friends and relatives in Peru (Garcilaso de la Vega [1609] 1985: I, 45). Perhaps the boldest statement about khipu sources appears in Martín de Murúa's *Historia general del Perú*, which corroborates the continued availability in the late sixteenth and early seventeenth centuries of the kind of narrative, historiographic khipu cited by the Inca Garcilaso. Murúa also echoes Polo de Ondegardo's claim that the khipu was the source of all information on the Incas:

By these knots they counted the successions of the times and when each Inca ruled, the children he had, if he was good or bad, valiant or cowardly, with whom he was married, what lands he conquered, the buildings he constructed, the service and riches he received, how many years he lived, where he died, what he was fond of; in sum, everything that books teach and show us was got from there and by means of the khipu I have come to know these things. All those who refer to things of this kingdom have acquired it and come to know it by means of this medium, the one and only way to understand the secrets and antiquities of this kingdom. (Murúa [1611] 1987: 373).[14]

Murúa's statement that all those who write about the Inca obtain their information from khipu may be an exaggeration, but there may be more truth to it than has previously been thought. The fact is that colonial historiographers rarely document the sources of specific pieces of information. The only exception to this tendency is the anonymous Jesuit's *Relación de las costumbres antiguas de los naturales del Pirú* (1594), which I will discuss

14 "Por estos nudos contaban las sucesiones de los tiempos y cuando reinó cada Ynga, los hijos que tuvo, si fue bueno o malo, valiente o cobarde, con quién fue casado, qué tierras conquistó, los edificios que labró, el servicio y riqueza que tuvo, cuántos años vivió, dónde murió, a qué fue aficionado; todo en fin lo que los libros nos enseñan y muestran se sacaba de allí, y así todo lo que en este libro se refiere del origen, principio, sucesión, guerras, conquistas, destrucciones, castigos, edificios, gobierno, policía, tratos, vestidos, comidas, autoridad, gastos y riquezas, de los Yngas, todo sale de allí y por los *Quipus* he venido en conocimiento de ellos. Todos cuantos refieren cosas deste reino lo han alcanzado y sabido por este medio, único y solo de entender los secretos y antigüedades deste reino" (Murúa [1611] 1987: 373).

in more detail below. The casual way in which the anonymous Jesuit cites khipu sources and names *khipukamayuq* informants in footnotes to his text resonates with Murúa's assertion and may suggest the possibility that other chroniclers who do not document their sources in this way also relied much more extensively on *khipukamayuq* informants without explicit attribution.

Juan Ossio has argued that Murúa was not much of an investigator himself. Murúa drew directly – in many cases verbatim – from the texts of other, primarily unpublished chronicles (Ossio 2004: 30), but this does not mean that his reference to khipu sources is a fabrication. The information that appears in Murúa's earliest known manuscript may have been researched and written by indigenous informants such as Guaman Poma (Ossio 2004). Although Guaman Poma does not explicitly grant the khipu such an exclusive role in his references to the sources on which he relied in composing his chronicle, he does cite the khipu as source. Like other chroniclers, Guaman Poma states that the native Andeans did not have writing, but for him this does not mean that they had no documented history. He explains that Andean history was retained on khipu, in *memoriales* and in *relaciones* (Guaman Poma de Ayala [1615] 1987: 11).

Ironically, the reduced historiographic activity of the post-Toledan period corresponds to an often more explicit and intriguing relationship to the khipu. In 1614, around the time that Guaman Poma was sending a final version of his manuscript to Spain, the Carmelite priest Antonio Vázquez de Espinoza arrived in the Andes and began collecting information for his *Compendio y descripción de las Indias occidentales*. Although the *Compendio* was submitted for publication only shortly before his death in 1630, Vázquez de Espinoza collected much of his information while living and working in the Andes from 1614 through 1620 (Velasco Bayón 1992: 12). Vázquez de Espinoza claims to have drawn from khipu records in composing this work. On two occasions he identifies specific historical narratives that came directly from khipu: the origin of the Incas and the origin of a cross in Carabuco (Vázquez de Espinoza [1630] 1992: II, 758, 805).

The Jesuits and Heterodox Khipu Historiography

The kind of specificity that characterizes the relationship between Vázquez de Espinoza's text and khipu sources appears particularly stark in late sixteenth- and early seventeenth-century Jesuit chronicles. After the *Relación de los quipucamayos* (1542), one of the chroniclers who most explicitly refers to khipu as the source of specific historiographic information is Blas Valera. Although Blas Valera does not appear to have participated in Toledo's inquests, he was in Cuzco in 1571 to preach to the Indians (Porras Barrenechea 1986: 462). Valera wrote a work titled *Historia occidentalis*, most of which was destroyed in the English attack on Cadiz in 1596. The fragments that survived the attack have been lost. Evidently Garcilaso de la Vega had access to the surviving portion of this text, and he incorporated parts of Blas Valera's chronicle into his own. Based on its influence, apparent in Garcilaso's history and others by Cabello Balboa and Anello Oliva, Valera's work appears to have been an extensive and detailed history of the Andes.

According to Garcilaso de la Vega, Blas Valera's papers also included a poem and a fable related to astrology, all transcribed from khipu. The text of the fable and the poem are the following:

They say that the Creator placed a maiden, the daughter of a king, in the sky with a pitcher of water which she spills when the earth needs it, and that one of her brothers breaks it occasionally, and the blow causes thunder and lightning. They say the man causes them, because they are the work of a fierce man and not of a tender woman. The maiden they say causes hail, rain, and snow, which are the works of her gentleness and softness and of such benefit. They say that an Inca, a poet and astrologer, made the verses in praise of the excellence and virtues of this maiden, which God had given her to do good to all the creatures of the earth.

. . .

Súmac ñusta	*Pulchra Nimpha*	Fair maiden
Toralláiquim	*Frater tuus*	Thy brother
Puiñuyquita	*Urnam tuam*	Thine urn
Paquir cayan	*Nunc infringit*	Is now breaking
Hina mantara	*Cuius ictus*	And for this cause
Cunuñunun	*Tonat fulget*	It thunders and lightens
Illapántac	*Fulminatque*	And thunderbolts fall
Camri ñusta	*Sed tu nympha*	But thou, royal maiden
Unuiquita	*Tuam lympham*	Your beautiful waters
Para munqui	*Fundens pluis*	You will give us raining;
Mai ñimpiri	*Interdunque*	And sometimes too
Chichi munqui	*Grandinem, seu*	You will give us hail
Riti munqui	*Nivem mittis*	And likewise snow
Pacharúrac	*Mundi factor*	The world's Creator,
Pachacámac	*Pacha cámac*	Pachacámac,
Viracocha	*Viracocha*	Viracocha,
Cai hinápac	*Ad hoc munus*	For this office
Churasunqui	*Te sufficit*	Has appointed thee
Camasunqui	*Ac praefecit*	And has created thee.

(Garcilaso de la Vega [1609] 1966: 127–128)[15]

15 Evidently there are a number of translation issues between the Quechua, Latin, and Spanish versions of the poem (Sabine Hyland, personal communication). For my purposes, it is not necessary to work through these issues. Here I have used Harold Livermore's English translation of the Spanish in the third column. However, I have modified a few of the lines slightly in order to bring it closer to the original Spanish version that appears in Garcilaso's text.

These passages pose several problems that appear to be unresolvable at this point. First, from among all of the other chroniclers who investigated indigenous traditions, none corroborate this type of poetry or the "literary" khipus on which it was allegedly recorded. Furthermore, Bruce Mannheim points out that Quechua poetry does not employ meter (Mannheim 1991: 125). Thus, the regularity of the four syllable verses in this poem would seem to suggest the influence of the Spanish poetic tradition. Of course, the lack of corroborative evidence does not necessarily mean that Blas Valera fabricated these details. If there had existed a tradition of khipu poetry, the numerical nature of the khipu would have been very conducive to a formal regularization in dialogic relation with the material nature of the medium and the type of semiotic conventions employed. If either the oral conventions of the poetry or the material conventions of the khipu included some awareness of syllabic segmentation, then the numeric conventions of the khipu and the Andean ontology of numbers (Urton 1997) might very well have led to this type of metrical formalization.

However, Garcilaso also states that "nowadays the mestizos have taken much to composing these verses in the Indian tongue, and others of various kinds, both sacred and profane" (Garcilaso de la Vega [1609] 1966: 128–129). Garcilaso assumes that these colonial innovations in Quechua poetry derive from an autochthonous tradition exemplified by the poem recorded by Blas Valera. However, it is possible that Blas Valera's poem was part of the same mestizo tradition to which Garcilaso refers, and that it was a colonial phenomenon influenced by the conventions of Spanish poetry. I would argue that this is the more likely scenario, although without additional evidence, there may be no way to resolve this issue definitively.

In either case, the possibility that the narrative fable was recorded on a khipu is a separate question. If we take Valera at face value, the difference between these two genres may correspond to different types of khipu conventions. If the fable was transcribed from a khipu as Valera suggests, then this passage may be one of a small set of direct khipu transcriptions and one of only two or three possibly direct transcriptions of khipu narratives. Unfortunately, there exist no other known transcriptions of this same genre that would make possible a comparative analysis on which more substantive inferences could be drawn.

The only surviving text often attributed to Blas Valera is the *Relación de las costumbres antiguas de los naturales del Pirú* (1594). Many scholars have attributed this text to Blas Valera,[16] but others argue that he could not be the author. I do not wish to enter into the debate about the authorship of this work. For my purposes, it makes no difference whether or not Valera

16 González de la Rosa 1907; 1908; 1909; Means 1928; Lopétegui 1942, 88; Loaysa 1945; Hyland 2003: 82–87.

wrote it. More important is the fact that it explicitly cites a number of different khipu as the sources of various types of information.

The organization and structure of the *Relación* is the result of a synthesis of information from a variety of sources. The text dates to 1594, but the author could have drawn from Valera's earlier investigations, the more comprehensive *Historia occidentalis* in particular, and from whatever other experiences he might have had in Peru. Throughout the *Relación*, the author includes notes identifying his sources for specific pieces of information. These sources include published and unpublished works, oral testimony ("común tradición"), and khipus. In some cases, he even identifies the khipus of a particular individual or region. At the very beginning of the text, he explains that for many years the Peruvians did not have idols, statues, or images, but rather worshiped the sun, moon, and the stars. As the source of this information, he lists Polo de Ondegardo's *Averiguación*, Juan de Oliva's *Annales*, Fray Melchior Hernández's *Anotaciones*, the common tradition, and the khipu of Yutu Inga and Huallpa Inga (Anonymous Jesuit [1594] 1968: 153, 154, 155). In other bibliographic notes he cites additional khipu sources with varying degrees of specificity: the khipu of Cuzco and other provinces (ibid.: 154); the khipu of Pacaritampu (154); the khipu of several *khipukamayuq* identified by name (ibid.: 155); khipu from Cuzco, Cajamarca, Tarama, Quito, and other provinces (ibid.: 156, 157); khipu from Cuzco and Sacsahuana (ibid.: 160); khipu from Quito (ibid.: 160); and the common tradition of the khipu in general (ibid.: 173). In the section on "Acllas, vírgenes religiosas," the text describes a sort of monastery that housed the *acllas*, virgins dedicated to service in the Temple of the Sun; and it refers to khipu containing accounts of widowed queens and princesses who voluntarily entered these monasteries to live for the rest of their lives (ibid.: 171). He explains that none of the khipu indicate that any of these virgins ever succumbed to the weakness of the flesh (ibid.: 172). He also cites the khipu in order to contradict Polo de Ondegardo's assertion that *acllas* who did not wish to remain in the Temple were sacrificed. The basis for this rejection is that no khipu contains any record of such practices (ibid.: 173).

The uniqueness of these references to khipu sources is perplexing. It is tempting to dismiss such statements as an exaggerated attempt to lend authority and credibility to an account that differs, and in some cases contradicts, other histories. This is essentially what Duviols has done in his claim that references to khipu sources were innocent frauds (Duviols 1979: 589). In some instances, this may have been the case, but the evidence does not support Duviols's overly general assertion. Even in texts such as this, if references to the khipu were intended to legitimize historical claims, one might expect an explicit discussion of the importance and validity of such sources. On the other hand, it is certainly true that the reliance on khipu in this text – whether actual or feigned – may relate to attempts to vindicate indigenous cultural achievements (Hyland 2003: 122–149).

At some point between 1601 and 1630, the Italian Jesuit Anello Oliva also began working on a text that explicitly identifies khipu sources, in this case from Cochabamba. Oliva arrived in Peru in 1597 before he had finished his education. He completed his studies in Lima probably around 1601, at which point he was sent to work in the Juli mission in Alto Peru on the shores of Lake Titicaca (Gálvez Peña 1998: xiii). More or less during the same time frame during which Murúa, Guaman Poma, and Vázquez de Espinoza were finishing or researching versions of their works, then, Anello Oliva may have begun collecting the information for his *Historia del reino y provincias del Perú* (1631). In 1628, Oliva was sent to Misque and Cochabamba (Vargas Ugarte 1963–1965: II, 27; Gálvez Peña 1998: xiv). Although Oliva would certainly have studied Spanish sources early on in his career, his extensive reliance on an informant from Cochabamba suggests that he may not have begun actually writing his own work until after 1628.

Oliva's history is most akin to the anonymous Jesuit's text in its relationship to the khipu. Like the anonymous Jesuit, Oliva claims to have interviewed numerous *khipukamayuq*, but he explains that, as in the case of the Spanish chronicles, many of the details of their histories differed (Oliva [1631] 1895: 19). In a few instances, Oliva cites the general khipu tradition (ibid: 26, 52), but he somehow decides that one *khipukamayuq* from Cochabamba by the name of Catari is the most credible. Oliva claims that this informant had been a *khipukamayuq* of the Inca and that he came from a family of *khipukamayuq* (ibid: 23). Of course, given that Oliva conferred with Catari while he was stationed in Cochabamba between 1628 and 1630, this informant could not have been a *khipukamayuq* under the Inca unless he was referring to the post-conquest Inca government of Vilcabamba. Either way, he very well could have come from a line of *khipukamayuq* who did serve the Inca. In any case, according to Oliva, Catari's khipu provided most of the information and apparently the structure for his text (ibid: 51).

Here again, Duviols would seem to reject such claims as fraudulent attempts to garner authority, but Oliva had no obvious need or desire to fabricate a khipu source. He explicitly identifies Catari and his khipu as the primary source and governing structure of his history (Oliva [1631] 1895: 51), but he is not dogmatic in his adherence to this khipu-based information. At the beginning of his text, Oliva criticizes Garcilaso for including in his *Comentarios reales* an obviously fabulous account of the origin of the Incas, and he explains that Catari's version is more credible

(Oliva [1631] 1895: 19).[17] Later, however, in Chapter 5, Oliva gives what he believes are two contradictory descriptions of the Inca Mayta Capac Amaro, one by Catari and the other by the Inca Garcilaso, and he leaves it up to the reader to decide which one to believe (ibid.: 42). At the end of this chapter, Oliva also points out certain deficiencies in Catari's khipu: they did not indicate where Mayta Capac Amaro died, how long he lived, or how long he reigned (ibid.: 44). In the case of other Incas, this information does appear on the khipu (ibid.: 50). In Chapter 10, Oliva actually rejects Catari's claim that Pachacuti was just another name for Inca Viracocha. Instead, Oliva favors the version that appears in the work of Garcilaso and other chroniclers who identify Viracocha and Pachacuti as two separate Incas (ibid.: 53).

Of course, one might argue that making Catari's khipu fallible in a few respects might have been a more effective way of validating the khipu, because it places this medium on a par with the other alphabetic sources cited. But this implicit comparison would have no bearing on an evaluation of the khipu. Unlike the khipu, the Spanish texts available in the sixteenth century that contain information on indigenous Andean history were historiographic rather than historical documents: they were only indirect sources of information on the pre-Hispanic past. Therefore, they do not mitigate the fact that prior to the conquest there existed no alphabetic script in the Andes that would have provided, if not a more consistent record, at least a more familiar basis on which to evaluate conflicting sources. The variability in the Spanish chronicles is merely the result of the variability in the accounts produced by native informants. If Oliva were fabricating the relationship to a khipu source in an attempt to validate this indigenous medium, then one would expect him to make Catari's khipu even more reliable than he does. There would seem to be no point, for example, in creating deficiencies in the khipu account such as the one involving missing information about Mayta Capac Amaro's place of death, age, and length of rule (ibid.: 44), or in privileging Spanish accounts over Catari's khipu with regard to the identity of Viracocha and Pachacuti (ibid.: 53). All indications seem to suggest that Oliva actually did rely primarily on the khipu-based information conveyed to him by Catari and supplemented by various Spanish sources such as Blas Valera, Garcilaso de la Vega, and others; and Oliva seems to be honest in his use and evaluation of these sources. Oliva decides to privilege Catari's khipu, but throughout his text he consistently cross-checks his information with other Spanish chronicles,

---

17 This criticism is ironic given that Oliva himself also includes events in his own history that are equally fabulous.

motivated by what appears to be a desire to provide the most credible history possible.[18]

As far as I am aware, the last colonial historiographical text to explicitly identify the khipu as a direct source is the second book of Fernando de Montesinos's *Memorias antiguas historiales y politicas del Peru*, which contains a list of over ninety rulers. The original version of Montesinos's text was completed in 1642. Sabine Hyland argues that the second book of Montesinos's work is actually a separate manuscript by an unknown author from the Quito region (Hyland 2007). Hyland points out the stark contrast in the style, content, and methodology between Book II and the other books of Montesinos's text. For one thing, the second book claims to derive entirely from indigenous sources, but nowhere else does Montesinos ever refer to having spoken with any indigenous informants. He relies exclusively on Spanish sources, in some cases copying directly from other texts (ibid.). Ultimately, Montesinos was not as interested in indigenous culture as he was in finding El Dorado or justifying Spanish dominion over the New World; and in any case, in his first book, Montesinos explicitly refers to a manuscript that he bought in Lima containing a history of Peru and its emperors (Seville ms., bk. 1, chap. 4; cited in Hyland 2007: 60). Evidently Montesinos was able to determine that the author of the manuscript originated in Quito. Evidence from the text itself reveals that the anonymous author produced the work at some point between 1609 and 1636 or 1641 (Hyland 2007: 61).

In addition to presenting the biographies of the Inca rulers, Montesinos's Quito manuscript includes a list of ninety-two pre-Inca kings dismissed by many scholars as historically worthless (Prescott 1947: 74–75; Rowe 1946: 197). However, more recent scholars have begun reconsidering this initial response (Hyland 2007: 5; Hiltunen 1999; Cahill 2002: 643, n.27). Of course, one might argue that no history of the Andean past conforms to the criterion of historical accuracy that John Rowe uses in dismissing this text (Rowe 1946: 197). Part of the problem for Rowe is that the Quito manuscript does not coincide with official Inca versions of Andean history. If Rowe's criterion of historical accuracy refers to some kind of literal and complete account of the past, then official Inca versions of Andean history

18 It is important, however, not to exaggerate the significance of Oliva's reliance on Catari's information for an understanding of khipu semiosis. One cannot simply infer a level of semiotic complexity based on such references. Textual analysis of colonial chronicles that rely on khipu may justify certain inferences about khipu semiosis, but merely the fact that a text refers to khipu as the source of its information establishes in the most general way only a connection between this medium and an indigenous genre of history. I will deal with the specific relationship between the khipu and alphabetic script in another study. Here, the focus is limited primarily to the history of this medium.

are not historically accurate either. They are just as much a construction of the past as Montesinos's Quito manuscript. It makes no sense, therefore, to dismiss other versions of Andean history merely because they do not reflect the historical ideology of the Inca Empire. On the contrary, for that very reason, they may be all the more important. In any case, regardless of whether or not the information contained in the Quito manuscript is historically accurate (whatever that means), its references to the khipu make it relevant for the history of this medium in the colonial period.

In a few instances in the Quito manuscript, the khipu appears within the history itself. In Chapter 16 on the origin of the Incas, when Mama Cibaco, the mother of the first Inca, presents a plan to her son designed to make him into a king, she refers to historical khipu containing records of a previous time of happiness and prosperity (Hyland 2007: 132). Chapter 17 contains a similar instance in which the now Inca Roca gives a speech to his people in which he invokes the military exploits of that bygone era as a justification for initiating his own campaigns of conquest. Later, Inca Roca convened a meeting with *amautas* and *khipukamayuq* in order to research the history of the old kings of Cuzco whose kingdom he wished to reconstitute (Hyland 2007: 135). Although these references to the khipu do not provide any details about the medium employed in the preservation of this account, it reveals that the khipu continued to occupy a place in the Andean historical imagination.

Other passages refer explicitly to a khipu source for the history contained in the Quito manuscript. In Chapter 10, which focuses on a ruler named Titu Yupanqui Pachacuti, the text reads: "For this reason, the ancient *amautas* say, and they learned it from their elders and they have it in memory through their khipu for eternal memory, that the sun tired of walking and hid his light from the living as his punishment, and he did not rise for more than twenty hours" (Hyland 2007: 121).[19] In Chapter 22, dealing with the reign of Inga Sinchi Rroca, the text states: "The *khipukamayuq* and the *amautas* whom the author of the aforementioned history consulted, say that there were so many Indians who were present at this triumph that they covered all of the hills and the plains around the city of Cuzco, that they acclaimed in loud voices the valor of the victor and the treason of the vanquished" (Hyland 2007: 142).[20] The author of the history referred to in this second passage is presumably the anonymous author of the original text

---

19 "Por esta causa, diçen los antiguos *amautas*, y lo aprendieron de sus mayores y lo tienen en memoria por sus *quipos* para eterna memoria, que el sol se canssó de caminar y ocultó a los viuientes, por su castigo, su luz, y no amaneçió en más de veinte horas" (Hyland 2007: 121).

20 "Diçen los quipocampos y amautas que alcançó el autor de la historia çitada, que heran tantos los indios que se hallaron en este triunfo, que cubrían todos los altos y los llanos de la rredonda de la çiudad del Cuzco, que a grandes vozes aclamaban la valentía del venzedor y traiçión de los vençidos" (Hyland 2007: 142)

that Montesinos incorporated into his larger work with some modifications. These are the only passages that are explicitly identified as deriving from khipu records, but they imply that the other details of this history come from the same *khipukamayuq* informants.

More often, the Quito manuscript refers to native informants as *amauta* rather than *khipukamayuk*; but the consistent pairing of *amauta* and *khipukamayuq*, both in Montesinos's text and in other colonial sources, suggests that the functions indicated by these two terms were either equivalent or overlapping in some significant way. In general, *amauta* is understood as a more generic term designating a wise man (González Holguín [1608] 1989: 24),[21] whereas *khipukamayuq* literally refers to those charged with khipu records. Thus, although all *amauta* may not have been *khipukamayuq*, all *khipukamayuq* officials at the regional and state-levels were probably *amauta*.[22]

Other references to *amauta* in Montesinos's Quito manuscript appear to corroborate this association. Chapter 8 contains an account of the appearance of two comets, which induces Manco Capac to convene a meeting of "astrologers and *amautas*" (Hyland 2007: 118–120). Guaman Poma explains that astrologers employed *khipu* (Guaman Poma de Ayala [1615] 1987: 349 [351]), and several chroniclers link the khipu to calendrics.[23] The Quito manuscript also contains an account in which Ayay Manco gathered together all of the *amauta* in Cuzco to reform the calendrical system. The kind of numerical operations described in this calendrical reformation by the *amauta* would inevitably have involved *khipu* (Hyland 2007: 124–125). The point here has nothing to do with the historical accuracy of this account but rather with the association between *amauta* and *khipukamayuq*, more specifically the identification of *khipukamayuq* as *amauta*. Perhaps the most compelling evidence in this regard is what appears to be an explicit association between *amauta* and khipu in Chapter 10 of the Quito manuscript cited above: "For this reason, the ancient *amautas* say, and they

21 Several rulers listed in the Quito manuscript are called *Amauta*. In the case of Lloquete Sagamauta, the term "amauta" appears to form a component of his name, and he is described as very wise (Hyland 2007: 122). The fact that the word "amauta" appears as a component of this ruler's name suggests either that such names were given after this quality manifested itself, possibly even after death, or that the quality of wisdom was attributed to this person merely based on the meaning of his name. In the case of other rulers, *Amauta* is appended to their name: e.g. Chinchi Roca Amauta, Topa Amaro Amauta, and Capac Raymi Amauta (Hyland 2007: 125).

22 I would stress the term "official" here. I am distinguishing between the official *khipukamyuq* who occupied positions of authority in indigenous communities and in regional and state-level Inca bureaucracies, on the one hand, and *khipukamayuq* who engaged in more popular practices that would not necessarily have involved *amauta*, on the other.

23 Román y Zamora [1575] 1897: II, 67–68; Gutiérrez de Santa Clara [c.1596–1603] 1968: 250; Murúa [1611] 1987: 372, 376. In the Quito manuscript, one of the rulers named Manco Capac is also called *Amauta* because he was wise and a great astrologer (Hyland 2007: 123).

learned it from their elders and they have it in memory through their khipu for eternal memory" (Hyland 2007: 121). Thus, when colonial chroniclers mention *amauta* informants, they may actually be referring to *khipuka-mayuq*; and such references appear numerous times throughout the Quito manuscript.

Taken all together, these references to khipu sources and *amauta/khipukamayuq* informants suggest that much of the information in the Quito manuscript was transcribed from oral renderings of khipu records. Further-more, at the end of this text as it appears in the Merced manuscript version of Montesinos's work, the writer explains: "Here, I just warn those who read this history that there is nothing falsified, but rather taken from the khi-pus and ancient memories, having worked to inform myself of everything" (Montesinos [1645] 1870: 404–405).[24] As in the case of other chronicles, if this is an attempt to invoke the khipu as a validating or authorizing gesture, it fails miserably. The vast majority of references to the indigenous source do not mention the khipu or *khipukamayuq* explicitly but rather the more general designation *amauta*. Moreover, although in most references to *amauta/khipukamayuq* informants, the text merely indicates what they say in a straightforward way such as "dicen los *amautas*," in several cases it reads "finxen aquí los *amautas*" (Hyland 2007: 115, 120, 151). In these latter cases, the text discredits the *amauta/khipukamayuq* informants, ostensibly because their version of Andean history violates the writer's criterion of historical accuracy. The text offers no clues as to whether these editorial comments were part of the original manuscript or were added later by Montesinos; but even leaving aside these statements, the text makes no attempt to validate the historical accuracy of the khipu. At the end of the book, the citation of khipu sources as a way to defend against accusations of falsification, then, does not imply any kind of universal reliability. The writer/transcriber himself points out several instances of what he identifies as falsity in the khipu. The apparent motive for this statement at the end of the work is to establish that he himself was not to blame for the falsi-fication. Any of the information in the book that might be dubious must be attributed to the khipu source rather than the writer/transcriber of the manuscript.

Sabine Hyland identifies a substantive relationship between Montesinos's Quito manuscript and the works of Anello Oliva and Blas Valera (Hyland 2007: 65–66). For the purpose of this study, it is not necessary to work through the details of this relationship. What is important here is that all of these late colonial texts exhibit an unusually explicit relationship to khipu

---

24 "Solo advierto aqui á los que leyeren esta historia, que no ai cosa en ella fingida, sino sacada de los quipos y de memorias antiquisimas, haviendo tenido el trabajo de innstruirme en todo" (Montesinos [1645] 1870: 404–405).

sources that raises difficult questions. They suggest that *khipukamayuq* still maintained historiographic khipu in different regions of the Andes. They are the only major historiographical texts to identify *khipukamayuq* by name since the 1542 inquest by Vaca de Castro. And other than the *Relación de los quipucamayos*, they are the most explicit in the way they tie specific information to khipu sources. After the second book of Montesinos's 1642 manuscript, no other sources refer explicitly to such direct access to historiographic khipu traditions.

For many years, these chronicles have been dismissed as imaginative embellishments of pre-Hispanic history and culture, but more recent scholarship has begun reevaluating this indictment (Hyland 2007; Cahill 2002; Hiltunen 1999). These chronicles pose problems because they draw from peripheral historiographic traditions that are not consistent with the majority of other colonial sources, which come from the Cuzco region. The dominance of the Incas means that the Cuzco-centric perspective is certainly important and significant, but it does not imply any kind of objective validity vis-à-vis other contemporaneous traditions. Cuzco-centric historiography itself is not completely consistent. As explained in Chapter 3, the highly contentious politics of the empire also played itself out in the realm of khipu-based historiographic discourse. Of course neither Cuzco-centric sources nor unorthodox regional traditions provide unfiltered access to pre-Hispanic history. Nevertheless, they both exhibit discursive characteristics that appear to derive from the conventions of the khipu medium.

The Transpositioning of Khipu Historiography

The reliance on khipu historiography by colonial chroniclers was not a benign process of translation. Whenever Spanish writers set out to compose histories of indigenous American societies, native informants were their only real source of information. In many cases, historiographic investigations took the form of inquests structured by a set of questions. Thus the resulting form of the historical discourse produced by such investigations often directly reflected the question-and-answer format of the inquest. Spanish chroniclers who produced more comprehensive histories tended to reconfigure the information they acquired according to the discursive paradigms of European historiographic genres, but the subject matter itself inherently required the chroniclers to modify and adapt these genres in one way or another. General histories, for example, had to tie in the origins of indigenous societies to the Biblical account that comprised the beginning of this genre. Modern readers have a natural tendency to identify these projects as imbuing an indigenous content with a European form; but some of the formal features of khipu historiography inevitably survive the transpositioning to alphabetic script.

The formal characteristics of khipu historiography are difficult to detect in texts that extensively reformulate and reformat khipu-based histories. During two periods, however, the context of production of some chronicles led to a relatively less mediated transpositioning. First, at the very beginning of the colonial period, the earliest investigations by the Spaniards evidently did not always follow the inquest format that characterized most later projects. Vaca de Castro's initial probe in 1542, which produced the *Relación de los quipucamayos*, purports to be a direct transcription of khipu. Unlike the later methodology criticized by Garcilaso, the Spaniards asked an open-ended question and let the *khipukamayuq* informants read from their khipu in response. The second period occurs at the end of the sixteenth and beginning of the seventeenth centuries when historiographic khipu still existed and the promotion of alphabetic literacy among native Andeans made it possible to compose alphabetic histories using their own criteria. Among the few examples of such texts, Guaman Poma's *Nueva corónica y buen gobierno* figures most prominently. Furthermore, this text is the most explicitly tied to khipu sources. Guaman Poma's work differs from many other chronicles in its details and format, but in many respects it essentially preserves the common Cuzco-centric perspective. The unorthodox account that appears in the anonymous chronicle incorporated as the second book of Montesinos's history may also belong to this group. The text differs markedly from Cuzco-centric sources, but it also evinces certain formal properties characteristic of other khipu-based discourses (Hyland 2007: 95–103).

I have argued elsewhere that many features of Guaman Poma's *Nueva corónica* reveal a relationship to the khipu medium: the page format; the culturally significant numerical organization of information into pairs, groups of five, and decimal units; and the decimal organization of the text as a whole (Brokaw 2002). In other words, in addition to transcribing portions of his text from khipu records, Guaman Poma appears to have constructed and formatted his alphabetic text according to the principles and logic of the khipu. This unique textual ontology becomes more apparent when compared to Murúa's manuscripts. The earlier 1590 version of Murúa's work would have retained more of the character brought to the project by Guaman Poma and possibly the other native scribes who worked for Murúa, and this version of the text exhibits a clear relationship to Guaman Poma's manuscript. Most importantly for the analysis here, they both employ a mode of presentation and conventions that appear to derive from the khipu (Mendizábal Losack 1963; Ossio 2004: 29–32). Murúa's later, revised manuscript from 1613, however, is more consistent with the model of European historiographic discourse to which Murúa himself aspired (Ossio 2004: 29–30).

In Chapter 3, I also identified a possible correlation between the convention of khipu color seriation and the hierarchy of information categories evident in transcriptions of both statistical and historiographic khipu. The histories of the Inca Empire that appear in *La relación de los quipucamyos* and Guaman Poma's *Nueva corónica* both take the form of a series of Inca biographies. The biographies of the *Relación* all follow the same format consisting of a series of information categories appearing in the same order: that is, conquests and achievements, the Inca's "queen," his oldest male child, younger children and the *ayllu* or *panaca* of their descendants, the length of time the Inca ruled, and finally his successor. Guaman Poma's biographies follow a very similar format with many of the same information categories in the very same order. This paradigmatic structure is highly consistent across all of the biographies (Brokaw 2003).

Sabine Hyland has observed that three of the Inca biographies in Montesinos's Quito manuscript follow this exact same paradigm, whereas others include the same categories but in a slightly different order (Hyland 2007: 95–103). Hyland notes that even when the text does not supply the information itself, the information category still appears. The biography of Capac Yupanqui, for example, does not tell how long the Inca lived or the number of years that he ruled, but it still includes the linguistic structure for that information: "he lived [blank] years, and of them he governed [blank] years" (Hyland 2007: 100, 139). A sentence like this, announcing the information category while omitting the information content, would be analogous to a khipu string without knots. As Hyland notes, a Christian ideology and the conventions of European discourse clearly inflect other portions of the Quito manuscript, but the Inca biographies appear to participate in the same discursive tradition tied to the conventions of khipu historiography that characterize *La relación de los quipucamayos* and Guaman Poma's *Nueva corónica*.

The Demise of Khipu Historiography

In his *Historia del Nuevo Mundo*, the final version of which was completed around 1653, Bernabé Cobo describes the khipu, but he does not seem to have consulted *khipukamayuq* in his historical investigations. Porras Barrenechea states that Alonso Topa Atau, a grandson of Huayna Capac, informed Cobo of pre-Hispanic traditions using khipu (Porras Barrenechea 1986: 512), but no evidence supports this claim. Alonso Topa Atau is mentioned in Cobo's text several times, and he appears to have been one of Cobo's primary informants in Cuzco; but nowhere does Cobo identify him as a *khipukamayuq* or imply that he drew from khipu accounts in any way. In fact, Cobo explains that although he interviewed informants such

as Alonso Topa Atau, the most extensive and reliable source of information
for his history comes from earlier colonial documents such as Ondegardo's
report of the inquest ordered by Cañete in 1559, the reports produced for
Toledo in the 1570s, and the account resulting from Cristóbal de Molina's
investigations from the same period (Cobo [1653] 1979: 99–100).

It is important to note that the late date of Cobo's text is misleading.
Cobo carried out his research on the Incas much earlier than 1653. He lived
in Peru from 1599 to 1629 or 1630, and again from either 1642 or 1650
until he died in 1657. Prior to returning to Peru in 1642 or 1650, Cobo
completed the initial draft of his manuscript, and in 1639 he attempted to
have it published in Seville (Hamilton 1979: xv). Thus, Cobo must have
carried out his research for the work during his initial stay in Peru from
1599 to 1629. Most of Cobo's research on the Incas may even date more
specifically to the period between 1610 and 1615. In his letter soliciting
publication from 1639, Cobo states that he had been working on his history
for twenty-eight years, which would mean that he began in 1611. In his
text, however, he mentions that he was living in Cuzco in 1610, where
he met Alonso Tupa Atau. Thus, although Cobo's work is a more general
history of the Indies, his research and writing on the Incas is contemporary
with Oliva's. Furthermore, Cobo was also a Jesuit, and it is virtually certain
that he and Oliva knew each other personally. They may have overlapped
in Lima as young students: shortly after arriving in Lima in 1599, Cobo
entered the Jesuit Colegio de San Martín (González de la Rosa 1935: ix;
Porras Barrenechea 1986: 510) as Oliva was completing his studies in
the Colegio Máximo de San Pablo at around the same time (Gálvez Peña
1998: xiii). Cobo was also sent to the mission at Juli in Alto Peru in
1615 while Oliva was working there (Torres Saldamando 1882: 99; Gálvez
Peña 1998: xiv). They also may have overlapped when Oliva returned to
Lima in 1630 as Cobo prepared to depart for Mexico. In 1636 Oliva was
serving as rector of the Colegio de Callao, the same position that Cobo
had occupied from 1627 to 1630. If Cobo returned to Lima in 1642 rather
than 1650, they may have overlapped again briefly before Oliva's death that
same year.[25] Cobo traveled extensively throughout other parts of the Indies,
and his work is a more general history; but he spent most of his time in
Peru, and he conducted his research in the first decades of the seventeenth
century.

Given this time-frame and the fact that Cobo's career path in Peru
seems to have been similar to that of Oliva, it may seem surprising that
their accounts are so different. But Cobo's work is indicative of changes that
were occurring in the production of colonial historiography at this time. By
the beginning of the seventeenth century, most of the native Andeans who

---

25 For brief biographies of Cobo and Anello, see Torres Saldamando 1882: 98–106, 107–111.

had a memory of life before the Spanish conquest had died. This corresponds
to an inevitable methodological shift in the production of New World historiography. Francisco Esteve Barba points out that seventeenth-century
chronicles tend to rework earlier texts informed by new social and political
contexts (Esteve Barba 1992: 19). This is not to say that no seventeenth-
century Spanish historiographers relied on indigenous informants, but the
textual production of the sixteenth century provides a tradition on which
most seventeenth-century writers feel compelled to rely heavily in the composition of their histories. With the exception of a few early-seventeenth-
century writers such as Guaman Poma, Vázquez de Espinoza, and Anello
Oliva, the historiographers of this period no longer invoke the khipu as a
direct source of information for their works. Cobo exemplifies this shift in
his disparaging attitude toward most native informants and in the way he
privileges the information collected in the sixteenth century:

Before all else, it is advisable to point out one very substantial thing about this
business, which is that not all the Indians knew how or were able to give explanations about these subjects at first and much less now, because to ask common
people such as *mitayos* and *yanaconas* to inform us about the Inca kings would be
as if someone wanted to ask in Sayago about the laws and *fueros* of Spain, or as if
someone were to discuss the statutes of a city with the average citizens, since very
few of them would know how to give an account or explanation except concerning
that which they deal in; and out of every ten with whom one talked, that many
different opinions would be forthcoming. Therefore, since all those who were concerned with government and religion resided in the city of Cuzco, only they were
able to understand and give explanations about what they were asked concerning
this, and the rest, for this purpose, are totally incompetent, because they had very
little to do with anything other than carrying out orders. It is stated that very few
of the common people understood the purpose of the tasks in which the Incas kept
them occupied, nor did they even have permission to ask about it. This is true to
such a degree that I have had personal experience with this situation numerous
times, and anyone who has had such experience will find this to be true: If we
ask about anything of this sort now of an Indian of the *hatunrunas*, who are, so
to speak, the country people, they do not know how to answer, nor do they even
know if there were Inca kings in this land; but upon asking the same thing of
any of those of the lineage of the Incas who live in Cuzco, at once he will give
a complete explanation of everything, of the number of Inca kings that reigned,
of their ancestry and conquests, and of the families and lineages from them that
have survived; therefore attention should be paid only to the reports that have
been made on this subject in the city of Cuzco. I will follow these reports in all
of this writing, especially the one made on the orders of Viceroy Andres Hurtado
de Mendoza, Marques de Cañete, and the first Archbishop of Lima, Fray Jeronimo
de Loaysa, by Licentiate Polo de Ondegardo in the year 1559, while he was the

corregidor of Cuzco; to this end Polo de Ondegardo brought together all of the old Indians who had survived the pagan era, including the Inca rulers as well as the priests and *quipo camayos,* or Inca historians. They could not be ignorant of matters pertaining to the government, rites, and customs of their own people, owing to the fact that they actually lived at the time of the Inca kings, held office then, and were questioned about their own experiences; the validity of their testimony is borne out by the record of their *quipos* and their paintings which were still intact. (Cobo [1639/1653] 1979: 98).[26]

Although Cobo relies primarily on the information collected in earlier colonial accounts, he recognizes that these alphabetic sources were originally based on the khipu. In fact, he even mentions this fact in support of the credibility of this medium: "the validity of their testimony is borne out by the record of their *quipos*" (Cobo [1639/1653] 1979: 99).

Cobo's argument that only native testimonies from Cuzco were credible sources of information on the Incas appears to have a certain intuitive logic, but it is misleading in its characterization of indigenous informants from other areas. As I suggested in Chapter 3, the kind of imperial khipu historiography transcribed in the *Relación de los quipucamayos* shortly after the conquest may have been a rather recent development practiced primarily in Cuzco, but based on the non-Cuzco-centric sources discussed above, it would appear that regional understandings of Inca history were also recorded in one way or another on khipu. Nevertheless, by the beginning of the seventeenth century, the availability of such khipu traditions was much more limited than in earlier periods. The institutions that supported Inca

26 "Ante todas cosas conviene advertir una muy sustancial en este negocio, y es que no todos los indios superion ni pudieron al principio, y mucho menos agora, dar razón destas materias, porque, pedir a la gente vulgar, como son *mitayos* y *yanaconas* nos informen déllas, sería como si en Sayago quisiese alguno preguntar por las leyes y fueros de España, o se tratase en una ciudad de los estatutos délla con la mayor parte de la gente popular, que muy pocos sabrían dar cuenta ni razón sino de aquello en que tratan; y de diez con quien se hablase sobre ello, se sacarían otras tantas opinones. Por lo cual, como en sola la ciudad del Cuzco residían todos los que trataban del gobierno y religión, solos ellos pudieron entender y dar razón de los que acerca desto se les preguntaba, y los demás, para este efecto, son de todo punto incapaces, porque tenían muy poca cuenta con más de lo que se les mandaba; y aun afirman que muy pocos déllos entendían el propósito de aquello en que los ocupaban ni aun tenían licencia de preguntarlo. . . . ; y así no hay que hacer caso más que de las informaciones que desta materia se han hecho en la dicha ciudad del Cuzco; de las cuales no me apartaré yo en toda esta escritura, en especial de la que por mandado del virrey don Andrés Hurtado de Mendoza, marqués de Cañete, y del primer arzobispo de Lima, don fray Jerónimo de Loaysa, hizo el licenciado Polo Ondegardo el año de 1559, siendo corregidor de aquella ciudad, haciendo junta para ella de todos los indios viejos que habían quedado del tiempo de su gentilidad, así de los Incas principales como de los sacerdotes y *quipucamayos* o historiadores de los Incas. Los cuales no podían ignorar lo tocante al gobierno, ritos y costumbres de los suyos, por haber alcanzado el tiempo de los reyes Incas y ejercitado en él todo aquello sobre que fueron examinados, y por los memoriales de sus *quipos* y pinturas que aún estaban en pie" (Cobo [1639/1653] 1956: 59).

historiography had dissolved with the conquest. The khipu that allegedly inform the histories of the Anonymous Jesuit, Guaman Poma, Vázquez de Espinoza, and Anello Oliva may represent the last vestiges of this particular historiographical khipu tradition. In any case, it would seem clear that in the seventeenth century the Spaniards stopped organizing *juntas* of *khipukamayuq*. The few texts that claim to rely on khipu in this period are vague about their informants (Vázquez de Espinoza) or their access to khipu (Guaman Poma), or they are based on a more limited investigation, possibly with a single *khipukamayuq* (Anello Oliva).

Nevertheless, other seventeenth-century chroniclers like Cobo often recognize that earlier histories had relied on khipu accounts, and in some cases they acknowledge the existence of narrative khipu containing reliable information. In this same period, Antonio de la Calancha actually goes into unusual detail in describing narrative khipu conventions, but he identifies his primary source of information about the pre-Hispanic period as earlier chronicles and other official documents such as Toledo's inquests from the sixteenth century (Calancha 1638: 90). Calancha acknowledges that the khipu were still in use, but he asserts that seventeenth-century khipu were not as complex as those used in the pre-Hispanic period (ibid.: 92). This raises a question about where he obtained the unusually detailed information about the khipu conventions that he describes in his text. Calancha may very well have observed community level practices that were not indirectly related to the kind of imperial historiographic records that played such an important role in the early to mid-sixteenth century. Thus, the disparity between the complexity of the conventions he describes and the allegedly less complex contemporary use that he observed may indicate that his description of narrative khipu conventions may be more the product of an hypothetical elaboration than an investigation of actual examples of specific khipu practices.

Cobo describes the continued use of such khipu at the local level in the early seventeenth century. According to Cobo, the khipu played an important role in the investigation of a case in which an Indian guide murdered a Spaniard. At that time, the investigation conducted by the governor from the town of Castro Virreina was unsuccessful in determining the killer. Six years later, when the body of another Spaniard was found in the desert, they renewed the investigation. At this point, the Spanish officials inquired about the identity of the Indian guide who had been assigned to the missing Spaniard six years earlier. The *khipukamayuq* of this area were able to identify the Indian in question using their khipu records. Cobo explains that this incident demonstrates "the extent of the achievement of the record and memory of these *quipos*" (Cobo [1639/1653] 1979: 254–255). It also reveals the continued use of community khipu sustained by local institutions independent of the Inca Empire.

The description of such community khipu as narrative in nature may be somewhat misleading if it is taken to imply a semiotic or even generic correspondence to the Inca tradition of imperial khipu historiography. Regardless of whether or not the conventions employed by these different khipu were the same, similar, or completely different, they clearly appear to involve different khipu genres. The khipu mentioned by Cobo may have been a community khipu that recorded the participation of its members in fulfilling community obligations. If guides were forcibly recruited from the community to serve the Spaniards, this service may have been incorporated into the administrative record of community obligations in order to avoid overburdening those who were taken away from their regular responsibilities by Spaniards.

Such khipu would have been analogous to the khipu actively employed by the community of Tupicocha through the late nineteenth century and possibly into the early twentieth (Salomon 2004). The Tupicocha khipu seem to have been yearly administrative records that were continually revised, providing a kind of running status rather than an historical record. But many communities in the pre-Hispanic and early colonial periods may have employed the same types of khipu for the preservation of an historical record. And the colonial-period statistical khipu to be discussed in the next chapter do produce narratives in some cases. Even though from our perspective these khipu were primarily administrative in terms of their function, the distinction between administrative and historical records may have been irrelevant to the way in which Andeans typically conceptualized the past at the local level.

With the exception of a few sometimes-ambiguous references in texts from the seventeenth through the nineteenth centuries, after the first half of the seventeenth century the genre of imperial khipu historiography disappears from the historical record. We cannot know for sure exactly how long Andean *khipukamayuq* preserved the historiographic khipu records relating to the Inca Empire, but after the first half of the seventeenth century, they no longer appear as sources in the historical investigations carried out by colonial chroniclers. This absence probably corresponds roughly to the disappearance of the last vestiges of this particular narrative tradition owing to the dissolution of Inca institutions that would have sustained such khipu practices; but it also reflects the changing concerns of Spanish historiographers. The hot political issues of the sixteenth century, which involved the rights of the Spaniards to conquer and govern the indigenous population of the Americas, demanded the kind of historical investigations carried out with indigenous informants. But by the seventeenth century, regardless of whether or not such issues had been resolved satisfactorily, in many respects the point was now moot. Pre-Hispanic history was still of some interest, but the authenticity of the account no longer had ramifications for the larger policy issues of the colonial administration. The last historical investigations into the Andean past to play a significant role in the determination of colonial policy were Toledo's inquests in the 1570s. The fact that Toledo's ordinances were still in effect in Cobo's time attests to the entrenched nature of colonial rule.

Just as in the Inca Empire, in the colonial period the widespread and consistent use of khipu to record any given type of information implies the existence of institutions that rely on such records. To a certain extent, the Spanish interest in khipu historiography through the 1570s may have actually contributed incidentally to the perpetuation of this form of khipu literacy. The Spaniards' interest in khipu historiography, however, was limited to what it could tell them of the pre-conquest period. They had no need to draw from khipu histories of the colonial period itself, and thus the institutional relationship with *khipukamayuq* would not have contributed to the preservation of continued historiographic documentation of contemporary events. Although the Spanish colonial government often merely replaced the Inca Empire, leaving local institutions intact along with their khipu record-keeping practices, the colonial administration itself had its own medium of alphabetic script. This is what led to the interaction between these two media examined in this chapter. Thus, even between 1532 and the end of Toledo's tenure as viceroy in 1581, Spanish institutions did not fill the void of whatever control the Inca might have exercised over the production of imperial khipu historiography. In other words, the institutional support for khipu historiography in the colonial period was only partial and indirect. The lack of interest in such records after Toledo's administration would have weakened any impetus derived from the early colonial historiographic investigations. This is not to say that individual *khipukamayuq* might not have continued to maintain historiographical khipu on their own initiative or as part of a community practice. In fact, the khipu that inform the texts produced by Guaman Poma, Vázquez de Espinoza, and Anello Oliva would all fall into this category. The lack of any institutional framework or continuing external impetus, however, appears to have meant the demise of this particular khipu genre, the last vestiges of which appear for the last time in these early seventeenth-century chronicles.

5

Spanish *Visitas* and Administrative Khipu

In addition to the historiographic research into the Andean past designed to produce evidence that would justify Spanish dominion over the Indians, the Crown also requested demographic and economic data in order to establish laws governing the collection of tribute and the granting of *encomiendas*. The quickest and easiest way to acquire this information was to translate and transcribe it from accounts provided by *khipukamayuq* who had maintained administrative records at the state, regional, and community levels. It is important to remember, however, that the Inca Empire was not necessarily the kind of monolithic polity that colonial sources describe (Pease 1982; Menzel 1959; Bauer 1992: 14). It may be impossible to construct in any detailed way an Inca theory of sovereignty, but archaeological research suggests that the incorporation of conquered ethnic groups by the Incas did not involve so much a thorough assimilation into a monolithic political administration as much as the imposition of an additional administrative layer that served as an interface between pre-existing local institutions and the imperial state. Local institutions may very well have changed in some way as a result of their new function within the Inca Empire, but they appear to have had a great deal of autonomy in devising whatever adaptations were necessary.

One of the dimensions of the administrative layer added by the Inca to whatever local institutions existed was khipu record keeping. As Juan de Betanzos's *Suma y narración de los Incas* (1551) suggests, many Andean communities already employed khipu, but any that had not already done so would have adopted it upon their incorporation into the Inca Empire, at least for use in the interface with the imperial administration. If some communities had not employed the khipu previously, the new record-keeping practices involved in their interaction with the Inca may have led to the adoption and adaptation of this medium for their own internal administration as well. In those communities and regions that already employed khipu, Inca practices would have entered into dialogic relationships with local conventions. Either way, the khipu-based administrative institutions of the Inca Empire resembled, to use a modern metaphor, a network more than a mainframe; and the Spanish conquest merely disrupted the network connections while, initially at least, leaving intact and functioning the various individual nodes. Thus, although the dissolution of the empire may have fatally crippled the institution of imperial khipu historiography, other levels of khipu literacy were initially unaffected.

Immediately following the conquest, the Spaniards employed an imperial model similar to that of the Incas, leaving intact community-level socioeconomic and political institutions. The local-level institutions about which we have the most information are related to the economic activities that most interested the Spaniards, who took the place of the Incas in the collection of tribute while maintaining the general structure of local pre-Hispanic communities. One of the essential differences in the new relationship between indigenous communities and the Spanish administration was the medium employed to control information: the khipu, on the one hand, and alphabetic writing, on the other. This meant that the colonial administration inevitably had to interface with the institution of khipu record keeping. It is no surprise, therefore, that statistical and economic khipu, specifically related to demographic and tribute information, are the most commonly attested khipu in colonial sources.

During the Spanish conquest, before the Spaniards had even learned the words "khipu" or "khipukamayuq," they observed the use of statistical khipu by the custodians of the Inca storehouses from which they requisitioned supplies (Pizarro [1533] 1920: 175, 178). Later, chroniclers who described the khipu explained that these devices functioned to record census and tribute information. These statistical or administrative khipu were employed both in the socioeconomic administration of local communities and in the institutions of the Inca state, and were perhaps the most common types of khipu both before and after the conquest. Although the nature of the narrative khipu discussed in the previous chapter is somewhat controversial, no serious disagreement exists with regard to these administrative khipu. This is not to say that all of the conventions of such khipu are understood, but the one dimension of khipu semiosis that has been deciphered is the decimal place system used to record numbers. With an understanding of the numerical conventions of the khipu, it is not difficult to imagine how other conventions such as color and cord configuration could have functioned to convey the qualitative information associated with quantitative data. During the first fifty or sixty years of the colonial period, Spanish officials would rely on these khipu records extensively in their attempts to incorporate Andean communities into the colonial system and to resolve administrative and legal issues that arose in this process.

As in the case of the historical texts examined in Chapter 4, the Andean and Spanish genres that recorded census and tribute information entered into a relationship in which each was affected by the other. The way in which

Spaniards and Andeans conceived of and recorded demographic and tribute data differed significantly. Documents from colonial inspections or audits contain traces of this conceptual and semiotic differential. In the early years of Spanish colonization, colonial authorities relied heavily on khipu records, because the khipu was the only source of tribute data prior to the conquest. But the Spaniards also relied on the khipu for current demographic data, because they often did not have the time or the personnel to conduct thorough censuses themselves, particularly during the first decades after the conquest. This inevitably led to the transpositioning of khipu-based conventions in the alphabetic records produced. The nature of these records establish precedents that often inform the expectations of the Spaniards in subsequent inquests. In some cases, the questionnaires prepared for these inquests, for example, anticipate the nature of khipu documentation. By the same token, the difference between the Inca and the colonial economies also forced *khipukamayuq* to adjust their record-keeping practices. In particular, the shift in emphasis from Inca labor tribute to commodity and monetary tribute required *khipukamayuq* to implement new conventions and/or adapt those of other genres for new purposes.

Spanish *Visitas* and Administrative Khipu Record Keeping

The colonial administration gathered demographic and economic data about the indigenous Andean population through the mechanism of the *visita*, which literally means "visit" but is more appropriately translated as "inspection," "audit," "survey," or in some cases "assessment." The *visita* was a peninsular institution normally referring to an inspection designed to ascertain the conditions of an administrative unit often associated with an extended geographical area. Guillermo Céspedes argues that initially the *visita* in the Indies was essentially the same as its peninsular counterpart but that over time it gradually developed into a unique institution tailored to the demands of the American context (Céspedes 1946: 985). I would argue, however, that even from the very beginning, at least the *visitas* of indigenous communities in the Americas were inevitably different from peninsular practices. First, the earliest *visitas* conducted by the Spaniards did not investigate the status of pre-established sociopolitical units within the Spanish administrative system; rather, they actually constituted such units. Of course, the local and in some cases regional sociopolitical units of the former Inca Empire were still intact, but they needed to be incorporated into an official Spanish administrative structure. In most cases, this required the division of the land and its population into *encomiendas* that were granted to Spaniards in recompense for their service in the conquest. The inspectors were typically charged with determining the "number of eligible tribute payers, the distribution of lands, the rights and successions of the ethnic lords during the reign of the Incas," and the nature of the tribute formerly paid to the Inca Empire (Diez Canseco 1966: 85). Thus, although the *visita de indios* was procedurally analogous to the peninsular institution, its purpose and substance differed significantly.

The Spaniards conducted numerous *visitas* of various areas of the Andes during the colonial period. Espinoza Soriano identifies at least four *visitas* that took place prior to 1536: Piura in 1532, Jauja in 1533, Cuzco in 1534, and Trujillo in 1535 (Espinoza Soriano 1967a: 6). These early *visitas* had the sole purpose of acquiring demographic and geopolitical information that would facilitate the granting of *encomiendas*. Most of the *visitas* formed part of *visitas generales*, inspections designed to cover the entire area over which the Spaniards maintained control in the Andean region. A general history of the *visitas* is difficult to reconstruct, because most of the *visita* records from the sixteenth century either have not survived or remain undiscovered. Based on the documents that are known, it seems that at least three and possibly as many as four or five *visitas generales* occurred in the sixteenth century.[1] In 1536 Pizarro received orders instructing him to carry out a *visita general* of the area that he had conquered. Although Pizarro began this *visita*, the political turmoil of the 1530s and 1540s prevented him from completing it (Rostworowski de Diez Canseco 1975: 15; 1978: 53). The same instructions were given to Vaca de Castro in 1542, Núñez Vela in 1543 (Rostworowski de Diez Canseco 1975: 53), and La Gasca, who finally completed this *visita general* in 1549 (Espinoza Soriano 1975: 50; Rostworowski de Diez Canseco 1978: 15). María Rostworowski has identified subsequent *visitas generales* from 1561, 1571, 1585, and 1591 (Rostworowski de Diez Canseco 1975: 74). The most important of the *visitas generales* identified by Rostworowski are the ones that took place in 1561 and 1571. The first, associated with Andrés Hurtado de Mendoza, marqués de Cañete, actually began much earlier. Cañete served as viceroy from 1555 to 1561, and most of the inspections that belong to this *visita general* date from 1558 (Aibar Ozejo 1968–1969; Espinoza Soriano 1978: 77) through 1562, which extends into the reign of the subsequent viceroy, Zúñiga y Velasco, conde de Nieva (Ortiz de Zúñiga [1562] 1967). The inspection of 1571 refers to the viceroy Francisco de Toledo's *visita general*, which actually ran from 1571 to 1573 or 1574, with additional *visitas* carried out as needed through 1581.

Here, there is no need to determine the parameters of the various *visitas generales* or define exactly what constitutes such a *visita*. Although the first *visita general* took an inordinately long period of time, these projects

---

1 For discussions attempting to identify the various *visitas generales*, see Céspedes 1946: 1012; Crespo 1977: 53; Espinoza Soriano 1964: 14; 1967a: 14; 1978: 77; Hampe Martínez 1979; Landázuri 1990; Rostworowski de Diez Canseco 1975: 74.

were inherently expensive and time consuming, and they normally extended over several years. Furthermore, the tribute rates established on the basis of these *visitas* generated subsequent legal petitions that sometimes involved *revisitas* [reinspections]. Many *visitas* also took place in order to reassign *encomiendas* that were left vacant at the death of an *encomendero*. Thus, throughout the sixteenth century, most governors and viceroys oversaw *visitas* to one extent or another. The main interest here is the role that the khipu played in all of these various *visitas* and related legal documents.

All *visita* documents do not explicitly refer to khipu or *khipukamayuq*, but as in the case of historiographical investigations, this absence does not necessarily mean that the informants did not use them. Whether or not *visita* documents explicitly identify khipu sources depends on a variety of factors, the most important of which was probably the whim of the scribe. In some cases, the way the scribe presents the information is conducive to mentioning the khipu; in other cases, it is not. Furthermore, cultural factors and the nature of the communicative context often may have contributed to a certain level of ignorance or indifference toward the khipu on the part of the scribe. The Spanish legal system's emphasis on oral witnesses essentially makes the *khipu* irrelevant from a Spanish perspective. Moreover, colonial officials conducted these interviews with the help of translators who would interpret the questions posed by the inspector for the native officials and then translate their answers for the Spanish scribes. Thus, the scribes who were creating the *visita* documents generally did not receive their information directly from the *khipukamayuq* informants but rather by way of the translator. This places the scribe at a remove from the khipu source and may have contributed to the tendency in many cases to exclude any reference to this medium from the *visita* record.

In a few instances, the context of the *visita* actually may demand reference to the khipu, because the accuracy of a prior khipu record is called into question; but in most cases, no compelling reason existed that would have obliged the scribe to identify the khipu as source. Nevertheless, many *visita* documents are clearly based on khipu records even though they do not always identify khipu as the source of their information. In the 1558 *visita* of Huaraz, for example, the scribe, Luis de Villareal, identifies the khipu as source at the beginning in reference to the census data for Ichoc Huaraz, but when he elicits the same type of information later from Llaguaraz, he does not mention any khipu (Espinoza Soriano 1978: 90, 132). Furthermore, another portion of this same *visita* does not cite the khipu in relation to testimony regarding the amount of livestock owned by the community (Aibar Ozejo 1968–1969: 6, 18). The use of khipu by Andean communities to maintain records of livestock is a well-documented practice. If the communities of Huaraz were using the khipu to record census data, they most likely would have employed this medium to keep track of their livestock as well.

Visitas from other areas provide additional corroboration of this disinterest in khipu as source medium. A document from 1563 related to the *visita* of Chillos near Quito, for example, does not refer to the khipu when the informants are able to answer the questions posed by the inspector, but it clearly implies that khipu records were the basis of the testimony: when the informants were unable to answer a question, they stated that they did not make a khipu record of that information (Landázuri 1990: 84–85).[2] This response implies that information given in answers to other questions came from khipu. In other cases, inspectors are unable to acquire the information requested, because a *khipukamayuq* had died and their informants had no khipu records.

The information gathered in the *visitas* primarily dealt with the demographics of indigenous geopolitical structures, economic resources, and data relating to pre Hispanic and colonial tribute. The recording of such information is precisely one of the major uses for which Andeans employed the khipu. Other factors to consider include the methodology employed by the inspector; but a close reading of the available *visita* documents suggests that when inspections rely directly on native informants who respond in any degree of detail to the inspector's requests for demographic and/or economic data, it is virtually certain that they are reading this information off of khipu, regardless of whether or not the document mentions this medium explicitly.

Demographic and Geopolitical Khipu

As discussed in Chapter 3, chronicles from the colonial period explain that the Incas employed khipu to record demographic information about the inhabitants of their empire. The information collected in these census khipu would have had to derive in one way or another from local-level officials. By the time the Spanish arrived in Peru, Andean communities had employed this medium at least for several hundred years, probably much longer. As argued in earlier chapters, the complex nature of local Andean socioeconomic organization was conducive to the development and perpetuation of a secondary medium that would facilitate its administration. In some areas, these local institutions maintained the use of khipu long after the conquest. Frank Salomon recently discovered that the community of Tupicocha in the Province of Huarochiri employed khipu in

---

2 For other passages from *visitas* that do not mention a khipu source, but probably relied on this medium, see Ortiz de Zúñiga [1562] 1967: 216; Diez de San Miguel [1567] 1964: 78–79, 123; Rostworowski de Diez Canseco 1978: 219, 222–223.

their internal administration at least through the late nineteenth and possibly into the early twentieth century (Salomon 2004). Originally, even if local communities did not maintain census khipu per se, they would have recorded demographic information incidental to other administrative practices. Salomon explains that in Tupicocha, one of the primary functions of local khipu was the administration of the service obligations of the members of the community. Although such administrative khipu may not have been designed to record census data for its own sake, in effect it would be possible to read them in this way. Of course, in the context of the Inca Empire, local officials also may have maintained separate local-level census khipu specifically in response to the demands of the administrative state.

Whatever the nature of local khipu practices, higher levels of the Inca administration extracted demographic data for regional and state-level administration. Given the nature of the Inca administration's involvement in the economic and political management of the population, it would be surprising if no census khipu existed at the regional and state levels. The Inca often relocated significant portions of certain ethnic groups from their home communities to other areas in order to facilitate political control, particularly in the case of recently conquered groups.[3] These relocated groups, known as *mitmaqkuna* or *mitimaes*, maintained their membership in their communities of origin, but they resided permanently in the areas to which the Inca assigned them. In the administration of this *mitmaq* system, demographic and geopolitical khipu would have been essential.

Furthermore, the Inca tribute system was based on labor service rather than rates of commodity production. In such a system, the levying and enforcement of labor-tribute obligations would require a record of the population. Several colonial sources indicate that the Incas kept a detailed record of the entire population organized into a number of age brackets (Aibar Ozejo 1968–1969; Espinoza Soriano 1978; Santillán [1563] 1968: 106–107; Guaman Poma de Ayala [1615] 1987: 193[195]-234[236]). Hernando de Santillán claims that the Incas updated this information every year in order to make any adjustments that were necessary for maintaining the official, decimal administrative structure of *pachacas*, *guarangas*, and so forth. This structure represented an ideal that rarely, if ever, corresponded to the actual configuration of sociopolitical units. Nonetheless, the decimal basis of the ideal Inca political structure suggests that it developed in a dialogical relationship with the khipu medium. Santillán states that the Inca sent out inspectors to conduct state-level censuses, which means that they probably took their khipu census records back to Cuzco. However, local officials would have been involved in the census, and they would

---

3 For example, see the discussion of the extent of the Inca state's involvement in the valley of Cochabamba in Gordillo and Del Río 1993: 20–22.

have maintained their own copies as well. As explained in Chapter 3, Gary Urton and Carrie Brezine have recently analyzed a set of archaeological khipu that appear to exhibit precisely this type of relationship in which lower level khipu are summarized at successively higher levels (Urton and Brezine 2005; Urton 2005). They do not identify these khipu as census records, but the same principle would apply to any state khipu involved in the administration of geopolitical units.

The demographic data recorded on local, regional, and state-level census khipu seem to have been involved in the first substantive interaction between Spaniards and Andean *khipukamayuq*. The most important component of the *visita de indios* was a census of the population organized according to traditional sociopolitical units. In fact, early attempts to ascertain the size of the indigenous population, whether or not they qualify as *visitas* or not, were limited to this demographic information organized according to indigenous geopolitical criteria and designed to provide the basis for dividing the land and its population up into *encomiendas* (Espinoza Soriano 1967a: 6). In some cases, *encomiendas* constituted arbitrarily in the early days after the conquest were later revoked and redistributed based on demographic and geopolitical information collected in a subsequent *visita* (Galdós Rodríguez 1975–1976: 59). Many of these early *visitas* appear to have relied exclusively on state, regional, and community khipu records.

Upon first arriving in Cuzco, Francisco Pizarro granted a number of *encomiendas* before surveying the area. Subsequently, he was forced to leave the Inca capitol. In 1535, after returning to Cuzco, he explains that the political turmoil of this early period had prevented him from acquiring the information necessary to make *encomienda* grants in an informed way. Thus, he revokes the earlier grants and redistributes the land based on more detailed demographic data presumably acquired by means of a *visita* (Pärssinen and Kiviharju 2004b: 391–393). Pärssinen and Kiviharju argue that this reassessment of an *encomienda* grant in 1535 was part of a larger redistribution project undertaken by Pizarro and described by Juan de Betanzos in the following passage:

And one day it occurred to the Marquis that it was good to know what *repartimientos* there were in the land and to distribute them to the Spaniards who were with him at that time and to populate the towns. He had Manco Inca called in and ordered him to bring there all of the accounts and reports of all the *repartimientos* that there were in the land; and Manco Inca went from there and called together all of the *llactacamayos*, which means overseers of the towns and those who were in charge of the accounts of what was asked for in the city of Cuzco, and he learned from them the *repartimientos* that there were and the Indians that each *repartimiento* had, and he brought to the Marquis the account of what he had asked; and the

Marquis distributed the *repartimientos* there in the city to the citizens who had settled there, which sufficed for the neighbors that settled there; and thus he did later in the other towns that he settled. (Betanzos [1551] 1987: 289).[4]

This passage does not mention the khipu explicitly, but the "cuentas" cited by Betanzos clearly refer to khipu records. Subsequent more detailed *visita* documents reveal that the *khipukamayuq* reported this kind of information for Spanish inspectors using khipu.

A more explicit example of this practice from around the same time period appears in an account of Alonso de Alvarado's distribution of *encomiendas* in Chachapoyas. After establishing Spanish authority in the region, Alvarado had to travel to Lima to meet with Francisco Pizarro. He charged an indigenous *curaca* by the name of Guaman with conducting a census of the population while he was away. According to the account of this event that appears twenty years later in a document from 1555, Alvarado actually instructed Guaman to prepare a khipu record of this census. When Alvarado returned a year later, Guaman presented the requested khipu records, and Alvarado used them to divide up the territory into encomiendas (Espinoza Soriano 1967b: 299).This text states explicitly that the distribution of *encomiendas* was based on the information from the khipus provided by Guaman. Other documents seem to imply that in some cases early *visitas* were based on actual head counts taken by the inspectors,[5] but most of the earliest references to demographic data appear to come from the testimonies of indigenous leaders and their *khipukamayuq*.

This exclusive reliance on the khipu in the early *visitas* caused problems, because the Spanish inspectors did not understand the nature of the sociopolitical system of the Inca Empire. Their ignorance of the nature of the *mitmaqkuna*, for example, led to a situation in which two separate encomiendas laid claim to the same tributaries. In the early years of the conquest, the *visita* of the towns where the *mitmaqkuna* lived and the *visita* of their original ethnic group both included them in their censuses. This effectively meant that the *mitmaqkuna* were obligated to pay twice as much tribute as other groups. This problem arose in the first place because many

---

4 "Y un día paresciéronle al Marqués que era bien saber los repartimientos que había en la tierra y repartirlos en los españoles que al presente estaban con él y poblar los pueblos mandó llamar a Mango Ynga y mandóle que la trujese allí por cuenta y memoria todos los repartimientos que había en la tierra y Mango Ynga se fue de allí e hizo llamar los llactacamayos que quiere decir mayordomos de los pueblos y los que ansi tenían cargo en la ciudad del Cuzco de tener cuenta de lo que ansi les pedían y supo dellos los repartimientos que había y los indios que tenían cada repartimiento y trújole al Marqués la cuenta y razón de lo que ansi le pedía y el Marqués repartió allí en la ciudad de los vecinos que allí había poblado los repartimientos que bastaron para los vecinos que allí pobló y ansi hizo después en los demás pueblos que pobló" (Betanzos [1551] 1987: 289).

5 See Galdós Rodríguez 1975–1976: 59. He cites a document that refers to an account that was based on an assessment of the inspector.

inspectors were relying on khipu census records. Otherwise, even if they had known about such groups, they would not have been able to determine their numbers in order to include them in the census of their original communities. The only way that an inspector could have acquired detailed census data about a group living outside the area under investigation would have been through the demographic khipu of the indigenous administrators. By the 1540s, Spanish officials had become aware of this problem, and many of the inspectors were charged specifically with resolving this issue (Espinoza Soriano 1967a: 18–19).

Between 1539 and 1540, Pizarro ordered more extensive *visitas* of areas outside of the Cuzco area (Pärssinen and Kiviharju 2004a: 53). These *visitas* were explicitly designed to reform the *encomienda* grants and to determine a basis for establishing tribute rates, which up to that point each *encomendero* had set arbitrarily (Espinoza Soriano 1967a: 10). Most of the documents produced during these *visitas* remain undiscovered, but the few that are known provide some insight into the role played by the khipu. The orders for these inspections instruct the officials to follow a methodology that begins with an interview in which they ask the *curacas* to testify to the number of Indians and the quantity of livestock in the communities over which they preside. The inspector is then to conduct a census of the area personally counting all of the inhabitants and the livestock visually ("por vista de ojos") in order to verify the *curaca*'s figures. In the case of any discrepancy, the inspector was to interview leaders of the individual towns and include their figures as well as the inspector's own opinions (Espinoza Soriano 1967a: 26–27; Espinoza Soriano 1964: 21). If followed, this methodology meant that the first account recorded by the inspectors would have been based on readings of khipu records. Unfortunately, it seems that the inspectors also threatened the *curacas* with consequences if they lied, which in at least some cases seems to have led to a refusal by the *curacas* to offer demographic information from their khipu.

The most detailed account from this round of *visitas* comes from Cajamarca. Regional Andean sociopolitical groups were typically divided into two administrative and geopolitical units, each with smaller subject units called *ayllus*. The Spanish inspectors often referred to the larger divisions as "parcialidades" and to the *ayllus* as "pueblos" [towns]. In the Cajamarca *visita*, the regional *curacas* claimed that they did not have an account of the total population, and they effectively told the inspector to go and count the people himself. But they also said that they were afraid to offer any figures for fear of the consequences in case their numbers differed from the result of the inspector's own census (Diez Canseco 1966: 86; Espinoza Soriano 1967a: 33). These regional leaders do provide the inspector with a list of the towns in the region and the names of their respective *curacas* (ibid.: 33–38). At this point the document from the Cajamarca *visita* makes no reference to khipu, but we know that these communities maintained khipu records. In 1567 and again between 1572 and 1574, the same communities drew on khipu records in a legal case brought against their *encomendero* (Espinoza Soriano 1967a: 24).

Furthermore, other *visita* documents indicate that the type of census data requested by the Spaniards and the information provided by indigenous communities was recorded in one way or another on khipu (Aibar Ozejo 1968–1969: 6; Diez de San Miguel [1567] 1964: 74, 89; Espinoza Soriano 1978: 89–90; Ortiz de Zúñiga [1567] 1967: I, 23–24, 85). The *visita* of León de Huánuco in 1562, for example, explicitly states that the *khipukamayuq* actually read the names of the leaders of the towns from a khipu, but as in the case of Cajamarca, they also claimed that they did not have population figures. They explained to the inspector that the khipu of each local unit recorded the population figures (Ortiz de Zúñiga [1562] 1967: I, 24). Similarly, in the *visita* of Chucuito in 1567, when asked the same question, the *curaca* of the *parcialidad* of Anansaya gave the names of the towns but explained that he did not have a record of the population figures. He informed the inspector that the *curacas* of each individual town would provide this information (Diez de San Miguel [1567] 1964: 14). In cases such as the inspection of Huaraz in 1558 where the *visita* interview does produce an account of the entire population based on khipu readings, it appears that this is due to the fact that the local *curacas* were also present with their demographic khipu.[6]

These and other documents indicate the practice of recording towns, *curacas*, and population figures on khipu, but some issues remain unclear. The Cajamarca and León de Huánuco *visitas* would seem to involve two different genres of khipu, one for the towns and their *curacas* and another for the population figures. In these cases, the regional *curacas* appear to have maintained only the first type, and the *curacas* of each town or *ayllu* kept khipu that recorded the demographic information for the members of their respective units. However, this inference may be misleading. The census khipu to which the regional *curacas* refer may have been the local records designed to facilitate the administration of community property and the obligations of its members. The demographic nature of such khipu may have been merely incidental to this administrative function.

If regional leaders maintained census khipu during the Inca Empire, as suggested by Betanzos, they may have constituted a distinct genre that contained a more abstract census of the entire region; and this census information would have been organized according to the geopolitical information categories such as *ayllus*, *guarangas*, *pachacas*, and their respective

---

6 For relevant passages from this *visita*, see Aibar Ozejo 1968–1969: 5–6 and Espinoza Soriano 1978: 89–90.

curacas. If this were the case, it begs the question of why the *curacas* of Cajamarca and León de Huánuco no longer did so, or claimed to no longer do so in their respective *visitas*. As I suggested above, they may have refused to read their census figures because they feared the punitive consequences threatened by the Spaniards if their numbers did not coincide with the inspector's own census data. The reluctance to provide regional census data suggests that the *khipukamayuq* knew that their figures would not coincide with that of the Spaniards.

A number of different reasons for this discrepancy are possible. As María Rostworowski argues, indigenous leaders may have attempted to hide the actual size of the population in order to lessen the tribute burden that would be established based on the *visita* (Rostworowski de Diez Canseco 1978: 86). By this time, the native Andeans understood the purpose of the *visita*, and ample evidence indicates that they attempted to influence the process in their favor. They could try to hide a portion of the population from the Spanish inspectors, but they would not have been able to predict the outcome of the head count. They could not give the actual figures, because that would reveal the deception; and they could not present fabricated figures, because they could not predict the success of their ruse. If this was the case in Cajamarca, then the *curacas* may have read off only the geopolitical information and suppressed the demographic data when reading their khipu for the Spaniards.

Another possibility is that they suppressed the demographic data simply because it was out of date. Based on colonial documents such as those from the *visitas* cited above, it seems that in many areas the genre of regional census khipu fell into disuse immediately after the conquest. The dissolution of the Inca Empire may not have been as devastating to the institution of census khipu as it was to khipu historiography, because census operations were more dispersed throughout the empire. Furthermore, regional census khipu would have been based on local records whose demographic data was probably incidental to the internal administration of the community. However, without a functioning Inca bureaucracy after the conquest, regional institutions no longer responded to the needs or demands of the empire.

Aside from references to census khipu by colonial chroniclers and *visita* officials, nothing is known about Inca census khipu. We do not know under what circumstances such censuses were ordered or if they were a regular or an occasional practice. In Spain, the government did not conduct large-scale censuses at regular intervals. In most cases, they carried out censuses for specific purposes, such as the accommodation of Moorish citizens who had been expelled from Granada in 1570 or in order to levy a tax to pay for the costs incurred by the Spanish Armada in 1591 (Ryskamp 2002: 16). Local lists or *padrones* designed to facilitate the collection of taxes at the local level, normally limited to lists of heads of household, are more common and more frequent (Ryskamp 2002). Regardless of Santillán's claim that the Inca updated their census annually, this same type of structure may have characterized Inca census practices as well: local-level records that maintained current population figures, probably incidental to the exigencies of their internal administration, and less regular regional censuses motivated by occasional circumstances within the Inca Empire. In any case, without any sort of consistent bureaucratic need, regional leaders would have had no motivation for updating the census records originally requested by the Inca. In other words, the issue may not have been that the regional census khipu had fallen into disuse, but rather that there had been no request prior to the *visita* to update them.

In the *visita* of Chucuito in 1567, initially the *curacas* of each *parcialidad* state that they are unable to provide census data from the time of the Inca, but they offer to search for this information among some old khipu that they have in their possession. Later, they returned with khipu that they claimed were the last regional demographic records from the time of the Inca (Diez de San Miguel [1567] 1964: 14–15, 27, 64–66, 74–75). The inspector transcribes the khipu account presented by Martín Cari, the *curaca* of Anansaya, which contains a census record of both his own *parcialidad* as well as that of Lurinsaya. According to this record, each *parcialidad* had a total of eight towns, and all of them except one share a name with a town in the other *parcialidad*. Although the transcription of this khipu does not include the names of the *curacas*, it lists each town and the number of its inhabitants broken down according to their ethnic identity, in most cases either Aymara or Uro. It appears clear that the population figures include only tributaries. Thus, the numbers probably correspond to households. The figures for the Anansaya towns of Juli and Pomata include 153 *mitimaes* from Chinchaysuyu and 20 *mitimaes* identified as Canas, respectively. By this time, inspectors were aware of the fact that *mitimaes* or *mitmaqkuna* belonged to their communities of origin, and the *visita* transcription of this khipu record accordingly does not include them in the census totals. The document explains that Martín Cusi's khipu account contained exactly the same information as Martín Cori's khipu, except in one detail. According to the Lurinsaya khipu, twenty-two rather than twenty Canas *mitimaes* resided in Pomata.

This document appears to confirm the existence of pre-Hispanic regional census khipu, and it has interesting implications for our understanding of khipu conventions, which I will examine in detail elsewhere. From the historical perspective focused on here, it also indicates that after the Spanish conquest, the regional *curacas* in Chucuito ceased maintaining these census khipu. Given that the León de Huánuco *visita* explicitly identifies the record of geopolitical information (names of towns and their *curacas*) as a khipu account, it may have belonged to this same genre of census khipu from the Inca period. By 1562, it had been thirty years since the arrival of the Spaniards, and the population figures from Inca times would no longer have been valid. Thus, the *curaca* of León de Huánuco may have read the geopolitical portion of his census khipu record and left out the out-of-date demographic information.[7] The geopolitical information would not have changed to the same extent as the population figures. Even if this portion of the khipu record was not completely up to date, the *curaca* could have easily revised it in the process of his oral rendition for the Spaniards in order to reflect whatever changes had occurred. In the Chucuito *visita*, on the other hand, when the *curaca* of Anansaya lists the towns of his province without census data in response to the question about the current population, he makes no reference to khipu. As argued above, this is no guarantee that the khipu was not used, but the later presentation of a pre-Hispanic census khipu found among a collection of older khipu records from the Inca period could indicate that the earlier account of the seven "cabeceras" in his province was done from memory rather than knotted cords.

In cases such as that of Cajamarca where the inspectors were not able to acquire census data from regional khipu, they often appear to count the population themselves rather than rely on khipu. However, these records may still reflect the information structure of khipu record keeping. The Spaniards employed two different census methods in order to comply with the "por vista de ojos" provision of the *visita* instructions. The first method involved calling all of the inhabitants of the area together in one central location. The second consisted of visiting each residence house by house in each town (Urton 2006: 158). In spite of the fact that the *visita* instructions specifically dictate a house-by-house method, the inspector often did not follow the instructions in every detail (Espinoza Soriano 1967a: 15; Galdós Rodríguez 1975–1976: 66–67). In Cajamarca, for example, the inspector seems to have used the central gathering method (Espinoza Soriano 1967a: 15). Cristóbal Landázuri observes that the Spaniards did not employ the house-by-house census method until the *visitas* of the 1550s (Landázuri 1990: 14). Nevertheless, in the central gathering method, the census was still organized around community units and their *curacas*. Indigenous officials would have been involved in organizing and presenting the members of their communities for the count by the Spanish inspectors. Thus, the *curacas* may very well have still used their khipu to organize the presentation of their people to the census officials charged with counting them.

---

7 The inspector also asked the informants from León de Huánuco about the size of the pre-Hispanic population, but the answer was given in terms of the ideal organizational units of 1,000 tributaries called "guarangas," of which there were allegedly four (Ortiz de Zúñiga [1562] 1967: 45).

The Discourses of Spanish and Khipu Censuses

Both the procedural and substantive nature of the interaction between indigenous leaders and Spanish officials inevitably meant that the demographic data collected passed through a filter that could not help but alter in unpredictable ways the nature of the information and the indigenous codes and discourses by means of which it was conceived, recorded, and transmitted. As Urton has pointed out, for example, the central gathering and the house-by-house census methods may have resulted in some differences in the way certain types of individuals were classified. A servant, for example, might be considered part of a household in the house-by-house method and an independent individual in the central gathering method (Urton 2006: 158). Even if this is the case, it is not clear which of these two categorizations reflects or more closely approximates indigenous conceptions. According to Hernando de Santillán, servants would not have entered into the count of tributaries at all (Santillán [1563] 1968: 107). In any case, an essential connection inheres between the nature of the *visita* documentation and the dynamics of the cultural and political relationship between Spaniards and Andeans. Although the Spanish administration knew more or less what kind of information it wanted about indigenous societies, the type of investigations undertaken in the *visitas de indios* involved a sort of paradox or hermeneutic circle: in order to most effectively collect information about Andean societies, the inspectors had to know what to ask; but in order to know what to ask, they required a prior understanding of indigenous society. This situation resulted in a dialogic interaction between the information acquired in the *visitas* – whether recorded in the accompanying documentation or not – and the formulation of *visita* questionnaires.

Documents from both Mexico and Peru evince this type of dialogic interaction between the answers to the *visita* questionnaires and the formulation of subsequent questionnaires. The most immediately obvious evidence of this interaction is the consciousness of indigenous terms and their corresponding social, cultural, or political concepts. Starting at least by 1540, the explicit instruction for *visitas* to determine the number of "guarangas" and "pachacas" (Espinoza Soriano 1967a: 26) already reveals that indigenous principles of geopolitical organization were informing the expectations of Spanish officials.

Another dimension of this interaction has to do with the nature and format of the demographic information collected in the *visitas*. Early *visitas* such as that of Cajamarca tend to give general population counts without breaking down the numbers into demographic categories, but later *visitas* provide much more detail. The instructions for such *visitas* dictate that a married man, his wife, and his children be counted as one tributary for purposes of the census and that the elderly not be included (Espinoza

Soriano 1967a: 26). In the earliest *visitas*, this resulted in a single number for an entire community or in some cases its constituent *ayllus* (Espinoza Soriano 1967a: 6; Urton 2006: 162). But later *visitas* begin breaking down the entire population into demographic categories and often provide other details such as the names of each individual within the most important categories (i.e., tributaries).

In 1558, for example, the *visita* of Huaraz presents a detailed demographic record that explicitly cites census khipu as the source of its information. This document first identifies the *curaca*, the number of towns over which he presides, and the total number of households. It then gives the name of a town with its total number of households and breaks down its population according to the following categories: (1) *casados* [married men]; (2) *biejos* [old men]; (3) *mozos* [unmarried young men between eighteen and twenty years old]; (4) *mozas* [unmarried young women between eighteen and twenty years old]; (4a) *{mozas}* *biudas* (if any) [widowed women between thirty and forty years old]; (5) *mochachos* [boys between six and thirteen years old]; (6) *niños* [children five years and younger]; (7) *biudos* [widows and widowers fifty or more years old]; and (8) *oficios* [craftsmen] (Aibar Ozejo 1968–1969; Espinoza Soriano 1978). The *visita* of Tiquipaya in 1573 also presents a census using demographic categories, but in this case there are only six: (1) the Cacique and his family; (2) married tributaries; (3) widowers and unmarried tributaries; (4) old men over fifty and handicapped individuals; (5) widows and single women with their children; and (6) orphans (Gordillo and del Río [1573/1603] 1993).

In their study of the Tiqupaya *visita*, José Gordillo and Mercedes del Río argue that the structure of the information contained in the document is based on an indigenous paradigm (Gordillo and del Río 1993). The earliest *visita* instructions do not request this type of detailed breakdown, and peninsular censuses from the same period do not appear to set a precedent for this level of detail. *Vecindarios*, the most common form of Spanish census, merely list the heads of household, limited to married men and in some cases widows or single women who owned property. The type of Spanish census referred to as *callehita* listed all inhabitants of a town, but the degree of detail in these records varies greatly. In some cases, they record the names, ages, relationships, occupation, and occasionally the financial worth of the members of the household (Ryskamp 2002: 14–15); but they do not divide the population into age brackets such as those that appear in the Huaraz and Tiquipaya *visitas*. Originally, the only category of interest to the Spanish administration in the Andes was that of married men who were not too old to work. In fact, although the instructions for the Cajamarca *visita* of 1540 acknowledge the presence of women and children, they explicitly state that the only individuals to be included in the census are married men (Espinoza Soriano 1967a: 26). Thus, the introduction of demographic categories appears to derive from the conventions of khipu record-keeping practices. These information categories, then, may correspond to the semiotic units of a khipu-census genre.

At least at the regional level, this particular khipu-census genre may be independent of other statistical information such as tribute obligations. The Huaraz khipu census, then, may be a vestige of the official census practices ordered by the Inca. According to Hernando de Santillán and Guaman Poma, the Inca census employed age brackets similar to the ones evident in the Huaraz and Tiquipaya *visitas*. Each of these texts divides the population in different ways: the Huaraz *visita* employs eight categories; Tiquipaya divides the population into six categories; Santillán reports twelve age brackets (Santillán [1563] 1968: 106–107); and Guaman Poma lists ten categories for men and ten for women (Guaman Poma de Ayala [1615] 1987: 193[195]–234[236]. Nevertheless, they all divide the population into a comprehensive set of demographic categories.

In 1561, a few years after the *visita* in Huaraz, the Crown issued a set of Andes-specific *visita* instructions that appear to assimilate the khipu-based nature of these demographic categories. These instructions, which are included with the documents from a *visita* of León de Huánuco in 1562, actually request an age breakdown of the population: "And knowing how many towns there are, you will endeavor to list each chief one by one with his Indians and subjects, naming the town and the chief and the rest of the Indian men and women, listing specifically the men and the women and the ages of each one, adding together how many there are of each age at the end of each town in accordance with the orders that you carry" (Ortiz de Zúñiga [1562] 1967: 13).[8] The document gives no clear reason for the change in the instructions. It certainly may be that the Spanish authorities wished to determine the size of the entire population for documentary purposes, but even so, the very notion of the possibility of such an account seems to have originated in the awareness gained through the earlier *visitas* that indigenous communities maintained more detailed demographic data on their local khipu. Either way, these later *visita* instructions appear to be a direct response to the form and substance of the earlier *visitas* derived from indigenous principles of representation linked to the khipu medium from which the information was read. Indeed, Francisco Pizarro's reliance on the khipu census provided by Manco Inca and Alonso de Alvarado's instructions ordering the Chachapoyan leader, Guaman, to prepare a census khipu in preparation for the granting of *encomiendas,* attests to the fact

8 "Item sabidos cuantos pueblos son procuraréis de poner cada principal por sí con sus indios y sujetos nombrando el pueblo y principal y los demás indios e indias poniendo muy específicamente los varones y las mujeres y las edades de cada uno sumando después en fin de cada pueblo todos en junto de cada edad cuantos son conforme a la orden que lleis" (Ortiz de Zúñiga [1562] 1967: 13).

that the nature of the khipu census genre impinged on the demographic discourse of the Spanish *visita* from the very beginning.

The changing nature of the *visita* may also reflect the disappearance of Inca-era regional census record-keeping practices and the increased reliance on local administrative records. Like the Spaniards, Inca censuses identified the "household" or "married male/head of household" as the primary demographic unit for purposes of tribute. In Inca censuses, the demographic category of imperial tributary appears to be an abbreviated version of local records. The community-level records from Huaraz, for example, list all members of each household, whereas regional Inca censuses such as that from Chucuito record a more abbreviated version limited to mature men.

At this point, it is impossible to determine in any definitive way the exact nature of official Inca census khipu and their relationship to regional and local record-keeping practices. The point here is merely to outline a few of the possibilities suggested by the khipu readings that appear in colonial *visita* documents. Unfortunately, the khipu appears in these documents only incidental to the acquisition of the information requested by the colonial inspectors. Most of the details about the type and extent of the data actually recorded on the khipu and the conventions employed must be inferred. The Huaraz khipu and a few others like it suggest the existence of a khipu census genre that recorded the entire population using a set of age brackets. It may be more accurate to call them life-stage categories, because in the indigenous tradition, age in quantified years was not the most important factor in determining the demographic category to which one belonged. In the colonial transcription of khipu censuses, such as the one from Huaraz, the age ranges given are probably approximate translations established in dialogue with the Spanish inspectors. Evidently, one of these categories consisted of tributaries, defined as married men who were not too old to work. This is also the definition of tributary that the Spaniards adopted in the colonial tribute system.

After the conquest, the impetus for maintaining administrative records designed for regional and pan-regional authorities shifted from the Inca to the Spanish colonial system. Initially, the Spaniards, much like the Inca, normally left native Andean social and political systems relatively intact, preferring to impose an administrative layer that would facilitate the extraction of tribute. The resulting system lacked uniformity at the local level. This was probably as true in the Inca Empire as it was in the colonial period. The variation in demographic categories reported in the Huaraz and Tiquipaya *visitas*, then, may reflect local variations, whereas the more rounded decimal and duodecimal categories in Guaman Poma's and Santillán's respective chronicles correspond to versions of the ideal structure that characterized official imperial records. After all, the *visita* documents are renderings of actual censuses, while the chroniclers are describing in more abstract terms the principles on which the census was based.

By 1558, it would make sense that in most cases the sort of detailed demographic data that appears in the Huaráz *visita* would probably have had to come from local community khipu records rather than regional Inca-style censuses. First, as explained above, it appears that whatever extent to which regional-level institutions still functioned, in many cases they no longer produced regional censuses that had been designed to facilitate the Inca administration. Second, the detailed nature of the Huaraz census would appear to be more consistent with the needs and interests of the local administration as opposed to the imperial one. Tristan Platt's characterization of the relationship between Inca imperial models and Inca census records is true of local levels as well: "formal models of . . . organization will be found to be inseparable from the nature of the mathematical and census techniques employed to control and direct demographic resources in a context of increasing specialization in productive activities" (Platt 1986: 256: cited in Urton 1998: 420). This means that census records inherently would have had an economic dimension at both local and regional levels.

It is important to keep in mind, however, that even the distinction between local and imperial records may not be sustainable in all cases. The extent to which the imperial and local levels (and their respective record keeping practices) impinged on each other is not exactly clear; but the political economy of each level would have been both dependent on, and informed by, the record-keeping practices designed to facilitate the administration of that level. Just as the administration of local communities involved the organization of labor, the Inca managed the population in order to provide the information necessary for the administration of the state, which was based on labor tribute. Imperial census records, then, may have always inherently represented the population in conjunction with the tribute activities in which it was engaged. If this was the case, then the few colonial transcriptions of pre-conquest census records that appear to contain exclusively demographic information would be partial readings prompted by the nature of the questions asked by the Spanish inspectors.

This would not necessarily mean that *colonial* census khipu also recorded both census and tribute data. Requests by Spanish inspectors for abstract population figures, on the one hand, and the collection of colonial tribute in commodities rather than labor service, on the other, could very well have induced a pre-conquest census-tribute genre to split into two separate genres: one to record census data and the other dedicated to documenting tribute obligations. As I will discuss in more detail below, the existence of a storehouse-khipu genre, which already recorded commodities independently from their associated labor activities, may have facilitated such a divergence.

Tribute Khipu

Prior to the conquest, all demographic khipu may not have been completely independent from tribute records. In the Inca Empire, census data were not merely abstract quantities. As in the colonial administration, Inca khipu censuses were designed at least in part to help determine tribute contributions, but the Inca and the Spaniards based the collection of tribute on completely different principles: the Inca exacted tribute in the form of labor, whereas the Spaniards imposed their demands in terms of specific quantities (Murra 1981, 1982; Urton 1998: 422). In many cases, of course, the labor-tribute rendered to the Inca also produced specific quantities of goods that would then belong to the Inca, but the tribute obligation was conceived of in terms of the labor itself rather than the resulting product. It is worth quoting Platt here again: "Inka formal models of imperial organization will be found to be inseparable from the nature of the mathematical and census techniques employed to control and direct demographic resources in a context of increasing specialization in productive activities" (Platt 1986: 256: cited in Urton 1998: 420). The demographic data in Inca census khipu, therefore, might have been combined inherently with a record of the labor-tribute obligations assigned to the population. Thus, it may be a mistake to draw a strict distinction in every case between census and tribute khipu genres. Furthermore, given the inherently temporal nature of labor tribute, the census-tribute khipu would also have had a calendrical dimension.

Gary Urton has argued that the Chachapoya census khipu discussed above that Guaman supplied to Alonso de Alvarado in 1535 may be among those discovered in 1996 in a burial site at Laguna de los Cóndores near Leymebamba (Image 19; see Chapter 3). The Chachapoya buried their dead at this site for many centuries prior to the conquest, and they continued to do so into the early colonial period (Urton 2001: 131–132). Thus, they may have interred Guaman's mummy there along with his census khipu. Khipu from the site are among the few that have been radiocarbon tested, the initial results of which date them from between 1426 and 1630 (Urton 2001: 146, n.6). Urton argues that the structure and content of the khipu in question, labeled UR6, encode labor tribute obligations over the course of two years. UR6 organizes the majority of the pendant cords into 24 paired sets with approximately 30 pendants per set for a total of 730 pendants, which corresponds exactly to the closest equivalent of whole days in a two year period (365 + 365 = 730). Thus, the 24 paired sets divide into two sections of 12 sets each, constituting two solar years. Each of the pendants in the paired sets would correspond to one day, and each of the 12 paired sets of pendant groupings for each year would comprise a synodic lunar month, which modern calculations determine to be 29.53 days. The 12 groupings of each solar year divide further into two half-year periods. The variation in the number of pendant cords in each month produces a distribution in which the number of cords in one of the six-month periods is virtually identical to the number of days in the perihelion, the time it takes the sun to move from the September to the March equinox; and the number of pendants in the other sixth-month period is essentially equal to the aphelion, the time between the March and September equinoxes (Urton 2001: 137). As Urton explains, the use of a two-year as opposed to a single-year calendar is consistent with the principle of pairing that constitutes an essential feature of Andean thought. In fact, given the Quechua ontology of numbers (Urton 1997), many features of which manifest themselves in other Andean cultures including the Chachapoya (Urton 2001: 138; Schjellerup 1997: 46; Lerche 1995: 58–61), it would be surprising if they did not conceive of years in pairs or divide them in half.

As suggested in Chapter 3, if this khipu belonged to a census-tribute genre that organized labor service obligations in a two-year cycle, then the knot values on each day-pendant might correspond to the number of individuals assigned to work on that day. The numerical value of the knots on these cords total 3,005. Adding the knot values of the extra pendants that supplement the paired sets comprising the main structural principle of the khipu results in a total of 3,085. Urton points out that these figures are remarkably close to an even set of three units of 1,000. The administration of the Inca labor-tribute system discussed in Chapter 3 involved the organization of the population into decimal units. A group of 1,000 tribute payers was called a *huaranga*, and Urton explains that colonial documents identify Guaman, the Chachapoya leader who governed the area immediately southwest of Laguna de los Cóndores, as a lord of three *huarangas*, or 3,000 tributaries (Urton 2001: 143; Schjellerup 1997: 315–316). Regardless of whether or not UR6 is actually the census khipu that Guaman read to Alonso Alvarado in 1535, Urton's analysis compellingly demonstrates how this khipu could have functioned as a census-tribute-calendar.

Colonial documents appear to imply the existence of distinct khipu genres for calendars, censuses, and tribute. For certain purposes and at certain levels, the Inca seem to have created distinct genres for calendrical, demographic, and tribute information, but local and regional khipu appear to integrate these data in a single genre, of which UR6 may be an example. The way in which the *visita* documents organize and present these various types of information does not necessarily imply a strict homology with the source. The apparent implication in alphabetic documents of a homology with the khipu sources from which they derive may reflect merely our preconceived notions with regard to such records and the way in which the Spaniards elicited information. When the Spaniards asked indigenous communities about population figures, they were not necessarily interested in tribute data. Likewise, when they requested information about tribute, they asked about the productive capacity of the population in terms of what they had produced for the Inca rather than in terms of periods and types of service rendered. Thus, the influence of khipu-based discourses on Spanish *visita* documents noted above worked in the opposite direction as well.

In the case of demographic data, it is difficult to determine exactly how demographic-tribute khipu might have influenced the way colonial officials recorded population figures, because the Spaniards drew this type of information exclusively from khipu sources for a relatively short period of time. Once they had completed the initial censuses and firmly established the colonial system, the Spaniards were more inclined to count the population themselves; and in fact this is what their instructions ordered them to do. In the case of tribute information, however, the khipu continued to play a more prominent role in Spanish-Andean interactions throughout the sixteenth and well into the seventeenth century.

In the early years immediately following the conquest, the colonial administration exercised very little oversight of the *encomiendas*, and *encomenderos* imposed tribute in an arbitrary way (Rostworowski de Diez Canseco 1975: 73). Furthermore, the *encomienda* grants were not always based on accurate information. Around 1540, in order to address these problems, the *visitas* begin shifting from an almost exclusively demographic focus designed to expedite the granting of *encomiendas* to include more expansive topics, and in particular the productive capacity of the population and their former tribute obligations to the Inca (Espinoza Soriano 1967a: 7–10). Among the known *visita* documents, this shift is most evident beginning with the inspections ordered by La Gasca around 1549. At this point, La Gasca ordered a moratorium on the collection of tribute at least throughout the province of Arequipa, because the civil unrest of the 1540s and unregulated tribute collection was jeopardizing the very survival of many inhabitants of the region. The native Andeans needed time to plant their crops and recuperate from years of exploitation. The *visitas* ordered by La Gasca at this time requested both information about pre-conquest tribute obligations rendered to the Inca and tribute that the *encomenderos* were currently collecting. As in the case of historical investigations, the instructions from the Crown explicitly charged the inspectors with seeking out all relevant sources of information (Santillán [1572] 1968: 101). The evidence from *visita* documents of this period often appears to corroborate the nature of the demographic-tribute calendar that Urton identifies in UR6.

In the 1549 *visita* of Ichoc-Huánuco, when asked about tribute rendered to the Inca, the informants explain that approximately one-third of their population had worked mining gold and producing goods for the

Inca. When asked about the tribute rendered to the Spanish *encomendero*, the informants give a very general response with very little quantitative information. They explain that they give the *encomendero* sheep and deer to eat and corn when asked. They also had sent two hundred Indians to Chuquibamba to extract gold. The instructions for the *visita* specifically requests information about goods given to the Inca, and the inspector makes it clear that he was looking for quantitative data. The report seems to indicate, however, that this is not the way that the community of Huánuco conceived of tribute under the Inca, which is why the inspector does not get a very specific response. The only quantitative bit of information has to do with the number of Indians dedicated to certain types of activities, which is consistent with the conceptualization and recording of tribute in terms of labor service (Espinoza Soriano 1975: 55–60).

In the *visita* of Atica and Caravelí in the same year, the informants evidently recorded the number of *mates* [a kind of cup] produced for the *encomendero*, but they demonstrate the same disparity in the conceptualization and recording of tribute. The *encomendero* states that the Indians delivered twenty pesos of gold every week. The indigenous informants, on the other hand, explain the same tribute in terms of labor: under the previous *encomendero* they provided fifty Indians to work in the gold mines of Chumilla and Chilpaca, and currently they send forty Indians for this purpose to Chumilla. In the end, the *curaca* informant also mentions that they delivered around ten pesos of gold to the *encomendero* each week, but this seems to be an estimate rather than part of a khipu record. It is clear that the number of individuals involved in the labor activity constitutes the primary unit of measure in the *curaca*'s report (Galdós Rodríguez 1975–1976: 69–70).

In most cases, the calendrical dimension of these khipu does not come through in the alphabetic documents, but in a few instances it does. In the 1549 *visita* of Chupaychu near Huánuco, as in the case of Atica and Caravelí, the informants explain Inca tribute in terms of the number of Indians dedicated to certain types of activities (Helmer 1993: 174–175; Mori and Malpartida [1549] 1967: 305–307); but they also give a detailed account of the different goods delivered to their *encomendero* at various intervals: a day, a week, every fifteen days, every month, and every three months (Mori and Malpartida [1949] 1967: 307–308).

In the *visita* of communities near Lima, *curacas* from Maranga and Guabra were unable to answer the inspector's questions about Inca tribute with any degree of specificity, because the elders and "camayoc" who knew this information had died. However, they do give a list of items given to the Inca in tribute such as clothing, fish, coca, and so forth. They also explain that they delivered these commodities directly to the Inca or to places such as Jauja, Bonbon, or Huánuco. When asked about what they currently paid in tribute to their *encomendero*, again they could provide only the types of goods produced without any specific quantities (Rostworowski de Diez Canseco1978: 220, 223–224). It is unclear whether or not any of this information derived from khipu records. However, during the very same *visita*, the informants from the community of Quiby give a more detailed account of Inca tribute, which presumably came from a khipu. They still do not give a specific amount of gold extracted for the Inca: they state merely that they gave all of the gold they acquired directly to the Inca's overseers. However, they give specific quantities of clothing, bags of coca and chili, pairs of sandals, and loads of jerky. They also list the number of Indians sent to serve the Inca as warriors, carriers, and servants (Rostworowski de Diez Canseco 1978: 229). These documents suggest the possibility that in at least some cases local khipu recorded both the labor tribute and the goods produced by that labor.

Nevertheless, as in the case of the census data, the implicit conceptualization of Inca tribute information requested by the Spaniards did not coincide with that of indigenous record keepers. There appears to have been a certain degree if incommensurability between the type of information demanded by the Spaniards and indigenous khipu record-keeping practices. Given the fact that the Inca levied tribute in the form of labor service, Urton suggests that tribute khipu would have been narrative in nature with subjects and verbs. Based on a comparison between the transcription of a khipu from Yacha and Chupaychu from 1549 containing a record of pre-conquest Inca tribute and a 1558 Huanca khipu transcription from Jauja of tribute paid to the Spaniards during the early colonial period, Urton argues that the Spanish system of commodity tribute effected a change in khipu record-keeping practices resulting in the loss of narrative conventions involving verbal concepts that characterized the pre-Hispanic labor-tribute record. Urton explains that the Inca tribute record contains a variety of verbs involved in labor service, such as "to make, take, guard, plant, carry," whereas the Spanish tribute record from Jauja required only one: to give (Urton 1998: 422).

Of course, as Urton recognizes, this does not mean that no pre-Hispanic khipu genre recorded commodities without reference to the productive process. In many cases, Inca labor tribute produced commodities that were then often placed in storehouses. The storehouse records themselves may have been merely commodity lists. The community of Ichoc-Huánuco mentioned above does not appear to have maintained such records. The informants state merely that they sent goods wherever the Inca ordered (Espinoza Soriano 1975: 60). If they sent the products of their labor-tribute to Cuzco or to storehouses administered by another community, then at this level they would have had no need for quantitative records of the goods produced. In other words, if this community did not maintain any storehouses, they would not necessarily have employed the storehouse genre that recorded goods without reference to the details of the productive process. If Huánuco did not employ a khipu genre designed to record goods as opposed to labor prior to the conquest, they may not have been able to adapt their record-keeping practices as readily to the model of Spanish tribute as other communities with *khipukamayuq* dedicated to maintaining storehouses and therefore versed in the khipu genre used in the accounting of storehouse commodities.

Storehouse khipu records evidently included entries equivalent to the Spanish accounting categories of "cargo" [deposits] and "descargo" [withdrawals]. The very first observers in Peru witnessed this accounting before the Spaniards had displaced the old system in order to impose their own. Pizarro, for example, observes *khipukamayuq* untying the knots on one cord and retying them on another as the Spaniards requisitioned supplies from an Inca storehouse (Pizarro [1533] 1920: 175). Thus, the storehouse khipu genre could very easily have been rendered in narrative terms, but it may not have emphasized this narrative dimension as much as the tribute genre itself. It certainly would not have involved necessarily the variety of verbs implied in the labor-tribute records. The khipu practices associated with commodity tribute obligations in the colonial period such as those of the Jauja khipu studied by Urton, therefore, may have adopted and adapted the storehouse genre rather than the more elaborate conventions of the pre-Hispanic tribute genre. The change identified by Urton, then, did not involve merely a kind of conventional atrophy in which certain lexical items were dropped but rather possibly the obsolescence of a distinct khipu genre.

If the informants from Maranga and Guabra, then, read the lists of non-quantified Inca-tribute commodities from a khipu, it would have been the labor-tribute genre. The quantitative information in this record would have consisted of the number and perhaps the identity of individuals dedicated to producing each of the commodities listed rather than the product of their labor. It may be no coincidence, therefore, that these communities are able to provide detailed demographic data for the census portion of the *visita*, which suggests a khipu source. If tribute and demographic information were inextricably linked at this level, then the list of commodities rendered in tribute to the Inca may have derived from the same khipu, regardless of whether or not this was the case in this instance. The fact that these communities sent the products of their labor tribute to other places such as Jauja and Huánuco may indicate that they did not maintain storehouses. Thus, their repertoire of khipu genres would not have included the storehouse genre adapted by other communities to record Spanish commodity tribute. This would explain the lack of quantitative data in their response to the inspector's question.

In the colonial *visitas*, therefore, the existence of quantitative commodity records may indicate use of the storehouse genre. If this is the case, one might expect Quiby, which provided quantitative data, to have been charged with storing the goods produced by labor-tribute in this area. Archaeological research may confirm this at some point, but the *visita* record does not indicate that this was the case. In fact, the Quiby informants say that they also sent commodities to the Inca. The major administrative center of Pachacamac is close enough that it may have served as the collection point for Inca tribute in this region, or they may have sent their goods directly to Jauja or Huánuco as they claim. Even so, the Inca system may have involved some sort of central control at the local level as well. If the Inca designated the community of Quiby as a low-level control center in the Inca tribute system, this would explain the fact that it maintained a quantitative record of tribute commodities while other communities in the area did not.

Labor-tribute records also may have commonly included a quantitative measure of the goods produced when applicable. In this case, the death of the elders and "camayo" from the communities of Maranga and Guabra would explain the inability of the informants to provide such information from the pre-conquest period. In such a case, if these communities still employed khipu, they should have been able to render a quantitative account of the tribute currently paid to their *encomendero*. However, this particular khipu practice may have died out with the elders who had maintained the pre-conquest records. On the other hand, the apparent deficiency may be the result merely of a difference between the understanding of the nature of tribute by the Andeans, on the one hand, and the Spaniards, on the other.

As in the case of other khipu genres, the narrative conventions of tribute khipu were dependent on the institutions that developed and perpetuated them. Once these institutions dissolved, the need or impetus for continued use of the semiotic practices associated with it would have disappeared as well. Of course, the Spanish imposed their own institution of colonial tribute, which served to perpetuate certain khipu practices. As Urton points out, the more complex narrative conventions implied in the record of pre-Hispanic labor tribute apparently fell into disuse at least at the level of the interface between many indigenous communities and the colonial administration. For a number of years many *khipukamayuq* preserved narrative, labor-tribute records from the time of the Inca; but Urton's analysis of the Jauja khipu transcription suggests that in many, perhaps most, cases they apparently no longer produced the labor-tribute genre to record colonial tribute rendered to the Spaniards (Urton 1998).[9] The

9 I should point out that this is not exactly what Urton concludes. Urton argues that the khipu
   undergoes a change involving the loss of narrative conventions. Although there may have been a very

fact that the Spaniards exacted colonial tribute primarily in goods rather than labor made the storehouse genre a more appropriate means of colonial accounting.

However, the apparent disappearance of the narrative conventions used to record labor-tribute from the khipu transcribed into the *visita* documents may be misleading. The adaptation of the storehouse genre to record colonial tribute does not necessarily mean that indigenous communities did not continue to employ a version of the labor-tribute genre in their internal administration. In fact, the Inca labor-tribute genre may have originated with local records used to administer community obligations, which were also conceived of in terms of labor. For communities that employed the khipu prior to their incorporation into the Inca Empire, then, the imposition of Inca labor-tribute would have entailed merely an expansion of local records that already employed sophisticated narrative conventions. Thus, the impoverishment of semiotic conventions in tribute khipu may reflect merely a shift from one genre to another within the relatively limited context of tribute accounting.

Some evidence supports the suggestion that indigenous communities continued to employ narrative conventions in their internal administration. The Spaniards exacted colonial tribute in both goods and money, and most of the khipu transcriptions of colonial tribute seem to consist of quantified commodity lists. However, each community had to acquire this tribute in some way. They usually produced commodity tribute (e.g., corn, coca, quinoa, and so forth) themselves. But in order to acquire money, either they sent individuals to work in the mines or they sold the products of their labor. In both cases, the indigenous authorities organized these activities according to the traditional socioeconomic system, which involved communal obligations conceived of in terms of labor service. Furthermore, although the Indians rendered their tribute primarily in goods and money, the Spaniards also imposed both formal and informal service obligations on groups and individuals under their control. In some cases, indigenous communities dutifully recorded these service activities on khipu.

In the 1560 *visita* of Totora, for example, the community leaders give an explicitly khipu-based account of labor service rendered to Gonzalo de Herrera and Gonzalo López Çerrato. This is a special case, because the groups involved were what was referred to as "en cabeza de su majestad," which means that they were in the service of the king rather than an *encomendero*. These communities rendered tribute directly to the king through the colonial administration. If other Spaniards wished to employ

close relationship between the conventions of labor-tribute khipu and storehouse commodity records, I prefer to think of these two types of khipu as distinct genres whose conventions are inextricably linked to the related but different institutional contexts in which they were employed.

them, technically they were supposed to pay them for their work. One of the main purposes of the *visita* of Totora was to investigate abuses against the communities in question. The *curacas* had two main complaints. First, they argued that the tribute paid to the king was excessive, because it had not been adjusted to account for the dramatic decline in the population. In Ucumare, for example, the population had declined from three hundred to just twenty, but the rate of tribute that they were paying was still based on the earlier figure (González [1560] 1990: 37–39). Second, two Spaniards, Gonzalo Herrera and Gonzalo López Çerrato, had obliged them to provide workers to clear land, sow crops, build houses, carry baggage, and so forth without any form of payment (González [1560] 1990: 37–38).

The testimony given by indigenous officials makes no explicit reference to the khipu, but the day before the inspection, the inspector requested that the *curacas* prepare khipu accounts. The report states that the informants gave their testimony "por su cuenta" [by their accounts]; and when the informants are not able to answer one of the questions, the document does not say that they do not remember but rather that "they do not have an account of it" ["no tienen dello quenta"] (González [1560] 1990: 37). In addition to the fact that in other documents the term "cuenta" commonly refers to khipu records, the inspector himself had requested the use of khipu. The khipu used to report information for the inspection relied on conventions of the traditional labor-tribute genre, possibly adapting Spanish temporal categories. The informants report the services rendered to Herrera and López Çerrato in terms of the activity engaged in, the number of Indians involved, and how long the labor service lasted. They explain, for example, that each year for three years they cleared enough land for López Çerrato to produce five *fanegas*[10] of corn. The first year five Indians worked for three Sundays and another four Indians for another two Sundays; the second year six Indians worked two Sundays; and in the third year, another six Indians worked for four Sundays (González [1560] 1990: 37).

The document clarifies that a "Sunday" refers to an entire week. This unit of measure, although articulated in European calendrical terms, is clearly not the conventional method employed by the Spaniards to measure time in this context. The first time it appears, the scribe actually converts it into a more familiar format in order to make subsequent references clear: "they began to clear [the land] until it was finished, time of about one month, which by their account had been four Sundays" (González [1560] 1990: 37).[11]

---

10 One *fanega* is about 1.58 bushels. This term is also used to refer to units of land. In its standardized form, one *fanega* of land was about 1.59 acres.

11 "Lo enpeçaron a desmontar hasta que se acabo tienpo de un mes [borrado: o quarenta dias] que por su cuenta dixo avia sido quatro domingos" (González [1560] 1990: 37).

Although several colonial chroniclers discuss the Inca calendar at the level of months of the year, they provide very little information regarding shorter units of time. The temporal units identified by Urton on UR6 include days, two unexplained sets of days, synodic lunar months, six-month periods, and periods of one and two solar years (Urton 2001). Four-month periods also may have been important. The *curaca* of the town of Totora itself maintained a khipu record of the tribute rate, because four years previously a Spaniard had taken away the original alphabetic text. This khipu recorded the tribute rate in terms of quantities of a certain commodity delivered per six-month period and labor service in three- and four-month periods (González [1560] 1990: 52–53). Local level officials probably used these same units in their internal administration, but they may have also needed shorter periods of time for the administration of community labor obligations. Guaman Poma explains that not all the areas outside of Cuzco employed the same calendrical model. However, he also states that the Andean calendar included a ten-day week (Guaman Poma de Ayala [1615] 1987: 235[237]). Given the importance of the decimal unit in Andean thought, in the Inca administrative system, and in khipu record keeping, this would make sense.

It may be no coincidence, therefore, that in the first reference to the units of time reported by the indigenous informants in the Totora *visita*, the scribe writes "time of one month or forty days" [tienpo de un mes o quarenta dias] and then scratches out the "or forty days." The ambiguity of this passage suggests a disconnect between the Spanish and Andean methods of measuring time. The scribe seems to have been trying to translate the indigenous temporal units into more standard European terms. According to the *visita* report, the khipu record actually recorded the number of Sundays, which the scribe identifies as a reference to week-long periods. But this may be misleading. "Four Sundays" may be merely the closest European calendrical equivalent of the units recorded on the khipu, which were actually closer to four Andean weeks or the "forty days" that the scribe scratched out. If the units of time recorded by the *khipukamayuq* were ten-day Andean calendrical units, this would explain the reference to forty days and provide the basis for a mistranslation into European weeks. The indecisiveness of the scribe in identifying the period first as forty days and then later as four weeks may reflect the difficulty in the translation process.

The Totora *visita* is unusual in that it reveals the symptoms of the translation process in more obvious ways than many other such documents. It is important to keep in mind that in many *visitas*, the Spanish inspectors worked through interpreters who conversed directly with the native informants. Thus, there were at least four opportunities for miscommunication to take place: (1) in the interpreter's comprehension and translation of the inspector's instructions into the native Andean language, usually Quechua or Aymara; (2) in the comprehension of the translation by the indigenous informants; (3) in the translator's understanding of the informants' response; and (4) in the inspector's understanding of the interpreter's translation of the informants' response. Thus, the translation process exacerbated the problems already inherent in the tremendous differential between Andean and European conceptual categories (e.g., nature of tribute, units of measurement, etc.).

Needless to say, misunderstandings were probably unavoidable. No standard methodology existed for avoiding miscommunication, resolving misunderstandings, or clearing up confusion on the part of either the native informants or the Spanish inspectors. In most cases, misunderstandings may have gone unnoticed. Even in the Totora *visita*, the possible symptom of the mistranslation identified above is merely a brief reference that does not explicitly reveal its significance. In general, the original *visita* methodology reveals the process through which information was acquired. The dialogue format, for example, produces a detailed record of how and when every bit of information was collected. However, the interview procedure and the discursive form with which it is associated was not designed to document the translation process. In most cases, the translation process is completely effaced in the final document, producing the appearance of a transparent interaction between the native informants and the Spanish official or scribe.

The Totora *visita* document is also unusual in its reference to the inspector's requests prior to the actual inspection that the *curacas* prepare khipu accounts. A request such as this implies the possibility that the informants created special khipu specifically for the purpose of the inspection. Although this does not necessarily mean that the khipu record was fraudulent, it certainly would have given the *curacas* the opportunity to fudge their figures if they desired to do so. Regardless, this constitutes another example of the kind of context in which the Spanish administration may have influenced the record-keeping practices of indigenous communities. One of the passages where this request appears actually suggests that the informants did in fact create special khipu for this purpose:

In the town of Ucumare on the seventeenth of the month of August of 1560, the said inspector ordered the said chiefs and Indians to gather together and to bring the khipu of the offenses that they had suffered from the Spaniards or from other chiefs to Indians of the chiefs, and he also ordered them to give him a khipu of the work that chiefs make the Indians do for the benefit of the coca fields and *chacras* and how they divide themselves into *mitas*; and understood by the chiefs and Indians through the *yanacona* Christian ladino interpreter Pedro and the said chiefs gathered together and among them they made their khipu as the said inspector ordered, and they gave an account of everything as follows.[12]

The inspector asks the *caciques* to prepare khipu in order to report on the internal administration of the *parcialidades*, referring to the way the *caciques* distributed the labor-tribute burden among their people. If these communities employed the khipu in their internal administration, one would not expect that they would need to create khipu specifically for the purpose of the *visita*. However, the document also says that they got together and made their khipu as ordered by the inspector. It is certainly possible that they prepared special khipu for the official inspection based on their regular community records. If so, it is doubtful that the inspector or the scribe who penned the *visita* document actually watched them do it. So this remark about the *caciques* preparing khipu as ordered by the inspector may be merely an inference. Even if the informants in the case did not create khipu specifically for the *visita*, this type of context would have provided an impetus to maintain the kind of records that would be useful in this type of situation. As I will argue in the next chapter, the interface between colonial officials and indigenous communities created a context conducive to the realignment and adaptation of khipu record-keeping practices to meet the needs of the new colonial context.

Explicit requests for khipu records was probably more common than was documented. As explained above, in one of the earliest censuses, for example, Alonso de Alvarado ordered the preparation of a census khipu to facilitate the distribution of *encomiendas*. The official record, however, did not require a description of the preparations for the *visita*. Furthermore, the *visita* activities involved a tremendous amount of detail, and the scribes who transcribed the interviews tended to focus primarily on the essential information elicited by the script and to leave out most, if not all, of the background details. Thus, a lot of behind-the-scenes activity does not show up in the *visita* documents. As time went on, such documents may have been less and less likely to make explicit references to khipu sources. The casual way in which documents such as the Totora *visita* refer to the khipu attests to its relatively mundane status. The ubiquity of the khipu in many areas would have quickly made its presence in *visita* proceedings

12 "En el pueblo de Vcumare en diez e siete dias del mes de agosto de myll e quynientos e sesenta años el dicho bisitador mando a los dichos caçiques e yndios se junten e traygan el quipo de los agravios que an rreçibido de algunos españoles o vnos caçiques de otros a los yndios de los caçiques e tanbien mando le den quipo del trabajo que dan los caçiques a los yndios en el benefiçio de las sementeras e chacaras de coca e como los rreparten por mytas entre si y entendido por los dichos caçiques e yndios por lengua de Pedro yanacona cristiano ladino e los dichos caçiques se juntaron y entre ellos hizieron sus quypos como el dicho bisitador se lo manda e de todo dieron rrazon en la forma siguiente" (González [1560] 1990: 45).

a commonplace that was not particularly noteworthy to the scribes who created the documentary record.

In the latter part of the sixteenth century, fewer and fewer references to the khipu appear in official *visita* documents. In addition to the reason given above, this reduction is due primarily to the fact that after the inspections completed in the 1570s during Toledo's administration, the Spaniards conduct far fewer *visitas*. The thoroughness of Toledo's *visitas* provided a basis on which the colonial administration relied throughout the rest of the sixteenth and into the seventeenth century, with additions and revisions made as the need arose.

However, the khipu gradually begins to fade from the documentary record at this point for several other reasons as well. Toledo oversaw the most extensive resettlement program to date (Málaga Medina 1974; Ramírez 1996; both cited in Urton 2006). The *reducciones*, which required the population of a region to settle in a central town in order to facilitate Spanish political and religious control, forced communities to reconfigure their indigenous social, political, and economic systems. This process of centralization also meant that those who had acquired alphabetic literacy would be more readily available to interface with the Spanish administration on behalf of a much larger segment of the population than was previously possible; and it created an environment more conducive to both the acquisition of the Spanish language by a greater number of monolingual Andeans and the teaching of reading and writing in alphabetic script, both of which were ordered by Toledo and other viceroys.

Although in many cases the khipu may very well have continued to play a vital role in the administration of the indigenous communities that comprised the *reducciones*, one of the implicit goals of these projects was to acculturate the Andeans. This acculturation involved the acquisition and use of alphabetic script, which in most cases resulted in the eventual abandonment of khipu record-keeping practices. In the early colonial period, however, even communities such as Jauja that actively participated in the colonial legal system often continued to maintain internal records using their khipu. Here again, then, the gradual disappearance of the khipu from official documentation does not necessarily signal the demise of the khipu or any particular khipu genre. Often it may merely signal the inevitable relegation of khipu record-keeping practices to the internal affairs of community administration at a level where the Spaniards did not interfere, at least not in any direct way.

6

The Khipu and the Colonial State

The previous two chapters have attempted to document the role played by the khipu in the interaction that took place between Spaniards and indigenous Andean communities in the sixteenth and the first part of the seventeenth centuries. Up to this point, I have organized this history around khipu genres or the type of information this medium recorded while at the same time recognizing that generic distinctions are not necessarily sustainable in all cases. Carmen Loza,[1] in contrast, frames her historical studies of the khipu as analyses of the role this medium played in the Spanish legal system (Loza 1998a, 1998b, 2000, 2001). Loza does not explicitly discuss the implications of this delimitation, but in some sense such an approach is unavoidable. With the exception of some chronicles and a few records from religious orders, all references to the khipu in the sixteenth and seventeenth centuries appear in what can be classified as legal documents. Most of the chronicles discussed in the chapter on khipu historiography are not legal documents per se, but their authors often acquired their information through their participation in official inquests. Thus, my own history up to this point is also limited in large part to the "legal" interaction between the colonial administration and indigenous communities or individual *khipukamayuq*.

The limitations of the colonial archive, with its almost exclusive emphasis on the colonial government's role in this interaction, obscures the enduring vitality of khipu record-keeping practices within indigenous communities themselves. Although the approach adopted in the previous chapters does not provide an open window onto the internal context in which these khipu were produced, I have attempted to keep that internal context more in mind, if not in view. However, unlike Loza's approach, my use of genre distinctions as the organizing principle of the historical analysis does not provide a more general view of the Spanish reception of, or reaction to, khipu records. Here, then, I propose a broader historical analysis of the

---

1 For other perspectives on the history of the khipu in the colonial period see Urton (1998, 2002b) and Assadourian (1998).

Spanish attitude towards the khipu in the sixteenth and early seventeenth centuries.

Chapters 4 and 5 make it very clear that initially Spanish officials relied heavily on various types of khipu in their investigations of Andean history, in the incorporation of the indigenous population into the colonial state, and in the administration of tribute obligations; but in the latter part of the sixteenth century, references to the khipu in official colonial documents become much more scarce. The contrast between the ubiquity of such references up until around 1580 and their relative scarcity from then on has constituted one of the main questions that the few historical studies of the khipu attempt to address. These historical analyses have established that as Andean communities became familiar with their rights under Spanish rule and the procedures involved in defending them, they began filing suit in colonial courts in order to seek redress for abuses committed by the Spaniards. In these cases, native plaintiffs had recourse to khipu accounts that challenged the claims made by Spaniards, who often did not keep detailed records. During the first five decades of colonial occupation, Spanish officials accepted and often actively promoted the use of khipu accounts. All of this is indisputable, and Chapters 4 and 5 have attempted to provide more thorough analyses of these phenomena. However, the dominant view has also maintained that as time went on the khipu increasingly came under attack as an unreliable medium maintained by heathens with a propensity to lie. This portion of the history of the khipu gains further support from evidence ostensibly indicating that Spanish priests viewed khipu as idolatrous objects that impeded the conversion of the Indians. Thus, the argument attributes the disappearance of the khipu from the colonial archive to a conflict that emerged between indigenous communities, on the one hand, and Spanish priests and *encomenderos*, on the other, culminating with an allegedly universal prohibition of this medium issued by the Third Lima Council in 1583. At this point, the Spaniards allegedly confiscated and destroyed many khipu, which led to the subsequent scarcity of khipu references in the colonial archive.[2]

A few short historical studies have made valuable contributions to our understanding of the khipu (Urton 2002b), but they all tend to follow this general paradigm or trajectory established originally by Pierre Duviols (Duviols 1971) and more substantially by Carmen Loza (Loza 1998a, 1998b, 2000, 2001). This version of the history of the khipu has also influenced other historical work that does not focus directly on this medium. Loza's research on the history of colonial khipu, in particular, has had so much influence because no one else has focused so directly or intensively on this topic. Loza's pioneering work addresses a glaring omission in scholarship

---

2 For versions of this argument see Loza (1998a, 1998b, 2000, 2001) and Urton (2002b).

both on the khipu as well as on the colonial Andes in general. As the first to propose this kind of historical project, however, it is inevitable that different perspectives emerge.

The fact that the history of the khipu as established by Duviols and Loza has been so influential means that I must present my study in dialogue with theirs. This is especially important, because this work has informed the understanding of the history of the khipu in the colonial period by other scholars, who have perpetuated some of the misconceptions either explicitly or implicitly conveyed in it. Here, I propose a different scenario in which neither the Third Lima Council nor the conflicts that occurred between indigenous communities and *encomenderos* played a significant role in the disappearance of the khipu from the colonial record. The relationship between the colonial administration and the khipu certainly changes to some extent in the course of the sixteenth century, but the reduced visibility of khipu record-keeping practices results more from the reduction in the administrative activities that required indigenous informants than from an overt campaign to destroy khipu. During the colonial period, the khipu falls into disuse throughout the Andes, but the process is a gradual response to the on-going assimilation, acculturation, and political and cultural domination.

The Four-Stage History of the Khipu in the Sixteenth Century

In "El uso de los quipus contra la administración colonial española (1550–1600)," Loza identifies two stages in the history of the khipu as used in the colonial legal system. In Loza's first stage, running from 1550 through 1569, Spanish officials who carried out *visitas* introduced the khipu into the Spanish administrative and legal system as a reliable source of information incidental to their official information gathering activities. In the second stage, from 1570 to 1581, Loza argues that the viceroy Francisco de Toledo officially incorporated the khipu into the colonial administrative system. Loza grounds her history of the khipu on documents identified as khipu transcriptions from official inspections (*visitas*) and court cases that took place between 1550 and 1581 in different parts of the Andes and on the ordinances instituted by Francisco de Toledo during his tenure between 1569 and 1581. She alleges a progression in which the colonial administration increasingly accepted the khipu as valid, culminating in Toledo's ordinances, which she argues give official legitimacy to khipu record-keeping practices. Although Loza does not explicitly extend her analyses beyond these dates, the argument implies two additional stages: one prior to 1550 and one after 1581 in which the khipu presumably would not have functioned in such contexts. The latter stage is the most explicit:

Loza makes reference to a prohibition of the khipu by the Third Lima Council in 1583, which allegedly reversed the incorporation of the khipu into the colonial administration and contributed to the demise of this medium (Loza 1998a: 156). Loza explicitly acknowledges that her study is not a history of the khipu in general, but rather a history of this medium as used in the sixteenth-century legal system. Nevertheless, her argument explicitly draws conclusions about the historical trajectory of khipu practices in general as well.

This argument makes certain assumptions regarding the nature of the documentary evidence presented and the inferences drawn from this evidence. Loza explains that she chose the inspections and the court cases from different dates and areas in the Andes in order to insure "an empirical base ample enough to demonstrate the conditions that permitted the use of the khipu as juridical proof, and to show that this was a phenomenon that occurred in different parts of the Andes throughout the sixteenth century" (Loza 2001: 65; my translation). Although Loza's samples are from different areas and dates, they do not necessarily demonstrate the kind of progression that she identifies, nor do they support a generalization about the history of the khipu. Documents that present themselves explicitly as direct transcriptions of khipu are very limited in number. The selection of these particular documents was also motivated by the fact that they were the only ones available: at the time these were the most well-known cases of explicit khipu transcriptions from the colonial period.

Furthermore, the claim that Toledo's ordinances officially incorporated the khipu into the colonial administration is very misleading. If this were the case, one would expect to find many more of such transcriptions from this period. Toledo's ordinances do create an official structure within which the *khipukamayuq* play a role, but this was merely an incidental recognition of the function that the *khipukamayuq* had been serving long before Toledo (and even before 1550), and would continue to serve long after 1583. And the prohibition by the Third Lima Council in 1583 was not a general prohibition of the khipu, as many have claimed.

The documents analyzed by Loza do indicate certain tendencies, but they are less representative examples illustrating the gradual incorporation of the khipu into the colonial legal system than they are individual occurrences within a much broader and more ambiguous history of the khipu in the Andes. As I have explained in previous chapters, numerous other documents make reference to the khipu in the context of economic and more general administrative interactions between Spaniards and indigenous communities. These documents do not always contain the same kind of explicit and detailed references to the khipu, nor do they always involve the kind of controversies evident in the documents cited by Loza; but they do provide the basis for a much more complete understanding of the history of the khipu in its relation to the colonial administration.

The Early Colonial Administration and Khipu Transcriptions

From the very beginning, the Spaniards demonstrated considerable confidence in, or at least a willingness to accept, the reliability of the *khipukamayuq* and their khipu. Other than oral accounts, this was one of the only durable media on which they could rely for information about Andean history, government, and society. The reliance on *khipukamayuq* for demographic data and historical information during the earliest *visitas* and other investigations into the history of the Incas such as that conducted by Vaca de Castro in 1542 (Collapiña, Supno, et al [1542/1608] 1974) set a precedent that the Spaniards confirmed repeatedly through their acceptance of khipu records as viable sources of information on which to base the allocation of *encomiendas*, the establishment of tribute rates, and the documentation of historical and genealogical claims.

The acceptance of khipu records by the Spaniards for their inspections and historical investigations may have made native Andeans more aware of the possibilities that such registers could play in the colonial legal system. At least by 1554, indigenous communities began using khipu records in support of legal petitions requesting recompense for goods and services rendered to the Spaniards. In fact, in the 1550s, Guacrapaucar, a Huanca leader from Jauja, used the same khipu observed by Hernando Pizarro in 1533 (Pizarro [1533] 1920: 175) and Cieza de León in 1548 (Cieza de León [1553] 1985: 59–60) to document his compensation requests for the goods and services rendered to the Spaniards during the conquest and subsequent civil wars. In their legal case, the indigenous communities in the valley of Jauja submitted alphabetic transcriptions of several khipu that recorded goods and services provided to Pizarro, or stolen by his men, in support of both the suppression of indigenous resistance and the Spanish civil wars in the Andes (Espinoza Soriano 1971–1972; Murra 1981; Loza 2001: 65–73). This is one of the most well-known cases of khipu transcriptions, and it is one of the four analyzed by Loza in her study.

The four sets of documents on which Loza bases the first stage in her history of the khipu are from: (1) Jauja, 1554–1561; (2) Chillos 1551–1559; (3) Chucuito, 1567; and (4) Sacaca, 1572–1578. Both the Chillos and the Chucuito cases are rather run-of-the-mill *visita* documents. The Chillos case is a reinspection carried out in order to verify the population figures recorded in an earlier khipu-based *visita*. The fact that colonial officials carried out the reinspection at the insistence of the *encomendero* does not constitute any sort of novelty. Nor does the successful demonstration by the *khipukamayuq* that the khipu record was accurate induce the Spaniards to recognize this medium by itself as legal proof. If anything, the fact that the first census was based exclusively on khipu records implies that the Spaniards were already accepting the khipu-based testimony as proof. In fact, they had been doing so since the 1530s.

The Chucuito *visita* is one of the examples cited in Chapter 5 of a khipu-based inspection. Loza points out that in this case the Spanish officials made the *khipukamayuq* swear orally to the accuracy of his khipu record and that this demonstrates the difficulty in accepting the khipu as proof in legal proceedings (Loza 2001: 78–79). However, the swearing of oaths was an integral part of Spanish legal proceedings, which was based primarily on oral testimony. Given the fact that *khipukamayuq* were giving oral renditions of their khipu records, Spanish procedure dictated that they swear to the accuracy of their statements just like other informants. Even if the witnesses had presented alphabetic documents, they still would have been made to swear orally to the accuracy of their testimonies. The complex dynamic between inspector, translator, *cacique*, and *khipukamayuq* certainly complicates the process, but this difficulty does not necessarily have anything to do with the perceived legitimacy of the khipu medium. In fact, I would argue that in some respects this procedure makes the khipu irrelevant from the Spanish perspective, because it identifies the locus of knowledge in the speaker rather than the khipu.

The Jauja and the Sacaca documents are different in that they involve legal proceedings that took place outside of the context of a *visita*. Between 1554 and 1561, the *caciques* from Jauja filed petitions requesting recompense for the goods and services rendered to the Spaniards during the conquest and subsequent civil wars. Loza explains that the case contains testimony from several witnesses called in to verify the reliability of the khipu-based record, which was eventually accepted (Loza 2001: 69–71). The essential issue here has to do with the significance of this process of verification. Loza suggests that the successful verification process implies the legitimation of the khipu medium. But here again, from the Spanish perspective, the legal process carried out in the Jauja case had nothing to do with the accuracy of the khipu per se but rather with the accuracy of the information specific to this case. The general accuracy of the khipu was not the topic of debate.

The Sacaca case involved a dispute between the heirs of Alonso de Montemayor and the Indians of his *encomienda* that took place between 1572 and 1579.[3] In 1572, motivated by Toledo's campaign to reign in abuses by the Spanish *encomenderos*, indigenous leaders from Sacaca filed suit, claiming

---

3 For a concise but thorough summary of the case and its issues, see Platt 2002: 235–237. For an in-depth analysis of the Sacaca case, see Assadourian 1998. A few of the documents related to the case appear in Pärssinen and Kiviharju 2004b: 269–298.

that some thirty years previously, during the four years from 1548 through 1551 immediately prior to the enforcement of a fixed tribute rate, they had paid excessive tribute to their *encomendero*. The testimonies offered by the *khipukamayuq* in support of the case provide documentation of the tribute paid in goods and services. Loza explains that the court "adheres" to the khipu in this case in that it explicitly recognizes this medium as the only source or proof of the tribute information in question (Loza 2001: 86–87). Nevertheless, as Tristan Platt points out, in this case, the court ordered the second khipu reading and compared it to the first in response to protests by the Spanish defendants (Platt 2002: 245). Ultimately, the testimonies of the *khipukamayuq* witnesses prevailed over that of Montemayor's heirs. As in the Jauja case, however, the concern was not the status of the khipu per se but rather the status of the information to which the witnesses testified.

In her analysis, Loza places a lot of weight on the fact that the Jauja petition was eventually successful and that in 1559 the *khipuakamyuq* of Chillos successfully defended their 1551 khipu census transcription against claims by the *encomendero* that they had reported fraudulent numbers (Loza 2001: 79–82). It may be that the Jauja case is the first instance in which indigenous subjects brought suit against the Spaniards using khipu accounts. If this is the case, such an event has a certain historical significance. But without a larger corpus of similar texts, constructing a more detailed history of khipu-based litigation is impossible. Regardless, this case does not represent a major event in the colonial administration's attitude toward the khipu. The khipu itself was never called into question. The khipu had been a commonplace in colonial legal proceedings since the 1530s. Thus, even if the validity of the khipu medium itself, as opposed to the information it recorded, had been challenged, it would not signal the beginning of a process in which the khipu was introduced into the colonial administration. Rather, it would constitute precisely the opposite: an attempt to undermine the legitimacy of the khipu, which had been accepted up to that point. But the fact is that the Spaniards were not overly concerned with the khipu as such.

In each of the cases examined by Loza, the Spanish officials attempted to formally verify or legitimize the khipu transcriptions in an effort to confirm the reliability of the account, not the medium on which it was recorded. In the case of Guacrapaucar and other Huanca *khipukamayuq* from Jauja (1554–1561), the court compared the written khipu transcription to oral testimony provided by witnesses (Loza 2001: 71). In the Lupaqa inspection and census from Chucuito (1567), the Spanish authorities required formal oaths from the *khipukamayuq* and other indigenous officials as to the veracity of the khipu record (ibid.: 76, 78–79). And in the Chillos case (1551–1559), although the original inspectors did not question the accuracy of the khipu-based census, eight years later the court required visual verification of the population figures (ibid.: 80).

The Sacaca case is somewhat different in that the first khipu reading is later verified by another *khipukamayuq* (Platt 2002: 245). Loza discusses these khipu transcriptions along with the others from the first stage, but they actually occur later between 1572 and 1578, which chronologically places them in the second stage. This would make sense within Loza's paradigm, because the second stage corresponds to what she identifies as the official recognition of the khipu's legitimacy. The verification of one khipu account by another one would appear to lend support to the historical model that Loza proposes. I would argue, however, that just as in the other cases, the only criterion relevant for determining the legitimacy of a witness is the validity of his or her claims to knowledge, regardless of whether or not that knowledge was also recorded on a khipu. The only reason that the officials in the Sacaca case relied on a second *khipukamayuq* was that he was the only person with the knowledge necessary to confirm the original account. Of course, he had this knowledge by virtue of his role as *khipukamayuq*, but this was incidental from the Spanish perspective.

This does not mean that the 1550s and the 1560s (Loza's first stage) are insignificant in the history of the khipu in relation to the colonial administration. By the 1550s, the political turmoil of the early years had settled down considerably, and colonial officials began a renewed effort to establish and maintain administrative control. Hernando de Santillán arrived in Peru in 1550 and worked with a commission to establish rates of tribute. In December of 1553, Felipe II sent out another royal *cédula* requesting information about the nature and quantity of indigenous tribute rendered to the Inca in order to provide a basis for setting limits on the tribute collected by the Spaniards (Esteve Barba 1992: xxv). In addition to relying on oral testimonies, this document explicitly orders the *audiencia* to look into whatever other secondary media that might contain relevant information, including "paintings or boards or other accounts that there may be of that time where what is said can be corroborated."[4] In response to this request, Santillán produced his *Relación del origen, descendencia, política y gobierno de los Incas* (1563). In his official research into pre-conquest tribute, inevitably Santillán would have had to deal with *khipukamayuq* informants, and he explicitly identifies the khipu as one of the principal sources of information about pre-conquest Andean history (Santillán [1563] 1968: 43). Thus, this was a period of intense administrative activity involving numerous *visitas*, which relied extensively on khipu records.

---

4 "Pinturas o tablas o otra cuenta que haya de aquel tiempo por do se puede averiguar lo que está dicho" (Santillán [1563] 1968: 101).

The difference between this and earlier periods has more to do with this increased level of activity than it does with any qualitative difference in the role of the khipu in the colonial legal system. These decades do not constitute an independent historical stage that establishes the probative value of the khipu.

In general, Spanish officials were not concerned about the khipu as such. Their focus was on the accuracy of the information rather than the legitimacy of the medium. The colonial sources discussed in previous chapters indicate that from the very beginning the Spaniards recognized the importance of the khipu as an essential secondary record-keeping device that facilitated the collection of statistical and historical information. But this recognition took place beginning in the 1530s when the Spaniards first arrived in Peru and continued throughout the sixteenth century.

Toledo's Reforms and the Official Recognition of Khipu Record Keeping

This revision of Loza's first stage does not necessarily undermine the second stage, which is based on other evidence. Loza argues that during Francisco de Toledo's tenure as viceroy from 1569 to 1581, the khipu gains a higher degree of legitimacy through Toledo's historical investigations and his ordinances, which she claims officially institutionalized the *khipukamyuq* in the position of "ayudante de escribano" [scribal assistant] (Loza 2001: 89–90). Loza explains, for example, that Toledo's historical investigations into the Inca past produced Sarmiento's khipu-based *Historia Indica* (Loza 2001: 89), but here again, this type of khipu-based historical investigation had been going on at least since 1542. The khipu clearly continued to play an important role during the 1570s. Of course, this was to be expected given the fact that Toledo's inspections were more extensive and more thorough than those of any other colonial administration, and the *khipu* were just as important to Toledo's *visitas* as they were to those carried out by earlier viceroys. In some ways, the extent to which Toledo advocated the use of the khipu is even greater than what is suggested from the evidence presented by Loza, but its effect is not exactly what the documentary evidence would seem to suggest. The actions of Toledo's administration, including his ordinances, may have given khipu record-keeping practices a higher level of visibility and official recognition, but these events must be understood in the broader historical context.

Only a few years before appointing Toledo to the position of viceroy, the Crown had gained firsthand knowledge of the key role often played by khipu transcriptions in colonial legal proceedings. The *cacique* of Hurin Huanca from Jauja traveled to Spain with his khipu transcriptions based on the khipu readings by Guacrapaucar and other *khipukamayuq*, where King

Phillip II ultimately accepted his petition and granted an award in 1563 (Loza 2001: 72; Espinoza Soriano 1971–1972: 183–185). The fact that indigenous leaders from Jauja litigate their case, in which they explicitly identify khipu records as the basis for their claims, all the way to Spain may have made peninsular officials directly aware of the value and importance of khipu record-keeping practices. In 1568, prior to his departure for the Indies, the Crown gave Toledo very specific instructions about reforms that he was to institute, many of which were informed by Juan de Matienzo's *El gobierno del Perú*, published just one year previously in 1567 (Zimmerman 1938: 48–52), and perhaps by the direct experience with the Jauja case of 1563. Matienzo's specific suggestions effectively recommend that the Spaniards take advantage of khipu literacy in the administration of colonial affairs (Matienzo [1567] 1967: 51, 55, 56, 92), and subsequently the king explicitly instructs official inspectors (*visitadores*) to rely on the khipu in order to determine the nature of Inca tribute, which would then determine the allowable amount of tribute to be collected by the Spanish *encomenderos*. In addition, he orders them to make the Indians record on a khipu all their community's goods and livestock (Toledo [1569–1580] 1986–1989: I, 22, 29–30).

After Toledo arrived in Peru in 1569, Matienzo served as one of his most important advisors (Zimmerman 1938: 89–90); and Toledo's own regulations and statutes continued to officially recognize, and depend on, the important function fulfilled by the *khipukamayuq*. After his inspection of the community and hospital of Paria in April of 1575, Toledo ordered that indigenous shepherds of this community keep track of the hospital's livestock with khipu (Toledo [1569–1580] 1986–1989: II, 44); and he identifies the *khipukamayuq* as one of the four people who should have a key to the community chest where communal funds and documents are stored (ibid.: II, 45–46). Perhaps even more significant was Toledo's reaction upon discovering that the priests of the hospital had failed to keep records of the tribute collected from the Indians. Toledo ordered the hospital administrator to interview the *khipukamayuq* of the community and to transcribe their khipu records containing the amount of goods and money they had given to the hospital. This record was then to be used as the basis for an accounting with the priests (ibid.: II, 41).

In Chucuito in July of the same year, Toledo officially recognized and statutorily legitimized the role of the *khipukamayuq* in accounting for livestock and sheered wool (ibid.: II, 76–81). In this case, he explicitly orders the use of both khipu and books:

Item, the cows that there are in this said province that support its community and hospitals, you will take care to later gather them together and count, brand, and breed them, and account for them in a separate book together with the said *khipukamayuq*... and I order that the said don Felipe Calisaya and don Felipe Copaca, general *khipukamayuq* of the said livestock, be notified so that they know, see, and understand that which they will be obligated to maintain and that they have accurate accounts in their khipu of the said principal livestock and the increase and what is sold. (Toledo [1569–1580] 1986–1989: II, 80–81).[5]

This ordinance identifies by name the *khipukamayuq* in charge of livestock, and appears to place their khipu records on at least an even level with written accounts. Two months later, in a meeting with indigenous leaders from Arequipa, Cuzco, and Collao (a region south of Cuzco), Toledo also ordered that community *khipukamayuq* use their khipu to keep track of the religious services provided by priests. These records were to record any absences or delinquencies by the priests so that the community could adjust their salary accordingly (ibid.: II, 92).

It is important to note that Toledo's viceregal decrees rarely constitute universal statutes that would apply indiscriminately to all Andean communities. He explicitly states on several occasions that he is personally conducting inspections – against the advice of some of his advisors (Zimmerman 1938: 85) – in order to formulate ordinances and statutes according to the nature and the needs of each individual town, province, or particular situation (Toledo [1569–1580] 1986–1989: I, 153, 367; II, 203–204, 217–218). By November of 1575, however, his local experiences prompted him to institute a set of more general ordinances for the constitution and administrative structure of local indigenous governments (Toledo [1575] 1989: 217–266). The list of officials and administrators named in the very first ordinance of the first title of this document does seem to institutionalize the khipu through an explicit juxtaposition of official scribes or notaries and *khipukamayuq*: "First, I order and command that... there be in it two mayors and four councilmen and one constable, and one scribe or *khipukamayuq*" (Toledo [1569–1580] 1986–1989: II, 218).[6] This is the statute cited by Loza in her assertion that Toledo created a position of "scribal assistant" for the *khipukamayuq*, thus officially incorporating the khipu into the colonial administration (Loza 2001: 90).

This "institutionalization" of the *khipukamayuq*, however, is not as definitive as the cited passage would seem to imply. Toledo's ordinance officially

---

5 "Item, las vacas que hay en esta dicha provincia que están aplicadas para la comunidad y hospitales de ella tendrá cuidado de que luego las junte y cuente y hierre y beneficie y se haga cargo de ellas en libro aparte juntamente con los dichos quipucamayos.... y mando se notifique a los dichos don Felipe Calisaya y don Felipe Copaca, quipucamayos generales del dicho ganado, para que sepan, vean y entiendan lo que han de ser obligados a guardar y que tengan razón en sus quipus del dicho ganado principal y multiplico y de lo que se vendiere" (Toledo [1569–1580] 1986–1989: II, 80–81).

6 "Primeramente, ordeno y mando que... haya en él dos alcaldes y cuatro regidores y un alguacil y un escribano o quipucamayo" (Toledo [1569–1580] 1986–1989: II, 218).

recognizes the use of the khipu in official documentation prior to 1569, but it is not designed to incorporate it more fully into the colonial administration. This inference rests on two false premises asserted in Loza's argument: (1) that Toledo creates an official position of "ayudante de escribano" for the *khipukamayuq*; and (2) the even more curious claim that Toledo ordered administrative documents transcribed from alphabetic script into khipu in order to make this information available to indigenous communities (Loza 2001: 89–90). These statements are based on a misreading of Toledo's regulations. None of the ordinances Loza cites – nor any other that I could find – establishes an official position of "ayudante de escribano" for the *khipukamayuq*. And nowhere does Toledo order that alphabetic documents be transcribed into khipu. In fact, he ordered exactly the opposite. In spite of the apparent option between an alphabetic or a khipu scribe, Toledo commanded that the scribe of the *cabildo* transcribe into alphabetic script everything that the community customarily recorded on khipus: "everything else that is possible, which the Indians record on khipu, it is ordered and commanded that it be reduced to writing by the said scribe so that it is more certain and enduring ... so that the practice of said official will be to the use and benefit of each town, reducing to writing the said khipus" (Toledo [1569–1580] 1986–1989: II, 238).[7]

Although Toledo's ordinances recognize the role played by the *khipukamayuq* in indigenous communities, they do not institutionalize the *khipukamayuq* as "scribal assistant." Toledo's initial juxtaposition of scribe and *khipukamayuq* recognizes the fact that alphabetically literate individuals were not always available to fill the position of scribe for each indigenous community; but this acceptance of the important role played by *khipukamayuq* did not mean that the khipu was on an even ground with alphabetic writing. For Toledo, a *khipukamayuq* sufficed, but only if an alphabetic scribe was not available. This coincides with Matienzo's own preference for alphabetic script: Matienzo recommends the use of the khipu only when an alphabetically literate scribe is unavailable (Matienzo [1567] 1967: 51, 55, 56). In addition, on one of the first stops on his inspection tour in 1570, Toledo ordered that the Indians of the valley of Jauja be taught to read and write Spanish (Toledo [1569–1580] 1986–1989: I, 61, 63). It is perhaps no coincidence that in this order Toledo explicitly cites the Hurin Huancas whose *cacique* had traveled to Spain to submit khipu transcriptions as part of their legal case in 1563. And the same document that affirms the role of the *khipukamayuq* in 1575 also commands that a school be established in

7 "Todo lo demás que ser pudiere, que los indios suelen poner en quipus, se ordena y manda que se reduzca a escritura por mando de dicho escribano, para que sea más cierto y durable ... porque vendrá a ser el uso del dicho oficio en utilidad y provecho de cada pueblo, reduciendo a escritura los dichos quipus" (Toledo [1569–1580] 1986–1989: II, 238).

order to teach the children of the community how to speak, read, and write Spanish (ibid.: II, 251).

All of the statutes that officially recognize the *khipukamayuq* as legitimate record keepers reflect Toledo's campaign to bring under control the abuses of the colonial system. The entire colonial period, including the years of Toledo's tenure as viceroy, witnessed widespread corruption and abuse by both secular and religious officials in Peru. One of Toledo's main goals was to reduce this corruption in both sectors and strengthen civil power (Zimmerman 1938: 127–129). With regard to the mistreatment of Indians and the collection of excessive tribute, this presented a problem because the Spaniards naturally had a tendency to not document their own violations of official colonial policy. During his inspections Toledo realized the value of the khipu as an alternate form of documentary evidence in combating these abuses. In fact, Toledo's ordinances reflect the same kind of pragmatism that characterizes the earlier *visita* officials. Toledo was perhaps more receptive to indigenous testimony in general, because of his mandate to eliminate Spanish mistreatment and the overburdening of the Indians. In his inspection of the Hospital of Paria, for example, Toledo explicitly instructs officials to give priority to indigenous records of the tribute they had paid (Toledo [1569–1580] 1986–1989: II, 41–46).

Toledo's reformist project favorable to the Indians may have led to a more generous attitude toward the khipu, but his ordinances constitute merely an official recognition of a pre-existing system on which the colonial administration had always relied to one degree or another for information about indigenous society. Furthermore, these statutes were more a temporary accommodation to the reality of Andean social practices in which khipu literacy was deeply imbedded than they were an elevation of the khipu to the same level as alphabetic literacy. Toledo maintained the prestige and primacy of alphabetic script, and he put in place programs and policies that would help indigenous communities transition from khipu to alphabetic records both in their official dealings with the Spanish administration and in their internal affairs. In the meantime, he also recognized and accepted the interface between alphabetic and khipu literacy as a pragmatic solution to the semiotic incompatibility between the Spanish colonial administration and the indigenous Andean socioeconomic system.

The reliance of a predominantly non-alphabetic community on alphabetic record keeping effectively concentrates the role of political and economic mediation between indigenous and Spanish administrations in the literate scribe with a unique understanding of both sides of the relationship. Such a position was conducive to fraud, because it would have constantly presented the scribe with tempting opportunities to take advantage of his unique knowledge and position for personal gain, especially if the community abandoned the khipu altogether. This is one of the reasons for

Phillip II's decree in 1576 that prohibited mestizos from occupying the office of notary and Toledo's similar order in 1577 (Mannheim 1991: 65, 253 n. 10). But Toledo's ordinances encouraged and promoted the use of alphabetic script by indigenous scribes who belonged to the community itself, and he recognized that in some cases this would mean that local records would take the form of khipu at least until sufficient numbers of the community were taught to read and write in alphabetic script.

A few years later in 1585, Luis de Capoche made the more radical recommendation that local records of indigenous communities be kept exclusively on khipu, because the "indios ladinos" who were alphabetically literate in these communities could not be trusted (Capoche [1585] 1959: 138). This appears to be a very marginal view with little influence in the colonial administration, but at least one other source from around the same time suggests that in fact Spanish officials often insisted on khipu record keeping. In 1589, Murillo de la Cerda writes that the Spanish *corregidores* required indigenous communities to maintain khipu records even when they had acquired alphabetic literacy and arabic numeracy (cited in Salomon 2004: 112–113), but Murillo de la Cerda may have based this claim on Capoche's text rather than any empirical experience. In any case, neither Toledo's ordinances nor any other documentary evidence corroborate this claim.

Khipu record keeping was a long standing and fairly ubiquitous institution in the Andes, and indigenous communities had already established well-defined mechanisms that verified and legitimated khipu records. Toledo's ordinances adopt a pragmatic approach that takes advantage of this tradition in an attempt to more efficiently administer colonial affairs. Andean communities demonstrated that they were highly adept at adapting to new situations. Those groups who were in constant contact with the Spaniards began using alphabetic script in their official dealings with the viceregal administration as soon as possible after it became clear that this was the more effective medium in the colonial system. This does not necessarily mean, however, that they immediately abandoned the traditional role of the *khipukamayuq* within their communities, but they were well aware that they had to harness the power of alphabetic writing in one way or another.

The use of khipu in legal proceedings such as those cited above and in previous chapters may have implicitly afforded a certain level of legitimacy to this medium throughout the sixteenth century, but I see no neat progression in which the khipu passes through a process culminating in the institutionalization of the khipu in the colonial administration during Toledo's tenure as viceroy. Rather, the legal cases and Toledo's ordinances reflect the ad hoc demands of political interests and pragmatic necessity. In the case of the inspections, the initial process was inherently more disinterested than subsequent inquiries undertaken as a part of legal proceedings between private parties, because its effects had not yet been determined. Furthermore, inspectors were officials of the Crown charged with collecting accurate demographic and economic information about a vast population spread over an enormous geographical area. The information available from *khipukamayuq* offered colonial officials a much more efficient and expeditious method for completing their inspections with the limited resources at their disposal.

The historical process revealed by all types of official documents that rely on khipu as sources of information is not one of legitimation, which was granted implicitly from the very beginning, or official incorporation into the colonial administration, but one of gradual, albeit irregular, obsolescence in this particular dimension of the interaction between Andeans and Spaniards. The need to transcribe khipu for use in legal cases highlighted the incompatibility between this indigenous record-keeping medium and the colonial system. Nevertheless, Toledo's statutes outlining the structure of indigenous government and his deference to the khipu in collecting evidence for cases of abuse by secular and religious officials would appear to carve out a continuing role for the khipu in the colonial legal system as Loza argues. It is important to keep in mind that Toledo made many enemies (Levillier 1921–1926: VII, 130–406), his orders were not always obeyed (Zimmerman 1938), and his term as viceroy ended in 1581; but in any case, whatever possible effect Toledo's ordinances might have had, it would have been limited to communities who were already using this device. In other words, Toledo's ordinances merely recognized and affirmed what was already happening. And his simultaneous literacy campaign reveals that this official affirmation of local khipu record keeping was only a temporary solution to a larger problem. The ultimate outcome in the interaction between khipu and alphabetic records must be understood in the context of the hegemonic power exerted by alphabetically based social and political institutions. Whatever impetus Toledo's ordinances may have given to khipu record-keeping practices, in most cases, it was only a temporary reprieve from the inevitable disappearance of this medium from the domain in which it served as an interface with the official colonial administration.

The Alleged Prohibition of the Khipu

Just as Toledo's regime of the 1570s did not represent a qualitatively distinct period in the history of the khipu in relation to colonial institutions, neither did the 1580s and beyond. It is often asserted that in 1583 the Third Lima Council issued a universal condemnation of the khipu, that the Spaniards then burned as many as they could find, and that this resulted in an abrupt decline in khipu record-keeping practices. This condemnation and the scarcity of khipu in official documents after this point serve as the basis on which Loza argues that from this point onwards colonial officials no longer admitted khipu-based testimonies in legal proceedings (Loza 1998a: 156). The alleged campaign to destroy the khipu is supposed to have interrupted the continuity of this medium, contributing to the eventual loss of khipu literacy with its associated conventions. However, this scenario is based on unfounded inferences that run contrary to the available evidence.

The Third Lima Council did mandate the destruction of khipu in 1583, but contrary to the claims of most modern scholars, this order applied only to khipus related to indigenous religious practices that threatened to undermine Catholic orthodoxy. The Third Lima Council's order to destroy idolatrous khipu is more relevant to the interaction between indigenous communities and Spanish priests, and it will be discussed more thoroughly in the next chapter. In the secular context of the colonial administration, the possible ambiguity in the distinction between secular and idolatrous khipu may have given secular authorities a convenient excuse to destroy any khipu that they felt might pose a threat to the colonial order. If a pretense was even necessary, colonial officials could always trump up charges of idolatry. However, there is no evidence of any campaign by secular officials to destroy khipu.

The use of administrative khipu clearly continued with the complicity of the Spaniards throughout the colonial period. Other genres may not have fared so well, but as far as I am aware, colonial sources record only one instance of a Spaniard actually destroying a khipu. In *Miscelánea austral* (1602), Diego de Avalos y Figueroa relates how he and the *corregidor* from Hatun Jauja came upon an old Indian with a rather large and colorful khipu. The Indian attempted to hide the khipu from the Spaniards, but the *corregidor* forced him to explain the purpose of such an elaborate account. According to Avalos y Figueroa, the Indian explained that his khipu was one of several that contained a record of all that had happened in the valley of Jauja since the arrival of the Spaniards, and that he was keeping this record in order to give an account to the Inca when he returned. The *corregidor* immediately confiscated the khipu, burned it, and punished the old Indian (Avalos y Figueroa 1602: 151). It is important to note that the *corregidor* asked about the content of the khipu before taking any action. If the *khipukamayuq* had told him that the khipu contained a record of tribute obligations, the *corregidor* likely would have left him alone.

In this case, the khipu itself was not the issue but rather the nature of the khipu's contents, accompanied as it was by such a boldly subversive statement about the return of the Inca. This is the only known account of a Spaniard destroying a khipu, but one must suspect that it may not have been an isolated incident. And the arbitrary criteria used in deciding which khipu to single out for destruction might possibly have induced

Andean *khipukamayuq* to conceal all of their khipu not directly related to their administrative interactions with the Spaniards.

Anti-Khipu Sentiment in Colonial Peru

This is not to say that no other overt opposition to the institution of economic or administrative khipu emerges, but it is scarce, indirect, and often ambiguous. For example, whereas Loza cites the Sacaca case as illustrating the official recognition and acceptance of the khipu by the colonial legal system, Urton uses this same case along with a passage from Juan de Solórzano y Pereyra's *Política indiana* (1629–1639) to argue the opposite view that the khipu came under direct attack in the later colonial period (Urton 1998: 430–431). Urton cites one of the *khipukamayuq* witnesses in the case who is compelled to defend the trustworthiness of his colleagues: "They appoint as *quipo*-makers in the said *repartimientos* the most credible Indians that there are in them [the *repartimientos*] by reason of which the said *quipos* were trustworthy and for this reason there is no fraud in them [the *quipos*] nor are there any lies" (AGI 1579: 409v, cited in Urton 1998: 430).

The Sacaca case has several implications for an understanding of the history of the khipu in its relation to the colonial administration. First, it was a dispute between private parties rather than a governmental inquest. The colonial administration had no direct stake in the outcome. Of course, the Spanish defendants faced with incriminating evidence in the form of testimonies by *khipukamayuq* would naturally do everything in their power to undermine the plaintiffs' case. Given the fact that the Spanish legal system relied almost exclusively on oral testimonies, only two defensive strategies were available: (1) provide a different account of the events in question; and/or (2) discredit the witnesses of the opposing side. In the Sacaca case, the inheritors of Alonso de Montemayor had no basis on which to counter the firsthand accounts of the indigenous witnesses who were the very individuals who had paid the tribute in question. Their only recourse, then, was to attempt to discredit the witnesses, who in this case happened to be *khipukamayuq*. But whatever challenge that this case might have posed to the legitimacy of the khipu in the Spanish legal system, its effect would have been limited by the parochial nature of the dispute, not to mention the fact that the Indians won the case.

Furthermore, the colonial legal system was not based on common law precedents. Spanish judges were charged with enforcing the Laws of the Indies and the various other ordinances and decrees that were in effect at the time and relevant to each case. The procedure through which the determination of facts took place consisted of oral interviews with pertinent witnesses. The locus of credibility was the person of the witness rather than any secondary record. The case hinged, therefore, on the credibility of the witnesses. All khipu records admitted as evidence in legal proceedings were rendered orally and transcribed into alphabetic script. Spanish officials treated these testimonies in the same way as any other oral testimony and subjected them to the same criteria of legitimacy. Legal proceedings admitted khipu transcriptions recorded by a notary prior to or during the proceedings themselves; but these transcriptions were possible only in conjunction with a reading by *khipukamayuq* informants whose legitimacy rested on their own personal knowledge or eyewitness testimony.

Other than historiographical khipu, for which the same expectations do not apply, the only possible exception of which I am aware is when *curacas* from Chucuito had to search for khipu records from the time of the Inca in order to respond to questions posed in the *visita* conducted in 1567 (Diez de San Miguel [1567] 1964: 26–27). In that case, it is unclear whether or not the *khipukamayuq* were the same individuals who had recorded the information for the Inca. In virtually all cases of economic and administrative records, however, it is clear that the *khipukamayuq* who appear as witnesses in colonial documents are also the ones who first created the khipu on which they rely to give their testimony. The fact that the witnesses are *khipukamayuq* who happen to have a material record of the events in which they were involved only adds further to their credibility. The Sacaca case makes this very clear in the insistence placed on the fact that the *khipukamayuq* who read the khipu were the same ones who had created them thirty years earlier. In other words, the legitimacy of the testimony rested on the firsthand knowledge of the *khipukamayuq*, who happened to have recorded that knowledge at the time using khipu. This emphasis on the trustworthiness of the witness is also reflected in Alonso Yanxi's statement, in which he ties the veracity of the khipu record to the credibility of the *khipukamayuq*. In other words, as in the case of written documents, the medium itself is neutral; the accuracy of the khipu is contingent on the trustworthiness of its author.

In theory, the defendants in this and other cases could have pursued a line of argument that attempted to demonstrate the fallibility of the khipu medium itself. However, this would have meant delving into the details of khipu conventions, which did not happen. No evidence has surfaced to suggest that the khipu was ever challenged in this regard. In fact, the overwhelming procedural precedent in the colonial legal system was that *khipukamayuq* were reliable witnesses and that the khipu was a highly precise and accurate medium.

The few texts that can be read as critical of the khipu exhibit the same emphasis on the credibility of the *khipukamayuq* as the Sacaca case. Murillo de la Cerda, for example, briefly links the credibility of khipu accounting to the trustworthiness of the *khipukamayuq*: "[This accounting] has good faith and credit only through some trustworthy Indians in those towns, whom they call quypo camayos, as majordomos of those accounts and as senior accountants" (cited in Salomon 2004: 112). However, as explained above, Murillo de la Cerda also goes on to make the erroneous claim, probably based on Capoche's radical recommendation, that Spanish officials actually demand that indigenous communities maintain their records with khipu rather than alphabetic writing.

The closest thing to an actual attack on the khipu itself appears in Juan de Solórzano y Pereyra's *Política indiana* (1629–1639), but even here the issue has more to do with the trustworthiness of the *khipukamayuq* than the khipu itself. Although this work was published between 1629 and 1639, Solórzano y Pereyra cites the Sacaca case from the 1570s as an example of unreliable *khipukamayuq*:

35. For this reason, in a law suit brought against don Alonso de Sotomayor, *encomendero* of Sacaca, over excessive tribute that was said to have been exacted from his Indians, I saw placed in doubt whether sufficient proof could be attributed to the assertion and deposition of the officials that the very Indians elected to collect these books and pay their *encomenderos* and which in the Kingdom of Peru are called *khipukamayuq*, because they have the account and reason of their khipu, which are bunches of threads of various colors, in which appear some knots with admirable agreement and correspondence, that serve them as letters and writings, of which Acosta and other authors have dealt.

36. Although I do not deny that this numeration and assertion carries great weight when it is done well, and as is fitting, because these *khipukamayuq* are like public officials, elected for this administration, whose books are customarily trusted completely and consulted as a mirror and source of the truth, according to the opinion of many doctors . . . , still I dare not place such, and so much faith and authority in these khipu, because I have heard those who understand something of them say that the form of making them and of explaining them is very uncertain, deceptive, and intricate; and also I do not know that it can be affirmed that the *khipukamayuq* are chosen with public authority for this office. . . .

37. Even leaving all this aside, they are Indians whose faith vacillates, and thus also the explication that they give of their khipu, as Baldo said of a similar case, teaching that the notary who is also a father cannot receive depositions in favor of his son; and even better Menoquio, and others referred to by the same Genao, that say that to the books of the tax collectors, or even to those of the Masarios of a given University, no credit should be given, nor do they testify in harm of a third party.

38. This would be more accurate if we were to add that these *khipukamayuq* in the said declarations deal with their exoneration, or at least they are part of that

repartimiento of Indians, in whose favor they testify; for this reason their deposition is less certain. . . . . (Solórzano y Pereyra [1629–1639] 1972: II, 308–309).[8]

Solórzano y Pereyra's reference to "seeing" this event seems to suggest that he was present during the Sacaca proceedings, but this would have been impossible. He was born in 1575, and he did not arrive in the Indies until 1610. His knowledge of the case, therefore, must have come from the colonial archive rather than from firsthand experience. Solórzano y Pereyra explains that the Sacaca proceedings questioned whether or not the testimony of *khipukamayuq* constituted sufficient proof in the case. Even so, he admits that the khipu is a complex device capable of recording accurate information when it is made well, but according to his informants "who know something of the khipu," "the method of making and deciphering khipu is uncertain, deceptive, and intricate." What this means, then, is that it is not the khipu itself that is unreliable but rather the Indian who uses it. Solórzano y Pereyra further emphasizes this point in his statement that just as the Indians' faith waivers, so will their explication of the contents of their khipu.

In paragraph 38, Solórzano y Pereyra states further that the most damning evidence against the reliability of the *khipukamayuq* witnesses is the fact that they are interested parties: they have a stake in the outcome of the case, which means that their testimony is not as reliable as it might otherwise be. Of course, the same is true of the Spanish witnesses, but evidently for Solórzano y Pereyra their Christian faith makes them less

8 "35. Por esta razon, en un pleyto reñido contra D. Alonso de Sotomayor, Encomendero de Sacaca, sobre tributos demasiados, que se decia haver llevado á sus Indios, ví poner en duda, si tendria por bastante probanza la asercion y deposicion de los Oficiales, que de los mismos Indios se eligen para recoger estos libros, y pagarlos á los Encomenderos, que en el Reyno del Perú se llaman *Quipocamayos*, porque tienen la cuenta y razon de sus *Quipos*, que son unos ramales de hilos de varios colores, en los quales ván dando unos nudos con admirable concierto, y correspondiencia, que les sirven como de letras, y escrituras, de los quales tratan Acosta, y otros Autores.

36. Porque aunque no niego que sea esta numeracion y asercion de gran peso quando se halla hecha bien, y como conviene, por ser estos *Quipocamayos* como Oficiales público, electos para esta administracion, á cuyos libros se suele dár entera fé, y recurrir como á espejo y fuente de la verdad, segun la opinion de muchos Doctores . . . , todavia Yo no me atreveré á dár tal, y tan grande fé y autoridad á estos *Quipos*, porque he oído decir á los que entienden de ellos, que es muy incierta, faláz, é intrincada la forma de hacerlos, y de explicarlos; y también no sé que se pueda afirmar que los *Quipocamayos* se elijan con autoridad pública para este ministerio. . . .

37. Quando aún faltára todo esto, son Indios cuya fé vacila, y asi tambien vacilará la explicacion que dieren remitida á sus *Quipos*, como en semejante caso lo dixo Baldo, enseñando, que el Padre Notario no puede recibir instrumento ante sí en favor de su hijo; y mejor Menoquio, y otros referidos por el mismo Genoa, que dicen, que á los libros de los *Exactores*, ni aún á los de los *Masarios* de alguna Universidad no se les dá crédito, ni hacen fé en perjuicio de tercero.

38. Esto sería más cierto, si añadiésemos que estos *Quipocamayos* en las dichas declaraciones tratan de su exoneracion, ó por lo menos son parte de aquel repartimiento de Indios, en cuyo favor deponen; con que vendrá a ser menos segura su deposicion" (Solórzano y Pereyra [1629–1639] 1972: II, 308–309).

inclined to deception. In any case, here again, the critique consists of an ad hominen attack on the reliability of the witnesses themselves rather than the khipu as such. In fact, Solórzano y Pereyra himself explains that the general consensus among learned writers on the subject is that the khipu is extremely accurate in the information it records.

The only other antagonistic attitude toward the khipu shows up in the more limited ecclesiastical context that I will discuss in the next chapter. The few anti-khipu sentiments that surface in colonial sources appear to be isolated instances motivated by particular political or personal conflicts rather than a more general trend. Historiographical khipu continue to inform late sixteenth- and early seventeenth-century chronicles, but these narrative khipu also experience an abrupt decline in official documentation after 1580. Frank Salomon and Karen Spalding recognize that the khipu did not disappear at this point, and they suggest that perhaps colonial officials began rejecting khipu-based testimonies (Salomon and Spalding 2002: 860). But they make this argument only in order to explain the false contradiction based on the specious perspective inherited from Duviols and Loza and according to which the Third Lima Council issued a universal condemnation of the khipu. In fact, the scarcity of khipu references after 1580 has nothing to do with a campaign to destroy khipu nor any general anti-khipu sentiment.

The Disappearance of the Khipu from the Colonial Archive

The number of references to khipu in colonial documents appears to drop off fairly dramatically in the late sixteenth century, but to claim that this medium disappeared from the colonial archive at this point would be a gross exaggeration. Furthermore, the reduced visibility of khipu in colonial sources does not even necessarily correlate to a reduction in its use. As explained in previous chapters, the khipu continued to appear in documents not only in the latter part of the sixteenth century but throughout the seventeenth century and to some extent in the eighteenth as well. Throughout the colonial period, the use of khipu genres clearly declined, but the rather abrupt reduction of khipu references in colonial documents after around 1580 is not a diagnostic indicator of this phenomenon. The disappearance of the khipu was probably a fairly uneven process that occurred at different rates in different communities, but in general it was more gradual than the documentary evidence would seem to suggest.

The *reducciones* carried out by the colonial administration, most significantly by Toledo in the 1570s, brought about a restructuring of social, economic, and political relations that had a tendency to displace the khipu and introduce alphabetic writing. In fact, throughout the sixteenth century, repeated orders required that the Indians be taught to read and write in order to facilitate both their conversion to Christianity and their assimilation into the colonial system; and it appears that in most of the domains in which alphabetic literacy took hold, the khipu eventually fell into disuse. However, this does not necessarily mean that alphabetic literacy immediately or completely eclipsed the khipu even within communities where it took hold. By the mid-sixteenth century, for example, communities in Jauja were already actively engaged in the colonial legal system, commissioning alphabetic documents for the law suits in which they were involved. These communities in particular were explicitly singled out for instruction in alphabetic literacy. Nevertheless, as Avalos y Figueroa observed, many years later they continued to maintain khipu records for their own internal use (Avalos y Figueroa 1602: 151).

The most important factor in the reduced visibility of both statistical and historiographic khipu in the late sixteenth century was the reduction in the number of *visitas* and other forms of administrative intervention in local community affairs. As explained in Chapter 5, the most prevalent evidence of khipu records appears in official *visitas*, and the Spaniards conducted far fewer *visitas* in the 1580s and 1590s than they had in the previous decades. Just as the intensive and extensive engagement with indigenous officials during Toledo's *visitas* and regulatory and administrative reforms of the 1570s produced a documentary record in which the khipu figured prominently, the diminished number of *visitas* and other administrative interventions after 1580 resulted in a decline in the documented uses of this medium.

Aside from the *visitas* and the historical investigations of colonial chroniclers, the only other contexts in which khipu readings appear in the colonial record are lawsuits between private parties. The distinction between legal cases involving two private individuals or groups and those in which the colonial government has a stake is sometimes difficult to make; but in any case, such lawsuits that are known to include documents identified explicitly as khipu transcriptions are rare even before 1583. As in the case of the *visitas* themselves, many lawsuits relying on *khipukamayuq* informants may not have identified them explicitly as such. Furthermore, given the clearly privileged status of alphabetic script and the colonial literacy campaign, indigenous communities would have begun producing alphabetic records for such cases as soon as they were able. Nevertheless, none of this necessarily implies the demise of the khipu in the internal administration of local communities.

The suggestion that after 1580 or 1583 *khipukamayuq* withdrew to an informal space where they continued their record-keeping practices (Loza 1998a: 156; Salomon and Spalding 2002: 860) is misleading. It is important to keep in mind that although some communities may have maintained khipu specifically for interactions with the Spaniards, most of the khipu transcribed into alphabetic script for *visitas* or other juridical proceedings were actually internal community records. Colonial tribute khipu, for example, served as records that could be used to document goods and services rendered to an *encomendero*, but they also served an internal administrative purpose. The diminished presence of the khipu in colonial documents, then, represents a withdrawal of the Spaniards more than of the *khipukamayuq*. And the space in which the *khipukamayuq* continued to work after 1583 was only informal in relation to the Spanish administration.

Furthermore, at no point does the colonial administration ever give any indication of any negative attitude toward the khipu. In fact, to the contrary, Spanish officials continue to recognize and condone the important role played by the khipu in the interface between local communities and colonial institutions. In 1602 the *Audiencia* of Lima asked colonial officials from Potosí to determine the amount of tribute owed by the Indians of Chucuito, and the order specifically instructs the officials to draw from the communities' khipu records (Audiencia de Lima [1602] 1981: 953–954). In the seventeenth century, *khipukamayuq* continued to function formally in their communities, as recognized and advocated by Toledo's ordinances. In *Noticias políticas de indias*, published in 1639, Pedro Ramírez del Aguila explains that the structure of indigenous community governments included a *khipukamayuq* official (Ramírez del Aguila [1639] 1978: 124–125). In 1644, Pedro de Berrio Manrique presented a series of what appear to be khipu transcriptions that document the participation of various villages in the *mita* in the Plaza de Armas (ADC, Legajo 14, Cuaderno 26). Assadourian even cites a document from as late as 1725 that reveals the continued use of khipu in the administration of a local community. The document refers to an "Indian always carrying a khipu of cords by which he knew all of the members of his *panaca* who owed *mita* (labor service), the names, their condition, the livestock and possessions of each one, 'but it is not known how they knew it'" (Assadourian 1998: 30).[9]

The reduction in the number of contexts in which *khipukamayuq* were called on by Spanish officials to read their khipu after 1580, resulting in the scarcity of khipu-based documents in the colonial archive, then, does not necessarily imply a diminished use by indigenous communities. The presence or absence of khipu readings in colonial documents in any given period does not constitute an accurate indicator of the rate or extent to which the khipu did or did not fall into disuse. To be sure, over time the khipu began disappearing, but the obsolescence of this medium was due

9 "Indio siempre cargado con un quipo de cordeles' por el cual conocía a todos los efectivos de su panaca que debían mita, los nombres, estado, ganados y haciendas de cada uno, 'pero no se sabe con que ciencia lo sabia'" (Assadourian 1998: 30).

more to the spread of alphabetic literacy and the deterioration of traditional Andean socioeconomic and political institutions than any overt prohibition or anti-khipu sentiment. The khipu continued to play an important role in the internal administration of many communities throughout the colonial period and beyond. Rising literacy rates and the increased availability of bilingual scribes naturally meant that the khipu would play a much reduced role in official documentation, but such developments were uneven. Furthermore, colonial sources confirm that khipu often continued to mediate the day-to-day economic interactions between Spaniards and many indigenous communities well into the seventeenth century.

7

Ecclesiastical Khipu and Spanish Evangelization

Perhaps one of the most interesting aspects of the interaction between khipu record keepers and the colonial administration has to do with the adjustments that appear to take place in the genres of both Andean and European discourses. The power differential may have forced Andean *khipukamayuq* to adapt their khipu genres more extensively than the Spaniards did their alphabetic models, but each affected the other to some extent. Spanish chroniclers and inspectors inadvertently imported into their texts the paradigmatic information structures that characterized both the historiographical and administrative data stored on khipu. For their part, Andean *khipukamayuq* adapted their khipu practices to record the type of information demanded by their new Spanish overlords. The preceding chapters deal in part with the adaptations that take place in the khipu genres involved in recording historical narratives, censuses, and tribute.[1] Khipu practices associated with the recording of these types of information are the easiest to document and analyze, because they were directly involved in the interaction between indigenous communities and the colonial Spanish administration. A similar interaction took place between Andean *khipukamayuq* and Spanish priests, but far fewer traces of it appear in the colonial archive.

Spanish priests distinguished early on between acceptable secular khipu and unacceptable idolatrous khipu related to indigenous religious beliefs and practices. Although they attempted to stamp out idolatrous khipu practices, they also actively promoted the use of khipu for Christian ecclesiastical purposes. In many cases, native Andeans used the same administrative khipu genres discussed in previous chapters for ecclesiastical purposes, which in addition to specifically religious content also often entailed maintaining census and tribute records. However, the documentary evidence that has come to light suggests that the adaptation of the khipu for Christian ecclesiastical use often involved a much greater departure from traditional

1 It is important to emphasize once again that these generic categories are heuristic tools for which I make no definitive ontological claims.

practices than that which took place in historiographical and administrative genres.

The Campaign Against Idolatrous Khipu

The main task of the priests who arrived with the first conquistadors was to evangelize the Indians and root out their idolatrous practices. Colonial chroniclers identify numerous khipu practices that Spanish priests would have targeted for extirpation from the beginning. Several chroniclers associate khipu records with *huacas*, which refer to objects or places that the Andeans revered or considered sacred by virtue of certain qualities distinguishing them from the norm (Murúa [1611] 1987: 442–445; Arriaga 1621: 88), and the ceremonies and rites associated with them (Molina [c. 1570–1574] 1989: 122–123, 127–128; Garcilaso de la Vega [1609] 1985: I, 112–113; II, 27; Calancha 1638: 91). Cristóbal de Molina states, and *The Huarochirí Manuscript* confirms, that *khipukamayuq* recorded the offerings made to these *huacas*, which were often features of the landscape such as springs, mountains, and so forth (Molina [1570–1574] 1989: 122–123, 127–128; Avila [1608] 1991: 112).

In the Cuzco valley, the geographical distribution of *huacas* formed a series of lines known as *ceques* emanating out from the temple of Coricancha (Zuidema 1964; Bauer 1992). The *huacas* along the lines of the *ceque* system were associated with specific dates on which offerings were made. Tom Zuidema argues that a khipu containing a record of the *huacas* would have constituted in effect a sort of calendar (Zuidema 1977: 231; 1982; 1986; 1989).[2] The temporal nature of this khipu genre might have led to its use in historical records as well. Needless to say, the Spaniards considered the veneration of *huacas* to be an idolatrous practice, and evidently, at least at this early stage, they condemned the khipu records associated with them.

If the Spaniards mounted a campaign to destroy such records, this would explain why this particular genre does not appear in any direct way in colonial sources. The only colonial text to explicitly identify the *huacas* of the Cuzco *ceque* system is Bernabé Cobo's *Relación de las huacas*, which is based on a text produced by Polo de Ondegardo in 1559. Chroniclers such as Ondegardo and Molina conducted their research at a time possibly before the use of allegedly idolatrous khipu disappeared, at least from the view of the Spaniards. The text of *The Huarochirí Manuscript* (1608) reveals that some communities still employed khipu in ritual contexts at the beginning of the seventeenth century (Avila [1608] 1991: 112, 142).

2 Marcia Ascher and Robert Ascher disagree with the specifics of Zuidema's argument, but they also propose that there were calendrical khipu linked to the *ceque* system. They even identify three archaeological khipu whose features are consistent with their theory (Ascher and Ascher 1989).

Although no actual record of an extirpation campaign to stamp out idolatrous khipu practices exists, at least two sources from the second half of the sixteenth century appear to refer to such a project. As explained in Chapter 6, the *Actas* of the Third Lima Council from 1583 contain an article identifying khipu as idolatrous objects and calling for their destruction:

Books that intentionally deal with, narrate, or teach lascivious or obscene topics are absolutely prohibited, because it is necessary to keep in mind not only faith but also the customs that are in this way easily corrupted by the lesson of books. Severely punish the bishops and those who eventually possess such books. The ancient ones, written by gentiles, can be permitted for their elegance and the propriety of their discourse, but they are not to be read to children for any reason. And because among the Indians who are ignorant of letters, there were instead of books certain signs of different cords that they call khipus and from these arise not a few testimonies of ancient superstition in which they maintain the secret of their rites, ceremonies, and iniquitous laws, let the bishops endeavor to completely destroy all of these pernicious instruments. (*Tercer Concilio Limense* [1583] 1990: 191).[3]

As should be evident, this order is not actually about khipu per se but rather the corrupting influence of lascivious and obscene topics normally contained in certain books. For the Third Lima Council, the analog of such books in native Andean society was the khipu, which preserved equally corrupting superstitions of the Indians. But the council does not universally prohibit books, only those that contain objectionable material. In isolation, the language of this passage does appear to condemn all khipu, but the larger context of the entire paragraph clearly implies that, just as in the case with books, only khipu with idolatrous or superstitious content are to be confiscated and destroyed.

My English translation of the Third Lima Council's order is based on Francesco Leonardo Lisi's Spanish translation of the original Latin text. Evidently, the Third Lima Council also produced its own Spanish translation. Lisi's modern translation is more faithful to the original Latin text,[4] but

---

3 "Prohíbanse absolutamente los libros que tratan, narran o enseñan intencionalmente asuntos lascivos y obscenos, porque hay que tener en cuenta no sólo la fe sino también las costumbres que de esta manera suelen ser fácilmente corrompidas, por la lección de los libros. Castiguen severamente los obispos a los que posean eventualmente tales libros. Los antiguos, escritos por los gentiles, pueden ser permitidos por la elegancia y propiedad del discurso, pero no se han de leer por ninguna razón a los niños. Y como entre los indios, ignorantes de las letras, había en vez de libros ciertos signos de diferentes cuerdas que ellos llaman *quipos* y de éstos surgen no pocos testimonios de antigua superstición en los que guardan el secreto de sus ritos, ceremonias y leyes inicuas, procuren los obispos destruir por completo todos esos instrumentos perniciosos" (*Terecer Concilio Limense* [1583] 1990: 191).

4 "Et quoniam apud Indos litterarum ignaros, pro libris signa quaedam ex variis funiculis erant, quos ipsi, quipos, vocant, atque ex eis non parva superstitionis antiquae monumenta exmemoriam

the fifteenth-century Spanish translation can be read in a way that lends further support to the idea of a more limited prohibition of khipu. A more or less direct translation of the last sentence of the fifteenth-century Spanish version of the order reads as follows: "let the bishops endeavor with diligence that all the accounts or khipus, that serve for their superstition, be taken away completely from the Indians" (Vargas Ugarte 1951–1954: I, 358).[5] The ambiguity lies in the status of the phrase "that serve for their superstition," which could be understood as either a restrictive or a non-restrictive clause. I would argue that the larger textual and sociohistorical context suggests that it is a restrictive clause, which would indicate that the order applied only to those particular khipu that contain superstitions.[6]

Even if one maintains that the instructions in the Third Council are possibly ambiguous, the *Tercero cathecismo*, which is really a book of sermons published by the same Council, clarifies the issue. The *Tercero cathecismo* actually states that the Indians are to make khipu in order to facilitate the confession of their sins: "The first thing, my son, you must think hard on your sins, and make a khipu of them: just as you make a khipu when you are *tambocamayo* [steward of the storehouse], of what you give out and what they owe: in this same way make a khipu of what you have done against God and against your neighbor, and how many times, if many or if few" (*Tercero cathecismo* [1585] 1985: [f.67v.] 482).[7] This makes it very clear that the Third Council's order was not a universal condemnation of all khipu but rather only those with idolatrous content.

Most scholars have ignored the apparent contradiction between these two orders. Pierre Duviols, for example, reads the order in the *Actas* as a universal condemnation of the khipu without accounting for the *Cathecismo* (Duviols 1971: 243). Recently, this view has received even more traction from Carmen Loza's research into the history of the khipu in the sixteenth-century legal system discussed in Chapter 6 (Loza 1998a; 2000; 2001).

conseervant, curent Episcopi, haec omnia pernitiosa instrumenta penitus aboleri" (Vargas Ugarte 1951–1954: I, 297).

5 "Procuren con diligencia los obispos que todos los memoriales o quipos, que sirven para su super-stición, se les quiten totalmente a los yndios" (Vargas Ugarte 1951–1954: I, 358).

6 According to modern conventions, the fact that this phrase is set off with commas implies that it functions as a non-restrictive clause. I have been unable to examine the original manuscript of the Actas, which were never published in the sixteenth century. It is unclear, then, whether Vargas Ugarte reproduced the original punctuation or inserted these commas in the process of editing the manuscript. In either case, fifteenth-century punctuation conventions were not standardized. The presence or absence of such commas in the original fifteenth century text, then, does not indicate one way or the other whether the clause was restrictive or non-restrictive.

7 "Lo primero, hijo mío, has de pensar bien tus peccados, y hacer quipo dellos: como hazes quipo, quando eres tambocamayo, de lo q[ue] das y delo q[ue] deuen: assi haz quipo delo que has hecho, contra Dios y contra tu proximo, y quantas vezes: si muchas, o si pocas" (*Tercer cathecismo* [1585] 1985: 482).

Not only do these studies fail to reconcile the prohibition in the *Actas* with the order to use khipu in the *Cathecismo*, they do not take into account the continued widespread use of khipu after 1583 in both secular and religious contexts. The continued use of khipu after 1583 means that either the Third Lima Council's order was not carried out or it was never intended as a universal prohibition.

More recent studies recognize that the khipu continued to play a vital role in the administration of local communities, and while accepting that the Third Council's prohibition was universal, they attempt to explain this apparent contradiction. Frank Salomon and Karen Spalding, for example, suggest that after 1583 khipu record-keeping practices receded into the "unofficial" domain of local community administration (Salomon and Spalding 2002: 860). As explained in Chapter 6, although this is certainly true in a certain sense, it is important to dissociate the decline in the prominence of khipu in official secular records from the Third Lima Council's order. The temporal proximity of these two events is completely coincidental: they have no direct relationship. The Third Lima Council took place shortly after the extensive administrative reforms based on a comprehensive *visita general* carried out by the viceroy Toledo. The comprehensive nature of the *visita general* and the reforms instituted by Toledo dramatically reduced the need for further *visitas*, and this was the primary context in which khipu were incorporated into official records. In other words, the increased paucity of references to the khipu in the colonial archive after 1583 results directly from the reduced level of administrative interaction with local community record keepers. Nevertheless, ample evidence of khipu use after 1583 exists, not only for the internal administration of local communities but also in the interactions with Spanish administrators. Thus, the Third Lima Council's order did not affect in any profound way the reaction by colonial officials to the use of khipu.

It is possible, as John Charles argues, that the apparent contradiction between the two orders issued by the Third Lima Council represents a difference of opinion among religious leaders in Peru at the time (Charles 2007: 18). According to this scenario, some religious officials would have been in favor of promoting khipu practices, whereas others were opposed to it. The anti-khipu faction, then, would have controlled the preparation of the Third Council's *Actas*, in which the prohibition appears, and the pro-khipu advocates would have produced the *Cathecismo*, which orders the use of confessional khipu. The participants of the Third Lima Council may have had differences of opinion, but I would argue that the simultaneous prohibition of idolatrous khipu, on the one hand, and the advocacy of confessional khipu, on the other, does not necessarily indicate a disagreement on this issue. The Council authorized the publication of both the *Actas* and the *Cathecismo*, and there is no indication that disagreements among council members played themselves out in these publications. Furthermore, no other sources from the period contain any indication of any suspicion of the khipu in general or any conflict of opinions about its status.

I would argue, rather, that the two orders do not actually constitute a contradiction, because very early on Spanish priests made a distinction between secular and idolatrous khipu. Spanish clergy evidently felt that they could harness secular khipu literacy to facilitate their own religious projects. The Third Lima Council's order to destroy khipu referred only to those genres that contributed to the preservation of idolatrous beliefs and practices. As explained above, the section of the *Actas* that contains the condemnation of the khipu actually begins with a prohibition of certain books. It does not ban all books, just those that contain religiously subversive material. The recommendation to use confessional khipu in the *Tercero cathecismo* further corroborates the idea that this limitation also applied to the condemnation of the khipu. In other words, not all khipu were idolatrous, just those that contained the secrets of "their rites, ceremonies, and iniquitous laws." The order to destroy these khipu comes at the end of the paragraph: "let the bishops endeavor to completely destroy all of these pernicious instruments" (*Tercer Concilio Limense* [1583] 1990: 191). In the colonial context in which the khipu was a fairly ubiquitous device on which both priests and colonial administrators relied, it would seem clear that the prohibition refers only to "pernicious" idolatrous khipu as opposed to non-pernicious secular genres. As explained above, this passage views books and khipu as similar: they are not inherently evil but rather neutral media that can be used in the service of either good or evil. Thus, the prohibition of khipu was not universal, and hence did not enter into contradiction with the Third Council's simultaneous order to use khipu for confession.

The Third Lima Council does not go into very much detail about the nature of the "idolatrous" khipu, but it states that the Andeans used them to preserve their rites, ceremonies, and laws (*Tercer Concilio Limense* [1583] 1990: 191). A number of colonial sources indicate that the Inca used khipu to record laws. In his description of Inca legal khipu, the Inca Garcilaso de la Vega states that "by the color of the thread and by the number of knots, they understood the law that prohibited this or that offense and the punishment given to those who broke it" (Garcilaso de la Vega [1609] 1985: II, 27). It is unclear exactly how the colors and knots conveyed this information, but the nature of khipu conventions suggests that numerical values may have been involved. The Inca Garcilaso actually draws an explicit parallel between the numerical nature of the khipu and not only the Ten Commandments but the articles of faith and works of compassion as well: "Such that each thread and knot brought to their memory what they contained, just like the commandments or the articles of our

Holy Catholic Faith and the works of compassion, which by their numbers we remember what each one commands us" (Garcilaso de la Vega [1609] 1985: II, 27).[8] This parallel would have troubled the Spanish priests from the very beginning, because they would have seen Inca law as simulating the Christian Ten Commandments; and simulation was one of the tools of the devil.

Garcilaso was not the first to notice this analogical relationship between legal khipu and Christian doctrine. The second reference to the early khipu-extirpation campaign deals specifically with this genre. In 1582, Bartolomé de Porras, Francisco Cocamaita, and Francisco Quiqua testify that the Incas maintained a record of laws and their punishments on khipu and that the Spaniards destroyed these khipu during the conquest (Porras et al. [1582] 1904: 284–285, 287). Unfortunately, the failure of the priests to document their activities in the early decades after their arrival, and the subsequent absence of "idolatrous" khipu from interactions between *khipukamayuq* and Spaniards, means that no further information about such khipu has surfaced. We may surmise, however, that the destruction of these legal khipu would have formed part of the extirpation campaign acknowledge many years later by the Third Lima Council.

I would argue that the Third Lima Council's reference to khipu practices in 1583 is rather insignificant historically in that it does not reflect any change in policy: both the prohibition of "idolatrous" khipu and the simultaneous use of this medium for ecclesiastical purposes had been in effect for many years by this time. The Third Lima Council's orders are merely an official statement about what had been common knowledge and common practice from the early years after the conquest. By 1583, the Spaniards had probably destroyed many idolatrous khipu and driven any surviving practices underground. At the same time, however, they continued to actively promote their use for ecclesiastical purposes.

The Adaptation of the Khipu for Ecclesiastical Use

In addition to the similarity in the numeric nature of Inca and Christian laws, the khipu also simulated certain Christian ecclesiastical objects such as the rosary, but this did not seem to incite any anxiety on the part of the Spaniards. In the early 1570s, Cristóbal de Molina compares the khipu to certain strings used by Spanish women when they prayed: "they are almost like the strings with which the old women in our Spain pray, except they

---

8 "De manera que cada hilo y nudo les traía a la memoria lo que en sí contenía, a semejanza de los mandamientos o artículos de nuestra Santa Fe Católica y obras de misericordia, que por el número sacamos lo que debajo de él se nos manda" (Garcilaso de la Vega [1609] 1985: II, 27).

have branches" (Molina [1570–1574] 1989: 58).[9] Around the same time, Fray Jerónimo Román y Zamora draws a similar parallel to the rosary and other cords used in ecclesiastical contexts: "This was a type of knot made on somewhat thick cords like *pater nosters*, or a rosary, or a cord of Saint Francis" (Román y Zamora [1575] 1897: 67).[10] In these texts, Molina and Román y Zamora point out the similarity between the Andean khipu and Spanish prayer strings merely as a means of describing the khipu in such a way that would help their readers visualize this object.

The function of the khipu in relation to ecclesiastical practices in the Andes, however, was not limited to this visual analogy. In the 1570s when Molina and Román y Zamora produced their descriptions of the khipu, native Andeans had already adapted them for Christian ecclesiastical uses. As early as 1555, for example, Archbishop Jerónimo de Loaysa ordered that native assistants maintain khipu records of births and illnesses for the priests (Durston 2008: 285).

From the very beginning of the conquest, one of the most prominent religious orders operating in Peru had been the Mercedarians.[11] It may be no coincidence therefore, that the Mercedarian missionary Diego de Porres[12] wrote the only known sixteenth-century document other than the Archbishop Loaysa's order in 1555 and the Third Council's *Cathecismo* of 1585 to explicitly and proactively advocate the use of khipu for ecclesiastical purposes. Carlos Assadourian suggests that this undated document, titled "Instruction and order that priests working in the indoctrination and conversion of the Indians must have" [Instrucción y orden que han de tener

---

9 "Casi son a modo de pavilos con que las biejas reçan en nuestra España; salvo ser ramales" (Molina [1570–1574] 1989: 58). In her study of khipu and confessional manuals, Harrison translates Molina's phrase "salvo ser ramales" rather liberally as "except that they are strings which twisted together come apart" (Harrison 2002: 267). Literally this expression would translate as "except they are strands." The meaning of the term "ramal" as "the end of a twisted cord" certainly supports Harrison's translation, but it does not account for the fact that this attribute is supposed to distinguish the khipu from the Spanish prayer cords, which would also have been made from twisted fiber. I would argue that in this context, "ramal" must be understood in its more general meaning as a part or division originating from or attached to something else. In the comparison with the Spanish prayer cords, then, "salvo ser ramales" would refer to the fact that the khipu consists of a main cord to which were attached a number of pendant cords. This interpretation is consistent both with the material characteristics of the khipu and Andean modes of thought.

10 "Esta era un género de ñudos hechos en unos cordones algo gruesos, á manera de *pater nosters*, ó de rosario, ó ñudos de cordón de San Francisco" (Román y Zamora [1575] 1897: 67).

11 In 1570, the Mercedarians claimed to be the first order to have arrived in Peru (Barriga 1933: I, 2), but the Dominicans also had a significant presence from the beginning.

12 Most scholars give the surname of this priest as Porres with an "e," which is consistent with almost every reference to him that appears in colonial documents. However, Eudoxio de Jesús Palacio cites a document in which this priest actually signs his name, and he spells it "Porras" (Palacio 1999: 159). Here, I maintain the "Porres" spelling in order to avoid confusion.

los sacerdotes que se ocuparen en la doctrina y conversión de los indios],
actually gave rise to the ecclesiastical practices observed by later chroniclers
and priests (Assadourian 1998: 31–32).

I have been unable to determine the date of this document in any
definitive way. The nature of the instructions and the trajectory of Porres's
career do not necessarily provide any indications as to when Porres might
have written it. He arrived in Peru as a soldier with the viceroy Antonio
de Mendoza in 1551, but began studying for the priesthood in 1552. He
was probably ordained in 1558 (Aparicio 2001: I, 196), and he dedicated
most of his career as a Mercedarian to the evangelization of the Indians. By
1570, Porres was working as the procurator of the Mercedarian convent in
Cuzco (Barriga 1933: III, 287). Based on the placement of the document
along with others from the 1580s that appear in Victor Barriga's collection
of sixteenth-century Mercedarian documents (Barriga 1933–1954: IV),
Severo Aparicio and Sabine Hyland date Porres's "Instruction" to some
time in the 1580s after the Third Lima Council of 1582–1583 (Aparicio
2001: I, 204; Hyland 2003: 136). However, most other scholars identify
it as having been written many years earlier, possibly as early as 1560:
Carlos Assadourian implies that Porres wrote the "Instructions" prior to
Acosta's exposure to ecclesiastical khipu in 1576 (Assadourian 1998: 31–
32); Carlos Estenssoro Fuchs dates it from between 1558 and 1565; John
Charles gives a date of 1560 (Charles 2007: 15); and Alan Durston believes
that Porres wrote it in the 1570s (Durston 2008: 285). Given the fact that
Porres was ordained in 1558, some of the earlier dates may be questionable;
but it is certainly possible that by this time Porres had already gained
sufficient experience on which to base these instructions. In any case, I
would argue that even if Porres wrote the instructions in the 1570s or
1580s, they reflect practices that had been in place for many years, as
indicated by the Jesuit observations in 1576 and 1578 that I will discuss
below.

One of Porres's instructions orders that everyone have their own copies
of prayer khipu: "Item. Further, every two weeks, let the constables check
all of the Christians, men and women, the prayers that they teach them,
if they know them or if they forget and if each one of them has their
khipu of it as it is ordered, and he who does not know and did not bring
a khipu, they give him three lashings" (Porres [c.1560] 1952: 34).[13] If
Porres's document reflects actual practice, the extent to which the khipu
was adapted for Christian ecclesiastical purposes in the religious life of the
Indians is remarkable.

13 "Yten más que de dos a dos semanas los alguaciles tomen quenta a todos los Xpianos y Xpianas las
    oraciones que les enseñan si las saben o se les olvida y si tiene cada uno su quipo para ello como
    dicho es y el que no la supiere y no truxere quipo le den tres azotes" (Porres [c.1560] 1952: 34).

One of the questions raised by the use of ecclesiastical khipu indicated in Porres's instructions and the Third Lima Council's order has to do precisely with the extent to which the members of any given community were versed in this particular form of khipu literacy. Many colonial sources indicate that in pre-Hispanic times various officials were each charged with maintaining different types of khipu records. Of course, most of these sources refer to official Inca *khipukamayuq*. Khipu record keeping at the local level also would have involved multiple genres, although they may not have been as extensive or varied in their content and conventions. I would suggest that the khipu conventions of community-level genres were not esoteric to the same extent as those developed for higher level imperial purposes such as the Inca biographies discussed in Chapter 3. In any case, Andean social roles are rather flexible in the way they are associated with cultural practices. Urton recounts an experience, for example, in which a woman from the community of Misminay near Cusco explained to him that only the men chewed coca; shortly thereafter an elderly woman joined them, asked Urton for some coca, placed it in her mouth, and began chewing it. He also notes the flexibility of gender roles in the same community (Urton 1981: 19–20). Any given practice, then, is not necessarily restricted to a particular class or group.

Although the purpose of Porres's instructions have to do with the evangelization of the Indians, they also stipulate certain procedures related to the administration of community affairs, particularly those that concerned their obligations to the church and to the hospital run by the priests:

Item. In addition, let the constables visit all the houses of the town each morning and each afternoon, and if they find a sick Indian, man or woman, let him take him to the hospital, and there watch over and care for him, and give him whatever may be necessary, and whoever may be weakened, encourage him and make him commend himself to God and give him something to eat, from the birds that they are obliged to give to the priest and to their *encomendero*, keeping an account so that it is deducted from their tribute. (Porres [c.1560] 1952: 31–32).[14]

These orders instruct the priests to make sure that the Indians maintain records of what is given to the sick in the hospital in order to subtract it from their tribute obligations owed to the priests. In another passage, it also orders that a khipu inventory be made of the possessions of those who die (Porres [c.1560] 1952: 36–37).

14 "Yten más que los alguaciles cada mañana, y cada tarde visiten todas las casas, del pueblo, y en hallando, yndio o yndia enferma lo lleben al hospital, y allí lo miren y curen, y den lo que ubiere menester, y el que estubiere muy debilitado, le animen y hagan que se encomiende a Dios y le den a comer, de las abes que son obligados, a dar al sacerdote y a su encomendero, tiniendo, su quenta, para que se desquente de su tasa" (Porres [c.1560] 1952: 31–32).

In some cases, the type of information to be recorded implies the kind of labor-tribute/census genre discussed in Chapter 5:

Item. The Christian Indian, man or woman, who being home is absent from the parish on Sunday and Wednesday, take from them a hen or a cuy or two or three pounds of wool as punishment, and this penalty that is exacted, let it be taken to the hospital of this town, and let the majordomo of the hospital take it as delivery and a deposit to give to the sick, having his khipu and account of from whom the penalty was taken and to which sick person it was given so that when the Father has come, he gives an account of it, and from he who is poor, do not take anything, [rather] give him five lashings there in the presence of everyone, and let the boys and girls gather together every day in the morning to pray and later go to help their parents and let them not gather together in the afternoon. (Porres [c.1560] 1952: 31).[15]

The information on this khipu was supposed to include the identity of the person who missed the indoctrination session, the type and quantity of the commodity levied as punishment, and to whom it was given in the hospital. This is precisely the kind of information that would have appeared on labor-service khipu in pre-Hispanic times. The *khipukamayuq* would have had to adapt the conventions of this genre in some ways, but the essential structure of labor-service khipu, which may have included data on both the service activities and the goods that it produced, would have served as the basis for these colonial records.

Porres's instructions also invoke the genre of calendrical khipu. The following passage instructs the Indians to maintain a khipu calendar of religious feasts and more generally the days and months of the year:

Item. Further, in the church is kept the account and calendar of the whole year with the holy days that they must observe all in order on a khipu and a tablet that declares that which is contained therein, which will take care to say and announce the holy days and fasts each Sunday and will make sure to count the days and months of said year together under penalty of being whipped if they are incorrect. (Porres [c.1560] 1952: 35).[16]

15 "Yten que el Yndio o Yndia Xpiano, que estando en su tierra faltare, el domingo, y miércoles, dicho de la doctrina, le lleben de pena una gallina, o cuy o dos o tres libras de lana, y esta pena que se llebaren se dé al ospital, deste pueblo, y se haga dello, entrega, y depositario, fu[turo], el mayordomo del dicho hospital, para que lo den a los enfermos, teniendo su quipo, y quenta, a quien se lleó la pena, y a que enfermo, se dió, para que benido el padre, le den quenta, dello, y al que, fuere pobre, no lleven, nada, denle cinco azotes, allí en presencia de todos, y los muchachos y muchachas se junten cada día, por las mañanas, a rrezar, y luego bayan ayudar a sus padres y no se junten a la tarde" (Porres [c.1560] 1952: 31).

16 "Yten más les queda en la dicha Iglesia la quenta y calendario de todo el año con las fiestas que an de guardar todo por su orden por un quipo y una tablilla que declara lo que alli se contiene lo qual tendrá cuydado fecho de decir y hechar las fiestas y ayunos cada domingo y tendrá cuidado de contar

Several chroniclers refer to an Inca calendar, and inevitably they link it to khipu record keeping (Molina [c.1570–1574] 1989: 58; Román y Zamora 1595: 67–68; Gutiérrez de Santa Clara [c.1596–1603] 1963: 548; Murúa [1611] 1987: 372, 376; Guaman Poma de Ayala [1615] 1987: 260[262], 361[363]). The nature of pre-Hispanic Inca calendrical accounting is not entirely clear, making the khipu's role in this activity even more difficult to ascertain. The Incas and other ethnic groups certainly made detailed astronomical observations that informed their methods of temporal accounting. In all cultures, such astronomical observations are inherently numerical in nature, and they are inevitably facilitated by some form of secondary medium used to maintain records over time. The Incas and other ethnic groups divided the year into lunar months and further into eight- and/or ten-day weeks (Zuidema 1977), but as Mariusz Ziolkowski points out, even in Cuzco itself, all forms of temporal accounting did not use a single calendrical system (Ziolkowski 1989: 129–130). The Incas seem to have made certain calendrical reforms, but these were relatively recent. Inca calendrical reforms may have eventually become a standard across various domains, but at the time of the conquest it seems that methods of temporal accounting were specific to the particular type of information recorded, although in many cases perhaps with some commonalities in their conceptual structures and semiotic conventions. Accordingly, the accounting of time was distributed across the various khipu genres that had a temporal dimension. Historiographical khipu seem to rely on a particular type of genealogical periodization (Brokaw 2003), and tribute khipu had an inherent but different calendrical dimension in that tribute obligations would have been divided into temporal units of three or four months, solar years, and two solar years (Chapter 5; Urton 2001). In creating a khipu record of the Christian calendar, then, the *khipukamayuq* could have adapted conventions from several different genres.

The inherent relationship between the astronomic phenomena on which calendrical data is based and religious or cosmological beliefs and practices may have led Spanish priests to include the most predominantly calendrical genre or genres in their early extirpation campaign. The colonial references that tie the khipu to explicit calendrical accounting of days and months are rather vague, and they don't appear until the 1570s. Thus, the Spanish chroniclers who describe pre-Hispanic calendrical khipu practices may have based their assertions more on their exposure to the colonial ecclesiastical khipu calendars than to pre-Hispanic genres. Martín de Murúa recounts his experience with one such khipu:

I will only relate, so that you see the curiosity of some Indians, that which I saw an old Indian and *curaca* do at a certain parish, where I was a priest. This Indian

los días y meses del dicho año juntamente fecho so pena de que será azotado si andubieren errados" (Porres [c.1560] 1952: 35).

had in a cord and a khipu the whole Roman calendar and all of the saints and holy days to be observed by their different months, and he told me that he knew all of it, and it turned out that he had asked a religious of my order who had been an indoctrinator there to read them and tell them to him, and as the Father was telling him, the Indian was setting it down in his khipu, and for the holy days to observe he placed a different, thicker knot, and thus it was a thing to behold how it was understood with the khipu, and he knew when the holy days were and their vigils. (Murúa [1611] 1987: 376).[17]

The Christian khipu calendar described by Murúa sounds remarkably similar to the khipu calendar described in Porres's instructions. Murúa explains that this calendrical khipu resulted from an interaction between the *khipukamayuq* and a member of his order who had worked previously in the same place. Murúa does not mention the name of the town or the identity of the other priest, but it could have been Porres himself. Both Porres and Murúa were Mercedarians, and they both seemed to have worked extensively in the south central highlands.[18] Thus, Murúa's text may indicate that at the very least Porres himself implemented his instructions. Murúa's account does not reveal in any definitive way who came up with the idea to create an ecclesiastical khipu calendar, but in either case the priest would probably not have been involved directly in determining the most appropriate conventions for this new colonial genre.

Although the use of khipu to record demographic, economic, and calendrical information would have potentially relied on well-established conventions from pre-Hispanic genres, Porres also orders the use of khipu for various ecclesiastical purposes that imply an apparently more radical departure from pre-Hispanic practices and possibly a direct intervention by the priests. The very first reference to khipu in the document mentions that the priest must give the *cacique* a khipu containing the orders of the Holy Synod, which Estenssoro Fuchs suggests probably refers to the First Lima Council that met from 1551 to 1552 (Estenssoro Fuchs 2003: 217):

And afterwards there in the presence of all, read them and declare to them that which the Holy Synod orders and give it to them on a khipu, to the *cacique*, so that

17 "Sólo referiré, para que se note la curiosidad de algunos indios, lo que vi en un indio viejo y *curaca* en cierta doctrina, donde fui cura, el cual tenía en un cordel y *quipu* todo el calendario romano y todos los santos y fiestas de guardar por sus meses distintos, y me dijo que lo sabía aquello, y fue que a un religioso de mi orden, curiosos, que había sido doctrinario allí, le había dicho se los leyese y diese a entender, y como el Padre se lo iba diciendo el indio iba en su *quipu* asentándolo, y a las fiestas de guardar ponía el nudo diferente y más grueso, y así era cosa de admiración cómo se entendía por el *quipu*, y sabía cuándo venían las fiestas y las vigilias de ellas" (Murúa [1611] 1987: 376).

18 Espinoza Soriano states that Porres worked indoctrinating the Indians in communities from several areas including Cuzco and Huamanga (Espinoza Soriano 1980: 150). Although most of the information we have about Murúa comes from his own work, he also served in the same capacity in this same general area.

they cannot pretend ignorance of what it obliges and orders them to do. (Porres [c.1560] 1952: 27).[19]

This passage implies that the priest actually creates this khipu. Subsequent paragraphs contain the same implication. Another passage, for example, instructs the priest to give the Indians khipu that record five prayers and the commandments:

Item. Further, there in the presence of all, give them the four prayers that they are obliged to know, and the commandments on khipu just as they pray with their pauses and syllables, and order them that no Indian old or young will pray without such a khipu so that from it they know the said prayers, and that they always bring it with them wherever they go, even if they are forced to leave their land, so that they have the order of Christians and they say the said prayers accurately wherever they are asked to do so and that which each prayer means. (Porres [c.1560] 1952: 28).[20]

As indicated by sixteenth-century catechisms and documents produced by colonial missionaries, the four prayers would have been Our Father, Hail Mary, the Apostles' Creed, and Salve Regina (*Doctrina* 1583: 1r-3v; Martínez [1576] 1954: 286; Charles 2007: 15). Although "mandamientos" [commandments] appears without a definite article, suggesting a more general reference, it certainly would have included the Ten Commandments. As Charles explains, confessional manuals instructed penitents to examine their conscience by going through the Commandments one by one (Charles 2007: 17).

The use of Andean media to record this kind of Christian ecclesiastical information was not limited to the khipu. Native Andeans also adapted for this purpose the *yupana* practices associated with khipu accounting. The Dominican Francisco de la Cruz, for example, observes the use of small stones in an ecclesiastical context (Abril Castelló 1992: I, 630: cited in Estenssoro Fuchs 2003: 217–218). In 1599, The Jesuit Pablo de Arriaga also explains that the Indians learned the prayers with their stones: "the whole time that a Father is in a town, in the morning upon awaking all the people gather together in the curacy, and they sit in circles according to the need of each one, they learn the prayers by means of their stones."

19 "Y luego [de reunirlos] allí, en presencia de todos, leerles y declararles lo que manda la sancta sínodo, y dárselo por quipo, al cacique, por que no pretendan ignorancia de lo que allí les obliga y manda" (Porres [c.1560] 1952: 27). In the passage cited here, I have modified the text to correct what appear to be obvious errors in the transcription.

20 "Iten más, allí en presencia, de todos, dalles las quatro oraciones que son obligados a saver, y mandamientos, por quipo, asi como lo rrezan por sus pausas y sílavas y mandalles que ningun yndio biejo ni muchacho daran sin el tal quipo para que por allí sepan las dichas oraciones, y que siempre lo traigan consigo doquiera que fueren, aunque vayan a fuerza, de sus tierras, para que tengan rregla de Xpianos y den rrazones de las dichas oraciones donde se las preguntaren y lo que cada oración quiere dezir" (Porres [c.1560] 1952: 28).

(Arriaga [1599] 1974: 728).[21] And an anonymous history of the Jesuits in Peru written in 1600 observes the use of small stones to learn the fifteen mysteries (Anonymous [1600] 1944: II, 101–102). These later observations appear to reflect further developments in the ecclesiastical practices referred to by Porres many years earlier.

Porres's instructions attempt to integrate the khipu thoroughly into the religious life of the Indians. It is unclear what kind of influence these instructions, or others like them, might have had, but the use of ecclesiastical khipu do not originate with them. As in the case of the Third Lima Council's order, Porres's instructions are clearly informed by a knowledge that could have derived only from experience with such khipu. The instructions are designed to help promulgate what evidently had been a successful practice in some communities. In most cases, actual ecclesiastical khipu practices were probably more limited in scope than those described by Porres. If every colonial parish had followed them, even more documentary evidence of ecclesiastical khipu would probably have come to light by now. Nevertheless, the kinds of practices described by Porres laid the foundation for further developments apparent in later Jesuit documents.

Jesuit Involvement with Ecclesiastical Khipu

Although Mercedarians and Dominicans observe the earliest use of ecclesiastical khipu, most references to such practices appear in Jesuit sources. The only known evidence of ecclesiastical khipu practices prior to the arrival of the Jesuits in 1570 are the order issued by Archbishop Loaysa in 1555 and, possibly, the instructions written by Porres, which may date to the 1560s; but this paucity of documentation is not surprising. Estenssoro Fuchs explains that there exists very little documentation related to the conversion of the Indians in Peru prior to the Third Lima Council, in part because earlier religious documents were often discarded or destroyed when they were superseded. The Third Lima Council established an enduring orthodoxy that resulted in a subsequently more thorough documentary record of evangelization efforts (Estenssoro Fuchs 2003: 32–34). Furthermore, the Jesuits, who played an important role in the Third Lima Council, documented their activities to a greater extent and in more detail than other orders. The Jesuits also spearheaded an initiative to establish the first printing press in Peru, which began operation in 1584 immediately after the Third Lima Council. In fact, among the first documents

---

21 "Todo el tiempo questá el Padre en un pueblo se junta toda la gente, por la mañana en amaneciendo, a la doctrina, y sentarse en ruedas diferentes según la necesidad de cada uno, deprenden las oraciones por sus piedras" (Arriaga [1599] 1974: 728).

to be printed in Peru were the materials produced by the Third Lima Council.

José de Acosta was one of the major figures of the Third Lima Council, but he and his fellow Jesuits were relatively recent arrivals. Spain did not allow the Jesuits to travel to the Indies until 1566, and the first group did not leave for Peru until 1568. Acosta arrived with the third group in 1572 (Mateos 1954: x). The Jesuits were committed to the conversion of the Indians, but many of them resisted any direct involvement in the running of *doctrinas* or missionary parishes, ecclesiastical units set up to evangelize the Indian population of a particular geographical area. They felt that the material and political exigencies of this activity were not conducive to the observance of many of the Jesuit Order's rules, and in some cases completely incompatible with them (Piras 2004: 116). Nevertheless, in 1570 the general of the Jesuit Order approved the participation of the Peruvian Jesuits in the running of *doctrinas* on a provisional basis under certain conditions. But by 1573, Toledo was already complaining to the Crown that the Jesuits had abandoned the *doctrinas* over which they had taken charge in 1570. In 1576, José de Acosta was appointed *provincial* of the Jesuits in Peru, and he convened a meeting in which he was able to convince the members of his order to accept *doctrinas* on a provisional basis as the need arose. At this time, the Jesuits agreed to take on the responsibility for a *doctrina* in Juli (Piras 2004: 116–117).

Pierre Duviols attributes the use of the khipu in the evangelization of the Indians to the Jesuits at Juli (Duviols 1971: 243), but it is very clear that the Indians in this area were already using ecclesiastical khipu by the time the Jesuits arrived. Diego Martínez, who arrived at Juli with the first group of Jesuits in late October of 1576, recorded his observations of ecclesiastical khipu on November 11th of the same year:

I forgot to say how I find these boys to be much better able to learn the doctrine than I thought; some of them know how to cross themselves in just one week, and the Lord's Prayer, the Hail Mary, the Apostle's Creed, and the Salve Regina in the language, by chance in the Sunday procession they went along singing it all, divided into thirds in the procession, and many men and women, and the boys and girls walked around all day with their khipu, like students that repeat a lesson. When we arrived here, the Spaniards said that there would be no way to indoctrinate the Indians except by force. Blessed be the Lord, who gives so much love to the Company [of Jesus]. (Martínez [1576] 1954: 286).[22]

22 "Olvidádose me ha de decir cómo en estos muchachos que aprenden la doctrina hallo mucha más habilidad de la que pensé; algunos dellos en una semana sólo, saben persignarse y santiguarse, y el Padrenuestro, Avemaría, Credo y Salve en la lengua, de suerte que en la procesión del domingo lo fueron todo cantando, repartidos por tercios en la procesión, y muchos hombres y mujeres, y los niños y niñas andan todo el día con sus quipos, como estudiantes que repiten lición. Cuando

José de Acosta's first annual report as head of the Jesuits in Peru in 1576 also contains several other accounts from different areas that describe the use of khipu by Indians to record the things they learned of Christian doctrine and the prayers they had to memorize:

The following Sunday I saw all day long the procedure followed in indoctrinating the Indians. In the morning, the Indians came to a large plaza that is in front of the church, and there divided into choruses of twelve or fifteen people each, the men separate from the women, they said prayers and doctrine, having one as teacher that taught them, and they went along passing some khipu or registers that they had, made of cords with knots, by which they remember what they learn, as we do with writing. (Acosta [1576] 1954: 287).[23]

In the mornings and the afternoons, the children, the old men, and the old women, which are many, come, and one of the four *ayllus* one week, and another another week, and even the *caciques* come with the children to learn the catechism, which they enjoy so much, that the old men spend all morning in groups of four and groups of six, continuously repeating it with their khipu; and the boys are so clever and desirous to know it that, it is true, they surpass the students of Cuzco; and we praise God for how well they accept it. (López [1576] 1954: 275).[24]

And some eighty- and ninety-year-old men come to me crying and showing me some cords, the knots with which they indicate the things that they had learned of the doctrine in those days. (Plaza [1576] 1954: 280).[25]

These references come from reports of ecclesiastical *visitas* or accounts of shorter missions in which the priests would travel to various locations from their home base without setting up a permanent *doctrina*. These Jesuit

---

llegamos aquí nos decían los españoles que no habría remedio de traer los indios a la doctrina, sino con alguaciles. Bendito sea el Señor, que tanto amor les da a la Compañía" (Martínez [1576] 1954: 286).

23 "El domingo siguiente vi por todo el dia el orden que se guardaba en doctrinar a los indios. Por la mañana venían los indios a una plazuela grande que hay delante la iglesia, y allí repartidos por coros de doce en doce o de quince en quince, los hombres aparte y las mujeres aparte, decían oraciones y doctrina, teniendo uno como maestro que les enseña, y ellos van pasando unos quipos o registros que tienen, hechos de cordeles con nudos, por donde se acuerdan de lo que aprenden, como nosotros por escrito" (Acosta [1576] 1954: 287).

24 "Acuden mañana y tarde los niños, viejos y viejas, que son muchos, y uno de los quatro ayllos, una semana y otro otra, y los mismos caciques vienen con los niños a aprender el catecismo, de que gustan tanto, que están toda la mañana los viejos de quatro en quatro y de seis en seis, maceando en él por sus quipos; y los muchachos son tan hábiles y tan deseosos de saberlo que, cierto, hazen ventaja a los estudiantes de Cuzco; y alabamos a Dios cuán bien lo toman" (López [1576] 1954: 275).

25 "Y algunos viejos de ochenta y noventa años acudían a mí llorando y mostrándome unos cordeles, los nudos con que tenían señaladas las cosas que habían aprendido de la doctrina en aquellos días" (Plaza [1576] 1954: 280).

reports make it very clear that the process of evangelization had already begun. López, for example, explains that the Indians already knew some of the catechism (López [1576] 1954: 275). Carlos Assadourian states that the ecclesiastical khipu observed by Acosta and the other Jesuits in 1576 were actually the result of Porres's instructions discussed above (Assadourian 1998: 31–32). In any case, the adaptation of the khipu for ecclesiastical purposes in Juli, which up to that point had been a major center of Dominican evangelization (Estenssoro Fuchs 2003: 220), and in other areas as well, had already taken place by 1576 when the Jesuits became more engaged in *doctrina* work. They merely took over where others had left off.

The Jesuit observations give no indication of how, when, or who first adapted the khipu for ecclesiastical use. Carlos Estenssoro Fuchs discusses this issue as if the only question was which of the religious orders first introduced this medium into the Christian ecclesiastical context (Estenssoro Fuchs 2003: 219–220), but secular clergy also engaged in evangelization efforts. Furthermore, the Andeans themselves may have begun adapting the khipu for use in ecclesiastical contexts. Throughout the sixteenth and seventeenth centuries, there were never enough priests to effectively serve the Andean population (Mills 1997: 9, 18). John Charles explains that in order to compensate for this lack of personnel, Spanish priests relied heavily on local leaders to run many of the day-to-day activities of the early *doctrinas*, and these activities included the teaching of doctrine (Charles 2007: 15, 19). In this context of loose supervision, local leaders, many of whom were *khipukamayuq*, inevitably would have drawn on the resources available to them in fulfilling their duties; and among the tools at their disposal were the highly flexible and adaptable conventions of the khipu that they used for similar purposes in their own internal administration. The general lack of training in alphabetic literacy among the Andean population would have made the use of khipu for recording catechistic information particularly helpful to the overburdened priests (Charles 2007: 18).

Identifying the adaptation of the khipu for ecclesiastical use as originally a native Andean endeavor does not mean that Spanish priests did not subsequently influence or intervene in this process. However, it is unclear to what extent they may have done so. Andean communities were using the khipu in an ecclesiastical context prior to the arrival of the Jesuits, which means that in addition to the secular clergy, Dominicans and Mercedarians could have been involved in this innovation. If the Jesuits made any novel contribution to ecclesiastical khipu practices, it would have been to the development of a confessional khipu genre; but even this is somewhat doubtful.

It is unclear to what extent Spanish priests actually confessed Indian converts in the sixteenth century. The First Lima Council, which took place from 1551 to 1552, actually orders that the Indians confess once every year (Vargas Ugarte 1951–1954: I, 19). However, Estenssoro Fuchs explains that with the exception of the Jesuits, Spanish priests did not generally consider confession to be absolutely necessary. This does not mean that they did not confess Indians at all, but often such confessions were limited to the native lords or *curacas* (Estenssoro Fuchs 2003: 206–207). Interestingly, Porres's instructions discussed above do not specifically mention the use of the khipu for confession. In fact, as Estenssoro Fuchs points out (Estenssoro Fuchs 2003: 220), the first reference to confessional khipu appears in a report from Juli in the Jesuit Annual Letter from 1578 prepared by José de Acosta:

An Indian approached a Father on his knees, with a great quantity of khipus, which are accounts that they bring of their sins, saying that he wanted to do a general confession, because he had always omitted a sin, and that some days previously there had appeared to him one night a very majestic lady along with many others and she said to him: Son, so many years you have kept this sin quiet, all the confessions that you have done do not benefit you; see to it that you confess well, that these who come here will be witnesses. The Indian confessed with such feeling and order about his whole life that, according to what that Father said, you could very well believe that the Queen of heaven had been his teacher. (Acosta [1578] 1954: 296).[26]

Although this is the first known reference to a confessional khipu, it does not indicate in any way that the Jesuits necessarily instituted this practice among the Indians. In fact, the Jesuit who recounts the episode portrays himself as merely an observer. Given the recency of the Jesuit arrival at this point and the rather elaborate nature of this confessional khipu, it is doubtful that the Jesuits initiated this particular practice (Estenssoro Fuchs 2003: 220). Furthermore, the fact that such references appear for the first time in Jesuit sources is not a surprise, because earlier ecclesiastical records by non-Jesuits is rather sparse.

Citing the Jesuits' annual letter from 1602, Alan Durston argues that the Jesuits in La Paz actually instructed Indians in the use of confessional

---

26 "Un indio se llegó a un Padre hincado de rodillas, con una gran suma de quipos, que son unos memoriales que traen de sus pecados, diciendo que se quería confesar generalmente, porque había callado siempre un pecado, y que tantos días había le aparesció una noche una señora con otros muchos de gran majestad, y le dijo: Hijo, tantos años ha que callas tal pecado, todas las confesiones que has hecho no te aprovechan; mira que te confieses bien, que estos que vienen aquí han de ser testigos. El indio se confesó con tanto sentimiento y orden de toda su vida, que, sigún decía aquel Padre, se podía bien creer que la Reina del cielo había sido la maestra" (Acosta [1578] 1954: 296).

khipu (Durston 2008: 286–287), but the document does not actually say this:

The workers of the Indian brothers and primarily of the blind who know well the doctrine and being instructed particularly for this cause, they go around the town teaching Christian doctrine to each person, what they must pray each day, how they must confess and prepare for communion and ultimately encouraging all the rest by whatever means they are able to confess and prepare to serve Our Lord. These Indians instruct the others to do general confessions with khipu; and the number of these general confessions and others that are done by necessity for never having confessed in one's life or in a large part of it, is so great that a Father who keeps track of all such confessions that he does in a given year, there are very few days in which [such a confession] was lacking; for they tell me that one Saturday of the year, he had ten of these confessions to do. (Cabredo [1602] 1986: 262–263).[27]

The instruction received by the Indian assistants from Spanish priests refers only explicitly to doctrinal information. It does not say that the Jesuits trained these assistants to "teach other Indians how to confess with quipus" (Durston 2008: 286–287). The instruction on how to confess with khipu takes place among the Indians themselves. I would suggest that this passage actually implies a more passive acceptance by the Jesuits of ecclesiastical khipu practices developed by the Indians themselves, possibly with the encouragement and perhaps some intervention by earlier priests.

The active promotion of indigenous adaptations of the khipu for ecclesiastical use may have originated with the Dominicans, the Mercedarians, and/or the secular clergy, but the Jesuits do seem to have advocated such practices to an even greater degree, particularly the use of confessional khipu. However, it is impossible to corroborate in any definitive way claims that the Jesuits were the *main* promoters of confessional khipu (Durston 2008: 286), because so little documentation exists from other orders. The use of confessional khipu seems to have emerged along with the other practices described by Porres, but the Jesuit emphasis on confession as part

---

27 "Ayúdanse aquí los obreros de los indios cofrades y principalmente de los ciegos, que saben bien la doctrina y siendo instruídos particularmente para este effecto, andan en el pueblo enseñando cada uno de la doctrina cristiana, lo que han de rezar cada día, cómo han de confesar y disponer para la comunión y al fin despertando a todos los demás por los medios que su capacidad les dicta para qué se confiessen y dispongan para servir a Nuestro Señor. Instruyen estos indios a los demás a que se confiessen generalmente por sus *quipos*; y el número de estas confesiones generales y de otras que se hacen por necessidad de no averse confesado en toda la vida o en gran parte de ella bien, es tan grande, que tomando un Padre muy a su cuidado las que en un año hacía, en muy pocos días faltó en la qüenta, pues me dicen que un sábado de los de entre año tuvo dies confessiones que hacer de éstas" (Cabredo [1602] 1986: 262–263).

of the sacrament of penance would have given additional impetus to the development of this particular genre.

In addition to recording sins for confession, the use of khipu to record the essential components of the catechism also would have been particularly attractive to the Jesuits, because their preferred evangelical procedures did not involve sustained daily contact with the members of the indigenous communities with which they worked. In spite of the fact that the Jesuits maintained their *doctrina* at Juli, most of their activities consisted of missions in which they conducted short visits to a number of different communities. As Pablo de Arriaga explains in his annual letter of 1599, this method meant that every community received a visit four times a year (Arriaga [1599] 1974: 727). Even in *doctrinas* with priests in full-time residence, however, they were never able to meet the demand for trained personnel (Charles 2007: 15). Thus, the Jesuits would have relied on local leaders to an even greater degree than the secular clergy or missionaries from other orders. Furthermore, the language barrier only reinforced the important role played by native helpers.

The Jesuits, then, do not seem to have played a role in the original adaptation of the khipu for ecclesiastical purposes, but they quickly recognized the usefulness of this medium. By the early 1580s, the Jesuits had become seriously engaged in evangelization efforts in Peru, and they dominated the Third Lima Council. As noted above, the *Tercero cathecismo* produced by the Third Lima Council and published in 1585 explicitly instructs Indians to create khipu records of their sins for use in confession:

The first thing, my son, you must think hard on your sins and make a khipu of them: just as you make a khipu of what you give and what is owed when you are in charge of the storehouse, in the same way make a khipu of what you have done against God and against your neighbor, and how many times: if it is many or few. And you must not only confess your actions but also your thoughts: when, if you were able, you acted on them, if you desired to sin with a woman, and you looked at her for this reason: if you wanted to steel the blanket or the sheep of another, but you did not so that the *corregidor* would not punish you, if you got mad at the priest or the *curaca* and you did not dare harm him, but in your heart you wanted to do it. All this my children, you must tell, because men are also condemned by the sins of the heart that are not seen. After thinking and making the khipu of your sins following the ten commandments or the best way you know how, you must ask God for forgiveness with much pain for having offended him. (*Tercero cathecismo* [1585] 1985: [f.67v.-f.68r.] 482–483).[28]

---

28 "Lo primero, hijo mío, has de pensar bien tus peccados, y hacer quipo dellos: como hazes quipo, quando eres tambocamayo, de lo q[ue] das ydelo q[ue] deuen: assi haz quipo delo que has hecho, contra Dios y contra tu proximo, y quantas vezes: si muchas, o si pocas. Y no solo has de dezir tus obras: sino también tus pensamientos malos: quando, si pudieras, los pusieras por obra si desseaste

The instruction draws a parallel between the administrative khipu used in community storehouses and colonial Christian penance khipu for use in keeping track of the type and number of sins committed. The pre-Hispanic genre of legal khipu might have been a closer analogy, but the Spaniards were not as aware of this genre. As noted above, Spanish priests had attempted to destroy this genre of khipu from the very beginning (Porras et al. [1582] 1904: 287). Even without Inca institutions, legal khipu may have persisted for some time, as was the case with historiographic khipu, but given the "idolatrous" nature of these objects, the *khipukamayuq* would not have publicized these particular record-keeping activities. In any case, the Third Lima Council's order to employ khipu for confession also represents more a recognition of established practices than the promulgation of a new policy. In fact, the order is rather limited in that it mentions only confessional khipu, leaving out any reference to the calendrical and catechistic khipu.

It is important to keep in mind that neither Porres's document nor the Third Lima Council's order is an account of actual events, but rather an instruction to be carried out; and there were no guarantees that such orders would be followed. But the observations made by Acosta and his Jesuit colleagues in 1576 reveal that in fact Andean communities were engaging in the kinds of practices encouraged by Porres's instructions. The Third Lima Council's order to employ confessional khipu, then, constitutes more an official recognition of common practices than the institution of a new policy. At the very least, Porres's instructions and the Third Lima Council's order recognize the fact that some communities had adapted the khipu for ecclesiastical use, and they advocate that the same be done in others.

As I will explain below, this does not mean that the Jesuits did not intervene more directly in the further development of ecclesiastical khipu genres. However, it is important to keep in mind that neither the missionary practices of the Spaniards nor the reaction by the Andeans was always uniform or monolithic. Durston's study of the interaction between Spanish priests and Andean communities reveals a great deal of variation in the details of parish life even within the Jesuit order itself (Durston 2008). Thus, the promulgation of a certain practice in one document or the observation of certain ecclesiastical khipu practices in one town does not necessarily constitute evidence of more widespread phenomena. The evidence does

peccar con fulana, y la miraste para esso: si quisieras hurtar la manta, o el carnero de otro, y lo dexaste porque no te castigasse el Corregidor, si te enojaste con el Padre, o con el Curaca, y no te atreviste a herille, pero en tu coraçon quisieras hazello. Todo esto hijos mios, aueys de dezillo: porque también por los peccados del coraçon que no se veen, se condenan los hombres. Despues de auer to pe[n]sado, y hecho quippo de tus peccados por los diez mandamientos, o como mejor supieres, has de pedir a Dios perdon con mucho dolor de auelle offendido" (*Tercero cathecismo* [1585] 1985: [f.67v.-f.68r.] 482–483).

suggest the widespread adaptation of the khipu for ecclesiastical use, but the particular methods and conventions that constituted this adaptation probably varied from one place to another.

Religious Syncretism and Innovations in Khipu Conventions

One of the main concerns of Spanish missionaries throughout the colonial period was the survival of indigenous religious concepts and practices under the guise of Christianity. Often initial jubilation that the Indians had readily converted to Christianity and accepted its beliefs gave way to frustration that they actually (mis)understood Christian doctrine in their own terms according to their traditional beliefs.[29] In many cases, of course, they also secretly continued to engage in traditional practices in addition to their official Christian obligations. Andean culture did not distinguish between the secular and the divine to the same extent as the Spanish; but even so the analogic relationship between indigenous cosmology and Christian theology would have been obvious to the Indians, if for no other reason than that the Spaniards explicitly pointed it out to them. Thus, given the fact that khipu practices were caught up in an Andean cosmology, the use of this medium in the Christian ecclesiastical context would have contributed to the conservation of "idolatries" in less direct ways than the explicit recording of information. The conceptual assimilation of Christian doctrine into the paradigmatic information structures that characterized much Andean knowledge and the structural conventions of khipu semiosis would inevitably imbue that doctrine with an indigenous significance. In other words, the transpositioning or rearticulation of European religious concepts using the Andean medium of the khipu would inflect those concepts with a significance derived from indigenous cosmology and vice versa. This phenomenon occurs in the cognitive domain anyway: the assimilation of anything new inevitably relates it to what is already known. Assimilation is not a purely receptive process but rather a creative one that accommodates the new within the context of the old. The use of a secondary medium focuses or channels this accommodation in particularly regimented ways.

The references cited above indicate that the Andeans adapted the khipu for a wide variety of functions in Christian ecclesiastical contexts. The khipu recording Christian doctrine to which Plaza refers (Plaza [1576] 1954: 280) would have been drawn from a fairly standardized text designed to teach the Indians the basics of Christian theology, which included essential prayers, the commandments, and other doctrinal information. It is impossible to determine to what extent the Andeans transpositioned the instruction of

---

29 For studies of sixteenth- and seventeenth-century evangelization efforts, see MacCormack 1991, Duviols 1971, Mills 1997, and Estenssoro Fuchs 2003.

the priests onto their khipu, exactly how they did so, or the relationship between these ecclesiastical khipu and pre-Hispanic khipu genres. In many cases ecclesiastical khipu would have drawn from the conventions of various pre-Hispanic genres: historiographic or "narrative" khipu and legal khipu perhaps being the most obvious possibilities. If the general principles of khipu semiosis are the same for the various genres, as I have suggested elsewhere in relation to khipu historiography (Chapter 3; Brokaw 2003), then much of the religious information recorded on the khipu would have been organized conceptually according to paradigmatic structures that would make the information compatible with the material conventions available to the *khipukamayuq*. However, given the semiotic heterogeneity that characterized khipu semiosis, the adaptation of the khipu for new types of information also may have involved a certain degree of innovation in khipu conventions.

The most explicit reference to ecclesiastical khipu conventions suggesting a specific type of semiosis appears to indicate a transpositioning of phonographic conventions by ecclesiastical khipu genres. In the *Instructions* cited above, Porres states: "there in the presence of all, give them the four prayers that they are obliged to know, and the commandments on khipu just as they pray with their pauses and syllables" (Porres [c. 1560] 1952: 28). Porres's intriguing reference to "pauses and syllables" can be read as implying syllabic conventions and a kind of metrics. In other words, the khipu texts of the prayers should record the pauses and syllables of their oral performance. If Porres is actually referring to syllabic conventions, then these khipu were almost certainly the result of direct interventions by Spanish priests. However, it is unclear whether or not this passage reflects an understanding of actual ecclesiastical khipu or even whether Porres envisioned priests engaged in the actual production of such khipu. No evidence has surfaced that would clarify this issue. Some Spanish priests may have encouraged the development of syllabic and metric conventions in ecclesiastical khipu, but the extent of such projects remains unclear.

Experiments with these types of khipu conventions may have given rise to certain apparently anomalous khipu that appear in the late sixteenth and early seventeenth centuries. Khipu conventions involving pauses and syllables effectively introduce a basis for the kind of metrics that would have been conducive to recording the poem reproduced by the Inca Garcilaso from Blas Valera's lost history and discussed in Chapter 4 (Garcilaso de la Vega [1609] 1966: 127–128). Given the fact that regular meter does not seem to have been a feature of organic Quechua-language poetics (Mannheim 1991: 125), the metric nature of the conventions of the syllabic liturgical khipu described by Porres's could have laid the groundwork for the possibility of creating a Quechua-language metric poetry. Very little information exists about this particular line of development in khipu conventions. They quickly disappear from the colonial archive, only to reappear oddly enough in Raimundo de Sangro's mid-eighteenth-century treatise, *Lettera apologetica* (1750), which defends the idea that the khipu constituted a writing system. Sangro actually describes a system of syllabic conventions that may have originated with Jesuit projects such as that of Blas Valera. An experimental or ideological project such as this would have had little chance of catching on at the popular level. It is surely no coincidence then that the sample syllabic text offered by Sangro happens to be the very same poem that Garcilaso transcribed from Blas Valera's history (Sangro [1750] 2002: 182–183).

However, the Jesuits also observe other atypical conventions in confessional khipu. Cabredo's annual letter from 1602 includes a reference to a confessional khipu that contains objects such as stones, bones, and feathers:

It was a marvelous thing to see the khipu that he made to confess. These Indians call *quipo* many cords tied together at one end and loose at the other in the form of scourges. In each of these, they tie their knots according to the account that each one has, in such a way that in one of these khipu, an Indian will have formulated an account with one-hundred [knots] so that he will never be able to forget that which he has once encoded in his *quipo*. This Indian made it six rods long with twisted cords and at intervals a thread that crossed it and some signs of stones or bones or feathers according to the nature of the sin that he had to confess, so that in the four days that he spent confessing, he did not doubt in a single thing and by touching the *quipo* and the signs placed in it, he confessed with such clarity and accuracy as if he had eyes and very great understanding, crying over his sins and detesting the idolatries with which the devil had deceived him. (Cabredo [1602] 1986: 214–215).[30]

According to the observer who recounts this episode, this confessional khipu employed objects such as stones and feathers in order to indicate different sins. The insertion of such objects in khipu strings is extremely rare. None of the archaeological specimens with which I am familiar exhibit this feature.

---

30 "Era cosa maravillosa ver el *quipo* que hizo para confessarse. Llaman estos indios *quipo* muchos cordones juntos atados por una cabeça y sueltos por otra en fomra de ramales de diciplina. En cada uno déstos atan sus ñudos según la quënta que cada uno tiene, de suerte que en un *quipo* de éstos tendrá un indio armada qüenta con ciento, sin que se pueda jamás olvidar de lo que una vez señaló en su *quipo*. Hízolo esto indio de seis varas de cordel torcido y de trecho en trecho un hilo que lo atravesava y algunas señales de piedras o güezos o plumas, conforme a la materia del peccado que avía de confessar, sin que en quatro días que gastó en confessarse, dudasse en cosa alguna y por el tiento del *quipo* y de las señales puetas en él, se confessó con tanta distinción y puntualidad como si tuviera ojos y muy grande entendimiento, llorando sus pecados y detestando las idolatrías con que el demonio le avía engañado" (Cabredo [1602] 1986: 214–215).

It may be significant that the Indian who made this khipu was blind. He may have begun inserting objects into the cords as tactile conventions in order to compensate for his inability to see the more traditional color coding. Cabredo suggests that blind *khipukamayuq* played a prominent role as assistants to the Spanish priests in their indoctrination of the Indians and that they taught other members of the community to confess using khipu (Cabredo [1602] 1986: 262–263). If these blind *khipukamayuq* played a role in the instruction of other Indians, then the practice of inserting objects into khipu may have become common in some communities even for those who were not blind.

As far as I know, the only khipu to exhibit these kinds of conventions derive from post-colonial contexts. At least one of the two khipu described briefly in the eighteenth-century drama *Ollantay* seem to employ this type of convention. Elsewhere I have argued that the understanding that informs the references to khipu in *Ollantay* derives from an exposure to the conventions of eighteenth-century khipu practices, possibly even ecclesiastical genres (Brokaw 2006). The modern *khipukamayuq* from Taquile insert small pieces of wood into their khipu (Mackey 1990b; Prochaska 1990: 95–98), and the patrimonial khipu from Rapaz contain inserted objects as well (Ruiz Estrada 1982). These khipu are not necessarily ecclesiastical in nature, but their conventions may have derived originally from the innovations in semiotic conventions that arose in the development of ecclesiastical khipu during the sixteenth and seventeenth centuries.

One possible exception is a khipu of dubious origin that Charles Wiener claims to have found in Paramonga in 1876 (Figure 7.1; Wiener [1880] 1993: 826). This khipu appears to contain tufts of wool tied into the cords. What Wiener identifies as two khipu is actually a single specimen that was displayed at the Peruvian exhibit of the Philadelphia World Exposition in 1876. Wiener lifted the illustration from an article that described the exhibit and contained several drawings of objects on display (Figure 7.2; Saffray 1876). He cut the illustration in two and passed it off as two separate khipu in his book. Wiener was actually in Paramonga at some point in the late summer of 1876. In theory, he could have found this khipu there, but it does not appear in his inventory (Wiener [1880] 1993: 92). Furthermore, at this point it would have been difficult to get the khipu to Philadelphia by late May or early June for the Exposition. At this time, Peruvian archaeology was still in its infancy, and very few archaeological khipu had been discovered. No other record of this khipu or its current whereabouts exists, but, assuming it is authentic, I would argue that it was most likely an ethnographic or patrimonial khipu acquired from a contemporary community rather than an archaeological specimen.

The adaptation of the khipu for ecclesiastical use would have been conducive to these kinds of innovations, but some elements of Christian

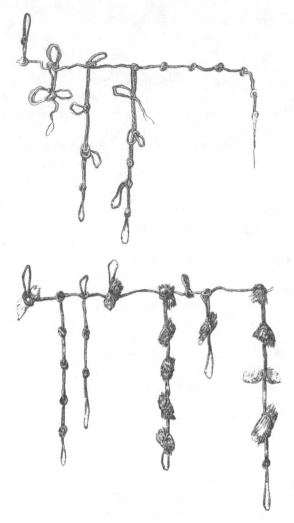

Figure 7.1. "Two" khipu that Charles Wiener allegedly discovered in Paramonga
(From Wiener [1880] 1993: 826).

doctrine would have lent themselves readily to the conventions of pre-
Hispanic genres. Any native Andean familiar with the numeric characteristics of Inca laws, for example, would inevitably make the association with
the ten Christian commandments. The numerically sophisticated khipu
could have encoded the Ten Commandments with relative ease (Charles
2007: 17–18). In fact, *khipukamayuq* could have easily adapted the color
and number conventions of the Inca legal khipu as described by the Inca

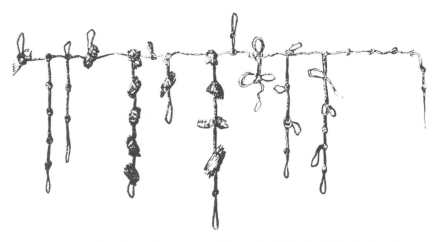

Figure 7.2. Khipu from the Peruvian exhibit at the Philadelphia World Expo in 1876 (Saffray 1876).

Garcilaso (Garcilaso de la Vega [1609] 1985: II, 27) to record the Ten Commandments by creating new color and number codes or recoding where necessary the signs that the Inca had used for their own laws. In some cases, then, ecclesiastical khipu would have employed many of the very same conventions on which "idolatrous" khipu had relied. If community-level *khipukamayuq* had never dealt with Inca legal khipu, they may not have employed the very same conventions as this pre-Hispanic genre in constructing colonial khipu to record the Ten Commandments; but the material record would evince the same structure of significance through which native Andeans accommodated this information.

The even decimal value of the Ten Commandments would have resonated with what Gary Urton calls a Quechua ontology of numbers in which the number ten carries metaphoric significance related to the social and political organization of Andean communities as well as the larger Inca Empire (Urton 1997). This decimal unit also seems to have informed the organization of historical narratives (Brokaw 2002; 2003). I would argue that the numerical characteristics of the Andean social world and of the Inca organization of historical periods derive directly from the use of the khipu to record information about them. Thus, the genre of legal khipu also may have articulated Inca laws using some sort of decimal paradigm. If this were the case, khipu adapted to record the Ten Commandments would have invoked a pre-Hispanic horizon of understanding even if they did not draw directly from the conventions of the legal-khipu genre.

Versions of these catechistic khipu recording the Ten Commandments may have also served as confessional khipu. Confessional manuals establish a structure for confession that follows the order of the commandments, and the Third Lima Council's *Cathecismo* suggests that the penitents follow the Ten Commandments in creating a record of their sins on khipu. As Juan Carlos Estenssoro Fuchs points out, the use of khipu to record sins would have contributed to an indigenous (mis)understanding of the Christian concepts of sin and penance. The Quechua term used by the Spanish to refer to sin was *hucha*, which Estenssoro Fuchs explains originally referred to an unresolved item of business, a pending matter that required resolution (Estenssoro Fuchs 2003: 217; González Holguín [1608] 1989:199).[31] From the Andean perspective, this concept referred not only to one's relationship with a deity, but also to other members of the community and to other communities with whom a relationship of reciprocity existed. The names given by Guaman Poma for the Inca officials charged with the economic accounting of the Inca Empire contain both this term "hucha" and "quipo": *hatun hucha quipoc* and *huchuy hucha quipoc* (Guaman Poma de Ayala [1615] 1997: 361[363]). Thus, the convergence of the indigenous concept of *hucha* associated with economic khipu record keeping and the use of this medium and its associated *yupana* practices to record sins and prayers inscribes the Christian notions of sin and penance, not to mention one's relationship to God in general, within the conceptual paradigm of Andean economic integration governed by the principle of reciprocity.

The use of confessional khipu also may have led to the tendency observed in the sixteenth century by Juan Pérez Bocanegra and Alonso de la Peña Montenegro to confess sins in even decimal units. Bocanegra explains with frustration that if an Indian confesses to swearing ten times, he also got drunk, fornicated, and committed robbery ten times each as well (Pérez Bocanegra 1631: 137; cited in Harrison 2002: 276). Peña Montenegro observes the same with confessions of lying, believing in dreams, failures to attend Mass, and so forth (Peña Montenegro [1688] 1985: 297; cited in Harrison 2002: 277). Regina Harrison suggests that these practices stem from instructions by native shamans and the use of the same khipu by various individuals for confession (Harrison 2002: 269–278).

Reactions Against the Use of Ecclesiastical Khipu in the Seventeenth Century

Spanish missionaries never seemed to have understood all of the mechanisms that preserved the idolatrous concepts and practices they were trying to extirpate. The obvious role that the khipu would have played in this preservation may be what led to the assumption by modern scholars discussed above that the condemnation of certain khipu genres by the Third

31 Also see Harrison 1994: 143; Urton 2009: 818–822; Horswell 2005: 212–213.

Lima Council was actually a universal prohibition of all khipu. However, in spite of the awareness that there existed idolatrous khipu and the effort to eradicate them, the early missionaries were not concerned about the adaptation of this medium for ecclesiastical purposes. The Spaniards were not necessarily incapable of perceiving the subtle way in which ecclesiastical khipu served as a locus of syncretism; rather they never seemed to have learned exactly how the khipu functioned. Nevertheless, their ignorance did not prevent them from incorporating this device into their official evangelization procedures.

For almost one hundred years after the conquest, there was never any objection to the use of ecclesiastical khipu. In 1631, however, Juan Pérez Bocanegra publishes his *Ritual formulario e institución de curas para administrar a los naturales*, in which he criticizes the use of confessional khipu. Pérez Bocanegra explains that the catechistic activities supervised by indigenous officials involved discussions of doctrine and extensive use of confessional khipu:

Let the Confessor also be very aware that in this city, and outside of it, certain Indians, men and women, who are called elder brothers and sisters do a certain thing among themselves: and you could call them Illuminati... about certain khipu knots, and memorials, that they bring to confess, like their writings, and memorials. Because these Indians, and particularly the women, teach others to confess with these knots and signs. (Pérez Bocanegra 1631: 111).[32]

He goes on to explain that the Indians first confess to these "elder brothers" and "elder sisters," who then teach them to make khipu of their sins and tell them what to say to the priest. In some cases, different individuals employ the same khipu for confession (Harrison 2002). For Pérez Bocanegra, the use of these khipu, then, undermines the validity of the confession, because they are not true confessions.

The role played by native officials in the indoctrination of the Indians reinforced the kind of religious syncretism discussed above. The personnel shortage forced Spanish priests to entrust much of the day-to-day administration of the parishes to indigenous officials. Alan Durston explains that these officials participated extensively in the production of catechetico-liturgical performance. The formation of self-regulating brotherhoods or *cofradías*, which also engaged in their own catechistic exercises, further added to the problem (Durston 2008: 282–283). Colonial *doctrinas* often

---

32 "Advierta tambien mucho el Confessor, que en esta ciudad, y fuera della hazen una cosa algunos Indios, è Indias que se llaman hermanos mayores, y hermanas mayores entre ellos mismos: y se les pueden poner nombre de alumbrados ... acerca de ciertos quipos ñudos, y memorias, que traen para confessarse, como escrituras, y memoriales dellos. Porque estos tales Indios, y particularmente las Indias, enseñan a otras a se confessar por estos ñudos y señales" (Pérez Bocanegra 1631: 111).

presented doctrinal information in the form of a dialogue between two individuals in which one asks a series of questions and the other responds. Ideally, the individual imparting the knowledge would be a priest, but in some cases, such dialogues were written as a conversation between two Indians who refer to each other as brothers. In Mexico, Pedro de Gante's mid-sixteenth-century Nahuatl *doctrina* follows this model (Gante 1553). Although Spanish priests working in the Andes produced fewer documents of this type and even fewer in native languages such as Quechua and Aymara, the indoctrination practices were often similar throughout the Indies. Of course, the very first priests to arrive in Peru came from other jurisdictions in the Indies and brought their methods with them. In Gante's Nahuatl text both participants in the dialogue refer to each other as "younger brother," but it was common to refer to lay individuals who occupied certain positions of authority as "elder brothers" and "elder sisters," particularly in the context of *cofradías* run by lay men or women.

In 1578, José de Acosta describes an Indian *cofradía* organized in Juli. The primary purpose of this organization was to root out idolatry and discourage drunkenness, but the members were also involved in indoctrinating other members. Acosta explains that entry into the association required an exam, and members were considered almost as priests by other Indians in the community (Acosta [1578] 1954: 296). As the documents cited above make clear, these native officials incorporated the khipu into their catechistic and liturgical practices.

Pérez Bocanegra objects to such practices because they undermine the legitimacy of confession. Normally the leaders of *cofradías* and the native assistants in colonial Peruvian parishes charged with teaching the catechism already occupied positions of authority in their communities. This convergence of traditional sociopolitical roles and new religious authority facilitated the indoctrination of the Indians, but it also created a context that invited syncretism. Pérez Bocanegra does not seem to have recognized, at least in this case, the syncretic nature of these practices. The problem for Pérez Bocanegra is not that the khipu are inherently idolatrous or unreliable, but rather that the "elder brothers" and "elder sisters" tell the Indians to confess sins they did not commit and to silence certain sins they did commit (Pérez Bocanegra 1631: 111–113).

Estenssoro Fuchs explains that the issue for Pérez Bocanegra is that these "elder brothers" and "elder sisters" were usurping the authority of the confessor (Estenssoro Fuchs 2003: 224–225). In other words, as Charles puts it, the danger was not merely one "of heterodox confession, but more important the question of who controlled the mechanisms of religious exchange and therefore power over the community" (Charles 2007: 32). Furthermore, these native assistants were the same officials who administered community affairs in accordance with indigenous cultural beliefs and practices. These officials inevitably would have imported these beliefs into their catechistic and liturgical practices, which the khipu facilitated. Pérez Bocanegra felt strongly enough about such practices that he instructs the *doctrineros* to confiscate and burn the confessional khipu: "teach them to confess this Confessional confiscating those accounts and knots; and burning them in their presence. And do not give them the Sacrament of the Eucharist until you have them reduced to the good order of confessing without such deceit and defects" (Pérez Bocanegra 1631: 114; Charles 2007: 32).[33]

Charles suggests that Pérez Bocanegra's objections to the use of confessional khipu may derive from his antagonistic relationship with the Jesuits who endorsed this practice (Charles 2007: 30). At some point prior to 1622, Pérez Bocanegra[34] was assigned to work as a parish priest in Andahuaylillas.[35] By this time, the Jesuits had evidently gotten over their reluctance to run colonial *doctrinas*. As Bruce Mannheim explains, in 1601 the Jesuits actually had begun campaigning for permission to set up a Quechua language training center in the Diocese of Cuzco modeled after the Aymara *doctrina* at Juli. After receiving a general authorization from the king, the viceroy issued a decree in 1618 granting them the parish at Andahuaylillas. The Diocese objected to this order, arguing that the Jesuits' true motivations had more to do with their economic interests in the area than any need for a Quechua language training center. The Jesuits continued their campaign, and the king finally issued a *cédula* in 1628 specifically granting the Jesuits the parish at Andahuaylillas. At first glance, it would appear that the Jesuits took over the parish in 1628 and controlled it until 1636, when the Diocese was able to reverse the king's order and return Pérez Bocanegra to his position (Mannheim 1991: 48, 250–251, n. 17). Durston explains, however, that the royal *cédula* from 1628 was contingent upon Pérez Bocanegra's willingness to cede the parish to the Jesuits, which he never did (Durston 2007: 399 n. 24). Thus, the Jesuits never occupied the parish. Even so, given the fact that the Jesuits had been campaigning to take over his parish for many years, Pérez Bocanegra may have developed

---

33 "Enseñarles á confessar este Confessionario quitandoles aquellas quentas, y ñudos; y quemandolos en su presencia. Y no darles el Sacramento de la Eucaristía, hasta tenerlos reduzidos, al buen orden de se confessar sin semejantes enredos, y defetos" (Pérez Bocanegra 1631: 114).

34 Torero argues that the church in Andahuaylillas was constructed by the Dominicans (Torero Fernández de Córdova 1987: 39), which would suggest that Pérez Bocanegra, whose name appears on the cornerstone laid in 1626 (Mannheim 1991: 251), belonged to this order. Irene Silverblatt, on the other hand, identifies Pérez Bocanegra as a Jesuit (Silverblatt 1987: 156). Bruce Mannheim explains that he was actually a third-order Franciscan, but assigned to Andahuaylillas by the Diocese (Mannheim 1991:250–251). Alan Durston suggests that in spite of his status as a third-order secular Franciscan, Pérez Bocanegra had stronger ties to the Dominicans (Durston 2007: 154).

35 Pérez Bocanegra's *Ritual formulario*, which he had completed by 1622 (Harrison 2002: 270), was informed by his experiences at Andahuaylillas.

a personal animosity toward the Jesuit order by 1622, which is the year in which the bishop of Cuzco granted the first approval for the publication of his *Ritual formulario* (Harrison 2002: 270).

However, the association between Pérez Bocanegra's possibly antagonistic feelings toward the Jesuits and his objections to the use of confessional khipu implies that the Jesuits played a special role in promoting this practice. Sabine Hyland has argued that the Jesuit Blas Valera was invested heavily in portraying the khipu as a sophisticated semiotic medium on a par with alphabetic writing (Hyland 2003: 129–149), but his focus was on what he alleged were pre-Hispanic practices. Furthermore, although the Jesuits tended to describe indigenous cultural achievements in favorable terms, Valera's project was marginal even within the Jesuit order. Sixteenth-century Jesuit documents make it clear that they advocated the use of confessional khipu, but the apparently heavier Jesuit investment in this practice derived more from the fact that the Jesuits emphasized sacramental confession more than the other orders or the secular clergy. Even so, the Jesuits were relative latecomers to the game. As explained above, when they arrived in Juli in 1576, for example, the Indians were already using confessional and other ecclesiastical khipu, probably encouraged by the Dominicans, who had worked in this area previously. And the most thorough endorsement of ecclesiastical khipu practices actually comes from the Mercedarian Diego de Porres in his instructions discussed above, possibly written before the Jesuits had even arrived in Peru. Although the Jesuits may have contributed much of the intellectual weight behind the Third Lima Council, its advocacy of confessional khipu was a collective act.

In his brief discussion of ecclesiastical khipu in the colonial period, Estenssoro Fuchs reads Pérez Bocanegra's text as an indication that from this point on the khipu was considered diabolical and rejected as a valid medium on which the Indians could base their confessions (Estenssoro Fuchs 2003: 223–228). Alan Durston is less definitive, but he also takes Pérez Bocanegra's text to represent a generalized negative reaction to the use of ecclesiastical khipu (Durston 2008: 287). It is important, however, to consider the significance of Pérez Bocanegra's *Ritual formulario* and the influence that it did or did not have. Although in his *Ritual formulario*, Pérez Bocanegra makes it very clear that he objects to the use of confessional khipu, I have been unable to find any evidence to suggest that others shared this opinion or that it had any influence beyond his own parish.

In fact, the limited evidence that does exist reveals continued support for confessional khipu. Several subsequent references attest to the persistent use of such ecclesiastical khipu throughout the seventeenth and eighteenth centuries. José de Arriaga's *Extirpación de la idolatría del Piru* (1621) reiterates the general support for the use of confessional khipu: "When you deal with them about confession, you must tell them to make a khipu in order to confess, because many confess very well with them" (Arriaga 1621: 81).[36] Arriaga's text, published in 1621, was contemporary with Pérez Bocanegra's *Ritual formulario*, which, although not published until 1631, was finished by 1622 at the latest. Moreover, in 1649, almost twenty years after the publication of Pérez Bocanegra's *Ritual formulario*, the archbishop of Lima, Pedro de Villagómes, began a renewed campaign to extirpate idolatrous practices in the Andes (Mills 1997: 143–147), and he published his own manual for the extirpators titled *Carta pastoral de exortacion e instruccion contra las idolatrias de los indios*. This text explicitly instructs the extirpators to have the Indians use confessional khipu: "When it is time to order them to come to confess, it is convenient to tell them to take time to think over their sins, and make their khipu in order to confess better with them" (Villagómes 1649: 54 recto).[37] Villagómes also encourages the use of khipu records of *huacas* and their associated practices, which is particularly surprising given the idolatrous nature of such content and the Third Council's prohibition of such records:

38. Finally, you must ask about the possessions that the *huaca* has, if it has money, which is usually held by its custodian or in the same place as the *huaca*, if it has gold or silver, *Huamas, Chacra, Hincas*, or *Tincurpas*, or *Aquillas* with which they give it to drink.

These things and other similar things, which are found in other parts, and that time will show, and experience will reveal, the inspector must ask, not all at once, nor very quickly, but rather very slowly, giving them time to remember what they forget; and to those who know how to write, giving them paper and ink so they can write down all that they know, or make a khipu of it, or count with corn, which is a common method among the Indians. (Villagómes 1649: 63 recto).[38]

In composing this text, Villagómes copies entire sections of José de Arriaga's *Extirpación de la idolatría del Perú* from 1621 (Mills 1997: 143). The instruction regarding confessional khipu is very similar to a passage from

---

36 "Quando se les trata de la confession se les a de dezir, que hagan sus quipos para confessarse, que muchos se confiessan muy bien por ellos" (Arriaga 1621: 81).

37 "Quando fuere tiempo de mandar que vengan a confessarse, conuiene decirles que con tiempo piensen sus pecados, y hagan sus quipos para confessarse mejor por ellos" (Villagómes 1649: 54 recto).

38 "38. A la postre se à de preguntar por la hacienda que la huaca tiene, si tiene dinero, que este suele estar en poder del que la guarda, ò en el mismo lugar de la huaca, si tiene oro, ò plata, *Huamas, Chacra, Hincas*, ò *Tincurpas*, ò *Aquillas* con que les dan de beber.

Estas, y las demás cosas semejantes, que en otras partes se hallaran, y el tiempo irá mostrando, y la experiencia descubriendo, à de preguntar el visitador, no todo de vna vez, ni muy a prissa, sino muy despacio, y dandoles tiempo para que piensen lo que se les oluida: y a los que supieren escribir dandoles papel, y tinta para que escriban todo lo que supieran, ò que hagan quipo dello, ó cuenten con maiz que es modo muy usado entre los indios" (Villagómes 1649: 63 recto).

Arriaga's text,[39] and the second reference to the documentation of *huacas* on khipu is for the most part a verbatim transcription.[40] However, Villagómes's reliance on Arriaga's earlier work was not merely a shortcut taken by an uninformed archbishop. Villagómes was a meticulous intellectual who involved himself in the details of the various posts he occupied. As his first act as bishop of Arequipa, he personally conducted a general inspection [*visita general*] of the region. He was already well-read on the topic of Andean idolatries, and in his *visita general* he gained extensive firsthand experience in attempting to stamp it out (Mills 1997: 140–146). Thus, the instruction encouraging the use of confessional khipu in the *Carta pastoral* is not a casual repetition of a colonial cliche but rather a judicious recognition of the valuable role the khipu played in the interaction between Spanish priests and Indian converts. The advocacy of ecclesiastical khipu by Arriaga and Villagómes is particularly significant given the fact that they were such fervent persecutors of idolatries. Their texts make it very clear that they did not consider the khipu a threat to Christian orthodoxy.

The passage cited above from Villagómes's *Carta pastoral* and Arriaga's earlier extirpation manual advocates not only the use of the khipu for confession but also khipu practices that had been targeted for destruction in the early extirpation campaign. The identity of *huacas*, their possessions, and their offerings were inherent parts of the rites and ceremonies that the Spaniards wished to eliminate. And the khipu that contained this information belonged to the genre explicitly condemned by the Third Lima Council in 1583 (*Tercer Concilio Limense* [1583] 1990: 191). It is tempting, but perhaps misleading, to interpret the difference between the attitude of early missionaries expressed by the Third Lima Council, on the one hand, and that of seventeenth-century extirpators such as Arriaga and Villagómes, on the other, as a reversal of policy. However, the objective of both early and later extirpation campaigns was to root out idolatry, which included the destruction of *huacas*.[41] It seems that early missionaries lumped the khipu records of *huacas* and their offerings together with the idolatrous practices with which they were associated. Failure to make a qualitative

---

39 Arriaga's text reads: "Quando se les trata de la confession se les a de dezir, que hagan sus quipos para confessarse, que muchos se confiessan muy bien por ellos" (Arriaga 1621: 81).

40 Arriaga's text reads: "Estas y las demas cosas de que se hace mencion en la relacion, que tendra muy bien vista, y entendidas el Visitador, y otras cosas semejantes, que en otras partes se hallaran, y el tiempo yra mostrando, y la experiencia descubriendo, a de preguntar el Visitador, a tres o quatro de las personas que se dixo arriba, o algunos otros que ellos citaren; no todo de vna vez, ni muy aprisa; sino muy espacio, y dandoles tiempo para que piensen, lo que se les olvida. Y a los que supieren escrevir, dandoles papel y tinta, para que escriban todo lo que supieren, o que hagan quipo de ello, o quenten con maizes, que es modo muy vsado entre los Indios" (Arriaga 1621: 88).

41 Of course, given the fact that many *huacas* were features of the landscape, it was impossible to destroy them all.

distinction between the khipu record and the *huacas* themselves may have led early sixteenth-century missionaries to snatch up idolatrous khipu on sight and destroy them; but they quickly came to realize that doing so undermined their project by making it more difficult to find and destroy the *huacas*. As the Spanish priests became more informed about Andean cultural practices, they began adopting a more pragmatic perspective. The Third Lima Council's order to destroy idolatrous khipu in 1583 appears to use the language of the more intolerant reaction by early missionaries who targeted all idolatrous khipu. Some of these idolatrous khipu would have been of no use to the extirpators: calendrical khipu unrelated to the *ceque* system and legal khipu, for example. By 1583, it appears that the initial, more intolerant campaign to destroy "idolatrous" khipu had run its course, for the pragmatic perspective is already evident in earlier writers. In 1559, for example, Polo de Ondegardo relied on khipu records in his investigation of *huacas*, and Matienzo endorsed this practice in 1567 (Matienzo [1567] 1967: 119).

Even so, the pragmatic tolerance of khipu records related to *huacas* and their associated ceremonies was probably more a change in methodology than in policy. It is clear that in general, the Spaniards implicitly distinguish between the legitimacy of the khipu medium and the content of the message. Even Pérez Bocanegra does not condemn the khipu in any general way. His objection has more to do with the usurpation of ecclesiastical authority and the way it had led to the corruption of the sacrament of confession than with the khipu per se. Likewise, for Arriaga and Villagómes, the idolatry does not reside in the khipu records of *huacas* but rather in the actual *huacas* themselves and the ceremonies in which offerings are made to them. This does not mean, however, that seventeenth-century extirpators did not destroy these *huaca*-khipu. The only reason for promoting the creation of such records was to facilitate the destruction of the *huacas* and the idolatrous practices associated with them. After achieving this goal, it is highly unlikely that either Arriaga or Villagómes would have allowed indigenous informants to walk away with their khipu, which could potentially serve as the basis for reconstituting the system of *huacas*. The extirpators using the manuals published by Arriaga and Villagómes surely would have confiscated and destroyed these *huaca*-khipus in the same way that Pérez Bocanegra evidently did with confessional khipu.

The essential difference between Pérez Bocanegra, on the one hand, and Arriaga and Villagómes, on the other, is that the former called for the destruction of Christian ecclesiastical khipu, whereas the latter promoted their use. It would appear that the more popular opinion was the one advocated by Arriaga and Villagómes, both of whom occupied much more influential positions than Pérez Bocanegra. The marginal view advocated by Pérez Bocanegra appears only in his *Ritual formulario*. The available evidence suggests that the use of confessional khipu, and Christian ecclesiastical khipu in general, was a widespread phenomenon endorsed, or at least accepted, by everyone who refers to it except Pérez Bocanegra.

From the beginning of the conquest through at least 1650, then, Spanish priests generally accepted, and in many cases actively promoted, the use of khipu for Christian ecclesiastical purposes. Although most khipu practices documented after 1650 are secular in nature, some evidence appears to indicate an enduring ecclesiastical khipu tradition as well. Teresa Gisbert and José de Mesa documented the use of ecclesiastical khipu by young girls in a church in Chipaya, Bolivia in 1966 (Gisbert and Mesa 1966: 497–506). Evidently, these khipu are formally more similar to archaeological specimens than modern pastoral khipu. Although Gisbert and Mesa were unable to investigate thoroughly this practice, they draw the following conclusions: (1) Chipaya khipu are used by women; (2) these khipus are kept tied to a cross; (3) they are used by girls for religious purposes under the direction of an older woman; (4) each khipu belongs to an individual child; (5) they are not used to pray, but rather to account for something personal specific to each child; (6) they are made of wool and are of different colors; (7) they are knotted according to the pre-Columbian system; and (8) they are generally more similar to pre-Columbian khipu than to the modern khipu (Gisbert and Mesa 1966: 505–506).

Regina Harrison reports that a priest from Chinchero, a community near Cuzco, also witnessed the use of confessional khipu as recently as the mid-twentieth century. The priest was even able to describe the scheme of color symbolism used in these khipu to denote various types of sin (Harrison 2002: 280–281). As with the ecclesiastical khipu reported by Pérez Bocanegra in the early seventeenth century, these twentieth-century ecclesiastical khipu practices do not seem to have been controlled, directed, or supervised in any way by the priests. In the Chipaya case, the girls were trained by older women, and the priest from Chinchero who described the confessional khipu appears to have been an observer. All of these practices are not necessarily identical to the kind documented in the colonial period, but it is very probable that they derive from them or similar colonial practices.

These are just two examples of enduring ecclesiastical khipu practices that researchers have happened to discover. Given the widespread use of ecclesiastical khipu in the sixteenth and seventeenth centuries, it would be surprising if other Andean communities have not preserved similar practices. However, a general survey of modern uses of ecclesiastical khipu would be a virtually impossible task at this point. The difficulty in conducting any sort of thorough ethnographic research on modern khipu in general is similar to that which hinders historical investigations: any methodology designed to discover the available sources of information would be prohibitively time consuming.

Surely a number of Andean communities preserve khipu traditions unknown to historians and anthropologists, but many more have probably abandoned this traditional record-keeping system. The historical evidence suggests that this has been a gradual process. As time has passed, the spread of alphabetic literacy and the socioeconomic forces that integrate in one way or another indigenous communities into the national and global spheres has exerted pressures that wreak havoc on the traditional models of social, economic, political, and religious interaction conducive to the survival of local khipu practices. This process continues today. Nevertheless, the few documented cases of enduring khipu traditions attest to the resilience of this medium and the cultural agency of those who have kept it alive.

Conclusion

In some respects, the division of the history of the khipu presented here into two sections focusing on the pre- and post-conquest periods, respectively, is a function of the different research methodologies that each of these periods demands; but it also reflects the different trajectories that the khipu follows in each of these general periods as a result of the corresponding differences in the socioeconomic and political contexts. In the pre-Hispanic era, the khipu emerges as a medium that both informs, and is informed by, the development of local, regional, and pan-regional socioeconomic institutions. In the historical development of the khipu and its conventions, then, the arrival of the Spaniards is less significant than the emergence of the Wari and Inca states. The significance of the transition from the pre-Hispanic to the colonial period resides in the fact that it marks a change in the institutional status of the khipu and the beginning of its gradual disappearance, which has continued up to the present. Although these two general periods differ in fundamental ways, the khipu evinces similar tendencies in each. In both periods, the khipu exhibits a dependence on the socioeconomic and political institutions that in turn depend on it. In some cases, the institutions, and thus the dynamics of the relationship, change, but the underlying principle of interdependence remains the same. Moreover, both before and after the conquest, the khipu enters into complex interactions with other forms of media.

In the first section of this study, the general historical outline of various Andean media leading up to and including the khipu is not an exhaustive survey; other relevant objects and practices abound, and surely many others are currently, and in some cases perhaps inherently, inaccessible. The details of pre-conquest Andean media and their function remain obscure, so this history must necessarily rely to some extent on conjecture. However, the available evidence suggests some general tendencies.

In the first few chapters, I examine some of the semiotic practices that belong to the context in which the khipu develops and the subsequent rise to prominence of this medium in the Wari and Inca Empires. The absence of the khipu from the archaeological record prior to the dominance of the Wari Empire does not mean that it did not exist until this point. The khipu is a perishable medium, the survival of which depends on institutional practices that would function to preserve it in some way. Given that semiotic media complex enough to facilitate the administration of a state bureaucracy are not invented overnight, the appearance of the khipu in the archaeological record suggests a prior history to which we will probably never have direct access. Thus, the semiotic practices that are evident prior to the archaeological debut of the khipu would have been contemporary with early khipu that have not survived. Furthermore, such media are not invented from scratch. Given the fact that early Andean media belong to the same context in which the khipu developed, I have argued that they may exhibit some of the same semiotic principles.

One of the implications of the larger argument presented here is the inherently heterogenous nature of all semiosis. In other words, the transmission of meaning in communicative interactions takes place through multiple channels that employ a variety of different types of semiosis. The primary context of interpersonal communication is perhaps the most heterogenous mode of semiotic interaction in that it involves gestures, facial expressions, posture, a variety of contextual indicators and pragmatic phenomena, as well as oral language itself with its many features and nuances that are unavailable to a medium like alphabetic script. The fixed nature of most secondary media make them more limited, but even so they all involve some degree of heterogeneity. In fact, most modes of secondary communication do not limit themselves to a single medium or type of semiosis. Even alphabetic script is often accompanied by images, for example. Pictographic or iconographic images inherently deploy diverse modes incidental to their mimetic nature.

The demands placed on secondary media by complex socioeconomic and political systems and the possibilities that such media afford lead to an increasing specialization and a concentration of semiotic functions in one medium relative to others. I would suggest that this is precisely what occurs with the khipu in the Wari and Inca Empires, during which this medium acquires a prominence commensurate with the needs of state bureaucracies. Although comparisons to the development of other media such as alphabetic script and its relationship to the emergence of states can be helpful, it would be pointless to push the analogy too far. The variables in each case differ significantly enough that no strict parallel exists. However, the correlation between the emergence of the Wari and Inca states and the simultaneous rise to prominence of the khipu corroborates the general principle of interdependence between secondary media and socioeconomic complexity.

The history of the khipu prior to the Spanish conquest can be divided into periods that correspond to the Andean polities of the Wari and the Inca precisely because their institutional practices involved the preservation of khipu in archaeological contexts. This is not to say that the khipu depended solely on state-level institutions. The khipu was just as important to local-level institutions as it was to the administration of pre-Hispanic states. In fact, state-level khipu would have built on and further developed pre-existing local practices.

Some of the best evidence we have for local practices actually comes from the modern community of Tupicocha in the province of Huarochiri. Frank Salomon discovered that this community continued to employ khipu for its internal administration up to the beginning of the twentieth century (Salomon 2004). Beginning in the late nineteenth century, the use of alphabetic *ayllu* books gradually displaced khipu record keeping, but the *ayllus* of this community have preserved a set of khipu as patrimonial objects symbolizing the authority and function of community officials. The modern alphabetic records of the community, then, give a good indication of the kind of information that would have been recorded on their khipu. Many of the details of community administration in Tupicocha certainly would have changed over the years, but its essential structure and function are highly consistent with what is known about the pre-conquest and colonial periods. Thus, in many respects the khipu practices that survived in Tupicocha into the early twentieth century appear to have been very similar to those of the fifteenth and sixteenth centuries. It may be no coincidence, therefore, that the material features of the patrimonial khipu from Tupicocha are also highly consistent with Inca and early colonial specimens. The Tupicocha case demonstrates the interdependence of organic local institutions and khipu record keeping, and it suggests that different levels of khipu literacy functioned more or less autonomously within the context of their respective institutions.

Modern scholars have had a tendency to view modern khipu as degenerate vestiges of a more illustrious medium. Around the same time that alphabetic books were displacing the use of khipu in Tupicocha in the late nineteenth century, Max Uhle documented the use of another khipu genre used by local officials to maintain records of livestock in Cutusuma and Challa, Bolivia (Uhle 1897; see Figure 8.1). Apparently unlike most archaeological specimens, these pastoral khipu rely on the size of the knots in order to determine decimal place values. Uhle himself argues that these khipu are undoubtedly direct descendants of pre-conquest khipu, but he maintains that their conventions differ significantly. Uhle's understanding of ancient khipu relies primarily on the Inca Garcilaso's explanation of the decimal place system (Garcilaso de la Vega [1609] 1985: II, 24–25), which is in fact an accurate description of the conventions evident in most archaeological khipu.

Arguments taking modern khipu such as the ones from Cutusuma and Challa as degenerate versions of Inca khipu make the unfounded assumption

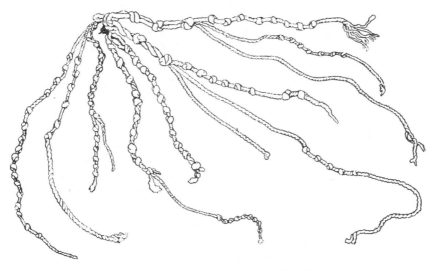

Figure 8.1. Modern khipu from Bolivia (After Uhle 1897).

that khipu conventions throughout the Andes were highly standardized and uniform in the pre-conquest and early colonial periods. It is true that the conventions of khipu genres involved in the administration of the Inca state were probably fairly standard throughout the empire. These genres related directly to those of local community record keeping in so far as they recorded the same types of information such as labor tribute, community or state obligations, and so forth. Thus, archaeological khipu preserved by the institutions involved in this type of record keeping both before and after the conquest closely resemble those employed by the *ayllus* of Tupicocha in the late nineteenth century.

However, colonial sources also indicate variations in khipu conventions. Jerónimo Román y Zamora, for example, describes the use of large and small knots: "they made the knots large and small with differences of color" (Román y Zamora [1575] 1897: 68).[1] Martín de Murúa appears to draw directly from Román y Zamora but also adds more detail: "by these they made units, tens, hundreds, thousands, and millions, and for the things that they wanted to say, to differentiate them, they made knots larger than the others . . . and according to the number, the knot was more or less thick" (Murúa [1611] 1987: 373–373).[2] Murúa appears to indicate

1 "Hacian los ñudos mayores y menores y con diferencias de colores" (Román y Zamora [1575] 1897: 68).

2 "Por éstos hacían unidades, decenas, centenas, millares y millones de millares, y para las cosas que querían decir, diferenciarlas, hacían unos nudos mayores que los otros . . . y según el número así era el nudo más o menos grueso" (Murúa [1611] 1987: 372–373).

that the thickness of the knots functioned to signal decimal values. This is not a convention of most archaeological khipu, but it appears on the modern khipu from Cutusuma observed by Uhle three hundred years later in the late nineteenth century, and it functions in precisely the same way (Uhle 1897). We may surmise, then, that the same variation between the modern conventions of the Tupicocha khipu and the Cutusuma khipu also existed between the ancient conventions of the Inca-era tribute khipu and less regulated local genres such as pastoral khipu.

The difference between the explanation of khipu conventions offered by the Inca Garcilaso and those described by Román y Zamora and Murúa appear to derive from exposure to different genres that function in different contexts. Garcilaso explicitly states that he gained his understanding of the khipu by working with the Indians from his father's *encomienda* (Garcilaso de la Vega[1609] 1985: II, 25–27). Given the fact that the *encomenderos* effectively took the place of the Inca state, the khipu genres used in this context would have been the same as, or very similar to, those employed by the local institutions in their interface with the Inca bureaucracy. Román y Zamora and Murúa, on the other hand, may have acquired their knowledge of khipu conventions from pastoral *khipukamayuq* who did not participate directly in state institutions.

All of this suggests the existence of different levels or domains of khipu literacy that often employed different types of conventions and exhibited different degrees of standardization based on the nature and relationship among the institutions functioning in each domain. The historiographical khipu discussed in Chapter 4 constitute perhaps the highest, most specialized level of khipu literacy. At another level, the vast majority of khipu genres would have been involved in the bureaucracy of the Inca state and the administration of local communities: censuses, storehouse records, and so forth. The necessary interface between state and local institutions would have served to standardize the conventions of the khipu employed at this level, effectively creating a corpus of standard administrative khipu genres that would form the bulk of the archaeological record. At perhaps the lowest level, shepherds charged with the care of communal livestock kept their own records that allowed them to render account to community officials. These khipu did not necessarily interface directly with the institutions of the Inca state. Thus, they would not have been subject to the same normalizing or regulatory pressure as higher level khipu genres. The various khipu practices that survived into the nineteenth and twentieth centuries, then, are not necessarily decadent vestiges of older, more complex conventions but rather continuities of particular levels of khipu literacy.

Even the most standardized genres probably never completely eliminated variation. Just as each individual develops his or her own alphabetic writing style, different *khipukamayuq* surely would have introduced their own stylistic idiosyncrasies into their khipu. In fact, one of the major difficulties for decipherment projects involves the distinction between actual conventions and mere stylistic variation.

The features of administrative khipu, both from Tupicocha and from archaeological contexts, differ one from another in many ways, but this variety must be understood in relative terms. Most administrative khipu are actually fairly homogenous compared to modern pastoral genres. Carol Mackey's study of modern ethnographic khipu illustrates that indeed, the conventions at this level differ significantly not only from archaeological administrative genres but also among themselves (Mackey 1970, 1990a). Given that this domain of khipu literacy did not interface directly with regional or state-level institutions, the semiotic conventions of such khipu differ not only from those of higher level genres but also from those of the same genre employed by other *khipukamayuq* from other communities or even perhaps within the same community. Mackey explains that even individual *khipukamayuq* often employ distinct styles in order to distinguish between their own khipu (Mackey 1970: 6–7). The majority of the differences among archaeological khipu may constitute stylistic variation, whereas the greater diversity of material features on pastoral khipu would correspond to conventional differences. At the level of pastoral literacy, then, one *khipukamayuq* would not necessarily be able to read the khipu of another. A familiarity with this level of khipu literacy appears to inform Bernabé Cobo's claim that any given khipu is an idiosyncratic device decipherable only by the *khipukamayuq* who made it (Cobo [1653] 1956: 143). However, all levels of khipu literacy would not have exhibited the same level of idiosyncracy. I would argue that the degree to which a particular khipu genre exhibited uniformity in its conventions and avoided idiosyncracies corresponded directly to the extent to which it was involved in the administration of the local, regional, or state institutions in which such standardization or uniformity occurs.

After the Spanish conquest, the normalizing pressure previously exerted by the Inca bureaucracy disappeared. For approximately fifty years thereafter, the institutions of the colonial state regularly demanded certain types of information from individuals and communities, thus indirectly compelling them to continue maintaining khipu records. However, the institutions of the colonial state employed alphabetic script and therefore did not exert any normalizing influence on the conventions of these khipu. In some cases, Spanish priests may have intervened in the adaptation of khipu for ecclesiastical uses, but the influence of these interventions seems to have been limited to the locale where they occurred. I would argue that for the most part, indigenous Andeans devised their own methods in order to meet the new record-keeping demands of the colonial context. *Khipukamayuq* throughout the Andes adapted the khipu in an ad hoc

way independently of each other. Even khipu genres that had been regulated by Inca institutions prior to the conquest, then, were susceptible
to idiosyncratic innovations in both conventions and content introduced
by *khipukamayuq* functioning independently or within independent communities in the colonial period. Thus, these genres would undergo the
same kind of divergent development that characterized the less regulated
pastoral khipu.

Khipu historiography was perhaps the pre-conquest genre most susceptible to divergent developments. The khipu historiographers who continued to maintain such records in the sixteenth and early seventeenth
centuries do not appear to have retained any connection to indigenous
institutions that would have constrained or coordinated the nature of their
practices. Throughout the sixteenth and to some extent in the first decades
of the seventeenth century, historical investigations by Spanish chroniclers
would have motivated khipu historiographers to continue maintaining
these records, but this relationship was never institutionalized or formally
regulated. Furthermore, after the conquest, khipu historiographers appear
to have operated for the most part independently from other *khipukamayuq*.
This may have contributed to the heterodox khipu historiography that
appears in the late sixteenth and early seventeenth centuries discussed in
Chapter 4.

Spanish officials also relied on community administrative khipu in gathering statistical information used to integrate indigenous communities into
the colonial system, but these genres did not depend on the kind of indirect
institutional support that contributed to the persistence of imperial khipu
historiography. After the conquest, the internal functioning of most local
institutions did not change in any essential way. The details of how local
community khipu interfaced with the Inca bureaucracy remains unclear.
Many of the Inca-era khipu that have survived may be local records, but
they appear to derive from the bureaucratic activities of the state. Similarly,
in the colonial period, many of the khipu records mentioned or transcribed
by *khipukamayuq* or colonial officials were local records, but they appear in
the colonial archive by virtue of their function within the colonial bureaucracy. If local *khipukamayuq* maintained certain khipu specifically for the
Inca administration, these genres would have enjoyed significantly more
institutional support than khipu historiography. Colonial officials engaged
with these khipu much more often than they did with historical genres, but
eventually the consolidation of the colonial system rendered them obsolete
as well.

It is unclear, however, to what extent the administrative khipu employed
in the Inca bureaucracy and, later, the colonial system differed from internal community records. Even if some khipu genres were specific to the
Inca and later colonial administration, their disappearance would not have

affected the khipu employed in the internal administration of the community itself. The genres used in the internal administration of local communities remained vital as long as their associated institutions continued to function without adopting alphabetic script. The *reducciones* carried out in the sixteenth century disrupted the nature and continuity of local institutions and hence almost certainly khipu practices as well. However, many communities preserved the structure and function of their internal administration for many years. The continued use of khipu in Tupicocha at the end of the nineteenth century may be an exceptional case of what would have been very common in the sixteenth and seventeenth centuries. The role of these khipu within community institutions would have provided a certain level of stability in the conventions they employed. This may explain why the conventions of the Tupicocha khipu appear to match so closely those of archaeological specimens.

In the case of ecclesiastical khipu, the situation is somewhat different. Although these khipu practices certainly draw from pre-conquest traditions, they essentially involve the creation of new genres that adapt European content to an indigenous medium. We know very little about this phenomenon or the innovations that it would have inherently involved. The first evidence of objects inserted into the strings of a khipu appears in this context (Cabredo [1602] 1986: 214–215; see Chapter 7), but it is unclear whether such conventions derive from popular khipu genres or colonial innovations. The use of this convention by modern ethnographic khipu (Mackey 1990b) may indicate the former, but it could have been originally an ecclesiastical innovation that then spread to community, pastoral, and perhaps even other genres (Brokaw 2006).

Beginning at the end of the sixteenth century, the sustained engagement between colonial and indigenous Andean institutions begins to subside. At this point, whatever impetus this engagement had given to the perpetuation of the khipu dissolves, and the survival of khipu genres depends solely on the preservation of formal or informal local indigenous institutions or idiosyncratic individual initiatives. It should be noted, however, that even prior to this point, many khipu practices remain almost completely obscure, because either the Spaniards targeted them for extirpation or they served no use or held no interest for the colonial administration.

The essential difference between the history of the khipu in the pre-conquest and colonial periods, then, resides in the particular types and levels of its institutional affiliation. I have suggested that the khipu originally developed in the context of local institutions that did not leave any direct evidence of these particular record-keeping practices. In the Middle and Late Horizons, the appearance of the khipu in the archaeological record corresponds to the development of complex state institutions that depend on this medium for the control and management of information. In the colonial period, indigenous Andean state level institutions dissolve. For several decades after the conquest, the administrative procedures involved in establishing and consolidating the colonial system rely heavily on khipu records, thus providing an impetus for the continued production of certain khipu genres that had been supported by the Inca state; but this was primarily an ad hoc, pragmatic response to the exigencies of the colonial context. Colonial institutions did not depend on the khipu in the same way as had indigenous Andean institutions. In fact, although the Spaniards took advantage of khipu record-keeping practices to further their own agenda, they actively worked to make the khipu obsolete by promoting alphabetic literacy. However, local Andean institutions that survived within the colonial system continued to perpetuate the khipu genres on which they relied for their internal administration.

In some ways, then, the colonial context resembles the period prior to the emergence of the Wari and Inca states in that the khipu functions only at the local level; and it becomes similarly difficult to trace its history. Our inability to follow the history of the khipu after the mid-seventeenth century illustrates the inherent difficulty of this type of investigation. The history of the khipu is inherently limited by the fact that the existence of evidence depends on either the survival into the present of ethnographic or patrimonial khipu that can be studied, as with the pastoral khipu examined by Mackey and the Tupicocha khipu discovered by Salomon, or some kind of interface between institutions of khipu literacy and those of alphabetic script, as occurred in the sixteenth-century chronicles and *visita* documents.

In spite of the differences in institutional diffusion, the khipu exhibits the same tendency to interact with other forms of media in both the pre-conquest and colonial periods. I have suggested that in the pre-conquest period, khipu semiosis appears to have some kind of genealogical relationship to Moche bean records, Chimu architectural conventions, and Wari practices that characterize architectural and textile structures as well as *yupana*-type record-keeping practices involving small objects deployed in a grid pattern. The semiotic principles on which the conventions of these media are based also appear to inform the conventions of the khipu. I have described this phenomenon as transpositioning: the transfer of semiosis from one code or medium to another resulting in a kind of intermediality. As the Inca state institutions developed and became more complex, the khipu took on a greater number of semiotic functions with increasingly important roles in Andean society relative to the functions of other media. But traces of the khipu's relationship to those media remains evident in the principles of its semiotic conventions.

Subsequently in the colonial period, the khipu enters into an inter-media relationship with alphabetic script in which each medium has an impact on the other. On the Spanish side, colonial officials and chroniclers transpositioned information from khipu records into alphabetic script. Given the inherently analogous nature of statistical and historical record keeping by socioeconomic and political institutions, the discourses of alphabetic Spanish and Andean khipu genres inevitably exhibited certain similarities. However, the profound difference between European and Andean institutions also means that these genres differed significantly. It is unclear to what extent the Spaniards consciously recognized these differences, but the process of transpositioning clearly involved a negotiation between both the form and the content of indigenous and Spanish discourses. In terms of content, the Spaniards selected the information that most closely matched the expectations of their discursive paradigms, and, whether consciously or unconsciously, often disregarded that which did not. Furthermore, they organized this information using familiar discursive patterns. Nevertheless, Spanish scribes and chroniclers were unable to completely assimilate indigenous discourses. Different documents and texts achieve different degrees of assimilation, but in one way or another they all import features of indigenous Andean discourses: census documents reproduce indigenous demographic categories; tribute records import an ordered hierarchy of ethnocategories; and chronicles inherit the paradigmatic information structures of their historiographic khipu sources.

The versatility that allows the khipu to adapt so easily to new functions is due not only to the heterogenous nature of its own semiosis but also to the general principle of semiotic heterogeneity that characterizes Andean secondary media more generally. The khipu itself employs several different types of conventions in conveying its message: color, number, cord configuration, and so forth. This semiotic heterogeneity informs, and is informed by, a corresponding mind-set. In other words, the very nature of the medium correlates to the way in which semiosis in general is conceived, which in turn tends to condition the nature and direction of further innovations or developments. In this case, then, the principle of semiotic heterogeneity would inform the way in which Andean *khipukamayuq* adapted their khipu for new uses and responded to alphabetic script. On the Andean side of this interaction, then, the administrative record-keeping practices of the Spaniards would have also impacted the khipu. Gary Urton has argued, for example, that the shift from the pre-conquest labor-tribute system to the colonial system, which levied tribute in the form of money or specified quantities of goods, effected a corresponding impoverishment of khipu conventions. He argues that the labor-tribute khipu would have recorded "fully grammatical . . . narrative constructions" composed of subjects, verbs, and objects, whereas the colonial tribute records only required nouns and numbers (Urton 1998: 410). It may be problematic to project onto the khipu notions of grammaticality derived from alphabetically biased linguistic theory, and in any case, as I suggest in Chapter 5, this shift may have merely involved the adaptation of a pre-existing storehouse genre. Nevertheless, the essential point of Urton's larger argument remains valid: the transformation of the tribute system effects a shift in khipu practices. The Spaniards impose commodity and/or monetary tribute rates, which native *khipukamayuq* duly record on their khipu by making the necessary conventional adaptations. Subsequently, they employ these conventions to maintain a khipu record of their tribute payments. In other words, the *khipukamayuq* developed or adapted khipu conventions specifically in response to the informational demands of the Spaniards.

Direct evidence for the transpositioning of statistical and historiographic khipu into alphabetic script far exceeds that of alphabetic script into the khipu. It may be that alphabetic transcriptions of khipu were more common than khipu reformulations of alphabetic texts, but the absence of evidence of the latter does not necessarily indicate this. The evidence for khipu transcriptions comes from alphabetic documents, which we can read. Although some evidence of transpositioning in the opposite direction appears in colonial documents, most of it would show up primarily in khipu themselves, which we do not understand in any complete way. Without a more complete understanding of khipu semiosis, research into this relationship may require the matching up of specific khipu with the documents or at least the types of document that they transposition. For a variety of reasons, such discoveries are difficult and in the end will probably be rare. Based on our understanding of the numeric conventions of the khipu, Urton has discovered a compelling relationship in the other direction between one of the khipu from Laguna de Los Cóndores and colonial census records (Urton 2001), but as yet we have no way to identify khipu that may have transpositioned alphabetic documents or even to know if any such khipu have survived.

The adaptation of the khipu for Christian ecclesiastical use presents the most prevalent and unambiguous, albeit indirect, evidence of this phenomenon. In some cases, the conventions of these ecclesiastical khipu may have derived directly from pre-conquest genres. Confessional khipu, for example, appear to be modified versions of Inca legal khipu. In other cases, however, ecclesiastical khipu would have required more extensive and innovative adaptations, resulting in the creation of new genres, possibly with new conventions. Although the church may have served as an institutional stimulus for the development of ecclesiastical khipu genres, it does not appear to have regulated khipu literacy in any consistent or uniform way. In some cases, Spanish priests may have participated directly in devising new conventions for ecclesiastical genres, but aside from the intriguing yet inconclusive reference to pauses and syllables in the sixteenth-century document written by Diego de Porres and discussed in Chapter 7, no other definitively authentic evidence of such activities from this period has surfaced.

Whatever involvement Spanish priests might have had in creating ecclesiastical khipu genres, these activities may have fed into a re-interpretive project instigated by a group of Jesuits in the late sixteenth and early seventeenth centuries (Hyland 2003: 129–149). This tradition appears to inform Raimundo de Sangro's apparently fanciful eighteenth-century treatise on the khipu, which describes syllabic conventions. Sangro claims to base his text on information from a seventeenth-century manuscript acquired from a Jesuit priest (Sangro [1750] 2002: 188–189; Hyland 2003: 135). The historical grounding of Sangro's work demands further investigation, but at the very least this treatise demonstrates the highly versatile nature of the material features that make up the khipu. However, it also reveals a disparity between actual khipu practices and European intellectual projects.

The reduction in the number of *visitas* in the latter part of the sixteenth century entailed a disengagement of the colonial administration from local institutions of khipu literacy. This effectively created a corresponding reduction in the frequency of references to khipu in the colonial archive. Mundane colonial documents continue to make reference to the khipu in a more limited and restricted way, but these sources do not form part of a larger more systematic engagement. Furthermore, by the seventeenth century, the Spaniards had effectively resolved the pressing issues of the early colonial period involving the status of the Indians, which had required the direct investigation of Andean history. In the seventeenth century, New World chronicles shift their focus from the investigation of pre-conquest history to a revaluation of the early colonial period based on sixteenth-century documents and chronicles. After the first few decades of the seventeenth century, the texts that do include a brief treatment of the pre-conquest period in their histories draw from earlier sixteenth-century chronicles, and in most cases they focus primarily on the Inca Empire without reference to the original sources of this information. Thus, they lose the implicit portrayal of the continuity of pre-conquest traditions that appears in sixteenth-century chronicles incidental to the methodology of engagement with *khipukamayuq* informants.

After the mid-seventeenth century, the khipu continues to experience the same gradual decline that had begun immediately after the conquest, but it continues to play the same role in Andean communities that it had up to that point. The general date of 1650, then, does not mark a transition in the history of the khipu itself, but rather a divergence between this history and European thought. In the eighteenth century, the emergence of the khipu in the popular and academic imagination evidenced by such works as Madame de Graffigny's *Letters from a Peruvian Princess* (1747), Raimundo de Sangro's *Lettera apologética* (1750), and William Robertson's *History of America* (1777) effectively relegate the khipu to the more illustrious past of the Inca Empire. These and later works from the nineteenth century rely almost exclusively on the Inca Garcilaso de la Vega's intriguing yet contradictory treatment of the khipu in his *Royal Commentaries*. These texts, or readings of them, tend to either denigrate the khipu as merely a mnemonic device that does not rise to the level of writing or romanticize it in order to attribute to this medium a prestige similar to that of alphabetic writing.

The divergence between actual khipu practices and the intellectual commodification of this medium raises its own issues and calls for further investigation. With the development of Latin American archaeology in the nineteenth and early twentieth centuries, this process of commodification extends to the material object itself. The first khipu specimens to appear in the nineteenth century function more as curiosities than objects of academic study, but by the end of the century serious researchers start to critically examine khipu specimens. From the very beginning, most khipu research focused either on attempts to decipher the meaning of khipu conventions or on the identification, description, and analysis of the material features of archaeological khipu in order to aid in future decipherment projects. Unfortunately, many of these decipherment projects make tacit assumptions about the nature of the khipu derived from the semiotic principles of alphabetic writing. Specifically, they often do not recognize the heterogenous nature of khipu semiosis, and they implicitly project onto the khipu the same degree of semiotic homogeneity that characterizes modern uses of alphabetic script.

This problem is evident from the very beginning. One of the first issues raised at the early stage of khipu research was whether or not the study of modern, ethnographic khipu would shed light on archaeological khipu from the pre-conquest period. Max Uhle believed that an analysis of modern ethnographic khipu could, in fact, illuminate the ancient Inca-era specimens that archaeologists had discovered in graves (Uhle 1897: 60–63; 1907). Enrique de Guimaraes argued to the contrary that modern khipu differ so significantly from archaeological specimens that they resemble ancient khipu only in the most superficial and limited way (Guimaraes 1907). In spite of their differences, however, both arguments assume that modern pastoral khipu derived historically from Inca khipu. The problem with the arguments on both sides of the issue is not that they fail to historicize the khipu, but rather that they do so incorrectly. Changes in khipu practices certainly must have occurred over time, but as explained above modern pastoral khipu did not result from the degeneration of more sophisticated Inca genres. Neither Uhle nor Guimaraes realized that the differences between modern and ancient khipu stem from the fact that they belong to different genres that employ different conventions and that such differences would have characterized pre-conquest practices as well.

Just as the semiotic principles of the khipu and other indigenous media inform a uniquely Andean mentality, the prominence of alphabetic script in modern Western societies conditions the way in which we think about secondary semiosis. I have argued that even alphabetic script involves a certain degree of semiotic heterogeneity in its incorporation of non-alphabetic signs such as arabic numerals and its reliance on non-alphabetic conventions such as punctuation, format, and so forth; but these non-alphabetic elements are ancillary to its primarily alphabetic nature. The alphabetic principle serves as the basis for all primarily alphabetic texts. An understanding of this principle allows any person versed in the script to read, at least at some level, any alphabetic document.

However, semiotic homogeneity is not inherent to all forms of Western textual practices. Other options are available: accounting ledgers, for example, rely on numbers and format more than alphabetic script; other types of texts such as comic books and graphic novels employ both images and script as primary media in conveying the message of the text. In some of these cases, alphabetic script may function as an ancillary element or not at all. The semiotic homogeneity of modern texts that rely primarily on alphabetic script, then, derives from the particular way in which the functions of alphabetic writing developed within the context of Western socioeconomic, political, and cultural institutions. The link to these institutions makes the homogeneity of alphabetic practices appear all the more natural. The resulting alphabetic mentality informs the very way in which we conceive of semiotic possibilities. In the case of the khipu, we have had a tendency to approach this medium as if it employed a uniform set of conventions across its various communicative functions and genres. An understanding of khipu practices as semiotically heterogenous may not provide the key to decipherment, but at the very least it explains one of the reasons why decoding the khipu has proved so difficult.

In this book, I have not approached the question of decipherment directly, but the principle of semiotic heterogeneity that emerges from the historical perspective adopted here has important implications for decipherment projects. It does not lead directly to any groundbreaking decipherment strategies. In fact, it essentially confirms the arguments about the nature of khipu semiosis that Marcia and Robert Ascher have been making for forty years (Ascher and Ascher 1969, 1971, 1975, 1981, 1989; M. Ascher 1983, 1986, 2002, 2005; R. Ascher 2002). The Aschers do not employ the term "semiotic heterogeneity," but this concept fits their understanding of khipu semiosis. Unfortunately, the semiotically heterogenous nature of the khipu makes decipherment very difficult. First of all, it means that the complete decipherment of one khipu will not necessarily make it easier to decipher others, because the conventions of one genre do not necessarily coincide with those of another. Furthermore, it will be difficult to determine what constitutes the complete decipherment of a khipu. The fact that khipu employed a variety of different conventions means that we can't be sure which features of a particular khipu are conventional and which are incidental. Gary Urton has recently documented a number of features on khipu that may constitute semiotic conventions (Urton 2003); but in most cases we have no way of knowing for sure if they actually were conventions, much less how they functioned (Brokaw 2005). Nevertheless, both the analysis of archaeological khipu and studies of ethnographic and patrimonial khipu have proven effective in advancing our understanding of this medium.

Decipherment projects and research activities designed to contribute to such projects have predominated in khipu studies. Early khipu scholars such as Leland Locke (1923), Erland Nordenskiöld (1925a, 1925b), Andres Altieri (1937, 1939, 1941), and Carlos Radicati di Primeglio (1949–1950, 1965, 1976, 1987, 1990) laid the groundwork for the later research by Marcia and Robert Ascher cited above, which employs a similar methodology of physical description and numeric analysis but on a larger scale. This methodology has been very productive in documenting the material features of the khipu and the patterns that emerge in the distribution of knot values, color sequences, and cord configurations, but it has become increasingly apparent that significant advances in further khipu decipherment require additional approaches and perspectives.

Over the last twenty years or so, a number of scholars have begun advancing the field of khipu studies in at least four areas. In most cases, these advances follow up on, and further explore the implications of, earlier work. Gary Urton has reinvigorated the project of material documentation begun by Locke, carried on by Radicati, and further advanced by the Aschers (Urton 2003). Martii Pärssinen (1992, 2004; Pärssinen and Kiviharju 2004a), Gary Urton (1998, 2001, 2006), and I (Brokaw 2002, 2003) have pursued the analysis of alphabetic transcriptions of khipu, an approach first adopted by John Murra (1968, 1981, 1982). Frank Salomon (2004) has also revived the study of patrimonial and ethnographic khipu originally undertaken briefly by Max Uhle (1897) and later more extensively by Carol Mackey (1970, 1990a, 1990b, 2002) and Arturo Ruiz Estrada (1982). Finally, recent research by Gary Urton (2002a, 2009), Carmen Loza (2000, 2001), Tristan Platt (2002), Regina Harrison (2002), Martti Pärssinen (2004), Monica Medelius and José de la Puente Luna (2004), Lydia Fossa (2000), and John Charles (2007) have all contributed to an emerging interest in the history of the khipu.

Each of these four approaches has its own theoretical, methodological, and substantive issues. Whereas the traditional examination and analysis of archaeological khipu have the sole aim of understanding the conventions of this medium, the other three approaches produce other types of knowledge whose value does not depend solely on their relevance for decipherment projects. Analyses of khipu transcriptions, for example, contribute to an understanding of cross-cultural interactions and the nature of indigenous discourses associated with the khipu. These issues hold their own interest for anthropologists and literary or textual scholars. For its part, the study of ethnographic and patrimonial khipu essentially involves ethnographic research into the cultural practices of modern communities. And investigation into the history of the khipu contributes to a better, more thorough understanding of the past.

In addition to the independent value of these lines of research, they have also demonstrated the potential to contribute to our understanding of khipu semiosis. Modern, ethnographic khipu practices derive from those of the pre-conquest and colonial periods, and in some cases they can provide insight into those earlier traditions. Transcriptions of khipu from the colonial period often retain the structure of indigenous discourses linked to khipu readings, which may correlate to identifiable khipu conventions. And historical analyses can uncover the relationship between the khipu and other Andean media, shedding light on their underlying semiotic principles. In conjunction with the analysis of archaeological khipu, all of these approaches contribute to a more sophisticated understanding of secondary media in the Andes.

A number of different studies have also contributed in one way or another to a fifth area or line of research that has received far less attention. Most scholars who conduct research specifically focusing on the khipu feel compelled to engage in some sort of theoretical discussion about writing or semiosis more generally and how it relates to the Andean medium of knotted cords. In most cases, these discussions serve as introductory sections of longer studies that segue into more empirical analyses. The lack of more extensive theoretical work is understandable given the fact that so little is known about the nature of khipu semiosis. In some ways this ignorance can be productive. Even the little that we do know about the khipu demands a reassessment of theories of writing and media more generally. In the Introduction, I proposed a revisionist theory about the relationship between secondary media and the development of socioeconomic complexity. Although here I have gestured toward alternative theories of semiosis, in a second volume on the khipu, I will build on the theoretical implications of work by Marcia and Robert Ascher, Gary Urton, Frank Salomon, Tom Cummins, and others through a series of more theoretically oriented studies that take indigenous American media rather than alphabetic script as their point of departure.

By way of conclusion, in addition to discussing the significance and the implications of the historical analysis presented here, I have attempted to outline the various dimensions of the field of khipu studies, because they are inherently interrelated. I would reiterate, then, the contingent and interdependent nature of all research on the khipu. The historical analysis presented in this study does not pretend to be comprehensive or definitive. Researchers will inevitably discover new ethnohistorical sources from the sixteenth and seventeenth centuries that will provide more complete information about both the history of khipu and, although perhaps to a lesser degree, its conventions. Such discoveries will certainly contribute to a more thorough, and perhaps even a different, understanding of the history of this medium, which in turn may provide additional insight into its material conventions and the semiotic processes through which it stores and conveys information. By the same token, advances in the analysis of the material medium itself, further research on colonial transcriptions of khipu, and new discoveries of modern ethnographic khipu practices are all essential, and they must be mutually informing projects. This is not an original observation. In practice, khipu research has always been an interdisciplinary endeavor. However, the history of this medium has never received a thoroughly systematic treatment. In the present study, then, I have attempted to set forth an initial historical perspective based on as many known primary and secondary sources as possible.

In some ways, this type of project is useful not only for what it reveals about what we know or can know based on the currently available evidence, but also for what it tells us about what we don't know or can't know at this point. As Slavoj Žižek has pointed out, there are four classes or states of knowledge: (1) there are things that we know that we know; (2) things that we know that we don't know; (3) things that we don't know that we don't know; and (4) things that we don't know that we know, or the "unknown knowns" (Žižek 2006). The first category ostensibly presents no problem at all. The second is a problem, but we can search for answers and devise methodologies to deal with it. The third and fourth categories, however, pose the greatest challenges for studies of the khipu. The interdisciplinary dialogue between historical, anthropological, ethnographic, theoretical, and textual analyses will help uncover information about the khipu that we currently don't even know that we don't know. Even more important, however, may be an attempt to reveal the "unknown knowns." The only way to address these "unknown knowns" is through more extensive and intensive theoretical investigations. The degree to which such theoretical investigations will be helpful in directly furthering our knowledge of the khipu remains to be seen, but their value also resides in their potential for exposing the cognitive and ideological biases of our own alphabetic mentalities. Such a project constitutes an equally important and necessary step toward a better understanding of this medium.

Bibliography

Abril Castelló, Vidal, ed. 1992. *Francisco de la Cruz, Inquisición, Actas I.* Madrid: Consejo Superior de Investigaciones Científicas.

Acosta, José. [1576] 1954. "Carta al P. Doctor Plaza, Visitador." *Obras del P. José de Acosta.* Ed. Francisco Mateos, pp. 286–290. Biblioteca de Autores Españoles, vol. 73. Madrid: Ediciones Atlas.

Acosta, José de. [1578] 1954. "Annua de la Provincia del Pirú del año 1578." *Obras del P. José de Acosta.* Ed. Francisco Mateos, pp. 290–302. Biblioteca de Autores Españoles, vol. 73. Madrid: Ediciones Atlas.

Acosta, José de. [1590] 1986. *Historia natural y moral de las indias.* Madrid: Historia 16.

Aibar Ozejo, Elena. 1968–1969. "La visita de Guaraz en 1558." *Cuadernos del seminario de historia* 9: 5–21.

Albarracin-Jordan, Juan. 1996. "Tiwanaku Settlement System: The Integration of Nested Hierarchies in the Lower Tiwanaku Valley." *Latin American Antiquity* 7.3: 183–210.

Albarracin-Jordan, Juan. 2003. "Tiwanaku: A Pre-Inka, Segmentary State in the Andes." *Tiwanaku and Its Hinterland, Archaeology and Paleoecology of an Andean Civilization,* Vol. 2: *Urban and rural Archaeology.* Ed. Alan L. Kolata, pp. 95–111. Washington, D.C.: Smithsonian Institution.

Altieri, Andrés Radames. 1937. "El Kipu peruano." *Revista geográfica americana* año 4, no. 40: 1–14.

Altieri, Andrés Radames. 1939. "Sobre un kipu peruano." *Notas del Instituto de Antropología {de la Universidad Nacional de Tucumán}* 1.1: 7–13.

Altieri, Radames A. 1941. "Sobre 11 kipu peruanos." *Revista del Instituto de Antropología de la Universidad Nacional de Tucumán* 2.1: 177–211.

Alva, Walter, and Christopher B. Donnan. 1993. *Royal Tombs of Sipán.* Los Angeles: UCLA Fowler Museum of Cultural History.

Anders, Martha B. 1986. "Wari Experiments in Statecraft." *Andean Archaeology: Papers in Memory of Clifford Evans.* Ed. Ramiro Matos M., Solveig A. Turpin, and Herbert H. Eling, Jr., pp. 201–224. Los Angeles: UCLA Institute of Archaelogy.

Anders, Martha B. 1989. "Evidence for the Dual Socio-Political Organisation and Administrative Structure of the Wari State." *The Nature of Wari: A Reappraisal of the Middle Horizon Period in Peru.* Eds. R.M. Czwarno, F.M. Meddens, and A. Morgan, pp. 35–52. Oxford: B.A.R.

Andrews, Anthony P. 1974. "The U-shaped Structures at Chan Chan, Peru." *Journal of Field Archaeology* 1: 241–264.

Anonymous. [1550] 1870. *Relación de todo lo sucedido en la provincia del Perú desde que Blasco Núñez Vela fue enviado por S.M. a ser visorrey della.* Lima: Imprenta del Estado.

Anonymous. [1600] 1944. *Historia general de la Compañía de Jesús en la provincia del Perú: Crónica anónima de 1600 que trata del establecimiento y misiones de la compañía de Jesús en los países de habla española en la América meridional*. 2 vols. Ed. Francisco Mateos. Biblioteca Missionalia Hispánica. Madrid: Consejo Superior de Investigaciones Científicas / Instituto Gonzalo Fernández de Oviedo.

Anonymous Jesuit. [1580–1594] 1968. "Relación de las costumbres antiguas de los naturales del Piru." *Crónicas peruanas de interés indígena*. Ed. Francisco Esteve Barba. Biblioteca de Autores Españoles, vol. 209. Madrid: Ediciones Atlas.

Ansión, Juan. 1990. "Como calculaban los incas." *Quipu y yupana: colección de escritos*. Ed. Carol Mackey, Hugo Pereyra, Carlos Radicati, Humberto Rodríguez, and Oscar Valverde, pp. 257–266. Lima: CONCYTEC.

Aparicio, Severo. 2001. *La Orden de la Merced en el Perú: Estudios históricos*. 2 vols. Cuzco: Provincia Mercedaria del Perú.

Arellano, Carmen. 1999. "Quipu y tocapu: Sistemas de comunicación Inca." *Los Incas: Arte y símbolos*, pp. 215–262. Lima: Banco de Crédito del Perú.

Arriaga, Pablo José de. [1599] 1974. "Annua de la Provincia del Pirú del año de noventa y ocho." *Monumenta peruana VI (1596–1599)*. *Monumenta Historica Societatis Iesu*, vol. 110. Ed. Antonio de Egaña, pp. 660–733. Rome: Apud "Institutum Historicum Societatis Iesu."

Arriaga, Pablo José de. 1621. *Extirpación de la idolatría del Piru*. Lima: Gerónimo de Contreras.

Ascher, Marcia. 1983. "The Logical-Numerical System of the Inca Quipus." *Annals of the History of Computing* 5.3: 268–278.

Ascher, Marcia. 1986. "Mathematical Ideas of the Incas." *Native American Mathematics*. Ed. Michael P. Closs, pp. 261–289. Austin: University of Texas Press.

Ascher, Marcia. 2002. "Reading Khipu: Labels, Structure, and Format." *Narrative Threads: Accounting and Recounting in Andean Khipu*. Eds. Jeffrey Quilter and Gary Urton, pp. 87–102. Austin: University of Texas Press.

Ascher, Marcia. 2005. "How Can Spin, Ply, and Knot Directionality Contribute to Understanding the Quipu Code?" *Latin American Antiquity* 16.1: 99–111.

Ascher, Robert. 2002. "Inka Writing." *Narrative Threads: Accounting and Recounting in Andean Khipu*. Eds. Jeffrey Quilter and Gary Urton, pp. 103–115. Austin: University of Texas Press.

Ascher, Marcia, and Robert Ascher. 1969 "Code of Ancient Peruvian Knotted Cords (Quipus)." *Nature* 222: 529–33.

Ascher, Marcia, and Robert Ascher. 1971 "Numbers and Relations from Ancient Andean Quipus." *Archive for History of Exact Sciences* 8.4: 288–320.

Ascher, Marcia, and Robert Ascher. 1975. "The Quipu as Visible Language." *Visible Language* 9.4: 329–356.

Ascher, Marcia, and Robert Ascher. 1981. *Code of the Quipu: A Study in Media, Mathematics, and Culture*. Ann Arbor: University of Michigan Press.

Ascher, Marcia, and Robert Ascher. 1989 "Are There Numbers in the Sky?" *Time and Calendars in the Inca Empire*. Ed. Mariusz S. Ziolkowski and Robert M. Sadowski, pp. 35–48. Oxford: B.A.R.

Assadourian, Carlos Sempat. 1998. "La creación del quipu con las cuerdas de los precios." *Población y sociedad* 5: 5–75.

Audiencia de Lima. [1602] 1981. "La Audiencia de Lima a los indios de Chucuito." *Monumenta peruana VII (1600–1602)*. *Monumenta Historica Societatis Iesu*, vol. 120. Ed. Antonio de Egaña and Enrique Fernández, pp. 953–959. Rome: Apud "Institutum Historicum Societatis Iesu."

Avalos y Figueroa, Diego de. 1602. *Primera parte de la Miscelánea Austral de don Diego Davalos y Figueroa en Varias Coloquias, Intercolutorea Delia y Cilena, con la Defensa de Damas dirigida a al excellentissimo don Luis de Velasco, Cavallero de la Oden {sic} de Santiago, Visorey, y Capitan general de los Reynos del Piru, Chile, y Tierra firme*. Lima: np.

Avila, Francisco de. [1608] 1991. "Tratado y relación de los errores, falsos dioses, y otras supersticiones y ritos diabólicos en que vivían antiguamente los Yndios de las provincias de Huarochirí. . . . " *The Huarochirí Manuscript: A Testament of Ancient and Colonial Andean Religion*. Trans. Frank Salomon and George L. Urioste. Austin: University of Texas Press.

Bakhtin, Mikhail. 1981. *The Dialogic Imagination*. Trans. Caryl Emerson and Michael Holquist. Austin: University of Texas Press.

Bakhtin, Mikhail. 1986. *Speech Genres & Other Late Essays*. Trans. Vern W. McGee. Austin: University of Texas Press.

Ballesteros, Manuel. 1984. Introducción. *La crónica del Perú*, pp. 7–54. Madrid: Historia 16.

Ballesteros, Manuel. 1985. Introducción. *El señorío de los Incas*, pp. 7–29. Madrid: Historia 16.

Bandera, Damián de la. [1557] 1965. "Relación general de la disposición y calidad de la provincia de Guamana, llamada San Joan de la Frontera, y de la vivienda y costumbres de los naturales de ella.–Año de 1557." *Relaciones geográficas de Indias–Perú*, vol. 1. Ed. Marcos Jiménez de la Espada, pp. 176-180. Madrid: Ediciones Atlas.

Bandera, Damián de la. [1582] 1925. Testimony of Damián de la Bandera. "Instrucción hecha en el Cuzco, por orden del Rey y encargo del Virrey Martín Enríquez acerca de las costumbres que tenían los Incas del Perú . . . ." *La imprenta en Lima*, vol. 1. Ed. José Toribio Medina, pp. 278–279. Madrid: Juan Pueyo.

Barriga, Victor. 1933. *Los mercedarios en el Perú en el siglo XVI: Documentos inéditos del Archivo General de Indias*. 3 vols. Rome: Boletín de la Orden de la Merced.

Barthel, Thomas. 1970. "Erste Schritte zur Entzifferung der Inkaschrift." *Tribus* 19: 91–96.

Barthel, Thomas. 1971. "Viracochas Prunkgewant (Tocapu-Studien 1)." *Tribus* 20: 63–124.

Bauer, Brian. S. 1992. *The Development of the Inca State*. Austin: University of Texas Press.

Bauer, Brian S. 1998. *The Sacred Landscape of the Inca: The Cusco Ceque System*. Austin: University of Texas Press.

Bawden, Garth. 1994. "La paradoja estructura: la cultura moche como ideología política." *Moche: propuestas y perspectivas*. Eds. Santiago Uceda and Elías Mujica, pp. 389–412. Trujillo: Universidad Nacional de la Libertad.

Bawden, Garth. 1995. "The Structural Paradox: Moche Culture as Political Ideology." *Latin American Antiquity* 6.3: 255–273.

Bawden, Garth, 1996. *The Moche*. Cambridge, MA: Blackwell.

Benjamin, Walter. 1968. *Illuminations*. Trans. Harry Zohn. New York: Shocken.

Betanzos, Juan de. [1551] 1987. *Suma y narración de los Incas*. Ed. María del Carmen Martín Rubio. Madrid: Atlas.

Betanzos, Juan de. [1551] 1996. *Narrative of the Incas*. Trans. Roland Hamilton and Dana Buchanan. Austin: University of Texas Press.

Biakolo, Emevwo. 1999. "On the Theoretical Foundations of Orality and Literacy." *Research in African Literatures* 30.2: 42–65.

Billman, Brian R. 2002. "Irrigation and the Origins of the Southern Moche State on the North Coast of Peru." *Latin American Antiquity* 13.4: 371–400.

Bird, Robert McK. 1972. "La agricultura en la visita de Ortiz." *Visita de la Provincia de León de Huánuco en 1562*, by Iñigo Ortiz de Zúñiga, vol. 1, pp. 363–367. Ed. John V. Murra. Huánuco, Perú: Universidad Nacional Hermilio Valdizán.

Boone, Elizabeth Hill. 2000. *Stories in Red and Black: Pictorial Histories of the Aztecs and Mixtecs*. Austin: University of Texas Press.

Brewster-Wray, Christine C. 1989. "Huari Administration: A View from the Capital." *The Nature of Wari: A Reappraisal of the Middle Horizon Period in Peru*. Eds. R.M. Czwarno, F.M. Meddens, and A. Morgan, pp. 23–34. Oxford: B.A.R.

Brokaw, Galen. 2001. "El khipu como fuente en la Nueva corónica de Felipe Guaman Poma de Ayala." *Guaman Poma y Blas Valera: Tradición Andina e Historia Colonial.* Ed. Francesca Cantú, pp. 417–429. Rome: Instituto Italo-Latinoamericano.

Brokaw, Galen. 2002. "Khipu Numeracy and Alphabetic Literacy in the Andes: Felipe Guaman Poma de Ayala's Nueva corónica y buen gobierno." *Colonial Latin American Review* 11.2: 275–303.

Brokaw, Galen. 2003. "The Poetics of Khipu Historiography: Felipe Guaman Poma de Ayala's Nueva corónica and the Relación de los quipucamayos." *Latin American Research Review* 38.3: 111–147.

Brokaw, Galen. 2005. "Toward Deciphering the Khipu." *Journal of Interdisciplinary History* 35.4: 571–589.

Brokaw, Galen. 2006. "Ollantay, the Khipu, and Eighteenth-Century Neo-Inca Politics." *Bulletin of the Comediantes* 58.1: 31–56.

Brotherston, Gordon. 1992. *Book of the Fourth World: Reading the Native Americas Through Their Literature.* Cambridge: Cambridge University Press.

Browman, David L. 1978. "Toward the Development of the Tiahuanaco (Tiwanaku) State." *Advances in Andean Archaeology.* Ed. David L. Browman, pp. 327–349. The Hague: Mouton.

Browman, David L. 1984. "Tiwanaku: Development of Interzonal Trade and Economic Expansion in the Altiplano." *Social and Economic Organization in the Prehispanic Andes.* Ed. David L. Browman, Richard L. Burger, and Mario A. Rivera, pp. 117–142. Oxford: B.A.R.

Burger, Richard L. 1992. *Chavín and the Origens of Andean civilization.* London: Thames and Hudson.

Burger, Richard L., and Ramiro Matos Mendieta. 2002. "Atalla: A Center on the Periphery of the Chavín Hoirzon." *Latin American Antiquity* 13.2: 153–177.

Burkholder, Jo Ellen. 2001. "La cerámica de Tiwanaku: ¿Qué indica su variabilidad?" *Boletín de Arqueología PUCP* 5: 217–249.

Burns Glynn, William. 1990. *Legado de los Amautas.* Lima: Consejo Nacional de Ciencia y Tecnología.

Burns Glynn, William. 2002. *Decodificación de quipus.* Lima: Banco Central de la Reserva del Peru / Universidad Alas Peruana.

Cabello Balboa, Miguel. [1578–1586] 1951. *Miscelánea antartica.* Lima: Universidad Nacional Mayor de San Marcos, Instituto de Etnología.

Cabredo, P.R. [1602] 1986. "Anua de la provincia del Perú del año de 1602." *Monumenta peruana VIII (1603–1604).* Ed. Enrique Fernández. Monumenta Historica Societatis Iesu, vol. 128. Rome: Apud "Institutum Historicum Societatis Iesu."

Cahill, David. 2002. "The Virgin and the Inca: An Incaic Procession in the City of Cuzco in 1692." *Ethnohistory* 49.3: 611–649.

Calancha, Fray Antonio de la. 1638. *Crónica moralizada del orden de San Agustín den el Perú.* Barcelona: Pedro Lacavalleria.

Campana D., Cristóbal. 1994. "El entorno cultural en un dibujo mochica." *Moche: Propuesta y perspectivas.* Eds. Santiago Uceda and Elías Mujica, pp. 449–473. Trujillo: Universidad Nacional de La Libertad.

Capoche, Luis. [1585] 1959. *Relación general de la Villa Imperial de Potosí.* Biblioteca de Autores Españoles, vol. 122. Madrid: Ediciones Atlas.

Castillo, Luis Jaime. 2001. "The Last of the Mochicas: A View from the Jequetepeque Valley." *Moche Art and Archaeology in Ancient Peru.* Ed. Joanne Pillsbury, pp. 307–332. New Haven: Yale University Press.

Castillo, Luis Jaime, and Christober Donnan. 1994. "Los mochicas del norte y los mochicas del sur: una perspectiva desde el valle de Jequetepeque." *Vicús*. Ed. Krzysztof Makowski, pp. 143–181. Lima: Banco del Crédito del Perú.

Céspedes, Gillermo. 1946. "La visita como institución indiana." *Anuario de estudios americanos* 3: 984–1025.

Chamberlain, Robert S. 1939. "The Concept of the Señor Natural as Revealed by Castillian Law and Administrative Documents." *Hispanic American Historical Review* 19.2: 130–137.

Charles, John. 2007. "Unreliable Confessions: Khipus in the Colonial Parish." *The Americas* 64.1: 11–33.

Cieza de León, Pedro. [1553] 1984. *La crónica del Perú*. Madrid: Historia 16.

Cieza de León, Pedro. [1553] 1985. *El señorío de los Incas*. Madrid: Historia 16.

Cobo, Bernabé. [1639/1653] 1956. *Historia del Nuevo Mundo*. 2 vols. Biblioteca de Autores Españoles, vol. 91–92. Madrid: Ediciones Atlas.

Cobo, Bernabé. [1653] 1979. *History of the Inca Empire*. Trans. Ronald Hamilton. Austin: Univeristy of Texas Press.

Collapiña, Supno, et al. [1542/1608] 1921. "Discurso sobre la descendencia y gobierno de los Incas." *Informaciones sobre el antiguo Perú*. Ed. Horacio H. Urteaga, pp. 1–53 Lima: San Martí.

Collapiña, Supno, et al. [1542/1608] 1974. *Relación de la descendencia, gobierno y conquista de los Incas*. Ed. Juan José Vega. Lima: Ediciones de la Biblioteca Universitaria.

Collon, Dominique. 1990. *Near Eastern Seals*. Berkeley: University of California Press.

Conklin, William. 1982. "The Information System of Middle Horizon Quipus." *Ethnoastronomy and Archaeoastronomy in the American Tropics*. Ed. Anthony F. Aveni and Gary Urton, pp. 261–281. New York: New York Academy of Sciences.

Conklin, William. 2002. "A Khipu Information String Theory." *Narrative Threads: Accounting and Recounting in Andean Khipu*. Eds. Jeffrey Quilter and Gary Urton, pp. 53–86. Austin: University of Texas Press.

Conlee, Christina A. 2003. "Local Elites and the Reformation of Late Intermediate Period Sociopolitical and Economic Organization in Nasca, Peru." *Latin American Antiquity* 14.1: 47–65.

Contreras y Valverde, Vasco de. [1649] 1982. *Relación de la ciudad del Cuzco*. Ed. María del Carmen Martín Rubio. Cuzco: Imprenta Amauta.

Cook, Alexandra Parma, and Noble David Cook. 1998. Introduction. *The Discovery and Conquest of Peru*, by Pedro Cieza de León. Ed. and trans. Alexandra Parma Cook and Noble David Cook, pp. 5–35. Durham: Duke University Press.

Crespo, Juan Carlos. 1977. "Los Collaguas en la visita de Alonso Fernández de Bonilla." *Collaguas I*. Ed. Franklin Pease, pp. 53–91. Lima: PUCP.

Czwarno, R. Michael. 1986. "Social Patterning and the Investigation of Political Control: The Case for the Moche/Chimu Area." *The Nature of Wari: A Reappraisal of the Middle Horizon Period in Peru*. Eds. R.M. Czwarno, F.M. Meddens, and A. Morgan, pp. 115–145. Oxford: B.A.R.

Czwarno, R. M. 1988. "Spatial Logic and the Investigation of Control in Middle Horizon Peru." *Separata of Recent Studies in Pre-Columbian Archaeology*, directed by N. J. Saunders and O. de Montmollin, pp. 415–456. BAR International Series 421. Oxford: B.A.R.

Day, Kent. 1982. "Storage and Labor Service: A Production and Management Design in the Andean Area." *Chan Chan: Andean Desert City*. Ed. Michael E. Moseley and Kent Day, pp. 333–349. Albuquerque: University of New Mexico Press.

Derrida, Jacques. 1974. *Of Grammatology*. Baltimore: Johns Hopkins University Press.

Diez Canseco, María. 1966. "Visitas de Indios en el siglo XVI." *Cahiers du monde hispanique et luso-brésilien (Caravelle)* 7: 85–92.

Diez de San Miguel, Garci. [1567] 1964. *Visita hecha a la provincia de Chucuito por Garci Diez de San Miguel en el año 1567*. Ed. Waldemar Espinoza Soriano. Lima: Casa de la Cultura del Perú.

Doctrina cristiana y catecismo para instruccion de los Indios. 1583. Lima: Antonio Ricardo.

Donnan, Christopher B. 1973. *Moche Occupation of the Santa Valley, Peru*. Berkeley: University of California Press.

Donnan, Christopher B. 1976. *Moche Art and Iconography*. Los Angeles: UCLA Latin American Center.

Donnan, Christopher B. 1985a. "Archaeological Confirmation of a Moche Ceremony." *Indiana* 10 (Teil 2): 371–381.

Donnan, Christopher B., ed. 1985b. *Early Ceremonial Architecture in the Andes*. Washington D.C.: Dumbarton Oaks.

Donnan, Christopher B. 1988. "Unraveling the Mystery of the Warrior-Priest." *National Geographic* 174.4: 551–555.

Donnan, Christopher B., and Luis Jaime Castillo. 1992. "Finding the Tomb of a Moche Princess." *Archaeology* 45.6: 38–42.

Donnan, Christopher B., and Luis Jaime Castillo. 1994. "Excavaciones de tumbas de sacerdotistas Moche en San José de Moro, Jequetepeque." *Moche: Propuestas y perspectivas*. Ed. Santiago Uceda and Elías Mujica, pp. 415–424. Trujillo: Universidad Nacional de La Libertad.

Donnan, Christopher B., and Donna McClelland. 1999. *Moche Fineline Painting: Its Evolution and Its Artists*. Los Angeles: UCLA Fowler Museum of Cultural History.

Durston, Alan. 2007. *Pastoral Quechua: The History of Christian Translation in Colonial Peru, 1550–1650*. Notre Dame: University of Notre Dame Press.

Duviols, Pierre. 1971. *La lutte contre les religions autochtones dans le Pérou colonial: l'extirpation de l'idolâtrie entre 1532 et 1660*. Travaux de l'Insitut Français d'Etudes Andine, vol. 13. Paris: Institut Français d'Etudes Andines / Editions Ophrys.

Duviols, Pierre. 1979. "Datation, paternité et idéologie de la «Declaración de los quipucamayos a Vaca de Castro» (Discurso de la descendencia y gobierno de los Ingas)." *Les cultures ibériques en devenir: essais publiés en hommage à la mémoire de Marcel Bataillon (1895–1977)*, pp. 583–591. Paris: La Fondation Singer-Polignac.

Engel, Frédéric. 1957. "Sites et établissements sans céramique de la côte péruvienne." *Journal de la Société des Américanistes* (new series) 46: 67–155.

Engel, Frédéric. 1958. "Algunos datos con referencia a los sitios precerámicos de la costa peruana." *Arqueológicas* 3: 53.

Engel, Frédéric. 1966. "Le complexe préceramique d'El Paraiso (Pérou)." *Journal de la Société des Américanistes* (new series) 55: 43–96.

Espinoza Bravo, Clodoaldo. 1962. "El Licenciado Pedro de la Gasca en Jauja." *Revista del Museo Nacional* 31: 165–167.

Espinoza Soriano, Waldemar. 1964. "El curacazgo de Conchucos y la visita de 1543." *Bulletin de l'Institut Français d'Etudes Andines* 3.1: 9-31.

Espinoza Soriano, Waldemar. 1967a. "El primer informe etnológico sobre Cajamarca. Año de 1540." *Revista peruana de cultura* 11–12: 5–41.

Espinoza Soriano, Waldemar. 1967b. "Los señores étnicos de Chachapoyas y la alianza hispano-chacha: visitas, informaciones y memoriales inéditos de 1572–1574." *Revista histórica* 30: 224–332.

Espinoza Soriano, Waldemar. 1971–1972. "Los Huancas, aliados de la conquista: tres informaciones inéditas sobre la participación indígena en la conquista del Peru, 1558, 1560, 1561." *Anales científicos de la Universidad del Centro* 1: 9–407.

Espinoza Soriano, Waldemar. 1975. "Ichoc-Huanuco y el señorío del curaca huanca en el reino de Huánuco, siglos XV y XVI: una visita inédita de 1549 para la etnohistoria andina." *Anales científicos (Universidad Nacional del Centro del Perú)* 4: 7–70.

Espinoza Soriano, Waldemar. 1978. *Huaraz: Poder, sociedad y economía en los siglos XV y XVI. Reflexiones en torno a las visitas de 1558, 1594 y 1712*. Lima: UNMSM.

Espinoza Soriano, Waldemar. 1980. "Los fundamentos lingüísticos de la etnohistoria andina y comentarios en torno al anónimo de Charcas de 1604." *Revista española de antropología* 10: 149–181.

Espejo Núñez, Julio. 1953. "El kipu peruano." *Cultura* (Lima) 2.3 (junio): np [5].

Espejo Núñez, Julio. 1957. *Bibliografía básica de Arqueología Andina VI: Kipu peruano*. Lima: Editorial San Marcos.

Estenssoro Fuchs, Juan Carlos. 2003. *Del paganismo a la santidad: La incorporación de los indios del Perú al catolicismo, 1532–1750*. Lima: Instituto Francés de Estudios Andinos / PUCP.

Estete, Miguel. [1534–1535] 1924. *Noticia del Perú (El descubrimiento y la conquista del Perú)*. Colección de libros y documentos referentes a la historia del Perú, 2nd series, vol. 8, pp. 3–71. Lima: Imprenta y Librería Sanmartí.

Esteve Barba, Francisco. 1992. *Historiografía indiana*. Madrid: Gredos.

Flores Ochoa, Jorge A. 1968. *Pastoralists of the Andes: The Alpaca Herders of Paratía*. Trans. Ralph Bolton. Philadelphia: Institute for the Study of Human Issues.

Foley, John Miles, ed. 1981. *Oral Traditional Literature: A Festschrift for Albert Bates Lord*. Columbus, OH: Slavica.

Foley, John Miles, ed. 1987. *Comparative Research on Oral Traditions: A Memorial for Milman Parry*. Columbus, OH: Slavica.

Foley, John Miles. 2002. *How to Read an Oral Poem*. Urbana: University of Illinois Press.

Fossa, Lydia. 2000. "Two Khipu, One Narrative: Answering Urton's Questions. "*Ethnohistory* 47.2: 453–468.

Frame, Mary. 2007. "Lo que Guaman Poma nos muestra pero no nos dice sobre Tukapu." *Revista andina* 44: 9–69.

Galdós Rodríguez, Guillermo. 1975–1976. "Visita a Atico y Caravelí (1549)." *Revista del Archivo General de la Nación* 4/5: 55–80.

Gálvez Peña, Carlos M. 1998. Prólogo. *Historia del reino y provincias del Perú* by Giovanni Annello Oliva, pp. ix-lix. Lima: Pontificia Universidad Católica del Peru.

Gante, Pedro de. 1553. *Doctrina cristiana en lengua mexicana*. Mexico: np.

García de Melo. [1582] 1925. Testimony of García de Melo. "Instrucción hecha en el Cuzco, por orden del Rey y encargo del Virrey Martín Enríquez acerca de las costumbres que tenían los Incas del Perú. . . . " *La imprenta en Lima*. Ed. José Toribio Medina, vol 1, pp. 271–278. Madrid: Juan Pueyo.

Garcilaso de la Vega, el Inca. [1609] 1985. *Comentarios reales*. 2 vols. Caracas: Biblioteca Ayacucho.

Garcilaso de la Vega, el Inca. [1609] 1966. *Royal Commentaries of the Incas, and General History of Peru*. Trans. Harold V. Livermore. Austin: University of Texas Press.

Gaur, Albertine. 2000. *Literacy and the Politics of Writing*. Bristol, UK: Intellect.

Gisbert, Teresa, and José de Mesa. 1966. "Los chipayas." *Anuario de Estudios Americanos* 23: 479–506.

Glowacki, Mary, and Michael Malpass. 2003. "Water, Huacas, and Ancestor Worship: Traces of a Sacred Wari Landscape." *Latin American Antiquity* 14.4: 431–448.

Glowacki, Mary, and Gordon McEwan. 2001. "Pikillacta, Huaro y la gran región del Cuzco: nuevas interpretaciones de la ocupación wari de la sierra sur." *Boletín de Arqueología PUCP* 5: 31–49.

González, Juan. [1560] 1990. *Visita de los Yndios Churumatas e Yndios Charcas de Totora que todos están en cabeza de su Magestad, 1560*. Ed. Raimund Schramm. La Paz, Bolivia: MUSEF.

González Holguín, Diego. [1608] 1989. *Vocabulario de la lengua general de todo el Perú llamada lengua Qqichua o del Inca*. Ed. Raúl Porras Barrenechea. Lima: Universidad Nacional Mayor de San Marcos.

González Pujana, Laura. 1993. *La vida y obra del licenciado Polo de Ondegardo*. Valladolid: Universidad de Valladolid.

González, Laura, and Alicia Alonso. 1990. Introducción. *El mundo de los Incas*, pp 7–25. Madrid: Historia 16.

González de la Rosa, Manuel. [1881] 1935. "El Padre Bernabé Cobo." *Monografías históricas sobre la ciudad de Lima*, pp. vii-xvii. Vol I. Lima: Gil S.A.

González de la Rosa, Manuel. 1900. "Polémica histórica: Las obras del Padre Valera y de Garcilaso." *Revista histórica* 4: 301–311.

González de la Rosa, Manuel. 1907. "El Padre Valera, primer historiador Peruano." *Revista histórica* 3: 296–306.

González de la Rosa, Manuel. 1908. "Los Comentarios reales son la réplica de Valera a Pedro Sarmiento de Gamboa." *Revista histórica* 2: 180–199.

Goody, Jack, ed. 1968. *Literacy in Traditional Societies*. Cambridge: Cambridge University Press.

Goody, Jack. 1977. *The Domestication of the Savage Mind*. Cambridge: Cambridge University Press.

Goody, Jack. 1986. *The Logic of Writing and the Organization of Society*. Cambridge: Cambridge University Press.

Goody, Jack. 1987. *The Interface Between the Oral and the Written*. Cambridge: Cambridge University Press.

Goody, Jack. 2000. *The Power of the Written Tradition*. Washington, D.C.: Smithsonian Institution Press.

Gordillo, José M. and Mercedes del Río. 1993. *La visita de Tiquipaya (1573): Análisis etno-demográfico de un padrón toledano*. Cochabamba (Bolivia): UMSS – CERES – ODEC/FRE.

Gose, Peter. 1993. "Segmentary State Formation and the Ritual Control of Water under the Incas." *Comparative Study of Society and History* 35: 480–514.

Guaman Poma de Ayala, Felipe. 1615. *El primer nueva corónica y buen gobierno*. Gl. Kgl.S. 2232, 4°. Copenhagen: Royal Library of Denmark.

Guaman Poma de Ayala, Felipe. [1615] 1980. *El primer nueva corónica y buen gobierno*. Eds. John V. Murra and Rolena Adorno. Trans. Jorge Urioste. Mexico: Siglo Veintiuno.

Guaman Poma de Ayala, Felipe. [1615] 1987. *Nueva corónica y buen gobierno*. 3 vols. Eds. John V. Murra, Rolena Adorno, and Jorge L. Urioste. Madrid: Historia 16.

Guimaraes, Enrique de. 1907. "Algo sobre el quipus." *Revista Histórica* 2: 55–62.

Gutiérrez de Santa Clara, Pedro. [c.1596–1603] 1963. *Quinquenarios o Historia de las guerras civiles del Perú*. 3 vols. Biblioteca de Autores Españoles, vols. 165–167. Madrid: Atlas.

Hamilton, Roland. 1979. "Introduction: Father Cobo and His Historia." *History of the Inca Empire: An Account of the Indians' Customs and Their Origin, Together with a Treatise on Inca Legends, History, and Social Institutions*. Trans. and ed. Roland Hamilton, pp. xiii-xxii. Austin: University of Texas Press.

Hampe Martínez, Teodoro. 1979. "Relación de los encomenderos y repartimientos del Perú en 1561." *Historia y cultura* 12: 75–117.

Hanke, Lewis, and Celso Rodríguez, eds. 1978. *Los virreyes españoles en América durante el gobierno de la casa de Austria*. 2 vols. Biblioteca de Autores Españoles, vols. 280–281. Madrid: Atlas.

Harris, Roy. 1986. *The Origin of Writing*. London: Duckworth.

Harrison, Regina. 1994. "The Theology of Concupiscence: Spanish-Quechua Confessional Manuals in the Andes." *Coded Encounters: Writing, Gender, and Ethnicity in Colonial Latin America*. Eds. Francisco Javier Cevallos-Candau, Jeffrey A. Cole, Nina M. Scott, and Nicomees Suárez-Araúz, pp. 135–150. Amherst: University of Massachusetts Press.

Harrison, Regina. 2002. "Pérez Bocanegra's Ritual formulario: Khipu Knots and Confession." *Narrative Threads: Accounting and Recounting in Andean Khipu*. Eds. Jeffrey Quilter and Gary Urton, pp. 266–290. Austin: University of Texas Press, 2002.

Hastings, C. Mansfield, and M. Edward Moseley. 1975. "The Adobes of Huaca del Sol and Huaca de la Luna." *American Antiquity* 40.2: 196–203.

Havelock, Eric, and Jackson P. Hershbell, eds. 1978. *Communication Arts in the Ancient World*. New York: Hastings House.

Havelock, Eric. 1963. *Preface to Plato*. Cambridge: Belknap Press of Harvard University Press.

Havelock, Eric. 1982. *The Literate Revolution in Greece and Its Cultural Consequences*. Princeton: Princeton University Press.

Havelock, Eric. 1986. *The Muse Learns to Write: Reflections on Orality and Literacy From Antiquity to the Present*. New Haven: Yale University Press.

Helmer, Marie. 1993. "La visitación de los Yndios Chupachos: Inka et Encomendero." *Cantuta: Recueil d'articles parus entre 1949 et 1987*, pp. 147–182. Madrid: Casa de Velázquez.

Hiltunen, Juha. 1999. *The Ancient Kings of Peru: The Reliability of the Chronicle of Fernando de Montesinos*. Helsinki: Suomen Historiallinen Seura.

Horswell, Michael. 2007. *Decolonizing the Sodomite: Queer Tropes of Sexuality in Colonial Andean Culture*. Austin: University of Texas Press.

Houston, Stephen. 2004. "The Archaeology of Communication Technologies." *Annual Review of Anthropology* 33: 223–250.

Houston, Stephen. 2008. "Overture to the First Writing." *First Writing*. Ed. Stephen Houston, pp. 3–15. Cambridge: Cambridge University Press.

Hyland, Sabine. 2003. *The Jesuit and the Incas: The Extraordinary Life of Padre Blas Valera, S.J.* Ann Arbor: University of Michigan Press.

Hyland, Sabine. [1642] 2007. *The Quito Manuscript: An Inca History Preserved by Fernando de Montesinos*. New Haven: Yale University Publications in Anthropology.

Innis, Harold. 1951. *The Bias of Communication*. Toronto: Toronto University Press.

Isbell, William H. 1977. *The Rural Foundation for Urbanism: Economic and Stylistic Interaction between Rural and Urban Communities in Eigth-Century Peru*. Urbana: University of Illinois Press.

Isbell, William H. 1986. "Emergence of City and State at Wari, Ayacucho, Peru, during the Middle Horizon." *Andean Archaeology: Papers in Memory of Clifford Evans*. Eds. Ramiro Martos M., Solveig A. Turpin, and Herbert E. Eling Jr., pp. 164–189. Los Angeles: University of California Institute of Archaeology.

Isbell, William H. 1989. "Honcopampa: Was It a Huari Administrative Centre?" *The Nature of Wari: A Reappraisal of the Middle Horizon Period in Peru*. Eds. R.M. Czwarno, F.M. Meddens, and A. Morgan, pp. 98–114. Oxford: B.A.R.

Isbell, William H. 1997. *Mummies and Mortuary Monuments: A Postprocessual Prehistory of Central Andean Social Organization*. Austin: University of Texas Press.

Isbell, William H. 2000. "Repensando el Horizonte Medio: El caso de Conchopata, Ayacucho, Perú." *Boletín de Arqueología PUCP* 4: 9–68.

Jackson, Margaret A. 2008. *Moche Art and Visual Culture in Ancient Peru*. Albuquerque: University of New Mexico Press.

Janusek, John Wayne. 2002. "Out of Many, One: Style and Social Boundaries in Tiwanaku." *Latin American Antiquity* 13.1: 35–61.

Jara, Victoria de la. 1970. "La solución del problema de la escritura peruana." *Arqueología y sociedad* 1: 27–35.

Jiménez de la Espada, Marcos. 1877. Introducción. *Tercero libro de las guerras civiles del Perú. . . .* by Pedro Cieza de León, pp. i–cxix. Madrid: M.G. Hernández.

Julien, Catherine. 1982. "Inca Decimal Administration in the Lake Titicaca Region." *The Inca and Aztec States, 1400–1800: Anthropology and History*. Eds. George A. Collier, Renato Rosaldo, and John D. Wirth, pp. 119–151. New York: Academic Press.

Julien, Catherine. 2000. *Reading Inca History*. Iowa City: University of Iowa Press.

Kant, Immanuel. [1790] 2000. *Critique of the Power of Judgment*. Ed. and trans. Eric Matthews and Paul Guyer. Cambridge: Cambridge University Press.

Kaulicke, Peter. 2000. *Memoria y muerte en el Perú antiguo*. Lima: PUCP.

Knobloch, Patricia J. 2000. "Wari Ritual Power at Conchopata: An Interpretation of Anadenanthera Colubrina Iconography." *Latin American Antiquity* 11.4: 387–402.

Kolata, Alan. 1982. "Chronology and Settlement Growth at Chan Chan." *Chan Chan: Andean Desert City*. Ed. Michael E. Moseley and Kent Day, pp. 67–85. Albuquerque: University of New Mexico Press, 1982.

Kolata, Alan L. 1990. "The Urban Concept of Chan Chan." *The Northern Dynasties: Kingship and Statecraft in Chimor*. Eds. Michael E. Moseley and Alana Cordy Collins, pp. 107–144. Washington, D.C.: Dumbarton Oaks.

Kolata, Alan L. 1991. "The Technology and Organization of Agricultural Production in the Tiwanaku State." *Latin American Antiquity* 2.2: 99–125.

Kolata, Alan L. 1993. *Tiwanaku: Portrait of an Andean Civilization*. Cambridge: Blackwell.

Kristeva, Julia. 1984. *Revolution in Poetic Language*. New York: Columbia University Press.

Landázuri N., Cristóbal. 1990. "El cacicazgo y la encomienda: anotaciones en torno a la visita de 1559 al valle de los Chillos." *Visita y numeración de los pueblos del valle de los Chillos, 1551–1559*. Ed. Cristóbal Landázuri N., pp. 11–47. Quito: MARKA & ABYA-YALA.

Lanning, Edward P. 1964. "Las culturas precerámicas de la costa central del Perú." *Revista del Museo Nacional* 33: 408–415.

Lanning, Edward P. 1967. *Peru Before the Incas*. Englewood Cliffs, NJ: Prentice-Hall Inc.

Lara, Jesús. 1947. *Poesía Quechua*. Mexico: Fondo de Cultura Economica.

Larco Hoyle, Rafael. 1939. *Los Mochicas*. 2 vols. Lima: Rimac.

Larco Hoyle, Rafael. 1942. "La escritura mochica sobre pallares." *Revista geográfica americana* 18.107: 93–103.

Larco Hoyle, Rafael. 1943a. "La escritura peruana sobre pallares." *Revista geográfica americana* 20.122: 277–292.

Larco Hoyle, Rafael. 1943b. "La escritura peruana sobre pallares." *Revista geográfica americana* 20.123: 345–354.

Larco Hoyle, Rafael. [1939] 2001. *Los Mochicas*. Lima: Museo Arqueológico Larco Herrera.

Larrabure y Unanue, Eugenio. 1935. "El quipu." *Manuscritos y publicaciones de Eugenio Larrabure y Uanue (1934–1936)*. Vol. 2: *Historia y arqueología*, pp. 123–131. Lima: Imprenta Americana.

Latcham, Ricardo E. 1922. *Los animales domésticos en la América precolombina*. Santiago, Chile: Museo de Etnología y Antropología / Imprenta Cervantes.

Laurencich Minelli, Laura. 1996. *La scrittura dell'antico Perù: un mondo da scopire*. Bologna: CLUEB.

Levine, Terry Y. 1992. *Inka Storage Systems*. Norman: University of Oklahoma Press.

Lerche, Peter. 1995. *Los Chachapoyas y los símbolos de su historia*. Lima: César Gayoso.

Levillier, Roberto. 1921–1926. *Gobernantes del Perú: Cartas y papeles, siglo XVI*. 14 vols. Biblioteca del Congreso Argentino. Madrid: Juan Pueyo.

Levillier, Roberto. 1956. *Los Incas*. Sevilla: CSIC.

Loaysa, Francisco. 1945. Introducción. *Las costumbres antiguas del Perú y la historia de los Incas (siglo XVI)*, by Blas Valera. Ed. Francisco Loaysa, pp. i–xxiii. Lima: np.

Locke, Leland. 1923. *The Ancient Quipu or Peruvian Knot Record*. New York: The American Museum of Natural History.

Lopétegui, León. 1942. *El Padre José de Acosta, S.I., y las misiones*. Madrid: Consejo Superior de Investigaciones Científicas.

López, Andrés. [1576] 1954. Carta al Padre Doctor Plaza, Visitador. *Obras del P. José de Acosta*. Ed. Francisco Mateos, pp. 275–276. Biblioteca de Autores Españoles, vol. 73. Madrid: Ediciones Atlas.

Lord, Albert Bates. 1960. *The Singer of Tales*. Cambridge: Harvard University Press.

Loza, Carmen Beatriz. 1998a. "Du bon usage des quipus face à l'administration colonial espagnole (1550–1600)." *Population* 53.1–2: 139–60.

Loza, Carmen Beatriz. 1998b. "Juger les chiffres: Status des nombres et pratiques de comptage dans les dénombrement andins, 1542–1560." *Histoire & Mesure* 13.1–2: 13–37.

Loza, Carmen Beatriz. 1999. "Quipus and Quipolas at the Museum für Völkerkunde, Berlin. Genesis of a Reference Collection (1872–1999)." *Baessler Archiv* 47.1: 39–75.

Loza, Carmen Beatriz. 2000. "El quipu y la prueba en la practica del Derecho de India, 1550–1581." *Historia y Cultura* (La Paz): 11–34.

Loza, Carmen Beatriz. 2001. "El uso de los quipus contra la administración colonial española (1550–1600)." *Nueva síntesis* 7/8: 59–92.

Lumbreras, Luis G. 1989. "Textiles and Ancient Peru." *The Textile Art of Peru*. Ed. José Antonio de Lavalle, pp. 17–23. Lima: Industria Textil Piura, PIMAX.

Mackey, Carol J. 1970. "Knot Records in Ancient and Modern Peru." Ph.D. dissertation, Department of Anthropology, University of California, Berkeley.

Mackey, Carol J. 1990a. "Comparación entre quipu inca y quipu modernos." *Quipu y yupana: colección de escritos*. Ed. Carol J. Mackey et al., pp. 135–155. Lima: Consejo Nacional de Ciencia y Tecnología.

Mackey, Carol J. 1990b. "Nieves Yucra Huatta y la continuidad de la tradición del uso del quipu." *Quipu y yupana: colección de escritos*. Ed. Carol J. Mackey et al., pp. 157–164. Lima: Consejo Nacional de Ciencia y Tecnología.

Mackey, Carol. 2002. "The Continuing Khipu Traditions: Principles and Practices." *Narrative Threads: Accounting and Recounting in Andean Khipu*. Eds. Jeffrey Quilter and Gary Urton, pp. 320–347. Austin: University of Texas Press.

MacCormack, Sabine. 1991. *Religion in the Andes: Vision and Imagination in Early Colonial Peru*. Princeton: Princeton University Press.

Mannheim, Bruce. 1991. *The Language of the Inka since the European Invasion*. Austin: University of Texas Press.

Martínez, Diego. [1576] 1954. Carta al P. Provincial. *Obras del P. José de Acosta*. Ed. Francisco Mateos, pp. 284–286. Biblioteca de Autores Españoles, vol. 73. Madrid: Ediciones Atlas.

Martínez Cereceda, José Luis. 1995. *Autoridades en los Andes: los atributos del señor*. Lima: Pontificia Universidad Católica del Perú.

Mateos, Francisco. 1954. Introducción. *Obras del P. José de Acosta*. Ed. Francisco Mateos, pp. vii–xlix. Biblioteca de Autores Españoles, vol. 73. Madrid: Ediciones Atlas.

Matienzo, Juan de. [1567] 1967. *Gobierno del Perú*. Ed. Guillermo Lohmann Villena. Travaux de l'Institut Français d'Etudies Andines, Vol. 11. Paris-Lima: L'Institut Français d'Etudes Andines / Ministère des Affaires Etrangères.

McAndrews, Timothy, Juan Albarracin-Jordan, and Marc Bermann. 1997. "Regional Settlement Patterns in the Tiwanaku Valley of Bolivia." *Journal of Field Archaeology* 24: 67–83.

McEwan, Gordon F. 1989. "The Wari Empire in the Southern Peruvian Highlands: A View from the Provinces." *The Nature of Wari: A Reappraisal of the Middle Horizon Period in Peru*. Eds. R.M. Czwarno, F.M. Meddens, and A. Morgan, pp. 53–71. Oxford: B.A.R.

McEwan, Gordon F. 1990. "Some Formal Correspondences between the Imperial Architecture of the Wari and Chimu Cultures of Ancient Peru." *Latin American Antiquity* 1.2: 97–116.

McLuhan, Marshall. 1994. *Understanding Media: The Extensions of Man*. Cambridge, MA: MIT Press.

McCown, Theodore D. 1945. *Pre-Incaic Huamachuco: Survey and Excavations in the Region of Huamachuco and Cajabamba*. University of California Publucations in American Archaeology and Ethnology, vol. 39, no. 4. Berkeley: University of California Press.

Means, Philip. 1928. *Biblioteca Andina: The Chroniclers, or, The Writers of the Sixteenth and Seventeenth Centuries Who Treated of the Pre-Hispanic History and Culture of the Andean Countries*. New Haven: Connecticut Academy of Arts and Science.

Medelius, Mónica, and José Carlos de la Puente Luna. 2004. "Curacas, bienes y quipus en un documento toledano (Jauja), 1570." *Histórica* 28.2: 35–82.

Mendizábal Losack, Emilio. 1963. "Las dos versiones de Murúa." *Revista del Museo Nacional* 32: 153–185.

Menzel, Dorothy. 1959. "The Inca Occupation of the South Coast of Peru."*Southwestern Journal of Anthropology* 15.2: 125–142.

Menzel, Dorothy. 1964. "Style and Time in the Middle Horizon." *Ñawpa Pacha* 2: 1–105.

Mills, Kenneth. 1997. *Idolatry and Its Enemies: Colonial Andean Religion and Extirpation, 1640–1750*. Princeton: Princeton University Press.

Mitchell, W.J.T., ed. 1980. *The Language of Images*. Chicago: University of Chicago Press.

Mitchell, W.J.T. 1986. *Iconology: Image, Text, Ideology*. Chicago: University of Chicago Press.

Molina, Cristóbal de. [1570–1584] 1989. *Relación de las fabulas y ritos de los Ingas*. Madrid: Historia 16.

Molina, Cristóbal de. [1570–1584] 1964. "An Account of the Fables and Rites of the Yncas." *Narratives of the Rites and Laws of the Yncas*. Ed. and trans. Clements R. Markham, pp. 1–64. New York: B. Franklin.

Montesinos, Fernando de. [1645] 1870. "Libro Segundo, Capítulo 28, Memorias antiguas historiales del Perú." *Revista de Buenos Aires* 22: 399–405.

Moore, Jerry D. 1992. "Pattern and Meaning in Prehistoric Peruvian Architecture: The Architecture of Social Control in the Chimu State." *Latin American Antiquity* 3.2: 95–113.

Mori, Juan de, and Hernando Alonso Malpartida. [1549] 1967. "La visitación de los pueblos de los chupachu, 1549." *Visita de la provincia de León de Huánuco en 1562* by Iñigo Ortíz de Zúñiga. Ed. John V. Murra, pp. 289–310. Huánuco: Universidad Nacional Hermilio Valdizan.

Moseley, Michael E. 1975a. "Chan Chan: Andean Alternative to the Preindustrial City?" *Science* 187: 219–225.

Moseley, M. Edward. 1975b. "Prehistoric Principles of Labor Organization in the Moche Valley, Perú." *American Antiquity* 40.2: 191–196.

Moseley, Michael E. 1978. "The Evolution of Andean Civilization." *Ancient Native Americas*. Ed. Jesse D. Jennings, pp. 491–541. San Francisco: W. H. Freeman.

Moseley, Michael E. 1982. "Introduction: Human Exploitation and Organization on the North Andean Coast." *Chan Chan: Andean Desert City*. Eds. Michael E. Moseley and Kent C. Day, pp. 1–24. Albuquerque: School of American Research / University of New Mexico Press.

Moseley, Michael E. 2005. "The Maritime Foundations of Andean Civilization: An Evolving Hypothesis." http://www.hallofmaat.com/modules.php?name=Articles&file=article&sid=85, July 26, 2005, 10:03 am.

Moseley, Michael E., and Kent C. Day, eds. 1982. *Chan Chan: Andean Desert City*. Albuquerque: University of New Mexico Press.

Murra, John V. 1968. "An Aymara Kingdom in 1567." *Ethnohistory* 15.2: 115–151.

Murra, John. 1972. "El 'control vertical' de un máximo de pisos ecológicos en la economía de las sociedades andinas." *Visita a la Provincia de León de Huánuco {1562}*. Iñigo Ortiz de

Zúñiga. Ed. John V. Murra, vol. 2, pp. 429–476. Huánuco, Perú: Universidad Nacional Hermilio Valdizán.

Murra, John. 1975. *Formaciones económicas y políticas del mundo andino.* Lima: Instituto de Estudios Peruanos.

Murra, John V. 1981. "Las etnocategorías de un khipu estatal." *La tecnología en el mundo andino.* Ed. Heather Lechtman and Ana María Soldi, pp. 433–442. México: UNAM.

Murra, John. 1982. "The Mit'a Obligations of Ethnic Groups to the Inka State." *The Inca and Aztec States, 1400–1800.* Eds. and trans. G.A. Collier, R.I. Rosaldo, and J.D. Wirth, pp. 237–262. New York: Academic Press.

Murra, John. 1998. "Litigation over the Rights of 'Natural Lords' in Early Colonial Courts in the Andes." *Native Traditions in the Postconquest World.* Eds. Elizabeth Hill Boone and Tom Cummins, pp. 55–62. Washington, D.C.: Dumbarton Oaks.

Murúa, Martín de. [1611] 1987. *Historia general del Perú.* Madrid: Historia 16.

Murúa, Martín de. [1590] 2004. *Códice Murúa: Historia y genealogía de los reyes Incas del Perú del Padre Mercenardio Fray Martín de Murúa: Codice Galvin.* Madrid: Testimonio Compañía Editorial.

Niles, Susan. 1999. *The Shape of Inca History: Narrative and Architecture in an Andean Empire.* Iowa City: University of Iowa Press.

Nordenskiöld, Erland. 1925a. "The Secret of the Peruvian Quipus." *Comparative Ethnographical Studies* 6.1: 1–37.

Nordenskiöld, Erland. 1925b. "Calculations with Years and Months in the Peruvian Quipus." *Comparative Ethnographical Studies* 6.2: 1–36.

Oliva, Giovanni Anello. [1631] 1895. *Historia del reino y provincias del Perú....* Lima: S. Pedro.

Ong, Walter. 1967. *The Presence of the Word: Some Prolegomena for Cultural and Religious History.* New Haven: Yale University Press.

Ong, Walter. 1977. *Interfaces of the Word: Studies in the Evolution of Consciousness and Culture.* Ithaca: Cornell University Press.

Ong, Walter. 1982. *Orality and Literacy: The Technologizing of the Word.* London: Methuen.

Ong, Walter. 1987. "Orality-Literacy Studies and the Unity of the Human Race." *Oral Tradition* 2.1: 371–382.

Ortiz de Zúñiga, Iñigo. [1562] 1967. *Visita de la provincia de León de Huánuco en 1562.* Ed. John V. Murra. Huánuco: Universidad Nacional Hermilio Valdizan.

Ossio, Juan. 2004. "Introducción." *Códice Murúa: Historia del origen y genealogía de los reyes Incas del Perú,* pp. 8–58. Madrid: Testimonio Compañía Editorial.

Owen, Bruce D. 2005. "Distant Colonies and Explosive Collapse: The Two Stages of the Tiwanaku Diaspora in the Osmore Drainage." *Latin American Antiquity* 16.1: 45–80.

Pachacuti Yamqui, Juan de Santa Cruz. [1613] 1968. "Relación de antigüedades deste Reyno del Peru." *Crónicas peruanas de interés indígena.* Ed. Francisco Esteve Barba. Madrid: Atlas.

Pachacuti Yamqui, Juan de Santa Cruz. [1613] 1995. *Relación de antigüedades de este Reino del Perú.* Ed. Carlos Araníbar. México: Fondo de Cultura Económica.

Palacio, Eudoxio de Jesus. 1999. *Provinciales del Cuzco de la Orden Mercedaria (1556–1944).* Roma: Instituto Histórico de la Orden de la Merced.

Pärssinen, Martii. 1992. *Tawantinsuyu: The Inca State and Its Political Organization.* Helsinki: Finnish Historical Society.

Pärssinen, Martii, and Jukka Kiviharju. 2004a. "Los textos incas y sus sistemas de escritura." *Textos andinos: Corpus de textos khipu incaicos y coloniales.* Eds. Martii Pärssinen and Jukka Kiviharju, pp. 23–75. Madrid: Instituto Ibero-Americano de Finlandia / Departamento de Filología, Universidad Complutense de Madrid.

Pärssinen, Martti, and Jukka Kiviharju. 2004b. *Textos andinos: Corpus de textos khipu incaicos y coloniales*. Vol. 1. Madrid: Instituto Iberamericano de Finlandia / Universidad Complutense de Madrid.

Patterson, Thomas C. 1971. "Central Peru: Its Population and Economy." *Archaeology* 24.4: 316–321.

Patterson, Thomas C. and Edward P. Lanning. 1964. "Changing Settlement Patterns on the Central Peruvian Coast." *Ñawpa Pacha* 6: 115–134.

Patterson, Thomas C. and Michael E. Moseley. 1968. "Late Preceramic and Early Settlement Patterns on the North Coast of Peru." *Journal of Ethnobiology* 3.2: 15–38.

Pease, Franklin. 1982. "The Formation of Tawantinsuyu: Mechanisms of Colonization and Relationships with Ethnic Groups." *The Inca and Aztec States, 1400–1800: Anthropology and History*. Eds. George A. Collier, Renato I. Rosaldo, and John D. Wirth, pp. 173–198. New York: Academic Press.

Pease, Franklin. 1984. Introducción. *Crónica del Perú: Primera parte*, pp. ix–liv. Lima: PUCP.

Peirce, Charles S. 1955. *The Philosophical Writings of Peirce*. Ed. Justus Buchler. New York: Dover.

Pereyra Sánchez, Hugo. 1990. "La yupana: complemento operacional del quipu." *Quipu y yupana: colección de escritos*. Ed. Carol J. Mackey et al., 235–255. Lima: Consejo Nacional de Ciencia y Tecnología.

Pérez Bocanegra, Juan. 1631. *Ritual formulario e institución de curas para administrar a los naturales*. Lima: Geronymo de Contreras.

Piras, Giuseppe. 2004. "El conflicto interno de la Compañía de Jesús sobre las doctrinas de indios en los años 1568–1608 y el papel de Diego de Torres y Martín de Funes en su solución." *El silencio protagonista: El primer siglo jesuita en el virreinato del Perú. 1567–1667*. Ed. Laura Laurencich Minelli and Paulina Numhauser Bar-Magen, pp. 115–126. Quito: ABYA YALA.

Pizarro, Hernando. [1533] 1920. "A los Magnificos Señores, los señores Oydores de la Audiencia Real de Su Magestad, que residen en la ciudad de Sancto Domingo." *Informaciones sobre el antiguo Perú*. Ed. Horacio H. Urteaga, pp. 16–180. Colección de libros y documentos referentes a la historia del Perú, vol. 3 (2ª serie). Lima: Sanmartí.

Platt, Tristan. 1986. "Mirrors and Maize: The Concept of Yanantin among the Macha of Bolivia." *Anthropological History of Andean Polities*. Eds. John Murra, Nathan Wachtel, and Jacques Revel, pp. 228–259. Cambridge: Cambridge University Press.

Platt, Tristan. 2002. "'Without Deceit or Lies': Variable Chinu Readings during a Sixteenth-Century Tribute-Restitution Trial." *Narrative Threads: Accounting and Recounting in Andean Khipu*. Eds. Jeffrey Quilter and Gary Urton, pp. 225–265. Austin: University of Texas Press.

Plaza, P. Doctor. [1576] 1954. "Carta al P. Maestro Piñas, rector del Colegio de Lima." *Obras del P. José de Acosta*. Ed. Francisco Mateos, pp. 277–284. Biblioteca de Autores Españoles, vol. 73. Madrid: Ediciones Atlas.

Polo de Ondegardo, Juan. [1561] 1940. "Informe al Licenciado Briviesca de Muñatones." *Revista histórica* 13: 125–196.

Polo de Ondegardo, Juan. [1571] 1990. *El mundo de los Incas*. Madrid: Historia 16.

Polo de Ondegardo, Juan. [1572] 1917. "Relación del linaje de los Incas y cómo extendieron sus conquistas." *Informaciones acerca de la religión y gobierno de los Incas*, segunda parte. Colección de libros y documentos referentes a la historia del Perú, vol. 4. Lima: Imprenta y Librería Sanmartí.

Polo de Ondegardo, Juan. [1572] 1964. "Of the Lineage of the Yncas, and how they Extended their Conquests." *Narratives of the Rites and Laws of the Yncas*. Ed. and trans. Clements R. Markham, pp. 151–171. New York: B. Franklin.

Ponte, Victor. 2000. "Transformación social y política en el Callejón de Huaylas, siglos III-X D.C." *Boletín de Arqueología PUCP* 4: 219–251.

Porras, Bartolomé de, Francisco Cocamaita, and Francisco Quiqua. [1582] 1904. Testimony of Bartolomé Porras, Francisco Cocamaita, and Francisco Quiqua. "Instrucción hecha en el Cuzco, por orden del Rey y encargo del Virrey Martín Enríquez acerca de las costumbres que tenían los Incas del Perú. . . . " *La imprenta en Lima*, ed. José Toribio Medina, vol 1, pp. 283–288. Madrid: Juan Pueyo.

Porras Barrenechea, Raúl. 1986. *Los cronistas del Perú (1528–1650) y otros ensayos*. Ed. Franklin Pease. Lima: Banco de Crédito del Peru.

Porres, Fray Diego de. [c. 1560] 1952. "Instrucción y orden que han de tener los sacerdotes que se ocuparen en la doctrina y conversión de los indios." *Revista del Archivo Histórico del Cuzco* 3: 26–37.

Prada Ramírez, Fernando. 1995. "El khipu incaico: de la matemática a la historia." *Yachay* 12.21: 11–37.

Prescott, William H. [1854] 1947. *History of the Conquest of Peru*. London: Richard Bentley.

Prochaska, Rita. 1990. *Taquile y sus tejidos*. Jesús María, Peru: Arius.

Protzen, Jean-Pierre. 2006. "Max Uhle and Tambo Colorado a Century Later." *Ñawpa Pacha* 28: 11–40.

Protzen, Jean-Pierre, and Craig Morris. 2004."Los colores de Tambo Colorado: Una Reevaluacion." *Boletín de Arqueología PUCP* 8: 267–276.

Quilter, Jeffrey. 2001. "Moche Mimesis: Continuity and Change in Public Art in Early Peru." *Moche Art and Archaeology in Ancient Peru*. Ed. Joanne Pillsbury, pp. 21–46. Washington, D.C.: National Gallery of Art.

Quilter, Jeffrey. 2002a. "Moche Politics, Religion, and Warfare." *Journal of World Prehistory* 16.2: 145–195.

Quilter, Jeffrey. 2002b. "Yncap Cimin Quipococ's Knots." *Narrative Threads: Accounting and Recounting in Andean Khipu*. Eds. Jeffrey Quilter and Gary Urton, pp. 197–222. Austin: University of Texas Press.

Quispe-Agnoli, Rocío. 2005. "Cuando Occidente y los Andes se encuentran: Quellqay, escritura alfabética, y tokhapu en el siglo XVI." *Colonial Latin American Review* 14.2: 263–298.

Radicati di Primeglio, Carlos. 1949–1950. "Introducción al estudio de los quipus." *Documenta: Revista de la Sociedad Peruana de Historia* 2: 244–339.

Radicati di Primeglio, Carlos. 1965. "La seriación como posible clave para descifrar los quipus extranumerales." *Documenta: Revista de la Sociedad Peruana de Historia* 4: 112–215.

Radicati di Primeglio, Carlos. 1976. "Los quipus: características y significado." *Revista de San Marcos de la Universidad de San Marcos* 14: 27–37.

Radicati di Primeglio, Carlos. 1979. *El sistema contable de los Incas: yupana y quipu*. Lima: Librería Studium.

Radicati di Primeglio, Carlos. 1987. "Hacia una tipificación de los quipus."*Libro homenaje a Aurelio Miró Quesada Sosa*. Vol 2. Eds. Eduardo Núñez H. et al, pp. 705–713. Lima: Villanueva SA.

Radicati di Primeglio, Carlos. 1990. "El cromatismo de los quipus. Significado del quipu de canutos." *Quipu y yupana: colección de escritos*. Ed. Carol J. Mackey et al., pp. 39–50. Lima: Consejo Nacional de Ciencia y Tecnología, 1990.

Ramírez del Aguila, Pedro. [1639] 1978. *Noticias políticas de Indias, y relación descriptiva de la Ciudad de la Plata Metropoli de las Provincias de los Charcas, y nuevo Reyno de Toledo en las Occidentales del gran Imperio del Piru*. Ed. Jaime Urioste Arana. Sucre: Imprenta Universitaria.

Ravines, Roger. 1968. "Un depósito de ofrendas del horizonte medio en la sierra central del Perú." *Ñawpa Pacha* 6: 19–46.

Regalado de Hurtado, Liliana. 1996. *Sucesión incaica: aproximación al mando y poder entre los incas a partir de la crónica de Betanzos*. Lima: Pontificia Universidad Católica del Perú.

Relph, E. 1976. *Place and Placelessness*. London: Pion.

Román y Zamora, Fray Jerónimo. [1575] 1897. *Repúblicas de Indias: Idolatrías y gobierno en Mexico y Perua antes de la conquista*. 2 vols. Colección de libros raros y curiosos que tratan de América, Vols. 14–15. Madrid:Victoriano Suárez. 67–68.

Rostworowski de Diez Canseco, María. 1975. "La 'visita' a Chinchacocha de 1549." *Anales científicos* 4: 73–88.

Rostworowski de Diez Canseco, María. 1978. *Señoríos indígenas de Lima y Canta*. Lima: Insituto de Estudios Peruanos.

Rostworowski, María. 1981. "Mediciones y cómputo en el antiguo Perú." *Tecnología en el mundo andino*. Edited by Heather Lechtman and Ana María Soldi, tomo 2, pp. 379–405. México: UNAM, 1981.

Rostworowski, María. 1990. "La visita de Urcos de 1562: un kipu pueblerino." *Historia y cultura* 20: 295–317.

Rostworowski, María. 1999. *History of the Inca Realm*. Trans. Harry B. Iceland. Cambridge: Cambridge University Press.

Rowe, John H. 1946. "Inca Culture at the Time of the Spanish Conquest." *Handbook of South American Indians*. Vol. 2: *The Andean Civilizations*. Ed. Julian Steward, pp. 183–330. Washington, D.C.: GPO.

Rowe, John. 1960. "Cultural Unity and Diversification in Peruvian Archaeology." *Men and Cultures: Selected Papers of the Fifth International Congress of Anthropological and Ethnological Sciences*. Ed. Anthony F.C. Wallace, pp. 627–631. Philadelphia: University of Pennsylvania Press.

Rowe, John H. 1962. "Stages and Periods in Archaeological Interpretation." *Southwestern Journal of Anthropology* 18.1: 40–54.

Rowe, John. 1979. "Standardization in Inca Tapestry Tunics." *The Junius B. Bird Pre-Columbian Textile Conference*. Eds. Ann Pollard Rowe, Elizabeth P. Benson, and Anne Louise Schaffer, pp. 239–264. Washington, D.C.: Dumbarton Oaks.

Rowe, John Howland. 1985. "Probanza de los Incas nietos de conquistadores." *Histórica* 9.2: 193–245.

Ruiz Estrada, Arturo. 1982. *Los quipus de Rapaz*. Huacho, Perú: Universidad Nacional José Faustino Sánchez Carrión.

Ryskamp, George. 2002. "Spanish Censuses of the Sixteenth Century." *BYU Family Historian* 1: 21–29.

Saffray, Eugène. 1876. "Exposition de Philadelphie." *La Nature* 4.182: 401–07.

Salomon, Frank. 2001. "Para repensar el grafismo andino." *Perú: el legado de la historia*. Eds. Luis Millones and José Villa Rodríguez, pp. 107–127. Seville: Universidad de Sevilla.

Salomon, Frank. 2004. *The Cord Keepers: Khipus and Cultural Life in a Peruvian Village*. Durham: Duke University Press.

Salomon, Frank, and Karen Spalding. 2002. "Cartas atadas con quipus: Sebastián Francisco de Melo, María Micaela Chinchano y la represión de la rebelión de Huarochirí de 1750." *El hombre y los Andes: Homenaje a Franklin Pease G.Y.* 3 vols. Ed. Javier Flores Espinoza and Rafael Varón Gabai, vol. 2, pp. 857–870. Lima: PUCP.

Sangro, Raimundo de. [1750] 2002. *Lettera apologetica*. Naples: Alós Edizioni.

Santa Cruz Pachacuti Yamqui Salcamayhua, Juan de. [1613] 1968. "Antigüedades deste reyno del Peru." *Crónicas peruanas de interés indígena*. Ed. Francisco Esteve Barba. Madrid: Atlas.

Santillán, Hernando de. [1563] 1950. "Relación del origen, descendencia, política y gobierno de los incas." *Tres relaciones de antigüedades peruanas*. Ed. by Marcos Jiménez de la Espada. Asunción, Paraguay: Editorial Guarania.

Santillán, Hernando de. [1563] 1968. "Relación del origen, descendencia, política y gobierno de los Incas." *Crónicas Peruanas de Interés Indígena*. Ed. Francisco Esteve Barba. Biblioteca de Autores Españoles, vol. 209. Madrid: Atlas.

Santo Tomás, Domingo de. [1560] 1951. *Lexicon o vocabulario de la lengua general del Peru*. Ed. Raúl Porras Barrenechea. Lima: Universidad Nacional Mayor de San Marcos.

Sarmiento de Gamboa, Pedro. [1572] 1988. *Historia de los Incas*. Madrid: Miraguano Ediciones / Ediciones Polifemo.

Schaedel, Richard P. 1966. "Incipient Urbanization and Secularization in Tiahuanacoid Peru." *American Antiquity* 31.3: 338–344.

Schjellerup, Inge R. 1997. *Incas and Spanish in the Conquest of the Chachapoyas*. Göthenberg: National Museum of Denmark.

Schmandt-Besserat, Denise. 1992. *Before Writing*. 2 vols. Austin: University of Texas Press.

Schmandt-Besserat, Denise. 1996. *How Writing Came About*. Austin: University of Texas Press.

Schreiber, Katharina J. 1987. "Conquest and Consolidation: A Comparison of the Wari and Inka Occupations of Highland Peruvian Valley." *American Antiquity* 52.2: 266–284.

Schreiber, Katharina J. 1992. *Wari Imperialism in Middle Horizon Peru*. Anthropological Papers No. 87, Museum of Anthropology, University of Michigan, Ann Arbor.

Shady, Ruth. 1982. "La Nievería y la interacción social en el mundo andino en la época huari." *Arqueológicas* 19: 5–108.

Shady, Ruth. 1989. "Cambios significativos ocurridos en el mundo andino." *The Nature of Wari: A Reappraisal of the Middle Horizon Period in Peru*. Eds. R.M. Czwarno, F.M. Meddens, and A. Morgan, pp. 1–22. Oxford: B.A.R.

Shady, Ruth. 2000. "Los orígenes de la civlización en el Perú: el área norcentral y el valle de Supe durante el Arcaico Tardío." *Arqueología y Sociedad* 13: 13–48.

Shady, Ruth. 2007. *The Social and Cultural Values of Caral-Supe, the Oldest Civilization of Peru and the Americas, and Their Role in Integrated Sustainable Development*. Lima: Instituto Nacional de Cultura / Proyecto Especial Arqueológico Caral-Supe.

Shady, Ruth, and Carlos Leyva, eds. 2003. *La ciudad sagrda de Caral-Supe: los orígenes de la civilización andina y la formación del estado prístino en el antiguo Perú*. Lima: Instituto Nacional de Cultura.

Shady, Ruth, Joaquín Narváez, and Sonia López. 2000. "La antigüedad del uso del quipu como escritura: Las evidencias de la Huaca San Marcos." *Boletín del Museo de Arqueología y Antropología, Universidad Nacional Mayor de San Marcos* 3.10: 2–23.

Shimada, Izumi. 1994. *Pampa Grande and the Mochica Culture*. Austin: University of Texas Press.

Silverblatt, Irene. 1987. *Moon, Sun, and Witches: Gender Ideologies and Class in Inca and Colonial Peru*. Princeton: Princeton University Press.

Solórzano y Pereyra, Juan de. [1629–1639] 1972. *Política indiana*. 5 vols. Biblioteca de Autores Españoles, vols. 252–256. Madrid: Ediciones Atlas.

Stanish, Charles. 2001. "Formación estatal temprana en la cuenca del lago Titicaca, Andes surcentrales." *Boletín de Arqueología PUCP* 5: 189–215.

Stone-Miller, Rebecca, and Gordon F. McEwan. 1990/1991. "The Representation of the Wari State in Stone and Thread." *Res* 19/20: 53–80.

Street, Brian. 1984. *Literacy in Theory and Practice*. Cambridge: Cambridge University Press.

Street, Brian. 1987. "Orality and Literacy as Ideological Constructions: Some Problems in Cross-cultural Studies." *Culture & History* 2: 7–30.

Tercer Concilio Limense. [1583] 1990. *Tercer Concilio Limense y la aculturación de los indígenas sudamericanos*. Ed. Frencesco Lenoardo Lisi, pp. 103–227. Salamanca: Universidad de Salamanca.

Tercero cathecismo y exposición de la doctrina christiana, por sermones. [1585] 1985. Corpus Hispanorum de Pace, vol. 26, no. 2, pp. 333–778. Madrid: Consejo Superior de Investigaciones Científicas.

Toledo, Francisco de. [1569–1580] 1986–1989. *Francisco de Toledo: Disposiciones gubernativas para el virreinato del Perú.* 2 vols. Seville: Consejo Superior de Investigaciones Científicas.

Toledo, Francisco de. [1570–1572] 1921. "Informaciones al Virrey Toledo." *Informaciones sobre el antiguo Perú.* Ed. Horacio H. Urteaga. Lima: San Martí.

Topic, John. 1990. "Craft Production in the Kingdom of Chimor." *The Northern Dynasties: Kingship and Statecraft in Chimor.* Eds. Michael E. Moseley and Alana Cordy-Collins, pp. 145–176. Washington, D.C.: Dumbarton Oaks.

Topic, John R. 1991. "Middle Horizon in Northern Peru." *Huari Administrative Structure: Prehistoric Monumental Architecture and State Government.* Eds. William H. Isbell and Gordon F. McEwan, pp. 225–254. Washington, D.C.: Dumbarton Oaks.

Topic, John R. 2003. "From Stewards to Bureaucrats: Architecture and Information Flow at Chan Chan, Peru." *Latin American Antiquity* 14.3: 243–274.

Torero Fernández de Córdova, Alfredo. 1987. "Lenguas y pueblos altiplánicos en torno al siglo xvi." *Revista andina* 5: 330–405.

Torres Saldamando, Enrique. 1882. *Los antiguos Jesuitas del Perú.* Lima: Imprenta Liberal.

Uceda, Santiago. 2001. "Investigations at Huaca Luna, Moche Valley: An Example of Moche Religious Architecture." *Moche Art and Archaeology in Ancient Peru*, Ed. Joanne Pillsbury, pp. 47–68. Washington, D.C.: National Gallery of Art / Yale University Press.

Uhle, Max. 1897. "A Modern Quipu from Cutusuma, Bolivia." *Bulletin of the Free Museum of the University of Pennsylvania* 1.2: 51–63.

Uhle, Max. 1907. "Algunas observaciones al artículo precedente." *Revista histórica* 2: 63–64.

Urton, Gary, 1981. *At the Crossroads of the Earth and the Sky.* Austin: University of Texas Press.

Urton, Gary. 1990. *The History of a Myth: Pacariqtambo and the Origen of the Inkas.* Austin: University of Texas Press.

Urton, Gary. 1994. "A New Twist in an Old Yarn: Variation in Knot Directionality in the Inka Khipus." *Baessler-Archiv (Neue Folge)* 42: 271–305.

Urton, Gary. 1997. *The Social Life of Numbers: A Quechua Ontology of Numbers and Arithmetic.* Austin: University of Texas Press.

Urton, Gary. 1998. "From Knots to Narratives: Reconstructing the Art of Historical Record Keeping in the Andes from Spanish Transcriptions of Inka Khipus." *Ethnohistory* 45.3: 409–38.

Urton, Gary. 1999. *Inca Myths.* Austin: University of Texas Press.

Urton, Gary. 2001. "A Calendrical and Demographic Tomb Text From Northern Peru." *Latin American Antiquity* 12.2: 127–147.

Urton, Gary. 2002a. "Codificación binaria en los khipus incaicos." *Revista andina* 35: 9–38.

Urton, Gary. 2002b. "An Overview of Spanish Colonial Commentary on Andean Knotted-String Records." *Narrative Threads: Accounting and Recounting in Andean Khipu.* Eds. Jeffrey Quilter and Gary Urton, pp. 3–25. Austin: University of Texas Press.

Urton, Gary. 2002c. "Recording Signs in Narrative Accounting Khipu." *Narrative Threads: Accounting and Recounting in Andean Khipu.* Eds. Jeffrey Quilter and Gary Urton, pp. 171–196. Austin: University of Texas Press.

Urton, Gary. 2003. *Signs of the Inka Khipu: Binary Coding in the Andean Knotted-String Records.* Austin: University of Texas Press.

Urton, Gary. 2005. "Khipu Archives: Duplicate Accounts and Identity Labels in the Inka Knotted String Records." *Latin American Antiquity* 16.2: 147–167.

Urton, Gary. 2006. "Censos registrados en cordeles con 'Amarres.' Padrones poblacionales pre-hispánicos y coloniales tempranos en los khipu inka." *Revista andina* 42: 153–196.

Urton, Gary. 2009 "Sin, Confession, and the Arts of Book- and Cord-Keeping: An Intercontinental and Transcultural Exploration of Accounting and Governmentality." *Comparative Studies in Society and History* 51.4: 801–831.

Urton, Gary, and Carrie Brezine. 2005. "Khipu Accounting in Ancient Peru." *Science* 309.12: 1065–1067.

Vargas Ugarte, Rubén, ed. 1951–1954. *Concilios limenses (1551–1772)*. 3 vols. Lima, Juan Cardenal Guevara.

Vargas Ugarte, Rubén. 1963–1965. *Historia de la Compañía de Jesús en el Perú*. Burgos, Spain: np.

Vázquez de Espinoza, Antonio. [1630] 1992. *Compendio y descripción de las Indias occidentales*. 2 vols. Ed. Balbino Velasco Bayón. Madrid: Historia 16.

Velasco Bayón, Balbino. 1992. "Introducción." *Compendio y descripcion de las Indias Occidentales* by Antonio Vázquez de Espinosa. Ed. Balbino Velasco Bayón, pp. 7–48. Madrid: Historia 16.

Villagómes Pedro de. 1649. *Carta pastoral de exortacion e intruccion contra las idolatrias de los indios del arcobispado de Lima. . . .* Lima: Iorge Lopez de Herrera.

Wassén, Henry. 1931. "The Ancient Peruvian Abacus." *Origin of the Indian Civilizations of South Americas*. Series: Comparative Ethnographical Studies, vol. 9. Ed. Erland Nordenskiöld, pp. 191–205. Göteborg: Elanders boktryckeri aktiebolag.

Wiener, Charles. [1880] 1993. *Perú y Bolivia: relato de viaje seguido de estudios arqueológicoss y etnográficos y de notas sobre la escritura y los idiomas de las poblaciones indígenas*. Lima: Instituto Francés de Estudios Andinos / Universidad Nacional de San Marcos.

Willey, Gordon R. 1953. *Prehistoric Settlement Patterns in the Virú Valley, Perú*. Smithsonian Institution Bureau of American Ethnology, Bulletin 155. Washington, DC: Government Printing Office.

Williams, Carlos. 1985. "A Scheme for the Early Monumental Architecture of the Central Coast of Peru." *Early Ceremonial Architecture in the Andes*. Ed. Christopher B. Donnan, pp. 227–240. Washington, D.C.: Dumbarton Oaks.

Yacovleff, Eugenio, and F.L. Herrera. 1934. "El mundo vegetal de los antiguos peruanos." *Revista del Museo Nacional* 3: 243–322.

Yacovleff, Eugenio, and F.L. Herrera. 1935. "El mundo vegetal de los antiguos peruanos (conclusión)." *Revista del Museo Nacional* 4: 31–102.

Zimmerman, Arthur Franklin. 1938. *Francisco de Toledo, Fifth Viceroy of Peru, 1560–1581*. Caldwell, Id.: Caxton.

Ziolkowski, Mariusz. 1989. "Knots and Oddities: The Quipu-Calendar or Supposed Cuzco Luni-sidereal Calendar." *Time and Calendars in the Inca Empire*. Ed. Mariusz S. Ziolkowski and Robert M. Sadowski, pp. 197–208. Oxford: BAR International Series.

Žižek, Slavoj. 2006. "Philosophy, the 'Unknown Knowns,' and the Public Use of Reason." *Topoi* 25: 1–2: 137–142.

Zuidema, R. Tom. 1964. *The Ceque System of Cuzo: The Social Organization of the Capital of the Inca*. Leiden. International Archives of Ethnography.

Zuidema, R. Tom. 1977. "The Inca Calendar." *Native American Astronomy*. Ed. A.F. Aveni, pp. 219–259. Austin: University of Texas Press.

Zuidema, R. Tom. 1982. "The Sidereal Lunar Calendar of the Incas." *Archaeoastronomy in the New World*. Ed. A.F. Aveni. Cambridge: Cambridge University Press.

Zuidema, R. Tom. 1986. "Cuzco, Quuipu, and Quadrant." *World Art: Themes of Unity in Diversity*. Vol 1. Ed. Irving Lavin, vol. 1, pp. 193–198. University Park: Pennsylvania State University Press.

Zuidema, R. Tom. 1989. "A quipu calendar from Ica, Peru, with a comparison to the ceque calendar from Cuzco." *World archaeoastronomy: Selected Papers from the 2nd Oxford International Conference on Archaeoastronomy Held at Mérida, Yucatan, Mexico, 13–17 January 1986.* Ed. Anthony Aveni, pp. 341–351. Cambridge: Cambridge University Press.

Index